lone

Norway

Svalbard
p302

The Far North
p275

Nordland
p244

Trøndelag
p219

The Western
Fjords
p183

Central
Norway
p113

Bergen &
the Southwestern
Fjords
p136

✪ OSLO
p42

Southern
Norway
p89

**Gemma Graham, Hugh Francis Anderson,
Anthony Ham, Annika Hipple**

CONTENTS

Plan Your Trip

The Guide

**Cycling in Norway
(p36)**

Hardangervidda National Park (p133)

Northern Lights, Tromsø (p278)

Smørbrød with smoked
salmon (p35)

TATIANA POPOVA/SHUTTERSTOCK ©

Preikestolen, Lysefjord (p179)

NORWAY
THE JOURNEY BEGINS HERE

Like most visitors who are lucky enough to have experienced Norway's dramatic fjords and forest-blanketed terrain, I've longed to return. Having grown up in Scotland, I already had an affinity for bleakly beguiling, glacier-hewn landscapes. Yet nothing could have prepared me for the first time I stood on Preikestolen (Pulpit Rock) and gazed up the Lysefjord, my heart thudding in my chest as the view seized my breath.

Gemma Graham

@gemmakgraham

Gemma is a writer and editor with a special interest in Scandinavia. She has worked with Lonely Planet, the UK's National Trust and more.

My favourite experience is dogsledding through Svalbard's wild landscape. When you harness up excitable dogs with names like McNugget, you know you're in for a joyful trip.

WHO GOES WHERE

Our writers and experts choose the places which, for them, define Norway.

Andøya's (p259) west coast is the alter ego of the nearby (and better-known) Lofoten Islands. Facing out to the Atlantic, this wildly beautiful coast echoes Lofoten's natural drama. But Andøya's long and empty roads, quiet villages and fine foods add a new dimension to your visit, making its west coast Nordland's special secret.

Anthony Ham

anthonyham.com

Anthony considers Norway to be a second home, with his countless visits here part of a travelling life that takes him to the Arctic for Lonely Planet.

The **Senja på Langs** (p284) is a breathtaking multiday hike that crosses Norway's second-largest island from north to south. It's been named Norway in Miniature, and you really get that sense when you pass through dense old-growth forests, up snow-capped mountains and across marshland plateaus. It's a place I've visited many times, and I'll be back again soon.

Hugh Francis Anderson

@hughfrancisanderson

Hugh is a writer specialising in adventure, the environment and travel.

There are countless picturesque spots along Norway's coastline, but none quite like **Runde** (p214). Driving the winding road from the mainland to this rugged, almost treeless island, I feel myself leaving the cares of civilisation behind to enter an elemental world of rocky beaches and jagged green cliffs.

Annika Hipple

@annikahipple

Annika is a Swedish-American travel writer, photographer and tour leader with Norwegian roots.

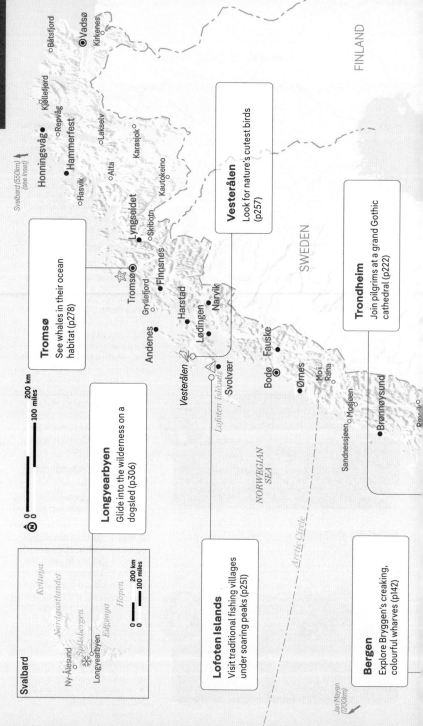

Svalbard

Kvitøya
Nordaustlandet
Ny-Ålesund
Spitsbergen
Longyearbyen
Edgeøya
Hopen

0   200 km
0   100 miles

Longyearbyen
Glide into the wilderness on a dogsled (p306)

Svalbard (550km)
(see inset)

Honningsvåg●   Kjøllefjord
Repvåg   Båtsfjord
Hammerfest   Vadsø
Kirkenes
Hasvik   Lakselv
Alta   Karasjok
Kautokeino

Tromsø
See whales in their ocean habitat (p278)

Lyngseidet
Skibotn
Tromsø◉
Finnsnes
Gryllefjord

Harstad
Andenes   Lødingen
Narvik

FINLAND

SWEDEN

Vesterålen
Look for nature's cutest birds (p257)

Vesterålen
Lofoten Islands
Svolvær
Bodø◉   Fauske
Ørnes
Moi
Mo i Rana
Sandnessjøen   Mosjøen
Brønnøysund
Rørvik

Trondheim
Join pilgrims at a grand Gothic cathedral (p222)

NORWEGIAN SEA

Arctic Circle

0   200 km
0   100 miles

Lofoten Islands
Visit traditional fishing villages under soaring peaks (p251)

Bergen
Explore Bryggen's creaking, colourful wharves (p142)

Jan Mayen
(200km)

6

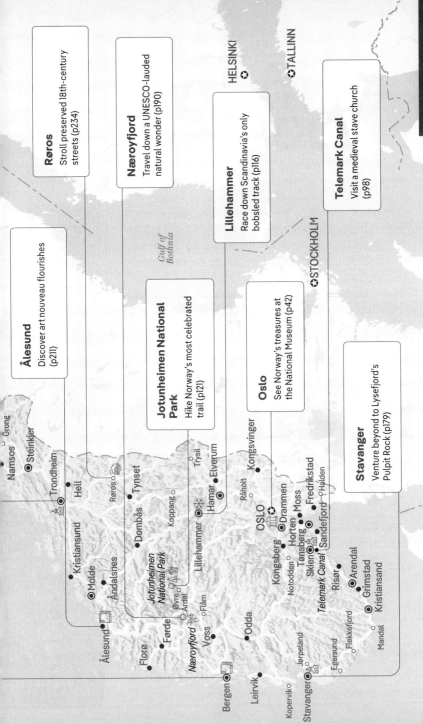

Røros
Stroll preserved 18th-century streets (p234)

Nærøyfjord
Travel down a UNESCO-lauded natural wonder (p190)

Ålesund
Discover art nouveau flourishes (p211)

Lillehammer
Race down Scandinavia's only bobsled track (p116)

Telemark Canal
Visit a medieval stave church (p98)

Jotunheimen National Park
Hike Norway's most celebrated trail (p121)

Oslo
See Norway's treasures at the National Museum (p42)

Stavanger
Venture beyond to Lysefjord's Pulpit Rock (p179)

Gulf of Bothnia

❂ HELSINKI

❂ TALLINN

❂ STOCKHOLM

Namsos Grong
● Steinkjer
Trondheim
Hell
Røros Tynset
Dombås
Kristiansund
Molde
Åndalsnes
Koppang
Jotunheimen National Park
Øvre Flåm
Årdal
Lillehammer Hamar ● Elverum Trysil
Voss
Førde
Flora
Nærøyfjord
Bergen
Odda
Råholt
Kongsvinger
Leirvik
Jørpeland
Notodden Drammen
Kongsberg Moss
OSLO Horten Fredrikstad
Tønsberg Halden
Telemark Canal Skien Sandefjord
Koperviko
Stavanger
Egersund
Flekkefjord Risør
Arendal
Grimstad
Mandal Kristiansand

7

FANTASTIC FJORDS

Norway's coastline is dominated by its monumental fjords. These astonishingly beautiful sea-flooded channels, carved by ice age processes, have steep mountainsides now decorated by rushing waterfalls, lush farmland and quaint villages reached by boat or switchback roads. The most famous fjords lie in the western and southwestern fjords regions, areas that draw millions to witness their majesty – and rightfully so – but beyond the UNESCO-listed big hitters you'll also find quieter alternatives if you'd like to escape the crowds.

Glacial Formation

Fjords are formed when glaciers slowly gouge and shape the path of an existing valley, creating a deep channel with characteristically high mountains on either side.

Norway's Record-breaker

At 205km long and 1308m at its deepest, Sognefjord in the western fjords is Norway's longest and deepest fjord and the world's second-longest after Greenland's Scoresby Sund.

Crowd Control

Some of the most famous fjords can be overwhelmingly busy during the summer peak. For fewer fellow fjord-goers, aim for late May or early September.

BEST FJORD EXPERIENCES

Get a priest's-eye view over **❶ Lysefjord** (p179) by hiking to the world-famous promontory Preikestolen (Pulpit Rock).

Take a boat trip to marvel at waterfall-curtained, UNESCO-listed **❷ Nærøyfjord** (Narrow Fjord; p190).

Journey deep into the **❸ Hardangerfjord** (p158) towards Ulvik and the fruit farms at the heart of what's known as the orchard of Norway.

Visit **❹ Hjørundfjorden** (p202) for a tranquil trip, with picturesque views of high mountainsides and hidden rural idylls, but with far fewer visitors than nearby Geirangerfjord.

Pack a picnic, jump on an electric ferry and go island-hopping in the **❺ Oslofjord** (p85), with beaches and forest walks to discover.

WILD ENCOUNTERS

When it comes to wildlife, Norway has few peers in Europe. While you may stumble upon polar bears and walruses (in Svalbard), Arctic foxes, Eurasian lynxes, wolverines, reindeer and other species, dedicated safaris in the Norwegian interior will take you within sight of the otherworldly musk ox, as well as the rather loveable elk (moose). Norway's birdlife is abundant – especially seabirds – while whale-watching outings are a staple of the Nordland coast.

Follow the Fish

Between late October and mid-January, orcas, humpbacks and fin whales arrive in northern Norway, especially around Tromsø and Vesterålen, attracted by the rich pickings of migrating herring.

Apex Predator

Around 3000 polar bears live on Svalbard. Lucky visitors might spot one from a distance but, for the bears' protection, safaris actively seeking them out are forbidden.

Responsible Whale Watching

All whale-watching operators in Norway must follow the National Guidelines for Whale Watching (norwhale. org). Some outfits, such as Brim Explorer, use quieter hybrid boats to minimise disturbance.

❶

❹❺

❸❷

BEST WILDLIFE EXPERIENCES

See walruses lolling and hunting for molluscs in the shallows at well-known hauling-out spot ❶ **Borebukta** (p312) on Svalbard.

Track down shaggy musk oxen on a safari through ❷ **Dovrefjell-Sunndalsfjella National Park** (p131) from Oppdal or Dombås.

Head to ❸ **Runde** (p214), near Ålesund, to see some of the 230 seabird species that frequent the island or nest here year-round.

Go in search of puffins, the pocket-sized seabirds with big personalities, on a birdwatching trip to ❹ **Bleiksøya** (p258) from Andenes.

Take to the waters off ❺ **Tromsø** (p278) from November to January to watch humpbacks, orcas and minke whales dining out on migrating herring.

NATALIA SOKKO/SHUTTERSTOCK ©

Snowmobile (p312) and the Northern Lights

FUN IN THE DEEP FREEZE

Norway offers an extraordinary range of activities throughout its long, dark winter. Many take place in the Arctic North: skiing is the most popular winter activity, but dogsledding and snowmobiling are thrilling pursuits too, and they require little experience – you'll be taught all the essentials you need to get started on your wintry adventure.

An Ancient Pastime

The word ski, from the old Norse 'skið', means 'split piece of wood' and Stone Age petroglyphs depicting humans travelling on skis have been discovered at Alta.

Licence to Drive

If you plan to try snowmobiling while you're in the Arctic, don't forget to bring your full, current driving licence, which needs to be recognised in Norway.

BEST WINTER SPORTS EXPERIENCES

Wear your warmest garb to zoom across Svalbard's wilderness on a snowmobiling trip from **❶ Longyearbyen** (p312).

Harness your own team of huskies and learn how to mush from a dogsledding master near **❷ Alta** (p288).

Hurtle down **❸ Lillehammer's** (p119) Olympic bobsled run at 120km/h in a 'Taxibob'...or take the gentler 'Bobraft' option at a positively sedate 100km/h.

Carve down the pistes at Norway's largest alpine skiing resort, **❹ Trysil** (p119), with 69 runs and 500km of cross-country trails.

Go ski touring through the **❺ Lyngen Alps** (p282), which offer experts the chance to traverse glaciers and navigate steep descents.

BEST VIKING EXPERIENCES

Hot-foot it to Oslo's ❶ **Museum of the Viking Age** (p67) when it reopens in 2026 for an unparalleled exposition of three magnificent Viking ships.

Travel to the ❷ **Lofotr Viking Museum** (p254) in Lofoten, which centres on the 83m-long longhouse discovered at Borg in 1981.

Visit ❸ **Tønsberg** (p101) to see the country's 'fourth Viking ship' and watch modern-day boatbuilders recreating Viking-era vessels.

Learn about Vikings' everyday life at the Viking Farm in ❹ **Avaldsnes** (p169) and visit in June for its annual Viking Festival.

Explore 10th-century history using 21st-century technology at ❺ **Viking Planet** (p53) in Oslo, which features an award-winning virtual reality experience.

Replica viking ship

VIKING DISCOVERIES

The coastal inlets along Norway's southern and southwestern coast are where the Vikings famously launched their longships in their quest for world domination and then returned with the spoils of victory. But evidence of the Viking legacy has been discovered across the country, from burial mounds and longhouses to precious artefacts and ships.

Origin Story

The word 'Viking' is thought to derive from *vik*, an Old Norse word meaning bay or cove, a reference to Vikings' homesteads when they weren't on raids.

Speed Boats

Viking longboats were fast and manoeuvrable. They could be more than 30m long, and some were capable of travelling up to 15 knots (28km/h) under favourable conditions.

WONDERS OF NATURE

The mystical aurora borealis; the duality of polar night and midnight sun; textured glaciers and rushing waterfalls: Norway's natural features, whether physical or ethereal, excite and inspire awe.Perpetual darkness can be discombobulating, but the potential to see the aurora borealis (Northern Lights) is reason enough to visit northern Norway in winter. The country's physical features shift, mould and shape: showy waterfalls burst with energy after rain, and ancient glaciers are imperceptibly carving a new landscape.

Magnetic Attraction

The aurora is caused when charged particles from the sun are drawn to Earth's magnetic poles and interact with nitrogen and oxygen atoms in the atmosphere, releasing light energy.

Up Your Chances

You'll have the best chance of spotting the Northern Lights on clear, dark nights between October and March, away from the light pollution of towns and cities.

Norway's Ice Box

Jostedalsbreen is mainland Europe's largest icecap and it feeds some of Norway's largest glaciers, among them Nigardsbreen and Briksdalsbreen, while Jotunheimen National Park is home to 60 glaciers.

❺ ❹
❶
❷❸

BEST NATURAL PHENOMENA EXPERIENCES

Whizz to the ❶ **Saltstraumen maelstrom** (p249) to feel the force of one of the world's most powerful tidal currents.

Enjoy the spray from ❷ **Hardangerfjord's waterfalls** (p158), including famed Vøringsfossen, a 182m-high torrent of white water.

Take a guided hike across the textured ice of Blåisen (the blue ice) glacier tip of ❸ **Hardangerjøkulen** (p135) for a deeper appreciation of Hardangervidda.

Journey to remote causeway ❹ **Ekkerøy** (p298) in Finnmark for gentle hikes, birdwatching and seeing the beaches bathed in the midnight sun.

Look up to witness nature's most mesmerising light show as the Northern Lights flicker, dance and swirl over ❺ **Tromsø** (p278).

Ishavskatedralen (p279)

STRIKING MODERNITY

Norway's modern and contemporary architecture scene is one of Europe's most exciting, combining the clean lines of Scandinavian design with forms inspired by Norway's natural environment. The results are often stunning: from rustic turf-roofed houses to soaring religious architecture and creative adaptations of Sami symbols and some Arctic landforms.

Norwegian 'Starchitects'

Oslo-based architecture firm Snøhetta (named after Dovrefjell-Sunndalsfjella National Park's highest peak) were the team behind the Oslo Opera House, Lillehammer Kunstmuseum and The Boulder cabins overlooking Lysefjord.

Architectural Conveniences

Norwegian public toilets as beautiful as their surroundings have become a tourist attraction in their own right, including undulating Ureddplassen, designed by Haugen/Zohar Architects, on the Helgeland coast.

BEST CONTEMPORARY ARCHITECTURE EXPERIENCES

Appreciate the timeless design of Oslo's
1 National Museum (p61) and look for the fossils in the foyer's limestone floor.

Cross Tromsøbrua towards the 35m-high triangular face of **2 Ishavskatedralen** (Arctic Cathedral; p279), its 11 ice-white, aluminium-coated concrete segments suggesting glacial crevices.

Discover Sámediggi, the **3 Sami Parliament** (p291), a building that evokes a traditional Sami meeting place resting in the woods in Karasjok.

Ice-skate in Hamar's **4 Viking Ship Sports Arena** (Vikingskipet; p118), the Olympic rink that resembles an upturned Viking longship.

Rest inside the undulating timber interior of **5 Viewpoint Snøhetta** (p130) as you look through the glass wall across Dovrefjell-Sunndalsfjella National Park.

LOUIELEA/SHUTTERSTOCK ©

Ålesund (p211)

**BEST TRADITIONAL
ARCHITECTURE
EXPERIENCES**

See how the riches of the
17th- and 18th-century
copper-mining boom
were ploughed into the
pretty wooden houses in
❶ **Røros** (p234).

Stroll the famous lanes
of ❷ **Bryggen** (p142),
Bergen's waterfront
warehouses; the
colourful buildings were
the focus of international
trade for centuries.

Make a pilgrimage to
Trondheim's Gothic
❸ **Nidarosdomen**
(Nidaros Cathedral;
p222), its soaring west
front laden with figures
carved by master
craftspeople.

Road trip along the
vista-packed ❹ **Lofoten
Islands** (p251) to discover
villages replete with
rorbuer (traditional
fishing cabins).

Find art nouveau
flourishes in ❺ **Ålesund**
(p211), a town rebuilt
with Jugendstil stylings
following a devastating
fire in 1904.

CABINS, CATHEDRALS & WHARVES

Timber and stone are the mainstays of
traditional Norwegian architecture and,
despite the WWII devastation in the north,
the rest of Norway retains many examples of
its distinctive wooden cityscapes. For a taster
of historical Norwegian architecture, it's
worth detouring to any of the excellent folk
museums dotted around the country, including
Maihaugen in Lillehammer.

High-tech Timber

The 16th-century introduction
of the water-powered saw
meant timber houses could
be clad with finer panelling,
influenced by refined European
styles but retaining a typical
Norwegian character.

Saints & Grotesques

Trondheim's Nidarosdomen,
the world's most northerly
Gothic church, is laden with
more than 5000 decorative
carvings, including saints,
notable historical figures and
mythical creatures.

MEDIEVAL MASTERPIECES

Norway's fantastical stave churches evoke a medieval past, with tarred-wood walls rising to turrets and ornamental flourishes. Once there were more than 1300 of these fairy-tale structures, but now only 28 remain across southern and central Norway. They were saved in the 19th century by the organisation now known as Fortidsminneforeningen (National Trust of Norway), a central figure of which was famous Norwegian artist Johan Christian Dahl, who campaigned to preserve the churches.

Oldest Standing

The timber used for Urnes Stave Church, commonly regarded as Norway's oldest, was felled between 1129 and 1131, but some decorative features are even older.

Norway Meets Poland

Vang Stave Church now stands in Karpacz, Poland, after Dahl bought it as an act of preservation, then sold it to Prussia's Frederick William IV.

Black Metal Burning

Fantoft Stave Church in Bergen was painstakingly reconstructed following an arson attack in 1992. Varg Vikernes of black metal band Mayhem was accused but not convicted.

BEST STAVE CHURCH EXPERIENCES

Find 13th-century **❶ Heddal Stave Church** (p98), Norway's largest, in Notodden, along the Telemark Canal; inside are 17th-century 'rose' paintings.

Visit Norway's oldest place of worship, the UNESCO-listed 12th-century **❷ Urnes Stave Church** (p193), sitting serenely by Lustrafjorden.

See **❸ Lom Stavkyrkje** (p123) and its unusual pair of naves, a structure atmospherically lit up at night and perfectly sited where valleys meet.

Note the carved dragon heads of the tar-black, exquisitely preserved **❹ Borgund Stave Church** (p193) and learn more about stave churches in the visitor centre.

Discover the perfectly proportioned **❺ Ringebu Stave Church** (p129), a lovely red-orange church set in a hillside meadow.

REGIONS & CITIES

Find the places that tick all your boxes.

The Far North

EMBRACE THE MAJESTIC NORTHLANDS

Mainland Norway's northernmost counties are sparsely populated but rich in Sami culture, diverse landscapes and huge skies for chasing the Northern Lights. The region is headed up by self-confident Tromsø, a hub for hiking and skiing, and remote towns such as Alta and Kirkenes brim with traditions such as dogsledding and fishing.

p275

Trøndelag

PAGE-TURNING HISTORY AND REGIONAL FLAVOURS

This is a region steeped in the nation's history. Gothic Nidaros Cathedral has drawn pilgrims to pretty Trondheim since legendary King Olav was martyred at nearby Stiklestad in 1030. Taste the produce of Trøndelag's fertile farmland in Inderøy, and discover windswept islands replete with Viking history and unique geology along its coast.

p219

Svalbard

FROZEN LANDSCAPES AND MINING HERITAGE

Svalbard's snow-iced mountain ranges rise from frigid fjords, calling would-be polar explorers to venture into its wilderness on foot, on skis or by dogsled. Longyearbyen, the archipelago's ruggedly charming main town, thrums with anticipation and a few quality museums, while research centre Ny-Ålesund recounts its part in the race to reach the North Pole.

p302

Svalbard
p302

Nordland

NORWAY'S GREATEST HITS

The Arctic Circle arcs through Nordland: inland, bucolic farms make way for mountains and ice fields, and the Kystriksveien Coastal Route reveals magical sea views. Culture capital Bodø leads to the serrated peaks and fishing villages of the Lofoten Islands. See sea creatures such as humpback whales, seals and puffins from Vesterålen.

p244

The Far North
p275

The Western Fjords

NORWAY'S FJORD HEARTLAND

Characterised by rugged, glacier-carved terrain and a coastline knitted together by a network of ferries, the landscape of the western fjords requires you to take time to explore it. The Flåmsbana Railway chatters to tiny Flåm at the head of Aurlandsfjord, while Geirangerfjord is a UNESCO-certified stunner. For small-town delights, Ålesund flourishes with art nouveau architecture.

p183

Central Norway

MOUNTAINS AND OUTDOOR ADVENTURES

Dominated by nature and outstanding national parks, including Jotunheimen, Rondane and Hardangervidda, central Norway is capillaried with hiking trails and home to the wildest of life, including reindeer and musk oxen. Tiny Lom punches above its weight with its culinary offerings, and Lillehammer's Olympic legacy lives on in its thrilling winter-sports facilities.

p113

Oslo

THE NEW NORDIC CULTURE CAPITAL

Norway's capital city is a triumph of reinvention, its harbourfront reimagined for culture and play, with hypermodern architecture and internationally significant art museums. Elsewhere, Oslo's green spaces bring nature and sculpture parks to a city watched over by centuries-old Akershus Fortress, while Grünerløkka, a former industrial quarter, works the night shift with bars and music.

p42

Bergen & the Southwestern Fjords

CAPTIVATING CITIES AND STUNNING NATURE

Cultured Bergen's Hanseatic history lingers around the colourful wharves of Bryggen, and Stavanger's preserved old town contrasts with its oil-funded modernity. Nearby fjords beckon too: Sognefjord is Norway's longest, and Lysefjord harbours the famed Preikestolen (Pulpit Rock). For the truly adventurous, extreme-sports capital Voss runs on pure adrenaline.

p136

Southern Norway

HISTORY, TRADITION AND COASTAL CHARM

The south coast 'Norwegian Riviera' pulls homegrown holidaymakers with its unspoilt whitewashed settlements and gleaming sea, as Kristiansand, the region's cultural hot spot, provides summertime excitement. Inland, Norway's south tucks away riches including stave churches, idyllic villages and orchards. The town of Rjukan leads to Gaustatoppen, the region's highest peak.

p89

Nordland
p244

Trøndelag
p219

The Western Fjords
p183

Central Norway
p113

Bergen & the Southwestern Fjords
p136

Southern Norway
p89

○OSLO
p42

21

ITINERARIES

Essential Bergen to Oslo

Allow: 5 days   **Distance:** 533km

Bergensbanen (the Bergen Railway), commonly known as the Oslo–Bergen train line, is equally beautiful whichever direction you travel, as it glides past rushing rivers and mysterious forests and across the beguilingly desolate Hardangervidda plateau. Break up the journey to take the vintage-style Flåmsbana (Flåm Railway) and float down two fjords en route to Oslo.

N
0 ___ 50 km
0 ___ 25 miles

START 1h 15min
1
Bergen

●Leirvik

❶
BERGEN ⏱1 DAY

Begin in **Bergen** (p142) with a stroll through the laneways between the creaking, colourful warehouses of UNESCO-listed Bryggen (pictured). Walk around the harbour to eat fresh seafood from Fisketorget Mathallen and then ascend Mt Fløyen on the Fløibanen funicular for breath-stealing views of the city. Walk back down to soak up world-class art at the KODE museums before dining at New Fjordic gem Lysverket.

❷
VOSS ⏱1 DAY

Arrive in **Voss** (p154) ready for adventure. June brings the world's largest extreme sports festival, when you can witness the pros BASE jumping, longboarding and more, but whenever you visit, you can find your own favourite thrill, from mountain biking to whitewater rafting. You can also choose a gentler pace with a walk around the scenic lake Vangsvatnet and a house-brewed beer at Voss Bryggeri.

❸
NÆRØYFJORD & AURLANDSFJORD ⏱½ DAY

From Gudvangen, take a ferry to experience the majesty of two offshoots of Sognefjorden: **Nærøyfjord** (pictured; p190) and **Aurlandsfjord** (p188). You'll journey through the narrow, steep-sided Nærøyfjord and then you'll glide into the similarly picturesque Aurlandsfjord – both have plunging waterfalls and deep-green forested fjord sides – before disembarking in Flåm.

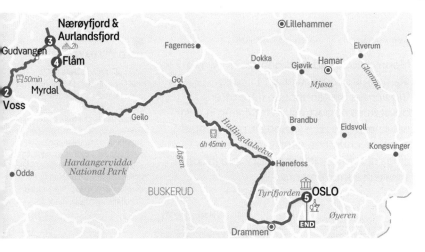

Nærøyfjord & Aurlandsfjord

⛴2h

Gudvangen

③

④ Flåm

🚠50min

② Myrdal

Voss

Odda

Hardangervidda National Park

Lillehammer

Fagernes

Elverum

Dokka

Gjøvik

Hamar

Glomma

Gol

Mjøsa

Geilo

Løgen

Hallingdalselva

🚂 6h 45min

Brandbu

Eidsvoll

Kongsvinger

Hønefoss

BUSKERUD

Tyrifjorden

🏛 OSLO

⑤

Øyeren

END

Drammen

④ **FLÅM** ⏱ ½ **DAY**

When you arrive in tiny, mountain-backed **Flåm** (p192), drop into Ægir Bryggeri for a hearty meal and be sure to visit the Flåm Railway Museum before you join the Flåmsbana (pictured) to make the impossibly scenic rail journey to Myrdal. You'll trundle through mountain tunnels, pass sheer drops and see tumbling waterfalls before you reach your destination to pick up the train to Norway's premier city.

⑤ **OSLO** ⏱ **2 DAYS**

When you reach **Oslo** (p42), take in the Norwegian capital's stately sights, such as the Royal Palace and Akershus Festning, and walk on the roof of the Oslo Opera House (pictured) for views across the fjord. Soak in the country's treasure chest of art, design and architecture at the National Museum and then take your pick of the many restaurants and bars at harbourside Aker Brygge.

Highlights of Central Norway

Allow: 6 days   **Distance:** 686km

Mountainous and wild, central Norway's scenery is spectacular, and a road trip across the landscape here offers boundless opportunities for hiking in vast national parks. The journey is punctuated by stave churches, pretty villages, and cities rich with ancient history and modern sporting achievements.

1
OSLO ⏱ 2 DAYS

Start your trip in **Oslo** (p42) and learn all about Norway's most famous artist, Edvard Munch, at the Munch Museum before taking the tram up to Grünerløkka for some vintage shopping and an evening of bar hopping. For a relaxing afternoon, stroll along the harbourfront and take an electric ferry to explore some of the islands in the Oslofjord.

Munch Museum (p57)

2
LILLEHAMMER ⏱ 1 DAY

Drive on to discover your inner Olympian in **Lillehammer** (p116), made famous by the 1994 Winter Olympics. Learn about the Games at the Norges Olympiske Museum (pictured) and climb to the top of the Lysgårdsbakkene Ski Jump for vertigo-inducing views across the town and Lake Mjøsa beyond.

🔸 *Detour: On your way northwards, veer off the E6 to see 13th-century **Ringebu Stave Church** (p129).*

PE3K/SHUTTERSTOCK ©

❸ RONDANE NATIONAL PARK
⏱ 1 DAY

Continue your journey towards the unspoilt and little-touristed Norwegian wilderness of your dreams: **Rondane National Park** (p127). Replete with crystal-clear streams and rocky mountain peaks, the park has trails for casual hikers and seasoned trekkers alike. But if you'd rather appreciate the landscape from afar, the scenic Rv27 road skirts the park on your way north and promises incredible vistas.

❹ RØROS ⏱ 1 DAY

Continue to **Røros** (p234), a UNESCO-protected former copper-mining town with perfectly preserved streets lined with wooden houses from the town's industrial heyday in the 18th century. Begin at Rørosmuseet Smelthytta – a smeltery turned museum – to explore the town's heritage. Then stroll the streets to discover the town's creative side in its many art galleries and quirky shops.

❺ TRONDHEIM ⏱ 1 DAY

Complete your journey in **Trondheim** (pictured; p222) as pilgrims have done since St Olav was laid to rest here in 1030. Visit Nidarosdomen, the sculpture-adorned Gothic cathedral said to stand on the site where Olav was buried. See the city from another angle on a kayaking tour down the meandering Nidelva River, then savour an expertly mixed cocktail at the refined bar of Britannia Hotel.

Glaciers & Archipelagos

Allow: 6 days   **Distance:** 723km

Weave your way along Nordland's fissured shoreline towards the Lofoten Islands as you cross the Arctic Circle. Travel part of the Kystriksveien Coastal Route, wending past quiet fishing villages towards Arctic culture hot spot Bodø, then continue to the fabled archipelagos of Lofoten and Vesterålen.

Vesterålen archipelago (p257)

T. SCHNEIDER/SHUTTERSTOCK ©

① SALTFJELLET-SVARTISEN NATIONAL PARK ⏱ 1 DAY

Start in Mo i Rana for **Saltfjellet-Svartisen National Park** (p264), where you can witness Europe's lowest-lying glaciers (pictured). You can catch glimpses of the bright white icefields from the road, but in July and August you can take a guided hike to get up close and personal with these huge geological wonders, the likes of which have been responsible for carving the country's landscape for millennia.

② BODØ ⏱ 1 DAY

Continue north along the Kystriksveien Coastal Route to **Bodø** (p248), European Capital of Culture for 2024. Take a thrilling RIB trip to the Saltstraumen maelstrom and experience the churning whirlpools created as millions of litres of water squeeze through a channel between two fjords. And don't miss Jektefartsmuseet, which tells the 400-year history of northern Norway's once-lucrative stockfish trade.

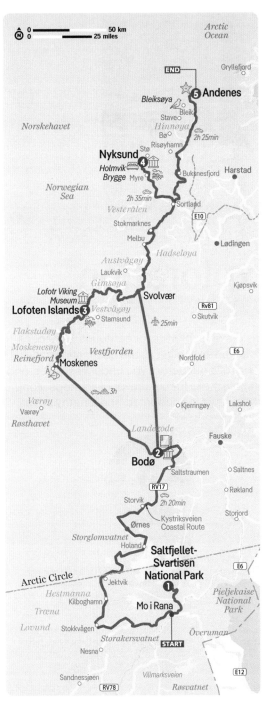

LOFOTEN ISLANDS ⏱ 2 DAYS

Next, take either a short flight to Svolvær or the car ferry to Moskenes and prepare to be wowed by the jagged peaks and impossibly pretty fishing villages of the **Lofoten Islands** (p251). Stop in at artists' workshops and cute cafes, and discover Viking history at the Lofotr Viking Museum on the roughly 130km journey between Å i Lofoten and Svolvær.

④

NYKSUND ⏱ 1 DAY

Travel northwards to the Vesterålen archipelago and the lovingly restored coastal haven of **Nyksund** (p260), a former fishing village and one-time ghost town that's now a thriving and creative community. Drop into the museum to learn the story of the settlement and while away a day in the galleries, shops and cafes before spending a night at rustic guesthouse Holmvik Brygge.

⑤

ANDENES ⏱ 1 DAY

Travel on to **Andenes** (p257) and finish your itinerary by taking in the wonder of the wildlife off the shores of Vesterålen. Join a whale-watching tour (pictured) for the chance to see orcas, humpbacks and fin whales. Or, at the other end of the size chart, you can go on a puffin safari to see the charismatic sea birds in all their comical glory at Bleiksøya.

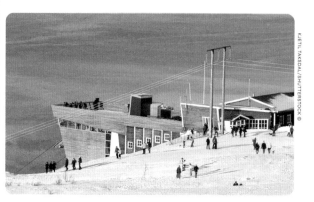

Fjellheisen cable car (p278), Tromsø

ITINERARIES

Arctic Exploration

Allow: 7 days   **Distance:** 736km

Norway's frozen north has drawn explorers for centuries. Distances are long, but the journeys are as appealing as the destinations: the expansive Arctic landscape rolls out before you under vast skies, and seemingly remote settlements make for culture-packed stops along the way. Factor in a few extra days to account for the lengthy drives.

① TROMSØ ⏱ 2 DAYS

Start your Arctic road trip in the 'Capital of the North', **Tromsø** (p278). Cross the gracefully arching Tromsøbrua towards the Arctic Cathedral, an ice-white prism backed by mountains. Take the Fjellheisen cable car for views over the snow-capped landscape – and maybe the Northern Lights too (pictured). And don't miss the town's legendary nightlife, with chic cocktail bars, relaxed brewpubs and live-music venues to choose from.

② ALTA ⏱ 1 DAY

Drive or fly to **Alta** (p287), a small town with a clutch of brilliant Arctic attractions. Marvel at the 7000-year-old petroglyphs along the trails at UNESCO-listed Alta Museum before harnessing up a team of huskies for a thrilling dogsledding trip. Then hunker down for the night in the Sorrisniva Igloo Hotel (pictured), rebuilt every year with ice from the lake Sierravann and carved by local artists and sculptors.

FROM LEFT: V. BELOV/SHUTTERSTOCK ©, MCDONALDKAR/GETTY IMAGES ©

❸ HONNINGSVÅG ⏱ 1 DAY

Continue to **Honningsvåg** (p289) and discover how the resilient seaside town was rebuilt after WWII at Nordkappmuseet. Next, make your way to the summit of Storfjellet for views over the town.

↪ *Detour:* You've come this far, so don't miss the chance to visit **Nordkapp** (pictured; p290), mainland Europe's northernmost point, for bragging rights and an unforgettable view out over the North Atlantic.

❹ KARASJOK ⏱ 1 DAY

Travel on to **Karasjok** (p291) – Kárášjohka in Sami. Start by joining a guided tour of the Sami Parliament building (pictured), a stunning larch-clad construction surrounded by tall pine trees, then spend some time exploring the Sami Museum to learn about the culture and traditions of Norway's Indigenous people, including *duodji* (Sami handicrafts) and the joik (traditional Sami singing).

WHEN **TO GO**

Norway is a year-round playground, with each season bringing a new way to discover its exciting cities and captivating landscapes.

Though summer can bring glorious sunshine and warm temperatures, in Norway there are no meteorological guarantees. But as the Norwegians say, *'Det finnes ikke dårlig vær, bare dårlige klær'* (There's no bad weather, only bad clothes).

Outside of the peak summer season (mid-June to mid-August), many attractions in smaller towns keep reduced opening hours or close altogether, so check the timings for any of your must-dos. With mild weather and fewer crowds, May and September can be ideal for very popular hiking trails. Meanwhile, clear, dark nights are best for Northern Lights spotting, so October and March are especially good times to head north of the Arctic Circle and look up.

Accommodation Lowdown

Demand for accommodation peaks across the country between June and August, while February and March are prime time for winter sports destinations; book well ahead during these times, especially close to outdoor activity hot spots such as national parks.

Northern Lights, Lofoten Islands (p251)

⊛ I LIVE HERE

THE COLOURS OF SPRING

Kristine Nygård is a social educator and tourist host who's based mainly in Volda, Møre og Romsdal, in spring and summer and in Bergen during winter.
@kneggolga

May is beautiful in western Norway: nature awakens and springs to life after a long, dark winter. The grey and brown hillsides explode in bright greens, while foaming white waterfalls and snow-covered mountain tops paint a stark contrast against the backdrop of a deep blue sky. Spring is like the Friday of the year.

TØRRFISK TEMPERATURE

Lofoten has the perfect climate for making *tørrfisk* (stockfish). The combination of the Arctic wind and a constant temperature of around 0°C prevents bacteria from proliferating, meaning that over the course of several months the fish dries out in the sun rather than rotting.

Weather Through the Year (Oslo)

JANUARY	FEBRUARY	MARCH	APRIL	MAY	JUNE
Ave. daytime max: -2°C	Ave. daytime max: -1°C	Ave. daytime max: 3°C	Ave. daytime max: 9°C	Ave. daytime max: 16°C	Ave. daytime max: 20°C
Days of rainfall: 12	Days of rainfall: 10	Days of rainfall: 8	Days of rainfall: 6	Days of rainfall: 10	Days of rainfall: 10

COASTAL CLIMATE

Mainland Norway sits between 58° N and 71° N, so there's a huge variation in climate from north to south. The warmth of the Gulf Stream means that Norway's climate is milder than that of other countries on the same latitude.

Traditional Celebrations

In February, Røros welcomes up to 70,000 visitors for **Rørosmartnan** (p236), five days of markets, music and merriment first instituted by royal decree in 1844.
☺ **February**

After months of polar night, Longyearbyen residents herald the return of the sun with **Sunfest** (p305), joining together at the old hospital steps at sunrise, followed by a week of cultural events across the town.
☺ **March**

All eyes are on Kautokeino in March for **Sami Easter**, a week-long celebration of Sami traditions including the World Reindeer Racing Championships and the Sami Grand Prix, a joik (traditional Sami song) competition.
☺ **March**

No celebration in Norway tops the patriotic enthusiasm that grips the country for **Constitution Day** every 17 May, when Norwegian flags fly for parades through towns and cities across the nation.
☀ **May**

A Good Sport

Head to Alta in March to catch the start and finish of **Finnmarksløpet** (p292), Europe's longest dogsled race, during which 160 teams make the punishing 1200km round trip over around six days.
☺ **March**

Since 1892, the annual **Holmenkollen Skifestival** (holmenkollenskifestival.no) has drawn competitive ski jumpers and biathletes to this hallowed winter-sports facility in Oslo, made internationally famous by the 1952 Winter Olympics. These days the snowy spectacle takes place each March.
☺ **March**

There's no gnarlier extreme-sports festival than the world's biggest, **Ekstremsportveko** (p156), held in Voss each June, when adrenaline-rush experts compete across disciplines including rafting, longboarding and BASE jumping.
☀ **June**

Endurance runners take to the streets of Tromsø in June for the **Midnight Sun Marathon** (msm.no), a 42km nighttime race with light provided courtesy of the polar summer.
☀ **June**

⬡ I LIVE HERE

OUTDOOR LIFE

Hugh Francis Anderson is a writer specialising in adventure, the environment and travel. Based in Tromsø, he enjoys skiing, hiking, and exploring Arctic mountains and plateaus. @hughfrancisanderson

Tromsø is the hub of outdoor pursuits in Arctic Norway, and I adore being able to access so many majestic mountains from my doorstep. Ski touring the Lyngen Alps, an hour from town, is a must – it's best in March and April, when the sun returns after the long polar night.

Skiing, Lyngen Alps (p282)

RECORD HIGHS & LOWS

Karasjok claims the record for the lowest temperature ever recorded – it plummeted to -51.4°C in 1886. At the other end of the scale, in 1970 the mercury maxed at a record 35.6°C in Nesbyen in Viken County, Central Norway.

JULY	AUGUST	SEPTEMBER	OCTOBER	NOVEMBER	DECEMBER
Ave. daytime max: **21°C**	Ave. daytime max: **20°C**	Ave. daytime max: **15°C**	Ave. daytime max: **9°C**	Ave. daytime max: **3°C**	Ave. daytime max: **-1°C**
Days of rainfall: 12	Days of rainfall: 12	Days of rainfall: 8	Days of rainfall: 9	Days of rainfall: 10	Days of rainfall: 12

LEFT: MUMEMORIES/GETTY IMAGES © FAR RIGHT/PHOTO 12/ALAMY STOCK PHOTO ©

Campers enjoying the Northern Lights, Lofoten Islands

GET PREPARED FOR NORWAY

Useful things to load in your bag, your ears and your brain.

Clothes

Day & evening wear: Style-wise, Norwegians are fairly relaxed, but they're always well put together. Smart-casual clothes are ideal for most situations, but if you're going to a particularly fancy restaurant, you'll feel more comfortable if you've packed something reasonably polished to wear.
Outdoor essentials: It is cold in Norway! Three essentials to pack are thermal underwear, a fleece, and a warm, windproof jacket.
Walking shoes: Sturdy walking shoes or boots are essential if you're going to head out into the mountains or forest trails. They'll also make city sightseeing a whole lot more comfortable.

Manners

Most people in Norway speak English fluently but do **make an effort to learn some Norwegian** – it's well received.

Greet people with a smile (along with a **firm handshake** in more formal situations).

Politeness is expressed by using a **friendly intonation** – always say '*takk*' (thank you).

Avoid boasting about your achievements – it's considered distasteful.

Reflectors: During dark nights, do as locals do and wear something reflective so you can be seen and stay safe.

📖 READ

Kristin Lavransdatter
(Sigrid Undset; 1920) The Nobel laureate's trilogy portrays life in 14th-century Norway from a woman's perspective.

Killing Moon (Jo Nesbø; 2022) Harry Hole hunts a serial killer in the 13th instalment of Nesbø's page-turning detective series.

Doppler (Erlend Loe; 2004) This subversive, modern-day fable sees Doppler turn his back on modernity and move to the forest.

One of Us (Åsne Seierstad; 2015) A harrowing account of the 2011 terrorist attacks that seeks to explain 'Why?'

Words

'Hei' is the universal way of saying 'hello', but you'll hear **'hei hei'** which is like 'hi there', **'god morgen'** (good morning) and the very informal **'heisann'** (similar to 'howdy'). You can also use **'hallo'**, especially when you answer the telephone.

'Ha det bra' (literally 'have it good') means 'goodbye', but you're more likely to hear it shortened to **'ha det'**.

'Takk' means 'thank you'. **'Tusen takk'** (a thousand thanks) is an even warmer way to show your appreciation. *Takk* can also be used in a similar way to 'please'; for example, if someone offers you something, you can say *'Ja, takk!'*

Vær så snill means 'please', although it's generally only used in the context of pleading for something;

you wouldn't use it when you're ordering a drink, for example.

Vær så god means 'you're welcome', but it's also used to say 'there you go' or 'here you are', so you'll often hear it in restaurants when the staff bring your food.

'Hvordan har du det?' is a polite way of asking 'how are you?'; a more informal phrase is **'hvordan går det'**, which is more along the lines of 'how's it going?' You can reply with **'(Veldig) bra, takk'** which means '(Very) well/good, thanks'

'Beklager' is the way to say 'sorry'.

Say **'unnskyld meg'** ('excuse me') or simply **'unnskyld'** to politely attract someone's attention. It's also another way of saying sorry, as in English.

📺 WATCH

Kitchen Stories (Bent Hamer; 2003; pictured) An unlikely friendship forms when a Swedish researcher studies the kitchen habits of a Norwegian bachelor.

Exit (2019–23) A dark TV drama following the depraved lives of four mid-30s men working in Oslo's financial district.

Witch Hunt (2020) An acclaimed one-season thriller in which a law firm employee attempts to blow the whistle on corruption.

Vikingane/Norsemen (2016–20) Every ludicrous scene in this gory Viking-themed comedy was filmed in both Norwegian and in English.

🎧 LISTEN

All My Demons Greeting Me as a Friend (Aurora; 2016) The elfin singer's debut album resurfaced when 'Runaway' trended on TikTok.

Sorry for the Late Reply (Sløtface; 2020) The Stavanger-based activist pop-punk band's second album features the irresistibly catchy single 'Telepathetic'.

De Mysteriis Dom Sathanas (Mayhem; 1994) The debut album by Norway's most influential (and infamous) black metal band.

Gula Gula (Mari Boine; 1989) The celebrated singer's first album; Boine blends the Sami joik with jazz and folk rock.

LEFT: AS FOODSTUDIO/SHUTTERSTOCK ©; RIGHT: SANDRA LOVISE/SHUTTERSTOCK ©

Fiskesuppe (fish soup)

THE FOOD SCENE

Norway is a locavore's delight: save up to savour some of the best locally sourced food in the Nordics.

The transformation of Norway's cuisine scene over the past few decades has been revolutionary. Forward-thinking chefs eager to showcase the country's flavour-packed produce and bounteous seafood and game use cutting-edge techniques to craft delicate dishes at refreshingly unstuffy restaurants all over the country.

International cuisine is easy to find too, though it tends to be adapted to suit local tastes, with less chilli in curries, for example. Sushi is especially popular in Norway and you can get your fill of *nigiri* in most larger destinations. Burger joints, pizzerias, taquerias and pubs are also ubiquitous.

Seasonal Menus

Heavily inspired by the New Nordic traditions pioneered by chefs such as Denmark's René Redzepi, seasonally evolving menus are now commonplace at quality restaurants across Norway. The very best hyper-local ingredients are crafted into inventive dishes, with menus changing as ingredients reach their best.

At higher-end restaurants offering tasting menus, you commonly won't know what you'll be served until you arrive. This may be thrilling or anxiety-inducing, depending on your point of view, but (with notice) chefs will do their best to accommodate allergies.

Norway's National Spirit

Aquavit (also spelled *akevitt*) is Norway's national spirit, a fiery, potato-based distillation flavoured with caraway and a combination of ingredients that might include dill, coriander (cilantro), anise or orange. It's then aged in 500L oak barrels for a minimum of six months, but some varieties can be matured for up to 12 years.

Since the monopoly on producing spirits in Norway was abolished in 2005, smallscale distilleries have flourished.

Meat-free Meals

While traditional Norwegian cuisine is heavy on seafood and red meat, options for vegetarians and vegans are improving and meat-free eaters are increasingly well catered for. Most restaurants in Norway will have at least one vegetarian option on the menu – though it may not be terribly imaginative – but vegans will have a harder time in smaller towns.

Local Specialities

Norway's classic dishes focus on fish and game, but there are some unusual delicacies for the epicure too.

Sweet Treats

Waffles Eat these heart-shaped treats with *rømme og syltetøy* (sour cream and jam) or *brunost* (brown cheese).

Skolebrød Sweet, cardamom-spiced buns filled with custard and sprinkled with coconut.

Multekrem A simple but decadent dessert of whipped cream, sugar and cloudberries.

Fårikål

Meaty Meals

Reinsdyrstek Roasted reindeer is commonly served with mashed potatoes, root vegetables and lingonberries.

Fårikål This lamb or mutton and cabbage stew is Norway's national dish; a winter warmer.

Bidos The traditional meal at Sami weddings, this reindeer stew sometimes features on menus in the far north.

Something Fishy

Laks (salmon) The quintessentially Norwegian fish is now mostly farmed – wild Atlantic salmon is rare (and expensive).

Tørrfisk (stockfish) Cod dried on racks in the perfect coastal conditions. Find it in Lofoten.

Fiskesuppe (fish soup) Norway in a bowl: creamy and filled with chunks of fresh fish.

Dare to Try

Brunost (brown cheese) A caramel-sweet cheese made from the whey of goat's and/or cow's milk.

Lutefisk Stockfish rehydrated in a lye solution, giving it a gelatinous texture.

Rakfisk One for the very brave: trout (or char) that's been fermented for up to a year.

FOOD FESTIVALS

Trøndersk Matfestival (Trøndelag Food Festival) Food and drink producers from around the region bring their flavours to Trondheim for three days in August.

Norsk Rakfiskfestival (Norwegian Rakfisk Festival) Up to 15 tonnes of the fermented fish delicacy are sold over this odoriferous three-day event in Fagernes in November, with coveted prizes for producers.

Norsk Eplefest (Norwegian Apple Festival) Telemark's orchards showcase their star fruits in late September, with all manner of apple-based produce to try.

Mat*Larm A two-day celebration of Norway-wide food producers in late August, with pop-up food markets and activities around Oslo.

Skalldyrfestivalen (Shellfish Festival) The second week in August sees up to 60,000 shellfish fans descend on Mandal, 40km from Kristiansand, for four days of markets, food and entertainment.

THE YEAR IN FOOD

SPRING
As the days lengthen, wild trout, earthy new potatoes and classic Norwegian rhubarb-based desserts such as rhubarb pudding grace seasonal menus. You'll smell pungent wild garlic while you're out in the woodlands too.

SUMMER
The fruits of the sea are abundant, with fried, grilled or steamed monkfish, tuna, plaice and lobster appearing on plates. Meanwhile, sweet peas, juicy strawberries and local honey are natural flavours to savour.

AUTUMN
Trees are laden with apples, mushrooms are foraged, and berries, including lingonberries and cloudberries, are ripe for picking. It's a good time for lamb; look out for *fårikål* (lamb or mutton and cabbage stew).

WINTER
Winter sees rich flavours with plentiful reindeer, beef and venison accompanied by hearty root vegetables such as beets and carrots. Winter also brings cod to the table, and vitamin-packed kale.

RUNAR VESTLI/GETTY IMAGES ©

Cycling, Hardangervidda National Park (p133)

THE OUTDOORS

Wherever you are in Norway at whatever time of year, there are infinite opportunities to experience the country's horizon-spanning mountain ranges, pine-scented forests and labyrinthine coastline.

The *friluftsliv* (open-air life) is part of Norway's national psyche and there's an astonishing range of activities available to anyone who wants to get out into nature.

You don't have to be an outdoors aficionado; Norway's peaks, gorges and glaciers are a playground for the experienced, but beginners are spoilt for choice too, with easy trails through stunning scenery and professional operators offering adventures to suit all abilities.

The excellent **ut.no** website (in Norwegian) details more than 16,000 marked hiking, cycling, kayaking, skiing and climbing routes.

Walking & Hiking

Norway is an outstanding destination for hiking, with over 22,000km of marked trails across achingly beautiful terrain. No matter your fitness or skill level, you'll find a route that suits. Most cities have at least one or two waymarked strolls amid local nature, while a multitude of long-distance wilderness treks awakens the explorer within – the only limits are your own.

Information boards in popular hiking areas describe and map out local routes, and established trails are marked by cairns or red 'T's at 100m or 200m intervals to keep you on the right track. The hiking season starts around late May and winds up in early October.

Majestic Jotunheimen National Park is Norway's premier hiking destination, but the trails criss-crossing nearby Rondane National Park tend to be less crowded. Glacier hiking in locations including Hardangervidda is possible in summer too, but

More Outdoor Fun

FISHING
Combine the patience of angling with the thrill of a churning whirlpool at the **Saltstraumen maelstrom** (p249).

CYCLING
Cycling pros can ascend to 1400m a.s.l to tackle the punishingly beautiful **Sognefjellet Rd** (p124) mountain pass.

ROCK CLIMBING
In **Åndalsnes** (p203), puzzle over climbs at the Norwegian Mountaineering Centre.

FAMILY ADVENTURES

Hire bikes and pedal a circular route around geologically fascinating **Leka** (p243), with its Viking burial mound and prehistoric rocks.

Follow in the footsteps of great explorers on Svalbard with a dogsledding experience leaving from **Longyearbyen** (p311).

Enjoy a gentle paddle down Trondheim's river, the **Nidelva** (p225), passing an ancient cathedral and colourful wharves along the way.

Raft gentler rapids with experienced guides on the **Sjøa River** (p128), so even young kids can enjoy the rush of white-water rafting.

Skiing for all levels with the ski school and 69 varied, well-groomed runs make **Trysil** (p119) a great choice for all abilities.

Feel the full force of physics on a summertime run in a wheelbob down Scandinavia's only Olympic bobsled track in **Lillehammer** (p119).

it's essential you trek with an experienced local guide.

Skiing

Winter-sports thrill-seekers have the pick of world-class ski centres here – including a legendary Olympic resort – and thousands of kilometres of cross-country ski trails.

As with all winter-sports destinations, Norway's ski season changes slightly from year to year (and across regions), though it usually runs from early December to April. Peak season is generally February and March. For a traditional skiing holiday, carve the

pistes at one of Norway's excellent down-hill ski resorts, including Trysil, Geilo and Lillehammer. The cost of lift passes and equipment hire is roughly comparable to costs at resorts in the Alps, though you'll undeniably pay more to eat out and enjoy an après-ski tipple – if you imbibe.

Cross-country skiers can set out independently on any of the marked, colour-coded wilderness trails across the country, but it's essential to be prepared with the appropriate kit and emergency supplies.

Kayaking

Norway's archipelago-speckled, fjord-slashed coastline is made for kayaking. Popular paddling sites include the Western Fjords, where an armada of operators offer guided excursions for all abilities at locations including Geirangerfjord and Sognefjord. Meanwhile, Vesterålen, north of Lofoten, is a magnet for sea kayakers.

Kayak hire is widely available, but most operators require a *vättkort* (wet card) as a condition of rental. Courses to earn one start at four hours, but companies set their own minimum requirement (DNT, for example, often requires a 16-hour course). Unless you plan to do a lot of paddling, you may find it more convenient to join a tour instead.

BEST SPOTS

For the best outdoor spots and routes, see map on page 38.

LILLIAN TVEIT/SHUTTERSTOCK ©

Kayaking on the Nidelva (p225)

WHITE-WATER RAFTING	BUNGEE JUMPING	PARAGLIDING & PARASAILING	ZIPLINING
The **Sjøa River** (p128) has white water for everyone, from Class I fun to unadulterated Class V exhilaration.	Take a deep breath and plunge a pulse-racing 84m from Norway's highest land-based bungee jump in **Rjukan** (p95).	Soar high at adrenaline-sports capital **Voss** (p154) with a paragliding or parasailing experience.	Adopt the steely nerves of a ski-jumper and glide from **Holmenkollen Ski Jump** (p86) on the 361m-long Kollensvevet Zipline.

ACTION AREAS

Where to find Norway's best outdoor activities.

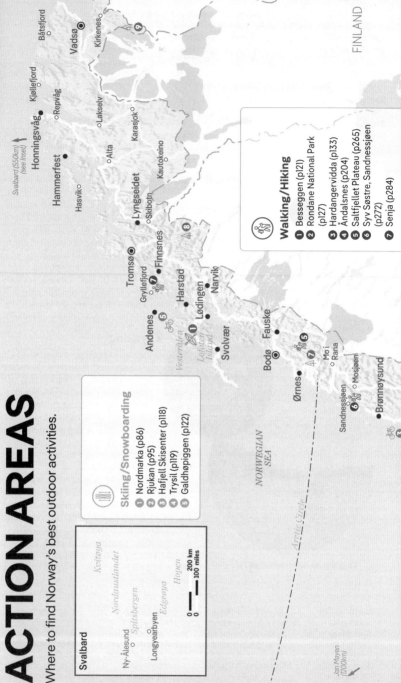

Svalbard

Ny-Ålesund
Longyearbyen   Spitsbergen   Edgeøya   Hopen   Nordaustlandet   Kvitøya

0 ——— 200 km
0 ——— 100 miles

Skiing/Snowboarding

1. Nordmarka (p86)
2. Rjukan (p95)
3. Hafjell Skisenter (p118)
4. Trysil (p119)
5. Galdhøpiggen (p122)

Walking/Hiking

1. Besseggen (p121)
2. Rondane National Park (p127)
3. Hardangervidda (p133)
4. Åndalsnes (p204)
5. Saltfjellet Plateau (p265)
6. Syv Søstre, Sandnessjøen (p272)
7. Senja (p284)

Svalbard (550km) (see Inset)

Båtsfjord
Vadsø
Kirkenes
Kjøllefjord
Repvåg
Honningsvåg
Lakselv
Hammerfest
Hasvik   Alta   Karasjok
Kautokeino

FINLAND

Lyngseidet
Skibotn
Tromsø
Gryllefjord   Finnsnes
Harstad
Andenes   Lødingen   Narvik
Svolvær
Vesterålen
Lofoten Island
Fauske
Bodø
Ørnes   Moi Rana
Sandnessjøen   Mosjøen
Brønnøysund

NORWEGIAN SEA

Arctic Circle

Jan Mayen (1200km)

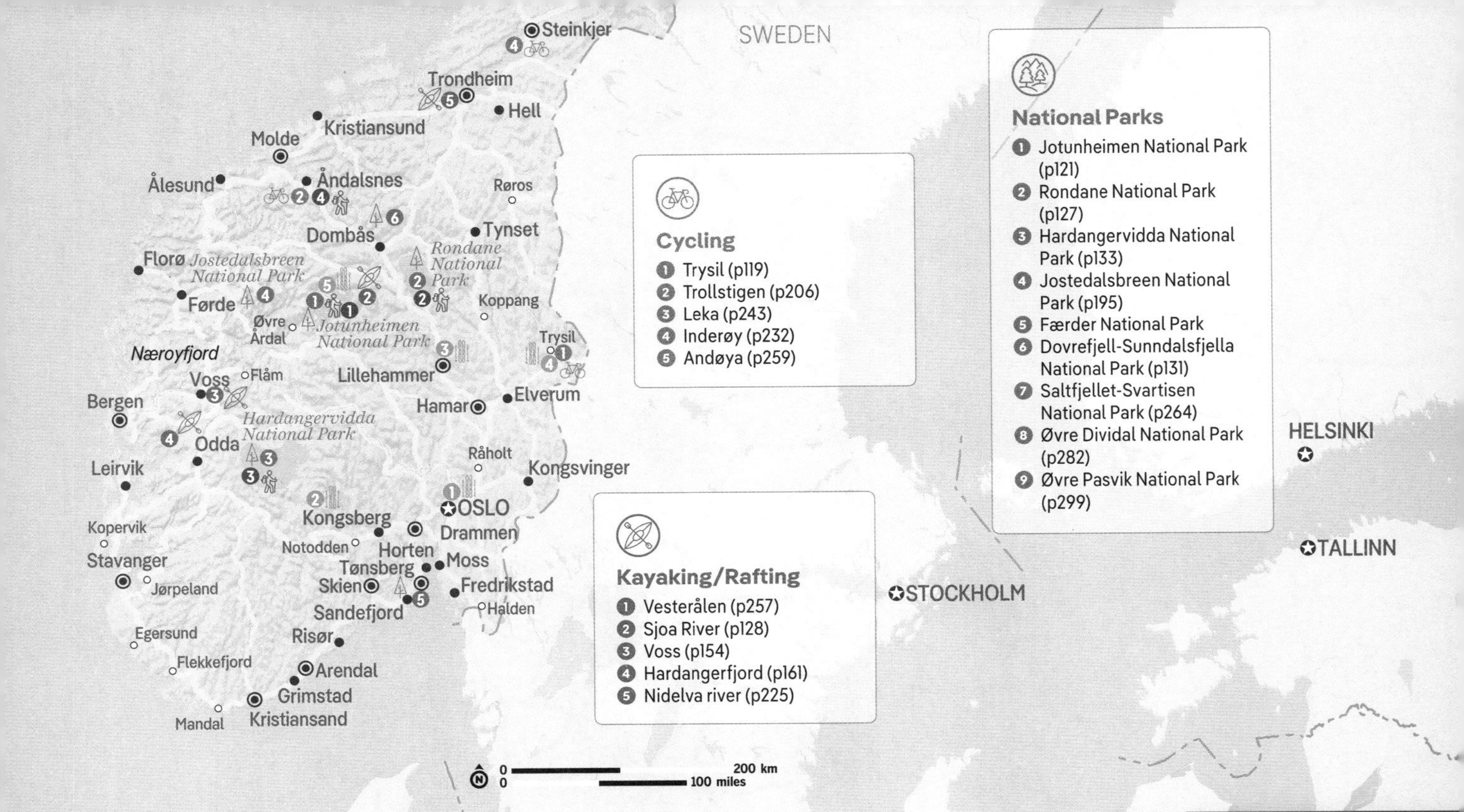

National Parks

1. Jotunheimen National Park (p121)
2. Rondane National Park (p127)
3. Hardangervidda National Park (p133)
4. Jostedalsbreen National Park (p195)
5. Færder National Park
6. Dovrefjell-Sunndalsfjella National Park (p131)
7. Saltfjellet-Svartisen National Park (p264)
8. Øvre Dividal National Park (p282)
9. Øvre Pasvik National Park (p299)

Cycling

1. Trysil (p119)
2. Trollstigen (p206)
3. Leka (p243)
4. Inderøy (p232)
5. Andøya (p259)

Kayaking/Rafting

1. Vesterålen (p257)
2. Sjoa River (p128)
3. Voss (p154)
4. Hardangerfjord (p161)
5. Nidelva river (p225)

SWEDEN

⊙ HELSINKI

⊙ TALLINN

⊙ STOCKHOLM

0   100 miles
0   200 km

⊙ Steinkjer
● Hell
Røros
Trondheim
Kristiansund
Molde
Andalsnes
Dombås
Tynset
Koppang
Rondane National Park
Ålesund
Flora
Førde
Jostedalsbreen National Park
Ardal
Øvre
Flåm
Jotunheimen National Park
Voss
Hamar
Lillehammer
Elverum
Trysil
Nærøyfjord
Odda
Hardangervidda National Park
Bergen
Leirvik
Notodden
Kongsberg
Horten
Moss
Tønsberg
OSLO
Drammen
Fredrikstad
Halden
Råholt
Kongsvinger
Kopervik
Jørpeland
Skien
Sandefjord
Stavanger
Risør
Arendal
Grimstad
Egersund
Flekkefjord
Kristiansand
Mandal

NORWAY

THE GUIDE

Svalbard
p302

Chapters in this section
are organised by hubs and
their surrounding areas.
We see the hub as your
base in the destination,
where you'll find unique
experiences, local insights,
insider tips and expert
recommendations. It's
also your gateway to the
surrounding area, where
you'll see what and how
much you can do from there.

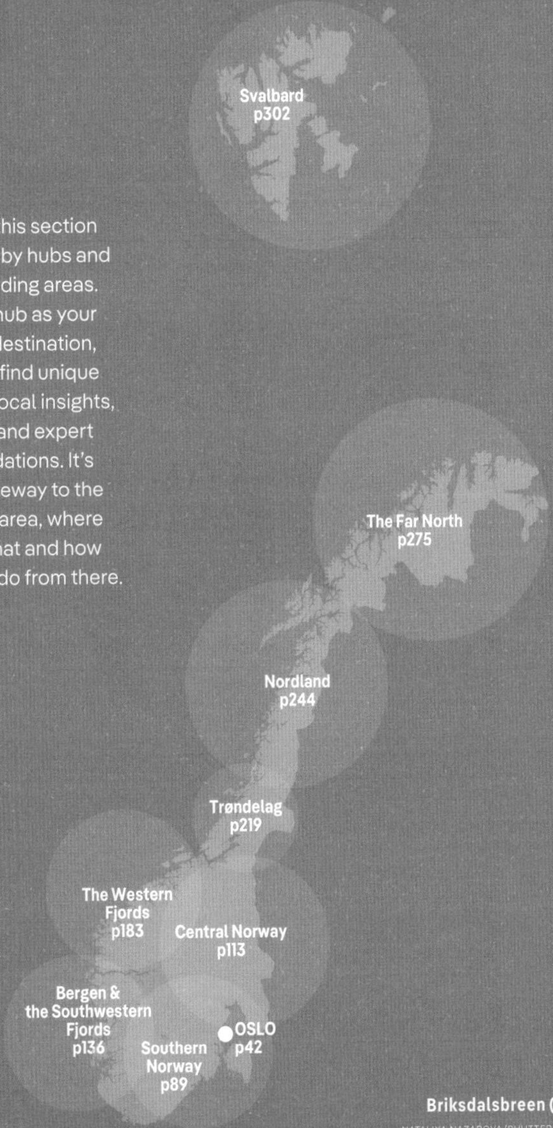

The Far North
p275

Nordland
p244

Trøndelag
p219

The Western
Fjords
p183

Central Norway
p113

Bergen &
the Southwestern
Fjords
p136

● OSLO
p42

Southern
Norway
p89

Briksdalsbreen (p197)

Oslo

THE NEW NORDIC CULTURE CAPITAL

Norway's quietly confident premier city is constantly evolving, with world-class cultural attractions and boundless opportunities for recreation.

Oslo has been playing a long game. Around a quarter of a century ago, it had to decide between redeveloping the neglected waterfront for industry or reimagining the area and creating accessible, enjoyable spaces for everyone. It decided on the latter, and in 2000 the municipality committed to creating Fjordbyen: the Fjord City.

Today, Oslo's locals and visitors are reaping the rewards, with outstanding cultural offerings, striking architecture, beaches, parks and a harbour promenade.

In 2008 the first of the star attractions opened: the Snøhetta-designed Oslo Opera House, all marble and glass and uncompromising angles. In hot pursuit came the Barcode development in 2011, packing a one-two punch of innovative architecture and roamable public realm. More recently, the immersive Deichman Bjørvika has redefined what a public library is, while the Munch Museum invites all to discover the works of one of the city's most venerated figures. And the National Museum, a 54,600-sq-metre celebration of art, design and architecture, opened in 2022.

The culinary scene has leapt forward too, with creative, seasonal menus becoming the norm at restaurants in every neighbourhood. Boundary-pushing chefs delight foodies, and Michelin stars twinkle across the city.

Since it was awarded the title of Green Capital of Europe in 2019, the city hasn't rested on its laurels, pledging to plant 100,000 trees by 2030 and encouraging citizens to reuse and recycle to reduce consumption.

Not all the developments have been welcomed by locals, though: in particular, the high-rise Barcode project was the most protested in Oslo's history. Yet a city so appealing attracts newcomers, and the municipality predicts that around 100,000 new homes will be needed by 2030. As the city faces pressure to accommodate its rising population, it remains to be seen whether the aversion to building upwards persists in this low-rise place.

As Oslo transforms, certain elements are constant: its lush forests, alluring fjord and ever-watchful Akershus Fortress endure, ensuring that the city will remain recognisable long into the future.

JHVEPHOTO/SHUTTERSTOCK ©

THE MAIN AREAS

GIEDRE VAITEKUNE/SHUTTERSTOCK ©

Left: Barcode district (p58); above: Astrup Fearnley Museum of Modern Art (p62)

FROGNER & WESTERN OSLO	GRÜNERLØKKA & VULKAN	GRØNLAND, TØYEN & EASTERN OSLO	BEYOND OSLO CITY CENTRE
Upscale real estate and elegant parks. **p69**	Buzzing bars and quirky shops. **p74**	Oslo's multicultural heart. **p79**	Outdoor activities and unexpected art. **p83**

Find Your Way

Compact Oslo's public transport is covered by Ruter's ticketing system and includes buses, trams, suburban and T-bane trains, and public ferries. Buy a ticket before boarding via Ruter's app or from physical service points. You'll find city bikes (oslobysykkel.no) and e-scooters (Voi, Ryde and Tier) everywhere for when your legs get tired.

FROM THE AIRPORT

Flytoget trains take you from Oslo Gardermoen International Airport to Oslo S train station in under 20 minutes and run every 10 minutes (less frequently between midnight and 6am). Regional Vy services are much cheaper, but there are only two or three an hour.

TRAM

Oslo's six-line tram service runs from around 5.30am to about 1am, and all except line 13 pass through Jernbanetorget, the square outside Oslo S train station. The tram stock is mostly modern, but line 12 still has small, old-style trams that aren't wheelchair accessible.

HOLMENKOLLEN

Emanual Vigeland Museum

Stasjonsveien

Beyond Oslo City Centre
p83

SKØYEN

ULLERN

△ *Vigelandsparken*
△ *Frognerparken*

Bøgstadveien

Kirkeveien

Trondheimsveien

Grünerløkka & Vulkan
p74

Mathallen

Ullernchassen

Vækerøveien

2 km

1 mile

Natural History Museum

Botanical Garden

Grønland, Tøyen & Eastern Oslo
p79

Bjørvika
p56

Opera House

Munch Museum

Sentrum
p48

Royal Palace

Akershus Festning

National Museum

Aker Brygge & Tjuvholmen
p60

Frogner & Western Oslo
p69

GIMLE

Ekebergparken

Ekebergveien

Valhallveien

Hovedøya

Bleikøya

Gressholmen

Heggholmen

Rambergøya

Lindøya

Nakholmen

Oslofjord

Langøyene

E18

Bygdøy
p64

Fram Museum

Paradisbukta

Drammensveien

T-BANE

Oslo's modern metro system, known as the T-bane (short for Tunnelbane), has five lines that snake out to the further reaches of the city and into the suburbs. All lines stop at Majorstuen, Jernbanetorget, Nationaltheatret, Stortinget, Grønland and Tøyen.

BUS

Buses weave across the city and run 24 hours, though there are fewer services overnight. Like trams, many buses stop at or close to Jernbanetorget. Buses have low floors, making them accessible for wheelchairs and pushchairs, and they all have screens announcing upcoming stops.

Plan Your Days

Start your day as the Norwegians do, with plenty of fresh black coffee – and perhaps some smoked salmon and eggs – before getting ready to hit the capital's high points.

GRISHA BRUEV/SHUTTERSTOCK ©

Aker Brygge (p60)

Day 1

Morning
● Devote the whole morning to the glorious **National Museum** (p61). Stop by the Munch Room to see the most vibrant version of *The Scream*.

Afternoon
● After lunch at one of **Aker Brygge's** quayside restaurants (p62), continue to **Tjuvholmen** (p62) and get a fix of contemporary art at **Astrup Fearnley Museum of Modern Art** (p62) before admiring the works in diminutive **Tjuvholmen Sculpture Park** (p62).

Evening
● Walk around the harbour and listen for the hourly **Rådhus** (p51) carillon chimes on your way to **Akershus Festning** (p51). Explore outdoors, then stroll to **Hitchhiker** (p53) for dinner and on to **HIMKOK** (p54) for cocktails.

You'll Also Want To...
Look for signs of Oslo's industrial heritage; step onto ships that took adventurers to the poles; and have a beach day, Oslo style.

WALK THE AKERSELVA
Meander along the **river** (p76) that powered Oslo, and see how former factories have been transformed.

SHOP AT SUNDAY MARKETS
Find a one-off souvenir at **Birkelunden Marked** (p77) or locally made artwork at **Ingensteds Sunday Market** (p77).

SEE ECLECTIC ARCHITECTURE
Find your way to **Barcode** (p58) via Akrobaten bridge to absorb the full effect of the futuristic high-rises.

GIEDRE VAITEKUNE/SHUTTERSTOCK ©, JJFARQ/SHUTTERSTOCK ©, DANNE_L/SHUTTERSTOCK ©

Day 2

Morning
● Pack a picnic and hop on the ferry to one or two of **Oslofjord's islands** (p85) for an escape away from the city centre.

Afternoon
● After lunch head to the **Munch Museum** (p57) and see beyond the artist's most famous work. Book a floating sauna session at **Oslo Badstuforening** (p59) or take a dip at **Sørenga Sjøbad** (p59).

Evening
● Visit the **Deichman Bjørvika** (p59) to marvel at the interior architecture, then walk onto the roof of the **Oslo Opera House** (p57) to see the sunset. Finish the evening at **SALT** (p59) for a casual bite and some up-and-coming acts.

Day 3

Morning
● Take tram 12 to **Vigelandsparken** (p70) to see Gustav Vigeland's life-size sculptures, then enjoy a takeaway lunch from **Happy Foods** (p71).

Afternoon
● Get to the **Royal Palace** (p50) in time for the Changing of the Guard, then tour the regal rooms (book ahead). Visit the **Queen Sonja Art Stable** (p55) to see the current exhibition from the royal collection. Jump a tram to Grünerløkka for some vintage shopping at **Frøken Dianas Salonger** (p77).

Evening
● Devour some noodles at **Hrimnir Ramen** (p78), then begin a Løkka bar crawl before ending the night with live music at **Blå** (p76).

EXPLORE THE POLES
Take the ferry to Bygdøy and venture onto polar-expedition ships at the **Fram Museum** (p66).

HAVE A BEACH DAY
Pack some snacks and take a trail through the forest to find some small-beach heaven at **Paradisbukta** (p65).

MEET THE VIKINGS
Time-travel back 1000 years to go on a virtual-reality raid at digital museum **Viking Planet** (p53).

LEAP FROM A SKI JUMP
Travel the T-bane to **Holmenkollen** (p86) and take the zip line from the top of Oslo's famous ski jump.

Sentrum

REGAL SIGHTS AND SHOPPING STREETS

☑ TOP TIP

It's difficult to get lost in Oslo's walkable city centre – if in doubt, just head for Karl Johans gate, the main shopping street running all the way from Oslo S train station right up to the Royal Palace. Jernbanetorget is a hub for public transport to any Sentrum sights and beyond.

Dominated by the imposing trio of Akershus Festning, the Royal Palace and Stortinget (the Norwegian parliament building), Oslo Sentrum is laden with history and packed with some of Norway's most significant buildings. In the city's thrumming heart, locals go about their regular commutes as tourists linger around all the stately sights. Sentrum's streets are lined with shops, restaurants and bars, with the marginally less tourist-trafficked places in the streets around Torggata.

The layout of the gridlike Kvadraturen area, etched behind the fortress, was created by Christian IV in the 17th century. After a fire in 1624 destroyed Oslo, which was then located further to the east, the king decreed that the city was to be rebuilt closer to Akershus Festning, and renamed Christiania. Four hundred years later the city centre is being transformed again: development of the new government quarter is underway following the 2011 terrorist attacks, with completion slated for 2030.

ANNA JEDYNAK/SHUTTERSTOCK ©

Rådhus (p51)

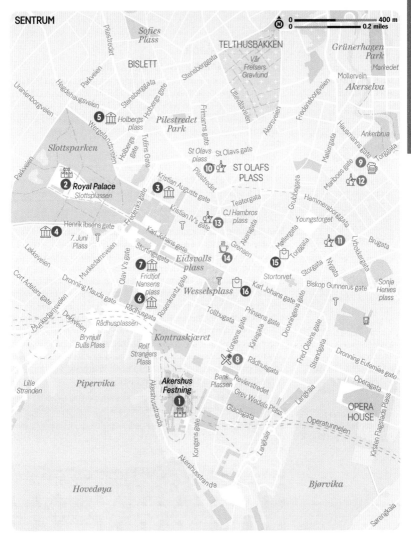

SENTRUM

0   400 m
0   0.2 miles

TELTHUSBAKKEN

Grünerhagen Park

Sofies Plass

BISLETT

Vår Frelsers Gravlund

Markedet

Akerselva

Pilestredet Park

St Olavs plass

St Olavs gate

ST OLAFS PLASS

Ankerbrua

Slottsparken

Royal Palace
Slottsplassen

Teatergata

CJ Hambros plass

Youngstorget

Henrik Ibsens gate

7. Juni Plass

Karl Johans gate

Grensen

Brugata

Eidsvolls plass

Fridtjof Nansens plass

Wesselsplass

Stortorvet

Karl Johans gate

Biskop Gunnerus gate

Sonja Henies plass

Tollbugata

Prinsens gate

Rådhusplassen

Brynjulf Bulls Plass

Rolf Strangers Plass

Kontraskjæret

Lille Stranden

Pipervika

Akershus Festning

Bank Plassen

Revierstredet

Grev Wedels Plass

Glaclsgata

Rådhusgata

OPERA HOUSE

Operatunnelen

Hovedøya

Bjørvika

HIGHLIGHTS
1 Akershus Festning
2 Royal Palace

SIGHTS
3 Historical Museum
4 IBSEN Museum & Teater

5 Kunstnernes Hus
6 Rådhus
7 Viking Planet

EATING
8 Rest

DRINKING & NIGHTLIFE
9 Crow Bar
10 Fuglen
11 HIMKOK
12 Papa Borracho

13 RØØR
14 Stockfleths

SHOPPING
15 Glasmagasinet
16 Steen & Strøm

QUEEN SONJA ART STABLE

Transformed into a gallery in 2017 in honour of the Queen's 80th birthday, the palace's stables now host changing exhibitions from the royal collection, with pieces mounted in the wooden stalls, which still have historic, hoof-level scratches in the wood.

Recent exhibitions have included *Craftsmanship of the Royal Palace*, celebrating the skills of artisans working for the royals, such as bookbinders and furniture upholsterers. Unlike the palace, the gallery is open all year round (except when a new exhibition is being mounted) and you can buy tickets at the door.

The Royal Palace
AN APPROACHABLE HOME FIT FOR A KING

Residence and office of the Norwegian Royals, the **Royal Palace** (Det kongelige slott) took 25 years to build, with construction spanning the reigns of two kings. Carl Johan (1763–1844) laid the foundation stone on Bellevue hill in 1825 but died before the palace was completed; his successor, Oscar I (1799–1859) inaugurated it in 1849.

The dignified, buttercup-yellow-and-white neoclassical building sits proudly at the top of Karl Johans gate, surrounded by the verdant **Palace Park** (Slottsparken) with its mature trees, duck-friendly ponds and shaded spots to read a book or watch the world go by.

Despite the palace being home to the Norwegian head of state, **Slottsplassen**, the square and parade ground directly in front, is completely open for visitors to wander around and appreciate the palace up close. If you're there around 1.30pm you'll see the Changing of the Guard, which tends to be more elaborate in summer, when the King's Guards march alongside a military band.

Between late June and mid-August you can join guided tours that give you a sneak peek inside a few of the palace's most significant rooms, including the gloriously gilded White Salon and the opulent banqueting halls. Ticket sales open in March for the upcoming season and you can book ahead through ticketmaster. Any remaining tickets are available at the door each day, but if you don't speak Norwegian it's better to book in advance as only five of the daily tours are presented in English.

TTSTUDIO/SHUTTERSTOCK ©

Royal Palace

Start in **1 Slottsparken**. Spend some time strolling the tree-filled park before walking towards the statue in front of the **2 Royal Palace**. The figure astride the horse is **3 Carl Johan**, king of Sweden and Norway from 1818 to 1844. Head down the steps and continue along the tree-lined avenue, focus of Constitution Day celebrations in Oslo every 17 May. Cross the road and continue until you see three grand neoclassical buildings on your left, the original **4 University of Oslo** complex, which opened in 1852. Today only the Faculty of Law remains at this site. Cross the road towards the park; directly ahead is a statue of Bergen-born writer and playwright **5 Ludvig Holberg** (1684–1754) standing between two of his characters, Henrik and Pernille. Walk around the raised flower beds to the front of the Henrik Bull–designed **6 National Theatre**, which

opened in 1899. The titan playwrights Henrik Ibsen and Bjørnstjerne Bjørnson are honoured with statues outside. Walk through the park, then cross the road towards the **7 Grand Café**, where Ibsen and Munch were regulars in the 1890s. Cross back over the road to reach **8 Stortinget**, Norway's parliament building. The H-shaped building overlooking Eidsvol plass is said to represent two arms outstretched towards the country's people. Walk down Stortingsgata, taking a left on Roald Amundsens gate. Continue towards the **9 Rådhus** (City Hall), which opened in 1950. Wander around the building to take in the array of sculptures and woodcarvings and listen out for the carillon marking the hours. Then head up Rådhusgata towards the medieval fortress **10 Akershus Festning**, where you can find an elevated spot to look out across the Oslofjord.

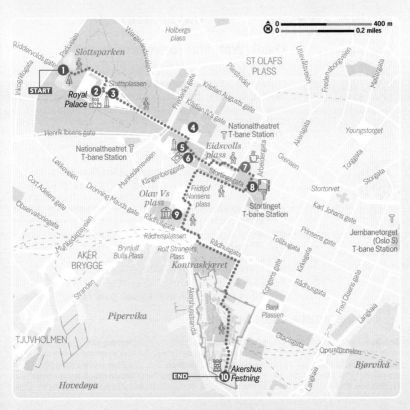

OSLO PASS: IS IT WORTH IT?

With free entry to most of Oslo's biggest attractions including the Munch Museum, the Bygdøy museums (plus the ferry) and a daily travel pass for Zone I, the Oslo Pass could save you some kroner, but do the maths before you buy one. As an example, if you plan to visit three attractions and make two single journeys on public transport in one day, a 24-hour Oslo Pass will likely save you money. Passes last for 24, 48 and 72 hours; the longer the pass, the lower the per-day cost.

Scan for more info:

Historical Museum

MORE IN SENTRUM

Oslo's Watchful Fortress

A MEDIEVAL SYMBOL OF POWER

Occupying a key defensive position on a promontory over-looking the fjord, the fortress **Akershus Festning** has been keeping guard over the city since it was built by Håkon V in 1299. The sprawling complex comprises around 30 notable structures, including walls with bastions, towers, powder magazines and gates as well as the palace itself. You can stroll around outside at leisure for free – it takes just under hour.

It's well worth the entrance fee to **Akershus Slott**, the medieval castle upgraded with Renaissance stylings by Christian IV from the early 17th century. The route inside takes you past a tiny but sinister dungeon and the restored Castle Church, as well as the Hall of Christian IV – used today for government receptions – with its astonishingly vibrant medieval tapestries. Kings and queens ancient and recent are interred in the **Royal Mausoleum**, including Håkon V and King Olav V, father of the present monarch. Don't miss the Hall of Olav IV: Emanuel Vigeland's radiant **Rose Window**, which was destroyed by an explosion in 1943, was painstakingly restored

 BUDGET BITES IN OSLO SENTRUM

Rice Bowl
Arrive with an appetite: portions are huge at this popular Thai cafe in Kvadraturen. €

Freddy Fuego
Freddy's secret marinade will make you want to fill up on these fresh, flavour-packed burritos. €

Nordvegan
Eat vegan cakes, freshly made salads and warming plant-based mains at this stylish canteen. €

and finally unveiled in 2023. Bring some headphones – you can scan QR codes along the route to listen to an accompanying audio guide.

Also in the complex is the **Norwegian Resistance Museum**, which documents resistance to the Nazi occupation of Norway during WWII, and the **Armed Forces Museum**, with its huge halls filled with weaponry and exhibits charting military history right up to the present day. The explanatory text at both of these museums is predominantly in Norwegian, though most exhibits have at least a summary in English too.

Archaeological Treasures

STONE AGE AND VIKING-ERA FINDS

Part of the Museum of Cultural History, the **Historical Museum** is the grand art nouveau display case for the country's largest collection of archaeological and ethnographic finds from the Stone Age onwards. Exhibitions guide you past objects illuminating nature's forces upon cultures and posing questions about humans' relationship with animals. There's also an emotive display of art and objects related to Norway's stave churches. Upstairs, the largest collection of coins in Norway spans 2600 years of glittering glory, while Egyptian artefacts are displayed with accompanying context about their acquisition at the peak of Egyptomania. The jewel in the crown, though, is the **VIKINGR** exhibition on the 3rd floor, with wonderfully preserved artefacts from the Viking Age including swords, gleaming gold and silver jewellery, and a Viking helmet from the 10th century, alongside details about the societal role of Viking warriors. Plan to spend around 1½ to two hours here.

Vikings for the Digital Age

MULTIMEDIA ROMP THROUGH VIKING LORE

Viking Planet, the world's first digital museum dedicated to the Viking era, takes you on a virtual visit to the Norway of 1000 years ago with immersive videos, interactive timelines of notable events and life-size holograms of fictional Viking Age characters. The star exhibit is *The Ambush,* an award-winning 12-minute VR movie transporting you onto a longboat during a Viking raid. It's pricey compared to other museums, but it's worth visiting for the digital renderings of the finds from the magnificent *Gokstad* and *Oseberg* ships alone. The exhibit is effectively a digital walkthrough of the Viking Ship Museum pre-renovation and, though the

BEST FOR DRINKS IN OSLO SENTRUM

Stockfleths
Visit the original branch at Lille Grensen for the perfect caffeine hit with a chaser of coffee history.

Fuglen
Caffeinating locals since 1963, Fuglen has house-roasted coffee, first-rate cocktails and mid-century modern style.

Crow Bar
A locals' favourite, with beer-loving staff who'll help you choose from more than 20 house and guest brews.

RØØR
Up to 74 beers and four meads on tap, with shuffleboard and an exclusively vinyl soundtrack.

Papa Borracho
Expertly mixed cocktails and good vibes guaranteed at this intimate *mezcaleria*.

 WHERE TO EAT IN OSLO SENTRUM

Dinner	Hitchhiker	Arakataka
Sleek, monochrome styling is the backdrop for comforting dim sum and other Cantonese and Szechuan classics. €€	Formerly in Mathallen, Hitchhiker brings East Asian street-food dishes to culture venue Sentralen. €€€	A set menu and small plates showcase Nordic seasonal fare in a relaxed, mural-accented dining room. €€€

two museums aren't connected, it's the closest you'll get to these treasures until 2026.

Sentrum Shopping
FIND YOUR PERFECT STYLE

Oslo's compact Sentrum squeezes a lot of fashion into its modest footprint, from high-street standards to designer giants. The eastern end of Karl Johans gate (nearest to Oslo S) is the place to go for ubiquitous retailers such as H&M, Zara and BikBok, while designer devotees should make a beeline for Nedre Slottsgate and Øvre Slottsgate, both lined with exclusive names such as Acne Studios, Hermès, Dior and Chanel. Upmarket department store **Steen & Strøm** is a stylish showroom for yet more high fashion (darling) including Gucci, while long-established **Glasmagasinet** is the place to go for design-forward homewares from brands including Illums Bolighus.

A Sustainable Menu
TURNING 'WASTE' FOOD INTO GOURMET GOLD

If you're planning to push the boat out on an extraordinary fine-dining experience, **Rest** will delight your palate and leave your conscience clear. Award-winning founder and head chef Jimmy Øien is on a mission to address the issue of food waste in the restaurant industry, and he creates exquisite food using ingredients that would otherwise be discarded. 'Ugly' vegetables are given a masterly makeover and produce is never overlooked simply because it's not considered to be the 'right' size or weight for an exclusive restaurant. The multicourse tasting menu is served in a courtyard restaurant decorated using secondhand materials. Book well in advance.

Drinks at HIMKOK
YOUR NEW FAVOURITE COCKTAIL BAR

A stencilled 'H' on the inconspicuous blue frontage is the only indicator that you've arrived at HIMKOK, a cocktail-quaffer's paradise. The name means moonshine and you sometimes have to ring the bell to enter, but there are no gimmicks here – just decadent drinks crafted by expert white-coat-wearing bartenders using premium house-distilled vodka, aquavit and gin. Knowledgeable servers are enthusiasts themselves and will help you find your next favourite from the selection of magic mixes on offer. Non-alcoholic concoctions are just as inspired. Then simply recline with your perfectly balanced

BEST MUSIC FESTIVALS

Øyafestivalen
A four-day Tøyenparken takeover each August, packed with big-name Norwegian and international acts.

Tons of Rock
For those about to rock...go directly to Ekebergsletta in June for four days of legendary rock and metal.

Inferno Metal Festival
Metal fans converge on Rockefeller Music Hall around Easter for an amalgam of black-metal bands.

Ultima Oslo Contemporary Music Festival
Genre-spanning, boundary-bending summertime festival staged over 10 days at venues across Oslo.

by:Larm
A three-day industry showcase of up-and-coming Nordic acts in September.

WHERE TO STAY IN OSLO SENTRUM

K7 Hotel	Citybox	Bob W
There's no party atmosphere, but the dorms at this hotel are decent and the location super central. €	How budget hotels should be done, with spacious rooms and boutique-chic communal spaces. €	Stylish, keycard-free rooms with smartphone-operated locks and free-to-use Instax cameras. €€

Aurora performing at Øyafestivalen

BEST ART IN OSLO SENTRUM

Kunstnernes Hus
Run by artists for artists, this independent gallery is housed in a functionalist building overlooking Slottsparken and hosts exhibitions and events celebrating contemporary art and film.

Queen Sonja Art Stable
Changing exhibitions of Norwegian art and items from the royal collection are displayed in the Royal Palace's exquisitely restored stable block.

Rådhus
The functionalist City Hall is laden with art, from Norse mythology–themed carvings and sculptures on its exterior to frescoes by Alf Rolfsen and Henrik Sørensen in Rådhushallen.

drink – chilled by a branded ice cube – in the chestnut-hued seating. There's also an outdoor area with a cider bar for those long Norwegian summer evenings.

Inside the Writer's Room
THE HOME OF HENRIK IBSEN

Join one of the hourly tours at the **IBSEN Museum & Teater** to see inside the apartment where renowned playwright Henrik Ibsen completed his last two plays and learn about his life and writing process. The home where he and his wife, Suzannah, lived out their final years is beautifully preserved, from the study where Ibsen worked – overlooked by a portrait of his literary rival August Strindberg as a means of motivation – to the bedroom where he exclaimed his final words: 'On the contrary!'. There's also a small exhibition on the floor below, with multimedia displays examining a selection of his works, including *Peer Gynt* and *Hedda Gabler,* and a separate room with an immersive animated experience projected across the walls, ceiling and floor. The last tour of the day begins one hour before closing.

 WHERE TO STAY IN OSLO SENTRUM

Smarthotel	Karl Johan Hotel	Hotel Continental
Near to Slottsparken with no-frills, compact rooms offset by a large, vintage-inspired guest lounge. €€	A city-centre retreat with neutral grey decor and a bountiful breakfast served in a light-filled atrium. €€€	Five-star luxury in prime National Theatre proximity with plush furnishings and Molton Brown toiletries. €€€

Bjørvika

FJORD-SIDE ARTS AND ARCHITECTURE

☑ **TOP TIP**

Oslo S is just a few minutes' walk directly to the north, and trams 13 and 19 (plus several bus services including regional routes) serve the Bjørvika stop. The Sukkerbiten and Sørenga areas are connected by a pedestrian bridge across the water.

If it's been a while since you visited Oslo, you'll scarcely recognise Bjørvika. Sure, the Opera House that opened in 2008 is still here, and still attracting visitors and locals up onto its sloping roof. But what was previously a jewel in an otherwise nondescript area is now simply one focal point in a stylish neighbourhood packed with show-stopping architecture and some rollicking good harbourside fun.

Bjørvika is very roughly '3'-shaped, running from Langkaia, which is lined with floating saunas, around to Sørenga, with its residential developments and harbour baths. The Sukkerbiten and Munch quays jut out into the water between them, while the tracks into Oslo S train station mark its upper boundary.

Between the traditional sights – the monumental Munch Museum and Oslo Opera House among them – there are quayside restaurants, bars and cafes, while 100m-long Operastranda beach and its surrounding park offer yet another reason to enjoy the harbour.

ROBSONPHOTO/SHUTTERSTOCK ©

Oslo Opera House

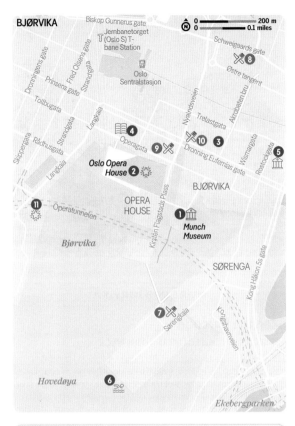

BJØRVIKA

Biskop Gunnerus gate

Jernbanetorget
(Oslo S) T-
bane Station

Schweigaards gate

Østre tangent

0 — 200 m
0 — 0.1 miles

Oslo
Sentralstasjon

Dronningens gate

Prinsens gate

Fred Olsens gate

Strandgata

Tollbugata

Skippergata

Rådhusgata

Langgata

Strandgata

Langgata

Nylandsveien

Operagata

Trelastgata

Akrobaten bru

Dronning Eufemias gate

Wismargata

Rostockgata

Oslo Opera House ❷

OPERA HOUSE

BJØRVIKA

❶ Munch Museum

Kirsten Flagstads Plass

Bjørvika

❶ Operatunnelen

SØRENGA

Kong Håkon 5s gate

Sørenkaia

Kongshavnveien

Hovedøya ❻

Ekebergparken

Munch Museum

CELEBRATING NORWAY'S MOST FAMOUS ARTIST

Opened in 2021, the hulking **Munch Museum**, dedicated to Edvard Munch, is the new home for the city's collection of his 26,000 artworks. Many of the most famous paintings are on display in the collection exhibition *Munch: Infinite,* while the immersive *Shadows* exhibition is themed around Munch's home in Ekely, just outside Oslo, with poignant displays of belongings, including the red-and-white bedspread depicted in *Self-Portrait: Between the Clock and the Bed.*

Three versions of *Skrik* (The Scream) are shown here: a painting, a print and a drawing. However, because of their fragility, only one is displayed at a time, rotating roughly once an hour.

Oslo Opera House

Still Hitting the High Notes

Home of the Norwegian Opera and Ballet, the marble iceberg **Oslo Opera House** on the harbourfront was designed by homegrown architect Snøhetta. Its 36,000 blocks of white Italian Carrara marble piece together to create its iconic sloping form, which seems to rise out of the fjord, water lapping the stone. Strolling up onto the roof to get an Opera House view of the city is an Oslo rite of passage. Inside, the ice-cool feel of the exterior melts away with the warmth of undulating oak panelling.

There's a full program of performances across its three stages; if you're fast you can snap up 100kr 'listening seats'. Meanwhile, excellent guided tours take you behind the scenes to see some of the 1000 rooms, workshops and rehearsal spaces, and if you're very lucky you might see the stage being reconfigured for a performance.

The sculpture just a few metres out in the fjord is Monica Bonvicini's *She Lies,* which twists and turns with the tide and gets locked in place when the fjord freezes in winter.

57

BEST PLACES TO EAT IN BJØRVIKA

Barcode Street Food
A small selection of options including tacos and poke bowls for when you and your companions can't agree. €

Bun's
Mouth-watering burgers and fjord views lure would-be swimmers away from the Sørenga pools. €

Salome
Italian classics and Venetian sharing plates to linger over under the orange terrace umbrellas. €€

Vaaghals
This Barcode trailblazer serves seasonal Norwegian fare conjured into creative dishes. €€€

Maaemo
Norway's only three-Michelin-star restaurant will serve you the meal of a lifetime. €€€

DIGITALMAMMOTH/SHUTTERSTOCK ©

Barcode

MORE IN BJØRVIKA

Scan the Barcode
SEEING AN ARCHITECTURAL SHOWPIECE

The 12 high-rise structures known collectively as **Barcode** have become a feature of Oslo's skyline since they were completed in 2016. Alternating between dark and light to resemble (you guessed it) a barcode, the individual buildings were designed by different firms according to an overall plan; each is architecturally unique, but they combine to form one cohesive development.

Initially, there was nothing between Barcode and the fjord but, since Bjørvika has developed, the best way to appreciate the overall effect is now from **Akrobaten** (The Acrobat), a pedestrian bridge spanning the train tracks leading to Oslo S. Walk over the bridge, take in the view, then stroll between the buildings to see the characteristics of each edifice. Aside from offices for major national and international companies, such as Deloitte, Barcode encompasses apartments, shops, restaurants and gallery spaces, notably **Kunsthall Oslo**, a small, not-for-profit gallery showcasing the work of national and international contemporary artists.

During the planning stages, there was fierce local opposition to the development, but over a decade later Barcode is here to stay and integral to Bjørvika's character.

 BEST BJØRVIKA CAFES

Mike's Corner
A selection of subs including *laab mih* (ground meat salad), plus beer, sodas and merch so you can 'Be Like Mike'. €

Talormade
Get a quality caffeine hit along with a fluffy doughnut at this pastel-pink shop in the Bispevika area. €

Åpent Bakeri
The Barcode-based outlet of this Oslo chain offers coffee, hearty salads and the freshest of pastries. €

A Library for All
Discover More Than Books

The six-floor **Deichman Bjørvika** is Oslo residents' one-stop community shop for books, events, workshops, films, courses and meeting spaces. Imagined by architects Lundhagen and Atelier Oslo, the striking building's cantilevered design maximises its footprint while maintaining a low profile. As you enter, your eyes are drawn upwards by dynamic angles and contrasting textures, all lit by three enormous skylights. Wandering around the building is a joy, with unexpected art installations and short films tucked away in tiny rooms like pearls. On the 2nd floor, don't miss Simone Hooymans' *Talking Plants* (Plantenes Stemme), an animated installation with an otherworldly soundscape and botanical drawings.

Fjord-side Fun at Sørenga Sjøbad
SWIMMING AT THE BUZZING BATHS

Osloites make the most of the short-lived Norwegian summers, and hundreds descend upon **Sørenga Sjøbad** sea baths on a hot sunny day to take advantage of the long days. But the floating oasis is popular year-round, with a beach, a fjord pool, diving platforms and a children's pool, plus a large green to simply relax on. As you walk towards the baths you'll pass a string of restaurants, a couple of which have dress codes (ie no board shorts).

If you want to try kayaking you can stop by the **DNT Friluftshuset** to book in for guided sessions. You might even spot Instafamous Fluffy (@friluftskattenfluffy), a lifejacket-wearing cat who sometimes joins the paddling sessions.

An Evening at SALT
AN INCLUSIVE CULTURAL SCENE

Reminiscent of the fish-drying racks seen along Norway's coast, this collection of pyramid-shaped buildings on Langkaia is **SALT**, a hub for culture and entertainment. The programme includes comedy, music, DJs and cinema, and aims to give a platform to amateurs and more seasoned artists alike. Even if you're not there for an event, you can book in for a sauna, lounge under fairy lights on the thrifted sofas and chairs at the bar inside, or enjoy a drink with harbour views on the terrace. Hungry? Grab a bite from one of the on-site food trucks. Originally planned to be in Oslo for just a year, SALT has been granted permission to stay until 2028.

FUTURE LIBRARY

Scottish artist Katie Paterson had a vision for a **Future Library** and, to realise her idea of a living, literary time capsule, 1000 trees have been planted in Oslo's **Nordmarka** forest. After a century, the trees will be felled and made into books, the stories for which are being written in secret, one a year, by renowned authors that so far have included Margaret Atwood, Karl Ove Knausgård and Tsitsi Dangarembga. The books won't be published until 2114, and until then a new manuscript will be added each year to its own locked drawer in the purpose-built, wood-lined Quiet Room, which you can visit for free on the top floor of the Deichman Bjørvika.

EXPLORING NORDMARKA
Venture beyond Oslo city centre to explore **Nordmarka** (p86), the forest where the trees for the Future Library have been planted. The 430-sq-km expanse of lush greenery is filled with hiking and skiing trails and is easy to reach by public transport.

 ## HARBOURSIDE SAUNAS

KOK	Oslo Badstuforening	SALT
Book two-hour shared or private sessions at Langkaia or Aker Brygge, or a sauna cruise out on the fjord.	Bringing 'saunas to the people' with a range of options both large and small at Langkaia and Sukkerbiten.	Book into your own 100-year-old aquavit barrel sauna or join a session with DJs spinning a sauna soundtrack.

Aker Brygge & Tjuvholmen

NATIONAL TREASURES AND WATERSIDE RESTAURANTS

☑ **TOP TIP**

Tram 12 stops at Aker Brygge outside the National Museum and you can walk alongside the waterfront to reach the bridges to Tjuvholmen. Alternatively, bus 21 runs directly to Tjuvholmen – it stops beside Skur13 skate park. Ferries to islands in the Oslofjord leave from Aker Brygge's platform E.

The connected areas of Aker Brygge and Tjuvholmen were once a warren of industrial wharves and coastal traffic. Aker Brygge was one of the first stretches of the harbour to be redeveloped as part of Oslo's three-decade-long waterfront transformation, and its offices in converted warehouses and stylish restaurants and bars are now a long-established feature of the city's ever-evolving personality.

Tjuvholmen – meaning 'Thief Islet' – wasn't far behind Aker Brygge in being rehabilitated. It was less than salubrious in the days of old (criminals were sometimes brought here to be executed in the 18th century), but its name has inspired a notable five-star hotel, and contemporary art galleries, harbour swimming spots, restaurants and a skate park have settled onto the islet over the past few decades. And the neighbourhood hasn't stayed still, with the opening of the outstanding National Museum in 2022 adding further weight to its appeal.

STEFANO ZACCARIA/SHUTTERSTOCK ©

National Museum

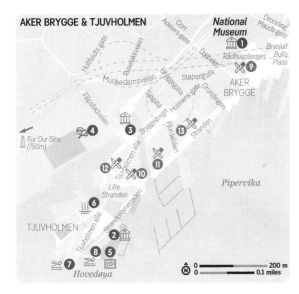

National Museum

NORWAY'S TREASURES OF ART AND DESIGN

Norway's long-awaited **National Museum** covers classic and modern art, design and architecture all under one Kleihues + Schuwerk–designed roof.

The main collection, arranged chronologically, is displayed in 86 rooms over two floors. On the 1st (ground) floor, precious objects from antiquity to the 1900s, grouped in themes such as 'Everything Norwegian is Danish', lead into rooms covering 20th-century design. One floor up, Norwegian and international artists from the 1500s to the present day are represented; prompts encourage you to ponder questions such as 'What makes a work of art beautiful?' The 3rd-floor Light Hall, with 9000 energy-efficient lights, hosts temporary exhibitions. Its lighting scheme can be seen from outside.

The **Munch Room** (Room 60) has the most vibrant version of *The Scream* of the four on public display in Oslo. If you want to guarantee you'll see the one you recognise, this is the place to come. In the foyer, don't miss *Pile O' Sapmi Supreme* by Sami artist Maret Anne Sara; the 400 reindeer skulls arranged in the form of the Sami flag speak to the injustices Sami people still suffer in Norway.

The museum is 54,600 sq metres – the equivalent of eight soccer pitches – so it's easy to get overwhelmed. Pause to scan the map first, and head for the rooms you're most interested in. If you have a multiday Oslo Pass, you can break up your visit over two days.

DESIGNING A MUSEUM

Intended by the architects to be timeless rather than fashionable, the National Museum's low-profile, L-shaped form is covered with textured Norwegian slate from Oppdal – 28,000 sq metres of it. An inviting courtyard leads into a spacious entrance foyer; be sure to look carefully at the floor: there are fossils in the limestone.

Such a vast exhibition space makes museum fatigue a real possibility. Happily, you're unlikely to suffer from it here, as carefully considered colour schemes create a boredom-beating visual difference between rooms.

BEST PLACES TO EAT

Bollebar
Get a decadent sugar hit with an iced, filled bun from this jolly shop by the National Museum. €

Døgnvill Burger
Try the Royale with Cheese (it *is* a tasty burger) and an 'X-rated' milkshake at this top-notch Norwegian minichain. €€

Yōkozo
Order your choice of sushi, small plates, ramen and salads via tablet at this relaxed restaurant. €€

Lofoten Fiskerestaurant
Savour perfectly presented seafood in an elegant setting with crisp white tablecloths and warm staff. €€€

xef
Spain meets Norway: traditional Spanish techniques transform local ingredients into tapas and tasting menus. €€€

GJEDRE VAITEKUNE/SHUTTERSTOCK ©

Canal alongside Astrup Fearnley Museum of Modern Art

MORE IN AKER BRYGGE & TJUVHOLMEN

Art to Steal Your Heart

PRIVATE GALLERIES AND PUBLIC ART

There's always new art to discover on Tjuvholmen, from one-off sculptures in public spaces to exhibitions in unique galleries showcasing contemporary artists. The sail-like wood-clad buildings connected by an over-canal walkway were created by Renzo Piano and form the **Astrup Fearnley Museum of Modern Art**. It celebrated its 30th anniversary in 2023 and continues to thrill art lovers with frequently refreshed exhibitions of the collection, which includes works by Damien Hirst, Jeff Koons and Børre Sætre. **Tjuvholmen Sculpture Park** comprises nine works, and most are displayed on the lawn between the museum and the fjord. The joyful collection includes the ambiguous *Eyes* by Louise Bourgeois and *Untitled* by Anish Kapoor. **FineArt Oslo** is a gallery representing more than 500 contemporary artists, including Håkon Bleken, and has 2000 sq metres of space for exhibiting regular solo shows. You'll find the gallery right between Tjuvholmen and Aker Brygge, over the bridge from Bryggetorget plaza.

WHERE TO GET A DRINK IN AKER BRYGGE & TJUVHOLMEN

Oh Dear
A dizzying wine selection from across the globe (even Denmark), with tapas snacks to nibble while you sip.

Underbar
If there's a liquor that this cosy and relaxed bar underneath the Beer Palace doesn't have, it's not worth it.

Thief Rooftop
Ask for the Spritz of The Week and watch the sun dip across the fjord from The Thief's rooftop terrace.

Splash Out
TJUVOLMEN'S SWIMMING SPOTS

At the furthest end of Tjuvholmen are a couple of inviting places to cool down on a hot day. **Tjuvholmen bystrand** is a petite shingle beach fringing the grassy sculpture park, and its gentle slope into the water makes it ideal for families with young children who only want to get their feet wet. Meanwhile, the **Tjuvholmen badeplass** swimming area is much livelier; join the sunbathers and energetic (and plucky) youngsters who leap into the chilly harbour from the floating wooden jetty. There aren't any changing facilities, so you'll have to get dressed under a towel, but it's all part of the harbour bathing experience.

Five-Star Relaxation
LUXURIATING IN THE THIEF SPA

The Thief hotel offers luxury lodgings in a prime spot on Tjuvholmen, but you don't have to stay overnight to enjoy a little of the five-star lifestyle. The **Thief Spa** offers sessions for nonguests and a selection of treatments to soothe travel-weary muscles or rejuvenate tired skin – its classic facial will leave you looking radiant and feeling reborn. Lie back and let the welcoming, well-qualified therapists pamper you before you float to the spa area, where you can sweat it out in the Finnish sauna and cool off with your choice of water therapy under a 'sensory sky' shower. Round out your afternoon of self-care by heading to the **Thief Rooftop** to watch the sun set over the fjord with a refreshing spritz.

Street Sports
SKATE PARK AND OUTDOOR GYM

The **Skur13** skate park, run by the Oslo Skateboard Association, is a 1500-sq-metre hangar filled with ramps, rails, ledges and stairs that was built for the X-Games street course in 2016. Now open to everyone, it's free all day on Wednesday and in the afternoons on other weekdays (there's a small charge on weekends). You can even borrow equipment for free if you haven't packed your own. Beside Skur13 there's an **outdoor gym**, with pull-up bars aplenty and a three-lane 100m running track – though you're more likely to see people strolling, rather than sprinting, down it.

FOR OUR SINS

In 2021 a young walrus nicknamed Freya was spotted along the coast of several European countries, far south of her usual Arctic habitat. By July 2022, 600kg Freya had arrived in the Oslofjord. Many people ignored pleas from authorities to keep their distance, and a few came close to being seriously injured. Citing issues of public safety, officials euthanised her, triggering international outrage. Critics argued that the people were at fault, and the walrus could have been relocated. Freya has been memorialised by Astri Tonoian's lifelike sculpture **For Our Sins**, unveiled in April 2023 at Kongens Marina, just over 1km from Tjuvolmen, along the harbour promenade towards Bygdøy.

WHERE TO GET ICE CREAM IN AKER BRYGGE & TJUVHOLMEN

Paradis	Hennig Olsen	Mövenpick
Choose from 20 flavours of Oslo's best gelato and sorbet at the chain's original shop. €	Norway's beloved ice-cream manufacturer has a kiosk by Aker Brygge's clock tower. €	There's always a queue at this kiosk serving creamy Swiss-style ice cream. €

Bygdøy

LEAFY MUSEUM PENINSULA

☑ TOP TIP

The Bygdøy ferry from Rådhusbrygga serves the museums at Bygdøynes. It's free with the Oslo Pass; otherwise, you can pay on board (Ruter tickets aren't accepted). It also stops at Dronningen for the Norwegian Folk Museum, but it's an 800m walk; bus 30 is more convenient as it stops right outside the museum before continuing to Huk.

A pretty peninsula to the west of the city, Bygdøy is mostly residential and offers a sedate alternative to the buzz of central Oslo. Distinguished white villas are strung along wide avenues lined with mature trees, and forested areas provide green spaces for recreation.

Sitting in among the exclusive abodes are some of the best-known and most frequently visited museums in the capital. Bygdøy also has a few scenic, rocky beaches that are perfect if you want to get away from the crowds at the harbourside bathing spots of Tjuvholmen or Sørenga.

The area at the tip of the peninsula is known as Bygdøynes and you could easily spend all day at the cluster of museums here – each is packed with information. Along the shoreline directly in front of the museums you'll find a lawn area and several benches – it's a perfect place for picnicking.

KON-TIKI – THE GREATEST SEA ADVENTURE OF OUR TIME

SAKOSP/SHUTTERSTOCK ©

Kon-Tiki Museum (p67)

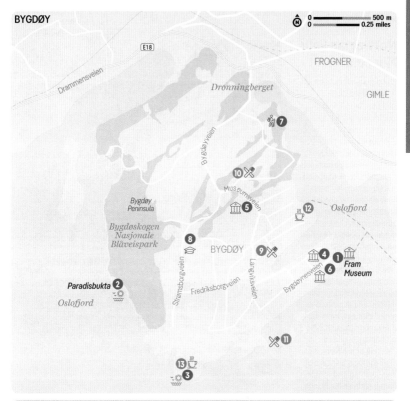

BYGDØY

HIGHLIGHTS
1. Fram Museum
2. Paradisbukta

SIGHTS
3. Huk
4. Kon-Tiki Museum
5. Norwegian Folk Museum

6. Norwegian Maritime Museum

ACTIVITIES, COURSES & TOURS
7. Havnepromenaden
8. Kongskogen

EATING
9. Café Hjemme hos Svigers
10. Gartneriet Kongsgården
11. Lille Herben

DRINKING & NIGHTLIFE
12. Le Crêpe D'Elen
13. Paahuk

Paradisbukta
BYGDØY'S PARADISE BAY

A little coastal haven on the western side of Bygdøy, rustic, forest-backed **Paradisbukta** (Paradise Bay) is a popular place to relax in the sun, wade into the water for a swim, or pause and gaze out at the sailboats in the fjord. From the bus stop at Huk, it's a 1km walk through the trees along Christian Frederiks vei. There are few amenities here – just a couple of portaloos and a drinking-water tap (the kiosk is currently closed), but it's all the more special for it.

Paradisbukta

GENLOCKI/GETTYIMAGES ©

Norwegian Folk Museum

NORWEGIAN LIFE IN A NUTSHELL

Discover what life was like for Norwegians in days gone by at the **Norwegian Folk Museum**. Peek inside centuries-old farmsteads transported from around southern Norway, and hear costumed guides tell stories of life in the countryside. Look out for medieval doodles etched on the pillars of 13th-century Gol Stave Church. The Old Town recalls city life, with an apartment block decorated across different time periods and social classes. Indoors, the Timescape exhibition presents the gilded lifestyle of the Norwegian elite through displays of fine clothing and trinkets acquired from far-flung lands. You'll likely spend longer here than you planned to – allow at least three hours.

FROM TOP: TRABANTOS/SHUTTERSTOCK ©: SAMOSP/SHUTTERSTOCK ©

Norwegian Folk Museum

Fram Museum

POLAR EXPLORATION BY SEA

Fram Museum

Delve into the history of polar endeavour at the **Fram Museum** and explore two legendary ships, *Fram* and *Gjøa,* which took pioneers Fridtjof Nansen and Roald Amundsen on expeditions to the poles. Step on board the *Fram*, surrounded by projections of a raging sea and the Northern Lights, then head below deck to imagine life as a seafaring polar explorer. Set over two buildings connected by an underpass, the museum is a (very) densely packed account of Arctic and Antarctic discovery. To learn chronologically, start with the introductory movie in the *Gjøa* building, then make your way to the top of the *Fram* building and work your way down around the galleried exhibits. Early mornings and late afternoons are quieter times to visit.

Maritime Endeavours
SEA-FARING MUSEUMS AT BYGDØYNES

Alongside the Fram Museum at Bygdøynes, the **Norwegian Maritime Museum** explores Norwegians' relationship with the sea, with exhibits covering transport and industry, the navy, and sailing for pleasure and competition. See Norway's oldest-known boat, a 2200-year-old dugout canoe discovered in Sørum, just east of Oslo. There's also a boat from the *Gokstad* find, on loan from the Museum of the Viking Age and, beside it, in the KLINK boat-building workshop, you can see a craftsperson using traditional techniques to build a replica. In a separate building, the Boat Hall houses a collection of archaeological finds uncovered during the remodelling of the harbourfront, including the wreck of a cargo boat thought to be from the late 16th century.

Also at Bygdøynes is the **Kon-Tiki Museum**, which charts the story of the 1947 Pacific voyage led by Norwegian explorer Thor Heyerdahl (1914–2002) to test Heyerdahl's hypothesis that it was possible to reach the Polynesian Islands from South America. The original balsawood raft, *Kon-Tiki*, is surrounded by displays telling the story of the expedition, and Oscar-winning documentary *Kon-Tiki* (1950) is shown daily at midday. There are further exhibits detailing Heyerdahl's subsequent expeditions across the Atlantic on the reed boats *Ra* and *Ra II*, which is also on display.

Bygdøy Hiking & Biking
REGAL FOREST TRAILS

It's easy to putter across the fjord on the Bygdøy ferry, take in the museums, and then putter back without realising that part of Bygdøy is blanketed in an inviting forest, **Kongskogen** (The Royal Forest), whose canopied trails are perfect for a short hike or cycle trip. A coastal path runs from **Huk** all along the western side of Bygdøy to Bygdøy Sjøbad, passing Paradisbukta (p65) and **Paraplyen**, a replica of the original wooden bridge and parasol-shaped pavilion first built in

MUSEUM OF THE VIKING AGE

One of the most revered museums in Norway for its collection of artefacts from the Viking era (most notably the *Oseberg* and *Gokstad* ships), the Viking Ship Museum closed its doors in 2021 in preparation for work to begin on a five-year renovation project. It will reopen as the **Museum of the Viking Age** with a brand-new circular glass extension and an exhibition space three times the former size, and will paint a more complete picture of the Viking era. It will also feature a climate-regulating system to preserve the millennium-old objects, as well as a lecture hall and research space. The new museum is slated to open in 2026.

ALTERNATIVE VIKING ATTRACTIONS

While the Museum of the Viking Age is under construction you can seek out Viking lore at the digital museum **Viking Planet** (p53) and at the VIKINGR exhibition at the **Historical Museum** (p53).

 WHERE TO EAT ON BYGDØY

Café Hjemme hos Svigers
Cosy family-run cafe with a menu of homemade burgers, salads and sandwiches. €

Lille Herbern
Hop on a tiny ferryboat to this casual seafood restaurant on the islet of the same name. €€

Gartneriet Kongsgården
On weekends, this greenhouse cafe serves small dishes made with homegrown organic produce. €€

MASSIMO BORCHI/ATLANTIDE PHOTOTRAVEL/GETTY IMAGES ©

Huk

WHY I LOVE OSLO

Gemma Graham,
writer

A Norwegian, a Swede and a Scot went on a road trip round southern Norway... not the start of a terrible joke, but my introduction to Oslo more than a decade ago. My friends and I did little more than stroll the city's parks and eat unholy quantities of ice cream, but I was enamoured by Oslo's proximity to nature, inspired by its public art and intrigued by all the construction. Since then, I've returned as often as I can and I've been captivated by its transformation every time. But I love that it's remained unpretentious, inviting all comers to explore what's new in the city and all that stays the same.

the 19th century. You can pick up an **Oslobysykkel** at the Huk bus stop to explore the pretty tree-lined avenues and window-shop for the villa you'll buy when you win the lottery.

Blue Flag Fun
BEACH-BASED ACTIVITIES AT HUK

Running all the way around the southwestern tip of the peninsula, rocky coastal hot spot **Huk** is a magnet for the local outdoor recreation crew, who descend here at the first sign of sunshine. There's a tree-shaded park with a volleyball and basketball court and grassy spots for picnicking. But it's the Blue Flag beach and natural bathing places between the rocks that really draw the crowds. **Paahuk** cafe offers refreshments. Follow the signs from the southern end of the Huk bus stop and car park, or take the route along Huk Ave, past the Center for Holocaust Studies and then down the forest trail behind it.

All Along the Waterfront
WALKING THE HARBOUR PROMENADE

Starting at Frognerkilen, a bay right at the top of Bygdøy, the 9km-long **Havnepromenaden** (harbour promenade) meanders a path mostly alongside the fjord right around to Kongshavn in the east. The route is marked by 14 unmissable orange pillars, each with historical photographs and stories. Even if you don't walk the whole way you'll notice the pillars in visitor-heavy areas such as Langkaia (by the Opera House) and Sørenga. If you make it the whole way to Kongshavn you can take the 85 bus from Loelva back to the city centre.

 WHERE TO GET A DRINK ON BYGDØY

Paahuk
A glass-fronted beachside cafe with hot and cold coffee drinks and sodas. There's pizza too.

Le Crêpe D'Elen
Enjoy a coffee or juice on the huge terrace at Lanternen, right beside the Dronningen ferry pier.

Kafe Fjord
There's a good selection of coffee and soft drinks in the spacious Maritime Museum cafe.

Frogner & Western Oslo

UPSCALE REAL ESTATE AND ELEGANT PARKS

Affluent Frogner was once part of the wider Frogner Manor estate, owned in the 18th century by Norway's then richest couple. The city's west end still attracts the wealthy set and is characterised by long, tree-lined boulevards, imposing villas, attractive parks, and apartment blocks with ornate wrought-iron balconies. Though there are only a couple of big-name sights across the neighbourhood, you'll find upmarket shops, restaurants and bistros around every sweeping corner. Much of the borough's appeal lies in doing as the locals do: living the good life and enjoying the green spaces and great food.

Most visitors make a beeline for Frognerparken to recreate the poses of the artworks in Gustav Vigeland's eponymous sculpture park, but the shops around Majorstuen and down Bogstadveien are ideal for some retail therapy. Elsewhere, busy Solli, which had a five-star facelift in 2022 with the grand opening of the Sommerro Hotel, offers opportunities to wine and dine.

☑ TOP TIP

Tram line 12 has stops at Solli plass for the National Library and right outside Frognerparken's main gate for Vigelandsparken. The line continues to Majorstuen, which is at the top end of Bogstadveien, for the shops. T-bane lines 1 to 5 all serve Majorstuen.

LUNNAYA/SHUTTERSTOCK ©

Vigelandsparken (p70)

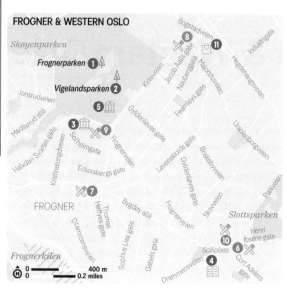

FROGNER & WESTERN OSLO

Sculpture,
Vigelandsparken

Frognerparken

WESTERN OSLO'S PLEASURE GROUND

Central Oslo's largest park is most famous for Vigeland's sculptures, but there's more to see besides. **Frognerparken** is popular with locals, who visit to walk dogs, exercise or just lie on the grass. Peaceful paths are lined with mature trees such as maples, sycamores and park limes, while the Frognerelva gently wends its way into the park's ponds (Frognerdammene). Norway's biggest collection of roses is here (more than 150 species), and there are a sizeable children's playground, drop-in tennis courts and an open-air swimming pool (Frognerbadet; enter from Middelthuns gate). Oslo City Museum is here too; it's in the Manor House.

NANISIMOVA/SHUTTERSTOCK ©

Vigelandsparken

THE WORLD'S LARGEST SCULPTURE PARK

A masterwork by Gustav Vigeland, **Vigelandsparken** is the world's largest sculpture park created by a single artist. The 214 expressive sculptures feature more than 750 stylised figures depicting emotions throughout all stages of life, from infancy to old age. Vigeland also designed the park's landscape and architectural elements, such as the stone and

wrought-iron gates of its main portal.

From the gates, the first sculptures you'll see are the 58 bronzes lining the bridge over the Frognerdammene ponds. Dynamic figures dance joyfully, pose strongly...and stomp angrily, in the case of the famous *Sinnataggen* (Angry Boy). All works lead to the arresting *Monolitten* (Monolith) and the 36

clusters of figures surrounding it. So called because it was carved from a single piece of stone, *Monolitten* took three full-time stonemasons 13 years to complete and was finished in 1943, just before the artist's death. You can also see a fountain, carved stone trees, *The Wheel of Life* and a number of works outside the main axis. Entry to the park is free.

An Artistic Evolution

GUSTAV VIGELAND'S STORY

Outside Frognerparken's southwestern corner is the **Gustav Vigeland Museum**. The City of Oslo gifted the museum building to Vigeland as studio and residence; in exchange, he donated his entire collection when he died so his works could be displayed to the public. You can see how Vigeland's style developed from the slender, classical figures he created as a younger artist to the fuller, more stylised sculptures he made towards the end of his career. The collection highlights his preoccupation with conveying vulnerability and emotion, from love and fear to anguish and loneliness. Even in the busts Vigeland created of famed Norwegians, such as mathematician Niels Henrik Abel and Henrik Ibsen, he presented the subjects with all their flaws, which was an unusual approach at the time.

Boutique Chic

SHOPPING IN FROGNER

Start at the Majorstuen end of **Bogstadveien** and the streets leading off it for a collection of independent stores and small chains, such as **StudioBazar**, which sells sustainable womenswear, and footwear shop **Lille Vinkel Sko**. The small department store **Valkyrien** has a selection of shops carrying high-end labels such as Acne Studios, while further down Bogstadveien you'll find inspiration for your next trip at **Chill Out Travel Store**. The 1km-long shopping street has more high-street labels the nearer to the bottom you go – if you walk the whole length you'll eventually reach the end at Slottsparken.

A Thousand Years of Oslo

DISCOVERING THE CITY'S BACKSTORY

Eighteenth-century Frogner Manor houses the **Oslo City Museum**, where you can take a time-travelling walk through Oslo's history, from its founding around 1000 and its survival after a devastating fire through to the 20th-century war years and the city's importance in the fight for women's rights, equality for

BEST PLACES TO EAT

Fatty Patty
Enjoy juicy smashburgers, crispy fries and and a chilled-out atmosphere on leafy Bygdøy allé. **€**

Hao
Tuck into Vietnamese comfort food with fresh, warming *pho* and rice bowls at this spot close to Majorstuen station. **€€**

Piazza Italia
Try thin-crust Roman pizzas and comforting classics such as carbonara at this independent modern Italian. **€€**

Brasserie Coucou
Settle in at this foliage-festooned French bistro, with a daily set menu and mains such as turbot with mushrooms. **€€€**

MORE FROM THE OSLO MUSEUM

The Oslo Museum is four museums: the Museum of Oslo (Bymuseet) and the Theatre Museum (Teatermuseet) in Frogner Manor; and the **Intercultural Museum** (Interkulturelt Museum; p82) in Grønland and the **Labour Museum** (Arbeidermuseet; p78) in Sagene.

 WHERE TO GET PICNIC SUPPLIES IN WESTERN OSLO

Fromagerie
A small deli packed with pungent cheeses, cold cuts and prepared salads for upmarket park snacks.

Happy Foods Takeaway
Pick up a sandwich or salad made with organic produce at this cute cafe close to Frognerparken.

Juels 33 Kolonial
Quality local grocer with abundant fresh fruit and shelves packed with tasty morsels to snack on.

BEST PLACES FOR DRINKS

Eckers
Pep up with a zingy smoothie (try the Mango Power) to go. Great fresh lunch options too.

Pust
This airy coffee bar attracts the laptop crowd with plenty of space and excellent caffeinated drinks.

Oslo Mikrobryggeri
Scandinavia's oldest microbrewery, crafting speciality brews for the good people of Oslo since 1989.

Viktors Vinbar
It's cosy and colourful inside, but the sun-dappled pavement tables are packed on a summer's evening.

F6
Classic cocktails and house concoctions in this relaxed bar just up from Solli plass.

the LGBTIQ+ community and the struggle for racial justice in Norway. Meanwhile, **The City Lab** has changing exhibitions created by locals, and on the 2nd floor the **Oslo Theatre Museum** celebrates all things theatrical.

Art Deco Afternoon Tea
TAKING TEA AT THE SOMMERRO

Opened in 2022 after a five-year renovation, the **Sommerro Hotel** hides a luxurious playground behind its monumental art deco brick frontage. For the ultimate afternoon of five-star frivolity, take traditional afternoon tea in the bright garden room of **To Søstre**. Work your way through three tiers of classic morsels: finger sandwiches such as rye bread with smoked salmon and tartare sauce, fluffy oven-fresh scones with clotted cream and jam, and bite-sized, dentist-defying sweet treats. They'll be accompanied by your perfect blend from the selection of teas (for a Norwegian twist, go for the Nordic Viking liquorice tea) or a teapot cocktail.

Norway's Archive
THE NATIONAL LIBRARY'S COLLECTION

A veritable vault, the **National Library** contains all manner of documents relevant to public life in Norway, from books, newspapers and maps to film, radio, TV and music. The 1914 building features frescoes by prominent artists such as Gustav Vigeland and Axel Revold, whose mural in the stairwell leading to the 2nd floor depicts Yggdrasil from Norse mythology. Second-floor **Kafe Å** is probably the calmest spot for coffee in Oslo.

Permanent and often surprising temporary exhibitions have covered such themes as the history of Norwegian black metal. Don't miss the **Map Centre**, a serene, modern pod filled with maps charting how the Nordics have been represented in cartography over the centuries.

 WHERE TO STAY IN FROGNER & WESTERN OSLO

Cochs Pensjonat
Clean, basic rooms (some with kitchenettes) in a prime Frogner location by Slottsparken. €

Camillas Hus
Boutique hotel with seven sumptuously decorated rooms in the former home of writer Camilla Collett. €€€

Sommerro Hotel
From mates-friendly 'lofts' with recessed beds to decadent suites, you're guaranteed a unique stay. €€€

Take bus 37 towards Nydalen T and alight at **1 Colletts gate**. Take the path forking uphill to the right and follow it into **2 St Hanshaugen Park** and around towards the **3 Tower House** (or take one of the steeper, more direct unofficial paths). The once rocky hill drew crowds for midsummer celebrations long before it became a landscaped park in the 19th century. Walk past the rectangular pool and take in the view towards the fjord over the tiered terraces. Stroll down through the park, exiting onto **4 Ullevålsveien**. Continue downhill past the street's inviting cafes, shops and restaurants, including Java for exceptional coffee, delicatessen and fine foods store Gutta på Haugen and Bib Gourmand–decorated Smalhans. Turn left when you reach Akersbakken and enter **5 Vår Frelsers gravlund** (Our Saviour's Cemetery). It's the final resting place of several notable Norwegians, including **6 Henrik Ibsen** and **7 Edvard Munch**. Leave the cemetery by the gate next to the **8 Russian Orthodox Church**. Turn right and then left down **9 Damstredet**, a pretty cobbled street of wooden buildings including the stable for Veslebrunen, 'horse and good friend' of writer Henrik Wergeland. Retrace your steps and turn right, continuing uphill until you reach **10 Gamle Aker Kirke**, Oslo's oldest remaining building (from 1150) and a stop on St Olav's Way. A sign outside marks 639km to Nidaros, the pilgrimage's destination. Double back and turn down **11 Telthusbakken**, an even more scenic lane of wooden houses. On the left, you'll see **12 Egebergløkka Parsellhage**, Olso's oldest allotments, established to combat food shortages during WWI. At the end of the lane, cross the road and finish at **13 Fyrhuset Kuba**, a pub in a former lighthouse.

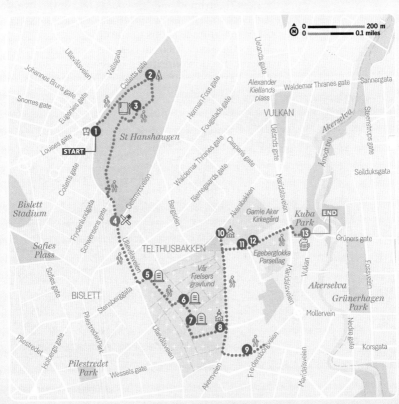

Grünerløkka & Vulkan

BUZZING BARS AND QUIRKY SHOPS

☑ **TOP TIP**

The borough of Grünerløkka is much bigger, but the area between the Akerselva and Toftes gate is the focus of the action. It's about 1.5km from Jernbanetorget, and trams 11, 12 and 18 head in the right direction. Vulkan is a hop over the river at Nedre Foss; it's on the 34 and 54 bus routes.

Grünerløkka was the epicentre for Norway's industrial revolution in the 18th and 19th centuries, with the area's factories and textile mills making use of the Akerselva to power their machinery. In the current century, this former working-class neighbourhood became famous for being Oslo's most alternative place to hang out, bristling with creativity as artists teetered on the edge of becoming The Next Big Thing.

Today, Løkka (as it's affectionately known) has become more mainstream, but despite not being quite the bleeding edge of cool it once was, artists, makers and creators still bring their originality to the neighbourhood and it remains one of the liveliest places in Oslo for a night out. It also has some of the best vintage shops in the city.

Across the Akerselva from Løkka is Vulkan, a densely packed collection of restored warehouses now home to a stellar food court and entertainment venues.

FOTO5693/SHUTTERSTOCK ©

Grünerløkka borough

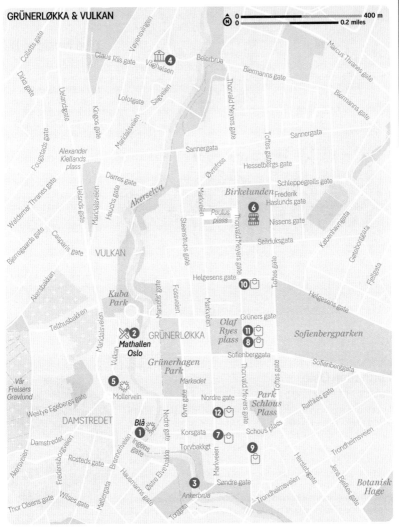

GRÜNERLØKKA & VULKAN

0 ⟶ 400 m
0 ⟶ 0.2 miles

HIGHLIGHTS
1 Blå
2 Mathallen Oslo

SIGHTS
3 Akerselva

4 Labour Museum

ENTERTAINMENT
5 House of Nerds

SHOPPING
6 Birkelunden Marked
7 Frøken Dianas Salonger
8 Retrolykkes Klær

9 UFF
10 Velouria Vintage
11 Vintage Wear
12 Xaki Vintage

FROM TOP: MICHAEL BROOKS/ALAMY STOCK PHOTO NANISIMOVA © J.FARO/SHUTTERSTOCK ©

Live Music at Blå

AN OSLO INSTITUTION

Named for the indigo factory that once stood on this stretch of the river, **Blå** was originally a jazz club, and today it's one of Oslo's favourite venues, staging talent of all genres from electronic to hip-hop to disco and everything in between. There are gigs throughout the week – check the schedule at blaaoslo.no.

The riverside terrace bar (card only) is equally popular; order a drink and a pizza and sit out under the fairy lights until the music gets underway.

Blå

Mathallen Oslo

OSLO'S PREMIER FOOD COURT

Located in a renovated red-brick warehouse in Vulkan, **Mathallen Oslo** is an epicurean adventure and a cut above the city's other food courts. A variety of vendors serve dishes for brunch, lunch and dinner, while others sell gourmet products. Kulinarisk Akademi runs a selection of long and short food courses, and coffee roasters Sohlberg & Hansen offer sessions that let you into the secrets of your favourite caffeinated drink. Pick up some luxury chocolate from Sebastien Bruno or a couple of tastebud-pleasing jars from Gutta på Haugen, or simply pull up a chair to chow down on dim sum from Hong's Bao Bao.

Produce store, Mathallen Oslo

Walk the Akerselva

THE RIVER THAT POWERED INDUSTRY

From its source at Maridalsvannet reservoir, the **Akerselva** snakes for 9km down through Oslo until it spills into the fjord behind the Opera House. For a riverside walk featuring signs of Oslo's industrial heritage, pick up the river anywhere around Grønland and

walk against the flow. You'll pass former factories now converted into offices, apartments and bars; waterfalls; a salmon ladder; and several bridges including **Ankerbrua**, aka the Fairytale Bridge after Dyre Vaa's four bronze sculptures depicting folk heroes

including Peer Gynt. Further up still you'll find the **Oslo National Academy of the Arts**, housed in a former sail factory and helpfully signposted by Gardar Eide Einarsson's rooftop installation *This Is It*. From the reservoir, the nearest transport back is at Kjelsås.

The Perfect Vintage

SHOPPING FOR RETRO FASHION

Whether your personal brand demands a neon puff-sleeved tea dress from the '80s or a leather jacket stylishly battered with age, Løkka has you covered. Markedsveien, Thorveld Meyers gate and the streets leading off them are a vintage-lover's dream, with myriad shops to riffle through for retro one-offs. Densely packed **Vintage Wear** squeezes in casual pieces such as T-shirts, sweatshirts and jeans, while airy **Retrolykkes Klær** feels more curated and boutique-like. **Xaki Vintage** is the place to go for Goth and punk pieces, and **Frøken Dianas Salonger** is a stylishly decorated place with a mix of vintage and small-label retro-inspired fashions. The rails at **Velouria Vintage** are chock-full of casual wear, while the Grünerløkka branch of the chain **UFF** has a mix of second-hand and vintage fashions for every occasion.

Weekend Markets

BRIC-A-BRAC AND HANDMADE CREATIONS

If you prefer to do your secondhand shopping outside, head to Birkelunden Park, near the top end of Thorvald Meyers gate, for **Birkelunden Marked** from noon each Sunday. You'll find an eclectic array of items, from sneakers and T-shirts to vintage glassware, prints, jewellery and quirky knick-knacks for that perfectly unique gift.

A shopfront for local makers, **Ingensteds Sunday Market** (in the same laneway as Blå) fills up with stalls inside and spills out into the street with creators selling wares such as handmade soaps, ceramics, hair accessories, drawings and prints.

Markets are some of the few places in Norway where you'll need to have some cash. Many vendors favour Vipps payments (not available without a Norwegian bank account), but check whether they'll accept cash or PayPal instead.

Gaming Nostalgia

PLAY RETRO DIGITAL AND ANALOGUE GAMES

If you get misty-eyed at the thought of your first games console, or you remember those heady, pixelated days of the original *Street Fighter*, you're in luck. **House of Nerds** has a bunch of old-school hardware including the classic Nintendo 64 – hooked up to old CRT monitors, of course. There's also a VR

TREAD CAREFULLY

Close to Oslo National Academy of the Arts, set amid mature trees and over a tranquil stretch of the Akerselva, is the much-photographed, white-painted iron bridge **Aamodt Bro** (also spelled Åmodt Bru). One of Norway's earliest suspension bridges, it dates to 1852, when it was first constructed over Drammenselva in Buskerud, a county to the west of the capital. Around a century later it was gifted to Oslo and rebuilt piece by piece in its current scenic setting. As you walk across its slightly wobbly wooden boards, you'll understand the cautionary wording embossed on a plaque on each side, which can be translated as '100 men I can carry, but falter under a tempo march'.

 WHERE TO GET COFFEE IN GRÜNERLØKKA & VULKAN

Tim Wendelboe	Sohlberg & Hansen	Supreme Roastworks
Choose from the seasonally updated menu to get your perfect caffeine buzz at this legendary coffee bar.	Norway's oldest roastery has a concept store in Mathallen Oslo; learn about the process over an espresso.	Home of champion roasters and a favourite with locals, who keep coming back to pore over their pour-over.

LØKKA'S BEST BARS

Hytta
A tiny corner bar with a varied craft-beer selection, occasional events and a cosy cabin vibe.

Meyers
This intimate spot has a tiny bar with a solid drink selection and effortless retro style.

Grünerløkka Brygghus
Warm, down-to-earth brewpub with a good variety of beers on tap and no-nonsense pub grub.

Territoriet
Choose from the list's 400 wines, then relax with a charcuterie board amid the greenery.

Dangerous Club
It's worth the walk from Løkka's main drag for exceptional classic cocktails and a vinyl soundtrack.

Grünerløkka Brygghus

escape room with a range of mind-melting scenarios to choose from, and for a break from the screens there's shuffleboard, board games and a bar. It's a welcoming place for groups, families and lone folks alike, just across from Mathallen Oslo.

Industrial History on the Akerselva
STORIES OF THE INDUSTRIAL REVOLUTION

In a former pharmacy in Sagene (meaning 'saws' after the saw-mills here in the 16th century), the **Labour Museum** tells the history of the factories and textile mills that sprang up along the Akerselva to process jute, hemp and cotton, through the stories of people who were instrumental in the factories' success. Voices include an industrial pioneer, a factory worker (70% of whom were women), and a campaigner who fought for workers' rights. Though much of the material is in Norwegian, there's an accompanying audio guide in English on the Useeum app. The museum is on Sagveien; for a scenic walk, follow the path up the river until you reach the footbridge beside the Anne på Landet cafe in Hønse-Lovisas Hus. Cross over and you'll see the museum directly ahead.

 WHERE TO EAT IN GRÜNERLØKKA & VULKAN

Brauð Toastbar
Toasted sandwiches are the main event, with options such as pulled pork, Taleggio and barbecue sauce. €

Cultivate Food
The mouth-watering aroma will draw you in, but the freshest of vegan fare will make you want to stay. €

Hrimnir Ramen
The menu may be concise, but the ramen is oh so umami and the service is impeccable. €€

Grønland, Tøyen & Eastern Oslo

OSLO'S MULTICULTURAL HEART

Home to students, young professionals and families, the mostly residential neighbourhoods east of Grünerløkka may be light on big-ticket attractions but they're filled with all the perks that go towards making a good life: speciality shops, parks, and unpretentious restaurants with first-rate cooking.

Closest to Oslo Sentrum, Grønland is the city's most diverse neighbourhood, and people visit from all over town to shop for good-value produce and quality international ingredients. Its popular large park, Grønlandsparken, is flanked by the city's prison, but don't let that put you off – it merges into Oslo's newest sculpture park, Klosterenga.

Sofienberg and Tøyen fan out seamlessly from Grünerløkka and each summer unassuming Tøyenparken hosts one of the capital's biggest music festivals. Also in Tøyen, the Botanical Garden offers a more manicured place to breathe some fresh air.

☑ TOP TIP

Though these residential neighbourhoods make for a pleasant stroll, you'll likely be visiting with a destination in mind. T-bane lines 1 to 5 stop at Grønland for the shops and at Tøyen for the park, while bus 31 stops at Sars gate, around 400m from the Botanical Garden entrance and the Natural History Museum.

ARTMEDIAFACTORY/SHUTTERSTOCK ©

Natural History Museum (p80)

79

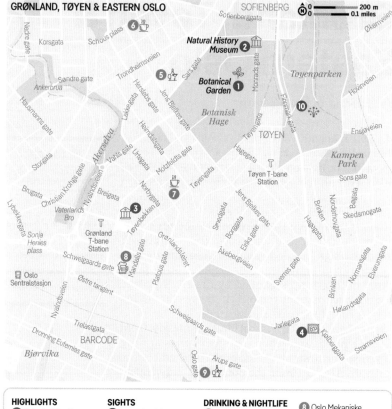

GRØNLAND, TØYEN & EASTERN OSLO

SOFIENBERG

HIGHLIGHTS
1 Botanical Garden
2 Natural History Museum

SIGHTS
3 Intercultural Museum
4 Klosterenga Sculpture Park

DRINKING & NIGHTLIFE
5 Gråbein
6 Kuro
7 Neongrut
8 Oslo Mekaniske Verksted
9 Preik

ENTERTAINMENT
10 Øya

Natural History Museum

EXPLORE NATURE'S PAST AND SHAPE ITS FUTURE

Take a whistle-stop tour through the wonders of the natural world, from the fossilised creatures of prehistory to the pressures facing the planet today. Arranged over two main buildings, Oslo's **Natural History Museum** has classic taxidermy exhibits of Norwegian and worldwide fauna arranged in themed 'habitats', while the building across the courtyard features more modern exhibits, with artfully laid out fossils (including Norway's only triceratops skull), a crystal cave, and brain-bending items that explore the vastness of space. In a separate building, the sobering, interactive displays at **Klimahuset** (The Climate House) empower visitors with knowledge about climate change and call on them to commit to being the change they want to see.

Botanical Garden

Botanical Garden

A TRANQUIL RETREAT IN TØYEN

Arranged in a series of themed areas unfolding downhill from the Natural History Museum, the 60-hectare **Botanical Garden** contains more than 5500 plant species and is perfect for a peaceful stroll. Gardens include the Scandinavian Ridge, a rocky area with a tumbling waterfall and a variety of mountainous flora; the Viking Garden, with its sculptural, sunken longboat featuring plants useful to the Vikings, such as hemp; and the steamy Palm House, which transports you to the tropics whatever the weather outside. The gardens are free to enter, and courtyard cafe **Handwerk Botaniske** serves organic light bites and drinks if you get peckish.

Øyafestivalen

OPEN-AIR MUSIC IN TØYENPARKEN

Bringing music to the Oslo masses for a quarter of a century, **Øya** takes over Tøyenparken for a four-day extravaganza each August, plus bonus gigs in clubs all over the city the night before the main event gets under way. Acts have included Lorde, Wizkid, Solange and Florence and the Machine. Spanning indie, hip-hop, electronica and more, it's one of Norway's most popular music festivals and it also aims to be among the world's greenest, using renewable energy, recycling 60% of its waste and eschewing plastic food packaging.

FROM TOP: ARTMEDIAFACTORY/SHUTTERSTOCK ©; PER OLE HAGEN/SHUTTERSTOCK ©

Sondre Lerche performing at Øyafestivalen

BEST CAFES & BARS

Preik
A locals' local, with crisp cool beers, small plates and evening stand-up in Gamle Oslo.

Neongrut
A warm welcome, champion baristas, and tasty plant-based sweet and savoury light bites.

Kuro
Minimalist-chic cafe with top-notch coffee drinks on the daily menu and wine on weekend evenings.

Oslo Mekaniske Verksted
Join the mixed crowd for beers amid the mismatched vintage furniture at this former workshop.

Gråbein
Buzzy corner bar with craft beers, cocktail classics and toasties to satisfy a snack attack.

Challenging Prejudices

A MUSEUM CONFRONTING BIASES

The **Intercultural Museum** sits at the heart of one of Oslo's most multicultural neighbourhoods and invites those who pass through its doors to consider the nature and origins of prejudice and racism. The main exhibition at this small, free museum leads visitors through a series of small rooms exploring themes such as hatred and fear, and an interactive artwork by Thierry Geoffroy (aka Colonel) asks them to confront their own biases and challenge injustice in society. Part of the Oslo Museum, the exhibition is curated from the perspective of Norwegian society, but the issues it raises are relevant wherever visitors hail from. The museum is just a few minutes' walk from Grønland T-bane station.

Oslo's Newest Sculpture Park

BÅRD BREIVIK'S CELEBRATION OF CULTURES

Officially opened in the summer of 2023, a new, small sculpture park within Klosterenga Park combines stone sculptures, architectural elements, a pool and planting schemes linked together by the Hovinbekken stream. Representing different cultures brought together in a spirit of mutual respect, the park was the vision of Norwegian artist Bård Breivik (1948–2016), who first began working on plans with the municipality in the 1990s. It's tucked away in a residential area of Gamlebyen (the Old Town), sandwiched between apartment blocks and the prison. Bus 20 from Tøyenparken stops nearby at Kjølberggata; walk a little further and enter Klosterenga Park at Jarlegata. The sculpture park is on the other side of the football pitch.

WHERE TO EAT IN GRØNLAND, TØYEN & EASTERN OSLO

Chowk
Eat aromatic small plates and classic curries at this casual Indian restaurant beside Tøyen station. €€

Golden Chimp
Try inventive dumplings amid retro decor, with set menu (book ahead) or à la carte options. €€

Restaurant Hot Shop
A sex shop turned Michelin-star spot serving unfussy but perfectly prepared bistro food. €€€

Beyond Oslo City Centre

OUTDOOR ACTIVITIES AND UNEXPECTED ART

Surrounded by inviting, deep-green forests on three sides and with a fjord filled with intriguing islands that beg to be explored, Oslo is immersed in the outdoors. Just a few minutes from the city centre you can be out in nature, exploring as the Norwegians do and enjoying the *friluftsliv* (open-air life).

Around 10km to the north are the forests of Nordmarka and the ski jump at Holmenkollen, an Oslo landmark that's visible from the city. While there are many excellent organised boat trips into the Oslofjord, you needn't join a scheduled cruise if you don't want to. Ferry trips to the islands and islets close to the city are cheap, quick and easily accessible with a standard Ruter ticket.

Meanwhile, there's some surprising art in the suburbs around Oslo: Ekebergparken sculpture park has delights at every turn, while the life of Emanuel Vigeland is memorialised at his mausoleum in Slemdal.

☑ **TOP TIP**

T-bane line 1 serves a number of sights and destinations up to Frognerseteren, the final stop on the line and gateway to Nordmarka's hiking, biking and skiing trails, while the B2 ferry routes from Aker Brygge will take you out to the islands Hovedøya, Gressholmen and Langøyene in the Oslofjord.

ARTMEDIAFACTORY/SHUTTERSTOCK ©

Hovedøya (p85)

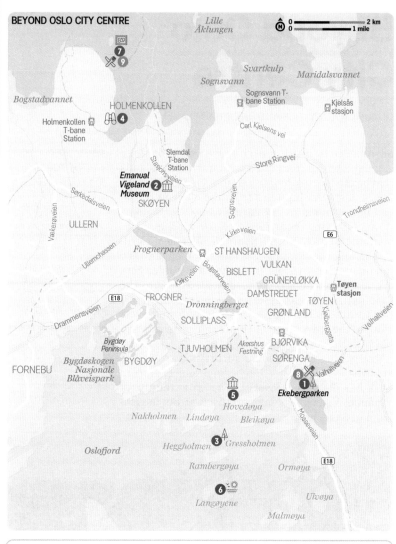

BEYOND OSLO CITY CENTRE

HIGHLIGHTS
1 Ekebergparken
2 Emanual Vigeland Museum

SIGHTS
3 Gressholmen
4 Holmenkollen Ski Jump
5 Hovedøya
6 Langøyene
7 Roseslottet

EATING
8 Ekebergrestauranten
9 Kafe Seterstua

Ekebergparken

OSLO'S HILLTOP SCULPTURE PARK

On a forested escarpment to the east of the city, this outdoor haven was transformed into a sculpture park in 2013. You'll find an ever-growing collection of works by classical and contemporary artists among the trees, including pieces by Rodin and Louise Bourgeois. Famously, a walk in this area inspired Munch to create his most famous work. Marina Abramovic's 2013 sculpture *The Scream* invites you to express your own angst. There's also a small visitor centre outlining the park's history and nature. Take tram line 13 or 19.

Ekebergparken

Emanuel Vigeland Museum

A FRESCOED MAUSOLEUM

The church-like **Emanuel Vigeland Museum** was planned as a museum to display the artist's works after he died. But Vigeland – younger brother to Gustav – changed his mind, bricked up the windows and created a mausoleum instead. After you enter the silent hall through the heavy door, it will take a few minutes for your eyes to adjust to the dark interior before the dramatic, erotic frescoes of his masterwork *Vita* (Life), depicting life from birth to death, slowly come into view. The museum is on a residential street about a five-minute walk from Slemdal T-bane station (Line 1) and is only open on Sunday; book ahead.

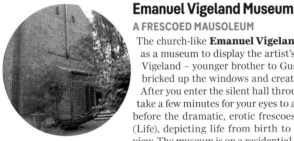

Emanuel Vigeland Museum

Oslofjord Islands

FERRY HOPPING ON THE FJORD

You can explore some of the most scenic islands in the Oslofjord with a Zone 1 Ruter ticket. Closest is **Hovedøya**, under 10 minutes from Aker Brygge on the B2 electric ferry. The forest-covered islet has the ruins of a Cistercian monastery, 19th-century military installations and an art gallery, all linked by a network of trails. Next stop is **Gressholmen** (actually three connected islands: Gressholmen, Heggholmen and Rambergøya). A little bit wilder, it was the site of Oslo's first airport, but now much of it is a protected nature reserve. You can stop by **Gressholmen Kro** for refreshments. Furthest away, lively **Langøyene** is the only island of the three that you can camp on, and there are trails, a kiosk and a beach.

360-Degree Views From Holmenkollen

SEE OSLO FROM ITS SKI JUMP

The hill at Holmenkollen has been used for ski-jumping competitions since 1892, when the winning jump was a very respectable 21.5m. Today the hill record stands at 144m and the futuristic curves of the modern-day structure are a beloved feature of Oslo's landscape. Get a ski-jumper's perspective by taking the funicular to the top of the 70m-high tower to peer over the slope. If you're brave enough, step onto the start platform and take the **Kollensvevet** zip line to the bottom. Alternatively, you can simply enjoy the majestic views down towards the Oslofjord and across the surrounding forest. The **Ski Museum**, renovated for its centenary in 2023, presents 4000 years of skiing history. From Holmenkollen T-bane station, head for the Kongeveien car park and look for the steps to the left. At the top, turn left and follow the bend up around to the right.

A Memorial Gallery

REMEMBERING THE WWII RESISTANCE MOVEMENT

Created by artist and art director brothers Vebjørn and Eimund Sand, the moving outdoor art installation **Roseslottet** (The Rose Castle) portrays the human stories of Norway's occupation during WWII. Around 270 portraits and large-scale paintings – varnished with epoxy resin to protect them from the elements – are arranged into series; one of the most affecting is *The Faces of History*, featuring portraits of courageous individuals connected to the resistance movement whom Vebjørn met in person. Other elements in the complex include the five gilded columns commemorating those who joined the five-year struggle for freedom. In a contemplative setting surrounded by trees beside Frognerseteren station, Roseslottet will remain in place until 2025.

NORDMARKA

The forests blanketing the landscape to the north of Oslo are a playground for outdoors enthusiasts, with marked hiking and biking routes and an extensive network of skiing trails for the winter months. In summer you can pack a picnic, hop on the T-bane to Voksenkollen or Frognerseteren, and pick up one of the trails from there. In winter head to **Skimore Oslo**, a small ski resort offering equipment rental and several fun-filled runs for skiers of all abilities.

WHERE TO EAT BEYOND OSLO CITY CENTRE

Kafe Seterstua
Canteen cafe serving traditional hot and cold Norwegian staples in a dark-wood chalet at Frognerseteren. €

Gressholmen Kro
Stop by on your island-hopping adventure for a drink and some tapas from the concise menu. €€

Ekebergrestauranten
Enjoy European classics, fine-dining style, in a gleaming-white art deco building in the sculpture park. €€€

Holmenkollen ski jump

87

Above: Setesdalen (p97); right: road to Kristiansand Botanical Gardens (p105)

Southern Norway

HISTORY, TRADITION AND COASTAL CHARM

Viking sites, white-painted seaside towns, folkloric traditions, canal cruises and gorgeous mountains: southern Norway is a charmer at every turn.

Though foreign visitors often overlook southern Norway in favour of the dramatic scenery of the west coast, the southern coastline draws Norwegian holidaymakers in droves come summer. This region rewards those who take the time to visit with a string of pristine coastal villages of whitewashed timber beside complex networks of bays and rocky islets and a shimmering sea, and its appeal is easy to understand. Inland, deep forests, rugged mountains and scenic river valleys draw hikers, climbers, skiers, rafters and paddlers, offering opportunities for just about any kind of outdoor activity you can imagine.

Southern Norway also has history and culture galore to keep you busy, and it's inspired the likes of Edvard Munch and other artists. The region is home to Norway's oldest city, Tønsberg, and has many interesting sites related to the Viking Age. It also played a major role in other eras, from the 19th-century maritime heyday of Arendal and Kristiansand to the industrial history of Rjukan and Notodden. In the heart of the region, the long valley of Setesdalen is known for its strong traditions and folklore.

All this makes southern Norway a place to savour, not simply pass through. Speaking of savouring, the region has plenty of great restaurants and food festivals to keep your taste buds happy too.

LILLIAN TVEIT/SHUTTERSTOCK ©

THE MAIN AREAS

Find Your Way

Travelling along the coast is relatively easy with good roads, rail service and local buses. Everything takes longer in southern Norway's interior, which has fewer buses and few train routes. The roads are also more sinuous and slower.

CAR & MOTORCYCLE
The E18 runs from Oslo to Kristiansand and then it's the E39 on to Stavanger. It's an excellent road, shadowed by smaller roads into the coastal towns. The E9 heads north from Kristiansand into Setesdalen and the interior.

TRAIN
Four or five trains run daily along the coast from Oslo to Kristiansand (4½ hours) and on to Stavanger (an additional 3¼ hours). Some stop at smaller stations and larger towns along the way.

Rjukan, p94
Tucked in a deep valley, Rjukan is a major jumping-off point in Norway's south for adrenaline-elevating adventures, including skiing, ice climbing and bungee jumping.

Fredrikstad, p92
Gamlebyen, Fredrikstad's old quarter, is an enchanted mix of wooden homes, cobblestone streets and a drawbridge in this fine fortress town.

Kristiansand, p104
Kristiansand combines a town beach with a walkable medieval core. It's a fine base for exploring the south and offers plenty of fun activities.

Tyrifjorden

OSLO

Kvitåvatn
Songevatnet
Flesberg
Vikersund
Rjukan
Hokksun
Lierbyen
Tinnset
Drammen
Hovden
Åmot
Kongsberg
Eidsfoss
Moss
Bykle
Brunkeberg
Bø
Tønsberg
Fredrikstad
Vråvatn
Norsjø
Blåsjøen
Fyresdal
Nisser
Skien
Sandefjord
Fyresvatnet
Brevik
Larvik
Sinnes
AUST-
AGDER
Gjerstad
Mølen
Ålgård
Byrkjedal
Åmli
Kragerø
Varhaug
Ørsdalsvatn
Tonstad
Byglandsfjord
Risør
Egersund
Evje
Tvedestrand
Stavanger
Arendal
Sogndalsstrand
Flekkefjord
Birkeland
Grimstad
Kirkehamn
Marnadal
Lillesand
Lyngdal
Kristiansand
North
Sea
Borhaug
Vigeland
Søgne
Mandal

Skagerrak

0   100 km
0   50 miles

MOSTOVYI SERGII IGOREVICH/SHUTTERSTOCK ©

Lindesnes Fyr (lighthouse; p111)

Plan Your Time

You could dip into the south en route between Oslo and Stavanger, but stay longer if you can. Focus on either the coast or the interior, and do both if you have time.

In Five Days

● Begin in Viking **Tønsberg** (p101) and then head to Henrik Ibsen's **Skien** (p107). Follow the coast and pause in **Risør** (p110) and **Grimstad** (p111) before visiting Norway's land's end at **Lindesnes** (p111). From **Kristiansand** (p104), detour to look for beavers and elk around **Evje** (p109) and then take the back road from Flekkefjord to **Jøssingfjord** (p111), **Sogndalstrand** (p111) and on to **Egersund** (p111).

If Time Is Tight

● Begin again in **Tønsberg** (p101) and then drive inland to **Telemark** (p98) for the lovely canal boat trip from Akkerhaugen to Lunde. Continue north via Notodden to peerless **Heddal Stave Church** (p98). Afterwards, it's more mountain roads to **Rjukan** (p94) for a couple of days of activities and fine views. Finish up with hiking and folk museums in **northern Setesdalen** (p97).

Seasonal Highlights

SPRING	SUMMER	AUTUMN	WINTER
As the days lengthen, **fruit trees** blossom in Telemark. In May, the **boating season** kicks off along the Telemark Canal.	The coast draws boaters and sunseekers, while the interior lures hikers.	It's harvest time in the fruit-growing region of Telemark, and the **Norwegian Apple Festival** takes place.	The ski resorts of Telemark come alive with **winter sports** enthusiasts seeking downhill thrills.

Fredrikstad

OSLO
Fredrikstad

GETTING AROUND

To cross the Glomma to Gamlebyen, you can either trek over the high and hulking Fredrikstad Bridge or take the free two-minute ferry, which shuttles across the water to the main gate of Gamlebyen regularly between about 5.30am and midnight. Exact times depend on the day.

Regular buses and trains connect Fredrikstad with Halden (30 minutes). Both towns lie along the main bus and train routes between Oslo and Göteborg, Sweden.

☑ TOP TIP

Stay in Halden and visit Fredrikstad from there. It may be a third of the size, but Halden has just as much choice when it comes to accommodation and far less traffic. Fredrikstad, on the other hand, has a more imaginative selection of restaurants to choose from.

Fredrikstad feels like a relic of unimaginable times, an era when Scandinavia was at war. Considered the best-preserved fortress town in the Nordic countries, Fredrikstad was established by King Frederik II of Denmark-Norway in 1567 during the Northern Seven Years' War. These days, those tumultuous times live on in the town's old quarter (which includes the fortress), with its timbered 17th-century houses, moats, city walls and even a drawbridge. The unusual proliferation of Norwegian flags is a reminder of how close this ancient border lies. Fredrikstad's 19th-century cathedral has a steeple that doubles as a lighthouse.

Nearby Halden is like a smaller version of Fredrikstad, with another imposing fortress, an even higher flag-to-rooftop ratio and a pretty location at the end of Iddefjord between steep rocky headlands. The stories of Fredrikstad and Halden run parallel: if Halden were to fall, Fredrikstad would soon follow, and it makes sense to visit them together.

Journey Back to the 17th Century

NORWAY'S BEST-PRESERVED FORTRESS TOWN

When King Frederik II built himself a formidable fortress in 1567, it replaced an earlier nearby structure that had been burned down by Swedish troops. The new fortress was closer to the mouth of the Glomma, a river that the king felt would be more easily defended. As things turned out, the only time Fredrikstad was attacked was in 1814, by which time the fortress had been allowed to deteriorate, enabling Swedish troops to capture it in just a few hours.

These days, **Gamlebyen Fredrikstad** (Old Town Fredrikstad) is a vibrant and beautifully maintained historic district across the river from the modern city centre, complete with ramparts, an old drawbridge and cobblestone streets lined with well-preserved wooden buildings.

FREDRIKSTAD

HIGHLIGHTS
1 Gamlebyen
Fredrikstad

SIGHTS
2 Kongsten Festning

SLEEPING
3 Hotel Victoria

EATING
4 Majoren's Stue og Kro

A kilometre away, the smaller **Kongsten Festning** provided essential protection for the main fortress. Bastions, moats and underground passages remain as evidence of the fort's strategic importance.

Climb the Ramparts of Halden's Fortress

FORTIFIED BORDER TOWN

With a population of just over 30,000, Halden is the only town mentioned in Norway's national anthem, under its old name of Fredrikshald. This pleasant, hilly town looms large in Norwegian history for one reason: the imposing **Fredriksten Fortress**, which has watched over Halden since 1661, guarding its strategic location just a few kilometres from the Swedish border. Climb the ramparts and bastions, peer into gun batteries and magazines, and admire the panoramic views of Halden and the fjord beyond. As you gaze out from the imposing heights, it's no challenge to understand how Fredriksten was able to withstand all attempts to capture it and remain essentially intact to the present day.

BEST PLACES TO STAY & EAT IN HALDEN & FREDRIKSTAD

Grand Hotell
Opposite the train station, the Grand is Halden's oldest hotel and is old-fashioned and comfortable. €€

Hotel Victoria
Fredrikstad's century-old hotel has period decor, appealing surroundings and plenty of parkland. €€

Fredriksten Hotel
Another historic hotel, this Halden belle has contemporary interiors and the best view in town. €€€

Majoren's Stue og Kro
Fredrikstad's best restaurant does slow-cooked meats, as well as international comfort food. €€

Rjukan

Rjukan ✪ OSLO

GETTING AROUND

Although Rjukan is easy to reach by bus, having a car really helps. In the valley, the local Bybuss runs from the Norwegian Industrial Workers' Museum, 6.5km west of Rjukan, to the eastern end of the valley. You can also hire bicycles from Rjukan Gjestegård.

Hidden away from the outside world in a long valley beneath impossibly steep-sided walls, Rjukan is filled with possibilities. Apart from a few museums, there's not much to do in the town other than admire the views, which you should do at every available opportunity. But the drama-filled backdrop issues an irresistible call to get out and explore: Rjukan is southern Norway's activities and adventure capital.

Above the valley rim to the north lies the vast and soulful Hardangervidda. Watching over Rjukan from the south is what many consider to be Norway's most beautiful peak, Gaustatoppen (1883m). These two giants of the natural world are the setting of some of Norway's best trails, not to mention the most spectacular (and unusual) cable car and funicular ride anywhere in the country. Skiing, ice climbing and bungee jumping are also essential elements of the exhilarating Rjukan experience.

Get High in Rjukan

SOUTHERN NORWAY'S BEST VIEWS

☑ **TOP TIP**

Narrow Rjukan stretches along the valley, straddling the Måna River for around 6km. Near the town's eastern end, tight switchbacks climb out of the valley to the south; 10km up this road lies Gaustatoppen, the main accommodation area for the ski fields and gateway for visiting Gausta.

High above the valley's western end, 9.5km from town, is a viewpoint overlooking the 104m-high **Rjukanfossen** waterfall. Park near the eastern end of the tunnel and take the 200m-long unsignposted gravel track.

Rjukan's valley is so deep that the sun doesn't reach the bottom from October to March (although there are now sun mirrors 450m above Rjukan's town square). In the 1920s, the local hydroelectric authority was so concerned for the sun-deprived mental health of its employees that it built them the **Krossobanen cable car** so they could climb out of the valley and see the sun. The cable car, which is signposted above the western end of town, takes you up and away from Rjukan's deep, dark recesses to Gvepseborg (886m). For fabulous views, climb to the roof platform atop the top cable car station; take one of the trails heading up the hill from the top station.

The summer-only **Gaustabanen Cable Railway** was built by NATO in the 1950s so its troops could reach the radio tower

RJUKAN

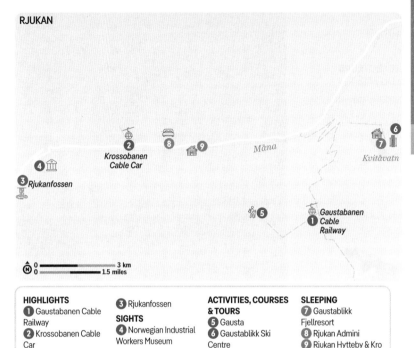

Måna

Kvitåvatn

Krossobanen Cable Car

Rjukanfossen

Gaustabanen Cable Railway

| 0 | 3 km |
| 0 | 1.5 miles |

HIGHLIGHTS
1 Gaustabanen Cable Railway
2 Krossobanen Cable Car

3 Rjukanfossen

SIGHTS
4 Norwegian Industrial Workers Museum

ACTIVITIES, COURSES & TOURS
5 Gausta
6 Gaustablikk Ski Centre

SLEEPING
7 Gaustablikk Fjellresort
8 Rjukan Admini
9 Rjukan Hytteby & Kro

near Gaustatoppen's summit no matter the weather. It's a two-part journey (open mid-June to mid-October) that takes you 850m into the mountain horizontally by electric tram, after which you switch to a funicular that ascends 1040m on a 39-degree gradient, alongside 3500 steps. After walking through a 100m-long tunnel, you emerge at 1800m, 675m higher in elevation than when you began. It's another 83m to the actual summit of the mountain. It's said that you can see one-sixth of Norway from up here on a clear day.

Get Active in Rjukan

GO THRILL-SEEKING ABOVE RJUKAN

Rjukan's surrounds seem custom-made for an adrenaline rush. The weekday-only tourist office can help with advice.

In the town itself, at the western end of the valley, it's possible to **bungee jump** from the bridge leading to the Norwegian Industrial Workers Museum. The 84m drop into the canyon is Norway's highest land-based bungee jump and is quite the thrill.

Rjukan is also famous as a premier place to go **ice climbing**, which basically means hauling yourself up a giant vertical icicle. There are more than 150 routes in the immediate area of the town.

After such hair-raising pursuits, skiing will feel positively serene. Overlooked by Gaustatoppen, the highest mountain

COLD WAR SECRETS

Few people know exactly what went on at NATO's facility at Gaustatoppen during the Cold War, but at the heart of the operations was NATO's need for intelligence and early warnings. Norway's geography and strategic location made it a valuable base for intercepting and relaying important information. Not until almost 60 years after tourism development in the mountain was first planned did Gaustabanen finally open to the general public.

SABOTEURS ON SKIS

During WWII, the occupying Germans began building a heavy-water production plant at Vemork, near Rjukan. 'Heavy water' is used in the production of nuclear weapons. In response, British and Norwegian insurgents mounted several sabotage missions. In 1943, saboteurs air-dropped onto Hardangervidda, wire-clipped the plant's perimeter fence and planted explosives that destroyed the facility. They then retreated on skis to Hardangervidda and avoided capture. In 1965, this story was made into the dramatic (albeit historically inaccurate) film *The Heroes of Telemark*, starring Kirk Douglas.

The plant is now the **Norwegian Industrial Workers Museum**, which has an interesting exhibition about the race to make an atom bomb, plus a fabulous miniature power station.

Rjukanfossen waterfall (p94)

in southern Norway, **Gaustablikk Ski Centre** has excellent runs across a range of levels. One option is to climb to the summit on Gaustabanen and ski back down.

One of Rjukan's best hikes is the trek up **Gausta**, the hiking alternative to Gaustabanen. From the trailhead at Stavsro – reachable by bus from Rjukan – it takes about 2½ hours to hike the 4.3km up to the summit, with an elevation gain of 710m. Alternatively, you can hike up the somewhat steeper route from Svineroi, a bit closer to Rjukan, a 4km (three-hour) trip each way, with an elevation gain of 883m. A great full-day option is to hike to the summit from Stavsro and then return to Rjukan on foot via Gausdalen. The whole hike is 16km and takes about six hours. The descent is steep, but the views are fabulous.

 WHERE TO STAY & EAT IN RJUKAN ─────

Gaustablikk Fjellresort
Beautifully refurbished in 2022, this lodge has incredible views (ask for a Gausta-facing room) and a top restaurant. €€€

Rjukan Hytteby & Kro
Right by the riverbank with excellent, warmly decorated cabins and hearty meals. €€

Rjukan Admini
Enjoy a historic country-house setting with four-poster beds, pastel tones and lush gardens. €€€

Beyond Rjukan

Rjukan
Heddal
Stave Church
Åsgårdstrand
Tretoppsvegen
Tønsberg
Setesdalen
Telemark
Canal
Setesdalsbanen

The mythic past is all around you in southern Norway's secluded valleys, towns and byways.

Hidden from the outside world by high mountains, dense forests and forbidding winters, southern Norway's interior is a little-known region that plays to the imagination. Alongside little-travelled byways and inhabiting deep, deep valleys, the region's attractions seem to spring from a minor medieval epic.

Nothing captures this spirit quite like Heddal Stave Church, with its aura of a more legendary past. Of the 20 Norwegian stave churches that remain with original features, none compares to Heddal. Folk museums dedicated to medieval architecture and Norway's oldest town (9th-century Tønsberg, built by Viking Harald Fairhair) add layers of fascination. And there's no better way to relax than on a slow boat through the Telemark Canal.

Get to Know Norway's Heartland in Northern Setesdalen

TRAILS AND TRADITIONS

Beloved by Norwegians but little known by just about everyone else, **Setesdalen** stretches 147km from Hovden in the north to Evje in the south, right through the heart of southern Norway. National Route 9 runs the entire length of Setesdalen, passing fjords, mountains, deep forests, the occasional waterfall and appealing villages. The area's diverse nature has made it a popular destination for outdoor activities, from biking and climbing to paddling, fishing and rafting on local rivers. **Hovden** is a popular winter ski resort, with hiking taking over during the summer months.

Setesdalen is also a regional heartland for traditions such as folk music and silverwork. In the valley's north, the **Setesdal Museum** consists of several sites with traditional farm buildings and workshops scattered throughout the valley, including **Rygnestadtunet** in Valle, **Huldreheimen** in Bykle and the **Bygland Museum** in the village of the same name. The building interiors are typically open from midsummer to mid-August and are free to visit. In **Rysstad**, the valley's

GETTING AROUND

Local bus services link the area's larger towns, including Rjukan, Kongsberg, Notodden, Seljord, Dalen and Tønsberg. They're fine if you're not in a hurry and don't mind changing buses a few times along the way. It's much easier to get around if you have your own vehicle. If you're travelling the Telemark Canal, you can drive or catch a bus to your starting point, take the boat and then get a bus back to your starting point; arrange this when booking your boat tour.

☑ **TOP TIP**

In summer, visit Heddal early to avoid the tour buses that crowd the site from mid-morning to 4pm.

SILVER FROM SETESDALEN

Setesdalen is famous for its handmade silver, particularly jewellery, often made to be worn with *bunad,* the Norwegian national costume. **RysstadSylv** is a third-generation family enterprise that makes a variety of pieces, including traditional costume jewellery. Master silversmith Trygve Rysstad carries on the tradition passed on to him by his father and grandfather, accompanied by his brother, Alfred, and wife, Inger, who are also trained silversmiths.

To watch the silversmiths at work, stop by **Sølvgarden** in Rysstad, where you can also admire (and perhaps take home) some of the finished products from the shop. During the summer, Sølvgarden has frequent folk music concerts, as well as a restaurant, bar, hotel rooms and a campground.

midpoint, the small main museum is open year-round (typically 11am to 3pm with a small admission fee) and has a permanent exhibit with tableaux illustrating different aspects of traditional Setesdalen life, as well as temporary special exhibits.

Marvel at Norway's Largest Stave Church
A FAIRY TALE TOLD IN WOOD

As you drive along the E134 west of Notodden, the rusting factories, residential homes and fenced farmland offer no hint of what lies ahead. And then, 67km by road southeast of Rjukan, **Heddal Stave Church** comes into view. On a rainy winter day, it emerges from the gloom like a silhouetted spectre. On a bright summer day, the sun glinting on its sharp angles and curlicue flourishes give it the quality of an apparition.

Built in the late Viking era, the church has intricately carved designs and dragon-headed gables, and the structure rises from a meadow alongside an otherwise unremarkable provincial roadside like the prow of a classic Viking ship. Twelve large and six shorter Norwegian pine pillars, each crowned by a truly terrifying carved face, support the structure. The church also has four carved entrance portals. The church took on its current form in 1242. The exterior bell tower was added in 1850.

Pay your entrance fee at the adjacent reception centre and then head inside the church to enjoy the superb 1668 'rose' paintings on the walls, a runic inscription in the outer passageway and the 17th-century bishop's chair. Its ornate carvings relate the pagan tale of the Viking Sigurd the Dragon Slayer, which has been reworked into a Christian parable involving Jesus Christ and the devil. The altarpiece dates from 1667, and it was restored in 1908.

The best – and really the only – way to get here without an inconvenient change of buses in Notodden is in your own vehicle.

Ride the Canal of Telemark
ALL ABOARD A HISTORIC BOAT

Built to facilitate the transport of timber, the **Telemark Canal** was a marvel when it was completed in 1892, creating an interconnected waterway 105km long from the coast to the interior of Telemark that linked cities and towns and provided access to the broader world. Kings, queens, presidents and other illustrious people came from far and wide to celebrate a waterway many called the Eighth Wonder of the World.

 WHERE TO STAY & EAT AROUND TELEMARK

Seljord Hotell	Dalen Hotel	Seljord Hotell Restaurant
Dating from 1858, this period hotel has individually styled rooms with fascinating historical touches. €€	This 1894 belle looks as though it wants to be a stave church; room 17 is said to be haunted. €€€	Seljord's best kitchen, the hotel restaurant is known for its perfectly prepared fish and game dishes. €€€

DALEN HOTEL

An elaborate fantasy in mustard-yellow wood, with towers and dragon heads inspired by stave churches and Viking history, **Dalen Hotel** opened in 1894 to serve the many royal and aristocratic guests who travelled to the Telemark Canal from throughout Europe.

During WWII, the hotel fell into decay, but it reopened in 1992. Accommodation ranges from comfortable rooms with shared bathrooms to ultra-luxurious tower suites with huge private balconies overlooking the garden and Bandak Lake. The restaurant serves exquisite four- and six-course tasting menus. There's a nightly gathering in the hotel lounge, during which you can hear more about the hotel's fascinating story.

Dalen Hotel is open from April to October only.

Telemark Canal

It took 500 men five years to build the canal, which has eight sets of locks with a total of 18 lock chambers to raise boats 72m between Skien and Dalen. A spur of the canal runs between Lunde and Notodden. The largest lock staircase is at **Vrangfoss**, where five chambers lift and lower boats a total of 23m.

There are plenty of routes along the canal to explore by bicycle or on foot. It's possible to take a bike or even a kayak with you on board the historic canal boats with advance reservation.

But the best way to experience the beauty of the Telemark Canal and the impressive feats of engineering that went into

WHERE TO STAY AROUND TELEMARK

Nutheim Gjestgiveri
Art-focused hotel in Seljord with 17 rooms, plus a restaurant with delicious set-menu meals. €€

Dalen Bed & Breakfast
Friendly and family-run, this B&B in Dalen has handsome rooms and information about local wildlife. €€€

Straand Hotel
Comfortable hotel in Vrådal with modern and historic rooms, plus apartments and cabins for rent nearby. €€€

SANDEFJORD & WHALING

Southwest of Tønsberg, **Sandefjord** keeps a low profile in international animal welfare debates, but this former whaling capital makes no secret of where its allegiances lie. The city has one of the few museums in the world dedicated to whaling and includes lots of photos and old whaling machinery, as well as information and displays on general Arctic and marine wildlife. It's well presented and does a good job of portraying both sides of the whaling debate. Sandefjord is a busy place, and it's also handy for Torp, Oslo's second airport.

Setesdalsbanen

its construction is to take a cruise along all or part of the waterway. Three historic canal boats make daily trips on the canal in summer: the M/S *Henrik Ibsen* and the M/S *Victoria* travel the full distance between Dalen and Skien in about nine hours, starting at opposite ends and passing each other at the Lunde locks. If you're interested in experiencing both vessels, plan your trip for a Monday, when each travels only half the distance between Dalen and Skien, turning around at Lunde.

The third canal boat, M/S *Telemarkens,* travels between Akkerhaugen and Lunde and back again, a journey of about

WHERE TO CAMP BEYOND RJUKAN

Seljord Camping Og Badeplass
Grassy campsites, a range of cabins and a telescope for spotting Selma the Serpent. €

Buøy Camping
Surrounded by water, this attractive place in Dalen has cabins, a restaurant and bike hire. €

Norsjø Ferieland
This superb waterside site has cabins, a private beach, lots of activities and a restaurant. €

3½ hours each way. All three boats have covered decks, saloons and onboard restaurants, and all pass through the most impressive lock staircase at Vrangfoss, where it takes about 45 minutes for a boat to get through all five chambers.

Ride a Historic Railway
ALL ABOARD

Join the rail buffs on a short leg of the 19th-century **Setesdalsbanen**. The original 78km-long narrow-gauge railway between Kristiansand and Byglandsfjord connected Setesdalen with the coast at Kristiansand. It operated from 1896 to 1962 and transported nickel from the Evje mines and local timber and barrel staves that were used in the salting and export of herring.

When rail and road transport became quicker and more reliable, the line fell into disrepair, but an 8km stretch of track remains in use from June to August, when steam- or diesel-powered locomotives pull old wooden carriages alongside the River Otra between Grovane (2km north of Vennesla) and Røyknes, a 25-minute journey one way. NSB trains connect Kristiansand with Vennesla.

Climb into the Treetops
ASCEND A WINDING WOODEN WALKWAY

Some 45km south of Dalen, the small town of **Fyresdal** makes a worthwhile detour thanks to an attraction opened in 2023 called **Tretoppsvegen**, a 1km elevated wooden boardwalk that winds from ground level to the height of the surrounding forest canopy, 15m above the ground atop the Klokkarhamaren rock formation. The walkway is designed to be accessible to everyone, including visitors in wheelchairs and families with pushchairs. From the top, enjoy fine views of Fyresvatn lake and the surrounding mountains.

Tretoppsvegen is located within **Hamaren Aktivitetspark**, which also has a lovely boardwalk attached to the cliffs along the lake, as well as cycling trails and outdoor play structures for children.

Explore Tønsberg's Medieval History
NORWAY'S OLDEST TOWN

To delve into Tønsberg's intriguing past, start at **Slottsfjellsmuseet**, situated just below the site of one of Scandinavia's largest medieval castles, Tunsberghus, destroyed in 1503. The

BURIAL MOUNDS & VIKING HISTORY

Borre Mounds (Borrehaugene)
On the western shore of Oslofjord, the 28 burial mounds (some Viking, some not) date back as far as 600 CE.

Midgard Viking Center
This museum, also at Borre, is dedicated to the Viking Age and can organise tours to the mounds.

Gokstad Mound (Gokstadhaugen)
Close to Sandefjord, this Viking burial mound dates to the 9th century; the *Gokstad* (at the Viking Ship Museum in Oslo) was unearthed here.

Kaupang Vikingbyen
Larvik's summer-only Kaupang Viking town is based around a Viking settlement, with volunteers in period dress and Viking-themed activities.

WHERE TO STAY BEYOND RJUKAN

Tønsberg Hostel
Well-run, friendly and well-equipped, this hostel has lovely public areas and excellent breakfasts. €

Thon Hotel Brygga
Occupying a converted wooden warehouse, this waterfront hotel has small but appealing rooms. €€

Hovden Høyfjellshotell
Hovden's finest accommodation option sits at the top of town with ski-resort facilities. €€€

BEARING FRUIT

In southeastern Telemark, **Fruktbygda** (the Fruit Village) has almost a million fruit trees planted from Notodden south along the Telemark Canal to Gvarv and Ulefoss. The orchards of Fruktbygda produce apples, cherries, plums and pears, a fair percentage of which are made into high-quality cider, apple juice, jam and other products. **Ole Christoffer Røste**, award-winning cidermaker and co-owner of NeRø Frukt og Sider, shares what makes Fruktbygda special.

'The climate in Fruktbygda is perfect for fruit production. Long, warm summers with relatively stable amounts of rain provide the right conditions for perfect maturation of the fruit. The lakes Norsjø and Heddalsvannet store warmth, protecting the vulnerable flowering in early spring. In mid-May, the views of flowering fruit trees are fantastic'.

museum's pride and joy is what it calls Norway's fourth Viking ship. Unlike other Viking ships found in burial mounds, the **Klåstad Ship** was a merchant ship that sank around the year 1000. Only bits of wood from the hull remain, but they provide an interesting focal point for exhibits on trade and society during the Viking Age. Slottsfjellsmuseet also has displays of whale skeletons, including the bones of the world's largest known blue whale, roughly 27m long.

Behind the museum, a tower atop the hill where Tunsberghus once stood provides historical information and panoramic views of the city. Nearby are a bronze model of the original castle and the foundation stones of a 12th-century church.

Viking shipbuilding techniques are still going strong at the southern end of Tønsberg's lively downtown waterfront. Expert artisans have recreated one of the most impressive Viking ships ever found, the Oseberg Ship, using only Viking Age tools and techniques. When not out sailing, the full-scale replica, **Saga Oseberg**, can be seen tied up along a nearby dock. The team is now working on recreating another famous Viking vessel, the Gokstad Ship, excavated in 1880 in nearby Sandefjord. You're welcome to watch the work in progress.

The original Oseberg Ship, now in Oslo, was excavated in 1904 at **Oseberghaugen**, a burial mound on the outskirts of Tønsberg. There's not much to see, but you can climb the mound and enjoy the view.

Enter the World of Edvard Munch

THE MASTER PAINTER'S SUMMER HOME

Norway's most famous artist, Edvard Munch, found an enduring source of inspiration in the seaside town of **Åsgårdstrand**, just outside Tønsberg. His first encounter with the place that would become his longtime summer residence occurred when he was 21 years old. While visiting a friend in Åsgårdstrand, Munch met his first great love, Milly Thaulow, a young married woman with whom he began a passionate and stormy relationship that greatly influenced his artistic development.

Though the affair eventually ended, Munch's love for Åsgårdstrand did not, and 13 years after his first visit, he bought a small yellow house in the town, overlooking the Oslofjord. Although Munch lived in various places during his life, Åsgårdstrand became the place that most represented home for him, and he kept his house there until his death in 1944. Now a museum – **Munch's Hus** – that's open in the warmer

---

 WHERE TO EAT NEAR THE COAST

Restaurant Havariet	**Roar I Bua**	**Hotel Kong Carl**
Popular option along the Tønsberg waterfront; offers solid pub grub in a warm and inviting interior. €€	This cute wooden shack in Tønsberg is half fishmonger and half seafood cafe. €€	Dine in Sandefjord in the second-oldest hotel in Norway, with a seafood-heavy menu and charming surrounds. €€

DESIGNIUM/SHUTTERSTOCK ©

FOR MORE CIDER

Setesdalen may be known for its orchards and apple cider, but **Hardangerfjord** (p158) is Norway's largest fruit-producing region, with picturesque fields of fruit trees rising from the water's edge and lots of opportunities to sample the local produce.

Saga Oseberg

SELMA THE SERPENT

Southwest of Heddal and not really on the road to anywhere, lakeside Seljord is famous throughout Norway as the home of Selma the Serpent, Norway's answer to the Loch Ness Monster that's said to inhabit the depths of the lake Seljordvatn.

Hikers in the hills around Seljord can also try and find the feuding troll women: Ljose-Signe, Glima and Tårån. Personally, we haven't seen them, but locals have assured us that they're there.

Cementing Seljord's reputation as a hub for fairy tales, it was also the inspiration for some of Norway's best-known folk legends, including Asbjørnsen and Moe's *The Three Billy Goats Gruff*.

months, it still contains many of Munch's personal belongings and looks almost as if the artist might return at any time. Admission is by guided tour.

Along the street where Munch lived and in other nearby locations are signs showing 13 of his paintings inspired by scenes in the town during his frequent long stays in the 1890s. Walk through the picturesque streets and you may well understand why this place and its people so captivated the brilliant yet troubled artist, who often yearned for its peace and beauty during his many trips abroad.

Kristiansand

❖OSLO
◗Kristiansand

GETTING AROUND

Agder Kollektivtrafikk (akt.no) operates buses in Kristiansand and to destinations up and down the coast and inland to Setesdalen. The website has a trip planner *(reiseplanlegger)* where you can search in English. To explore the city centre, park the car and get out and walk.

Norway's city of the south feels like nowhere else in the country. Its claims to being Norway's top resort town are both accurate and a little overblown: the lone palm tree by the town beach suggests that calling itself the country's sunniest city only goes so far. But the longer you're in Kristiansand, the longer you'll want to stick around.

Centred on a tight grid of streets lined with medieval facades and filled with museums, parks and even its own fortress, Kristiansand has a lot to like. It could also be the best place to shop in southern Norway. The location, too, is a winner: its position equidistant between Stavanger and Oslo makes Kristiansand an excellent base for exploring the white villages of the south coast or the quiet back roads of Setesdalen. Best of all, it's a thoroughly walkable city, and families love the town's outstanding children's park and zoo.

☑ TOP TIP

If you're here outside the summer months (when hotels are often full), visit during the week if you can. On weekends, domestic visitors from across southern Norway descend on the city in search of sunshine. Dyreparken can also get chronically overcrowded on weekends.

Family Fun at Dyreparken
NORWAY'S LARGEST ZOO

If you're travelling with children or love to see animals, **Dyreparken** (the Kristiansand Zoo and Amusement Park) is worth a stop. The park has more than 100 animal species from around the world and works in partnership with various international organisations to conserve wildlife and habitats around the world. Nordic species, such as moose, lynxes, wolverines and wolves are showcased here, along with wildlife from Africa, Asia and beyond.

In summer, you can stay overnight in glamping-style tents at **Dyreparken Safaricamp** or in themed apartments at the pirate harbour, **Abra Havn**. There's also a water park and a theme park based on the classic Norwegian children's book, **Kardemomme By** (Cardamom Town), where eight of the houses are available for overnight stays.

KRISTIANSAND

Otra

Lundsbrue

Posebyen

Town Square

Bystranden

Giestehavn

0   500 m
0   0.25 miles

HIGHLIGHTS
1. Bystranden
2. Posebyen

SIGHTS
3. Baneheia
4. Dyreparken
5. Kristiansand Botanical Gardens
6. Ravnedalen

SLEEPING
7. Scandic Kristiansand Bystranda
8. Sjøgløtt Hotell

EATING
9. Bønder i Byen

DRINKING & NIGHTLIFE
10. Drømmeplassen

Explore Green Kristiansand

CACTI AND CONIFERS

Kristiansand doesn't just have Norway's only wild palm tree. It also maintains its delusions of tropical or desert warmth with Norway's largest cactus collection at **Kristiansand Botanical Gardens**. Barely 1km from the city centre, across the Odd-ernes Bridge, the gardens cover 50 hectares with meandering paths, a rose garden that dates from 1850 and greenhouses that shelter the cacti from the cold Kristiansand winters.

North of downtown Kristiansand, **Baneheia** and **Rav-nedalen** are like smaller versions of Oslo's Nordmarka wilderness area, thanks to the lakeside hiking (summer) and cross-country skiing (winter) trails. Laid out in the 1870s, the two parks have benefited from the planting of more than 150,000 conifers over the years and, not surprisingly, it is a favourite escape for Kristiansand city folk.

BEST PLACES TO STAY & EAT IN KRISTIANSAND

Scandic Kristiansand Bystranda
This outstanding place by the beach has a few zany contemporary touches. €€

Sjøgløtt Hotell
Small but swish rooms, friendly owners and big windows make this a good midrange choice; enjoy free tea-time waffles. €€

Drømmeplassen
This bustling bakery is wildly popular for freshly baked *boller* (raisin rolls) and big bowls of soup. €

Bønder i Byen
The menu riffs on the best produce from the coastal hinterland. €€€

Kristiansand's compact nature makes it ideal for exploring on foot. Start your walk at graceful **1 Kristiansand Cathedral**, the fourth church to occupy this spot, and then follow the pedestrian street to **2 Kristiansand Rådhus**, the red-brick city hall. In front of the building, a **3 statue of King Haakon VII** stands tall, honouring the monarch who chose to go into exile during WWI and lead the Norwegian resistance from abroad rather than submit to the Nazis during the occupation of Norway. Continue past City Hall to **4 Posebyen**, the only part of Kristiansand that remains from before the devastating fire that levelled the city in 1892. White-painted wooden houses, most from the early to mid-19th century, line **5 Gyldenløves gate**, **6 Kronprinsens gate** and the surrounding streets.

From Posebyen, walk southeast along Kronprinsens gate until you reach the waterfront. Soak in some sun at **7 Bystranden**, Kristiansand's city beach, or turn right onto **8 Strandpromenaden**, the waterfront boardwalk. You soon reach **9 Christiansholm Festning**, a stone fortress built in 1672.

Continue through **10 Otterdalsparken** with its large granite fountains and past another small beach to Kristiansand's main harbour district, which has a variety of seafood restaurants and other dining options at **11 Fiskebrygga**, as well as live music on the quay every Tuesday in summer.

If you have time, cross the bridge to Odderøya to admire the architecturally striking **12 Kilden Performing Arts Centre**, whose wave-inspired facade in wood and glass is designed to harmonise with its seaside setting. Nearby, **13 Odderøya Museumshavn** offers a variety of family-friendly maritime-themed activities.

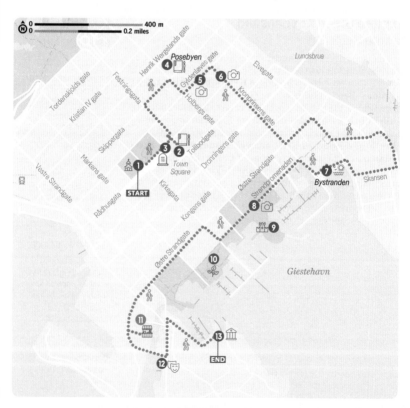

Beyond Kristiansand

- Skien
- Evje
- Setesdal Mineral Park
- Kristiansand

The Kristiansand shore is a picturesque meeting of beautiful coastline and dazzling white villages. It's one of the country's better-kept secrets.

Perhaps inspired by Norway's only palm tree near the beach at Kristiansand, Norwegians call their southern coast the Norwegian Riviera. Were it not for the weather, they might have a point.

From Tønsberg to Egersund, this coast is a succession of pretty white villages wrapped around natural harbours and looking out towards an island-studded sea. For the most part, the road travels inland, leaving these postcard-perfect hamlets to themselves. While each town has its devotees in summer, international tourists have yet to discover this corner of the country in any numbers. The result is a region with a distinctly Norwegian character, and its echoes of Henrik Ibsen at Skien and Grimstad only strengthen that feeling.

A Literary Walk Through Ibsen's Hometown

FOLLOWING IN IBSEN'S SKIEN FOOTSTEPS

Norway's most famous playwright, Henrik Ibsen, was born in **Skien** at the southern end of the Telemark Canal in 1828 to parents from two of the town's most powerful merchant families.

Unfortunately, a great fire in 1886 destroyed Skien's city centre, so there are few locations left from Ibsen's childhood, though a memorial plaque marks the site of **Stockmannagården**, the home where Ibsen lived during his earliest years. Henrik's father, Knut Ibsen, had a general store selling imported foreign goods, such as fabrics and wine.

After Knut Ibsen lost his fortune in 1835, the family was forced to move out of town to their country home in **Venstøp**, 5km away. This house is the only authentic location from Ibsen's time in Skien, which he left at age 15 to work as an apprentice apothecary in Grimstad. At the time of research, the family home was undergoing restoration but was open for guided tours on request. The **Henrik Ibsen Museum** on the site is open in the summer and has created a virtual reality experience based on Ibsen's play *Peer Gynt*.

GETTING AROUND

If you're flying into the area, Kristiansand is the main gateway. The city's Kjevik airport has infrequent flights from Oslo, Bergen, Stavanger and Trondheim, as well as a service from Copenhagen, Denmark.

Southern Norway is well served by NSB trains from Oslo, although parts of the coast are accessible only by bus from Oslo, Kristiansand or Stavanger.

By car, take the E18 from Oslo or E39 from Stavanger.

☑ TOP TIP

Bus and train services in this area are infrequent, so it's best to have your own car to get around.

A VIKING DETOUR

From the 8th to the 11th centuries, Norway's coastline was the domain of Vikings, but the cape at Lindesnes, where the waters of the Skagerrak and the North Sea collide, proved a challenge even to these formidable seagoers. Their solution? In a spirit of creative engineering that Norway's road builders would later emulate when faced with daunting geographic forms, the Vikings carved a canal across the Lindesnes Peninsula at Spangereid (once a home port of Viking chieftains) to avoid the dangerous seas of the cape. In 2007, a replica canal was opened to recreate the Viking detour.

Whitewater rafting on the River Otra, Setesdalen

Skien has also chosen to honour its famous native son in other ways, including the **Ibsen stairs**: 127 steps, 32 of which are engraved with quotes from *Peer Gynt*. The **Ibsenhuset** (Ibsen House) has more than 700 titles related to Ibsen, as well as several sculptures of Ibsen and characters from his plays. A gorgeous new **Ibsen Library** designed to harmonise with the surrounding park is scheduled to open in time for the 200th anniversary of Ibsen's birth in 2028.

WHERE TO STAY BEYOND KRISTIANSAND

Café Ibsen B&B
A great central B&B in Grimstad with character-filled rooms in a historic house. €€

Lillesand Hotel Norge
This boutique hotel dates from 1837 and overflows with period touches, particularly in the public areas. €€€

Sogndalstrand Kultur Hotell
This historic hotel occupies nine early-19th-century Sogndalstrand houses and sits right on the river. €€€

Seeking Thrills Around Evje

WHERE GEOLOGY MEETS WHITEWATER RAFTING

Geologists get very excited about the rocks in this corner of the country, and in southern Setesdalen, you can join in their excitement. Around 10km south of Evje in the town of **Hornness**, **Setesdal Mineral Park** is where you can see displays of local rocks in all their colour and splendour; many of the pieces are for sale. Ask here about where to go prospecting for your own samples; the park itself is a good place to start, but the staff have their favourite local spots.

If looking at and for rocks is a little sedate for your liking, **Evje** is otherwise all about exploring the great outdoors. You can arrange to go on a wildlife-watching safari – elk (moose) and beaver are the main prizes to spot.

As you drive along National Route 9 through the deeply forested valley, there's a good chance you'll see cars pulling trailers weighed down with canoes and kayaks. The pristine, ice-blue rivers of Setesdalen are perfect for whitewater rafting. River kayaking, water-skiing and riverboarding are also possible. Excursions range from a few hours to a few days and are usually possible from May to September. Drier options include rock climbing and mountain biking.

As proof that Evje and the lower Setesdalen have become an activities hub of southern Norway, you'll also encounter Oslo office workers undertaking team-building sessions with paintball and the like. **TrollAktiv** (trollaktiv.no) is a professional and reliable outfitter in these parts.

FESTIVALS OF SOUTHERN NORWAY

Kongsberg Jazz Festival
Four days of world-class jazz in early July with local and international acts.

Shellfish Festival
All the seafood you can eat in Mandal in the second week of August, plus lots of live music.

PUNKT
Kristiansand is the place to be in September for edgy electronica, specialising in live remixes.

Canal Street Jazz & Blues Festival
A fine jazz offering in Arendal, with plenty of blues thrown in as well as international crossover stars.

Kristiansand to Egersund

Norway's south coast is a stunning drive. This route begins in a venerably old town, slows down to enjoy a succession of white-washed coastal villages and then leaves the main road for some glorious coastal scenery. The mix of natural beauty and human-made picture-perfect coastal villages is a winning combination and makes for a delightful road trip.

1 Tønsberg

Your journey begins in Tønsberg, Norway's oldest town. Built by Viking Harald Fair-hair in the 9th century and later a capital of the country, Tønsberg has a crumbling medieval fortress and Viking-era ruins.

The Drive: Take the E18 and track southwest, passing Sandefjord, Larvik, Skien and Kragerø. The Rv416 turnoff to Risør is easy to miss; it leaves the E18 just after Akland.

2 Risør

White-as-white Risør wraps around a U-shaped harbour and is one of the pret-tiest coastal hamlets in southern Norway. Colourful fishing boats bob on gentle wa-ters, watched by 17th-century houses.

The Drive: Return to the E18 and then take the Arendal exit. Parking can be a nightmare: park after the tunnel and walk.

3 Arendal

Arendal is southern Norway's sophisticate. It has a lively main harbour (known as Pol-len) and an excellent contemporary art gal-lery, Bomuldsfabriken Kunsthall. The town swings to a world-class jazz festival in July. Charming Tyholmen district has 17th- to 19th-century timber buildings.

The Drive: Return to the E18. Some 16km southwest of the Arendal turnoff, follow signs to Grimstad's Sentrum.

TUPUNGATO/SHUTTERSTOCK ©

Wildflowers, Egersund

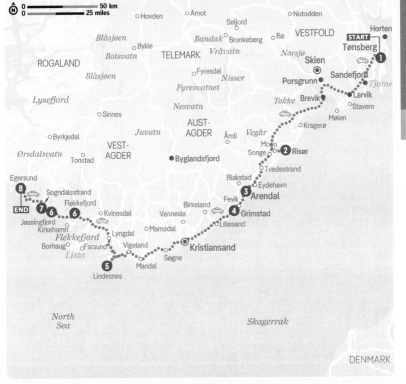

4 Grimstad

Grimstad's cobblestone streets and white-washed wooden buildings rise from a pretty harbour. Playwright Henrik Ibsen lived here in the 1840s and worked in the town's pharmacy, now the Ibsenhuset Museum.

The Drive: Follow the E18 past Lillesand, Kristiansand and Mandal, and then take the turnoff for Lindesnes. The road traverses a wind-scoured landscape strewn with boulders.

5 Lindesnes

Perched atop Norway's southernmost point, Lindesnes Fyr (lighthouse) is an evocative spot. When the wind blows (which is often), there's a wonderfully wild cast to the ocean.

The Drive: Drive back to the E18 and then detour and descend into Flekkefjord.

6 Flekkefjord & Jøssingfjord

Flekkefjord dates from 1660 and has a pretty historic centre. Explore on foot and then take the Rv44 through barren, bouldered hills and steeply down to Jøssingfjord, punctuated by a waterfall and two 17th-century houses crouched beneath an overhanging cliff known as Helleren.

The Drive: Follow the Rv44 northwest. Sogndalstrand is so small that it's unmarked on many maps – it's 2.5km south of Hauge i Dalane.

7 Sogndalstrand

Sogndalstrand's picturesque 16th- and 17th-century timber homes and ware-houses, perched over the river, adorn many tourism posters.

The Drive: It's 30km northwest along the Rv44 to Egersund.

8 Egersund

Lovely Egersund more than holds its own when it comes to appealing white-wood villages along the coast. It's a suitably tranquil place to rest at journey's end.

YURIY CHERTOK/SHUTTERSTOCK ©

Above: Voringsfossen, Hardangervidda National Park (p133); right: reindeer, Hardangervidda NP (p133)

Central Norway

MOUNTAINS AND OUTDOOR ADVENTURES

Central Norway's high mountains provide inspiration, backdrop and the necessary natural drama for some of the country's richest outdoor adventures.

Too many visitors race through central Norway on their way to the fjords out west or the country's Arctic North. That can only be because they don't know what they're missing.

This is a region where nature very much holds sway. Some of Norway's most beautiful national parks – Jotunheime, Rondane, Dovrefjell-Sunndalsfjella and Hardangervidda – reside here, and each issues an irresistible call to the wild. There's wildlife to enjoy – reindeers in Hardangervidda, musk ox high in Dovrefjell-Sunndalsfjella – and summer hiking trails that take you to scenic places that few other parts of Norway can rival. The country's most rewarding whitewater rafting is also found here. Road trips

GLENN PETTERSEN/GETTY IMAGES ©

– or what Norwegians call, with considerable understatement, scenic drives – also take you places where few other countries would build roads, whether over the high mountains or down remote valleys in pursuit of characters of literary legend.

But all of that natural beauty exists alongside two towns that rank among the loveliest in the Norwegian interior. By-the-lake Lillehammer is the proud standard-bearer for Norway's Olympic obsession, an enduring model for other Olympic cities to keep the flame burning long after the world's attention has shifted elsewhere. And Lom – more a village than a town – is a centre for culinary excellence, to go with its stave church and other fine ways to spend an afternoon.

THE MAIN AREAS

LILLEHAMMER
Olympics, history and paddle steamers. **p116**

JOTUNHEIMEN NATIONAL PARK
Spectacular mountain road and realm. **p121**

HARDANGERVIDDA NATIONAL PARK
Hiking, glaciers and reindeer. **p133**

Find Your Way

Central Norway clings to the heights and cuts through the deep valleys in between. Most of the main activities are close to the E6, and Lillehammer, Otta, Dombås and Lom are the best bases for exploring.

CAR & MOTORCYCLE

The best way to get around central Norway is with your own wheels. This will allow you to explore the quiet back roads where no public transport ventures.

BUS

Buses travel frequently up and down the E6, stopping at Lillehammer, Otta and Dombås en route. Less-frequent services run through Jotunheimen National Park and west from Lom into fjord country.

Jotunheimen National Park, p121

Summer skiing and mountain adventures via northern Europe's highest road; the gateway town of Lom is a real gem.

Hardangervidda National Park, p133

Hike alongside reindeer and peer down into crevasses from atop a glacier on the magnificent high plateau of Hardangervidda.

Lillehammer, p116

The Winter Olympics comes alive in this pretty lakeside town, with bobsled runs, ski jumps, paddle steamers and historical sites.

0 — 100 km
0 — 50 miles

Besseggen (p121)

Plan Your Time

So much to do and so little time. Norwegian summers may be short, but they're incredibly intense. These itineraries help you make the most of your time.

Pressed for Time

● Begin with a couple of days in **Lillehammer** (p116): stare down the ski run, ride the bobsled and paddle steamer, and visit the excellent historical sites. Stop at **Ringebu Stave Church** (p129) on your way north, then pause for a night or two in **Lom** (p123). Then head for the fjords by driving the **Sognefjellet Road** (p124) through **Jotunheimen National Park** (p121).

An Active Summer Week

● Enjoy **Lillehammer** (p116), then join a whitewater rafting excursion on the **Sjoa River** (p128), hike the high trails of **Rondane National Park** (p127), and go on a musk ox safari in **Dovrefjell-Sunndalsfjella National Park** (p130). Rest a little with a rail journey down **Romsdalen** (p130) before hiking **Besseggen** (p121) and skiing under the summer sun at **Galdhøpiggen** (p122), both in Jotunheimen.

Seasonal Highlights

SPRING
A lovely time to visit, as temperatures warm and locals look to summer, but some roads (including Sognefjellet) remain closed.

SUMMER
Roads, hiking trails, rafting operators and everything else should be open in the small window of summer (July and August).

AUTUMN
Early snows on the high peaks may close some roads. Except early in the season, rafting and hiking are no longer possible.

WINTER
A beautiful time to visit, although most activities outside of skiing won't be possible. Many high mountain roads are closed.

Lillehammer

Lillehammer
OSLO

GETTING AROUND

Lillehammer is about 2½ hours from Oslo and 4½ to 5½ hours from Trondheim by train and by bus. You'll arrive at Lillehammer Skysstasjon, where you can pick up a taxi.

Most sights are at the top of town, uphill from the station. Olympiaparken is on the B3 and B6 bus routes (stop Stampesletta Håkons Hall), while the B7 is best for Maihaugen. Download the Innlandstrafikk app to buy paperless bus tickets.

Hunderfossen and Hafjell are geographically close, but separated by water. Getting to Hafjell is easier by bus (141 or 142), while Hunderfossen is easier by train.

☑ **TOP TIP**

Download the Bolt or ShareBike apps to pick up an on-demand electric scooter or e-bike for an easier climb up to Olympiaparken. Otherwise, it's either a long walk or an expensive taxi ride. If you have your own vehicle, there's parking near most of the sights.

If it weren't for the 1994 Winter Olympics, Lillehammer would just be one of Norway's loveliest lakeside towns. Arrayed along a wide and beautiful valley, Lillehammer has a pretty, compact core above the northern end of Lake Mjøsa, beyond which the town climbs the surrounding hillsides where ski slopes wind between farms and forests.

Lillehammer's former Olympic venues, in particular, have been artfully transformed into a fascinating collection of sites. Some celebrate Olympics past, such as the Olympic Museum. Others that hosted Olympic events (ski jumps and slopes, the bobsled run) remain in use by locals and visitors from across Europe. Lillehammer also has one of Norway's best open-air museums and an excellent amusement park. And with the confidence of a medium-sized town assured of its place in history, Lillehammer's many places to eat and drink hum nightly with activity, and never more so than during the winter ski season.

Dive into Olympic History

RELIVE THE 1994 WINTER GAMES

Norwegians are very proud of their Olympic history, and rightly so. Twice the country has hosted the Winter Olympics (Oslo in 1952 and Lillehammer in 1994). And despite the country's population of around 5.5 million people, the country's athletes regularly top the medal table. In Beijing in 2022, they finished with 37 medals overall, including 16 gold, putting them in first place ahead of Germany, China and the United States.

It should thus come as no surprise that the Norwegians have built a museum worthy of such passions. The **Norges Olympiske Museum**, located to the southeast of town, takes you through the history of the Games, from the ancient Olympics to the modern era. There's a refreshing lack of patriotic chest-thumping and the clear-sighted celebration of all things

LILLEHAMMER

Lillehammer Golf Park

Olympic Bobsled Course (13km)

Olympiaparken

SIGHTS
1 Bjerkebæk
2 Lillehammer Kunstmuseum
3 Maihaugen Folk Museum
4 Norges Olympiske Museum

ACTIVITIES, COURSES & TOURS
5 Lysgårdsbakkene Ski Jump

SLEEPING
6 Mølla Hotel
7 Scandic Lillehammer Hotel
8 Stasjonen

EATING
9 Heim

10 Nikkers
11 Oliven Bistro & Delikatesse

TRANSPORT
12 Lillehammer Skysstasjon

winter sports. The museum covers past Olympics, the exploits of Norwegian athletes and the Lillehammer games in equal measure. The historic posters announcing each of the Summer and Winter Games are a highlight. And don't miss the 180-degree video presentations in the cinema room, that take you inside the games with great footage.

 ## WHERE TO EAT & DRINK IN LILLEHAMMER

Heim
This warm, welcoming gastropub is popular with everyone from hipsters to ale enthusiasts. €€

Oliven Bistro & Delikatesse
A bit of the eastern Mediterranean has travelled north, with spanakopita, fresh olives and dips. €€

Nikkers
Everyone's favourite winter hangout: a brewpub-bar-bistro with a riverside terrace and reindeer stew. €€

CENTRAL NORWAY FOR FAMILIES

Hunderfossen Familiepark
One of Norway's best parks for children, with rides, fairy-tale palaces, wandering trolls and an epic rollercoaster.

Stave Churches
Seeming to spring from a child's imagination, these fanciful structures are found at Lom and Ringebu.

Whitewater Rafting
Join a family rafting expedition down safe but exciting rapids near Sjoa, one of Norway's best rafting destinations.

Musk Ox Safari
Search for prehistoric musk oxen that look like a figment of Steven Spielberg's imagination in Dovrefjell-Sunndalsfjella National Park.

Fifteen kilometres north of Lillehammer, **Hafjell Skisenter**, the Olympic downhill venue, remains a popular winter ski centre. In summer, mountain-biking trails take over. Around 50km north of Lillehammer, **Kvitfjell Alpine Facility** hosted Olympic cross-country skiing and still draws Nordic skiers. In Hamar, 62km southeast of Lillehammer, the graceful 20,000-seat **Viking Ship Sports Arena** evokes an upturned Viking ship and hosted the speed skating in 1994. From late July to mid-August, it opens to the public for ice-skating.

Stand atop the Ski Jump
IMAGINE YOURSELF AS AN OLYMPIC ATHLETE

A trail behind the Olympic Museum takes you on a long, slow climb through the area known as **Olympiaparken**. There you'll find the **Lysgårdsbakkene Ski Jump**, the Olympic site most likely to evoke a sense of actually being at the Games back in 1994. Unmissable on the horizon from many places around town, it's easily the most accessible Olympic evocation for those with no intention of skiing the slopes or riding the bobsled.

Take the **Lysgårdsbakkene Ski Jump Chairlift** up to the top of the ski jump tower; you could also walk the steep 952 steps, although most visitors take the chairlift up and then walk back down. The views from the tower are superb, extending far across the hills towards western Norway.

And then, almost without warning, you're standing atop the ramp. Even for those not susceptible to vertigo, it's difficult not to feel the frisson of fear and excitement, to sense the feelings of expectation and destiny that must have occupied the minds of those about to launch in a bid for gold and glory, as you peer down the steep 37.5° ramp, which extends 136m down to the landing slope far below. As if the height alone weren't enough reason to admire the bravery of ski-jump athletes, remember this: the speed at takeoff is around 86km/h, and the longest leap at the Olympics was 104m. Parallel to the main (K120) ramp, the shorter K90 ramp often has budding Olympians honing their skills.

It wasn't just the ski jump event that was held here: Lysgårdsbakkene was also the venue for the opening ceremony for Lillehammer 1994: the **Olympic flame tower**.

WHERE TO STAY IN LILLEHAMMER

Stasjonen	Mølla Hotel	Scandic Lillehammer Hotel
More hostel than hotel, friendly Stasjonen has basic yet comfortable rooms and dorms above the train station. €€	Modern rooms added to the side of the town's old mill, with brick walls and Olympic memorabilia. €€€	Sports-themed wallpaper, plus gym, swimming pool, sculpture park and spa, in a residential spot near Olympiaparken. €€€

LUKIPIX/SHUTTERSTOCK ©

Skiing in Trysil

Bobsled Like the Jamaicans

RACE DOWN THE MOUNTAIN

Unless you're an expert skier ready for the Olympic black diamond runs, the **Olympic Bobsled course** in Hunderfossen is where you'll live out your Olympic fantasy. If you already stood at the top of the Lysgårdsbakkene ski run and wondered just how fast you could race down the mountain, here's where you get to find out.

If you're a little nervous about hurtling down the mountain at speed, take the 'slow' option: the wheeled bobrafts take five passengers and hit a top speed of just 100km/h. But even the famous Jamaican bobsled team went faster than that. That's because they were in the real thing. In a bobsled, you and three other passengers might reach 130km/h as you careen down the icy run, riding the high walls of the sharp bends and losing all sense of time as everything becomes a blur. It's frightening and exhilarating in equal measure, and you'll be down the bottom in just 70 seconds (although you may feel as though your stomach hasn't quite arrived until some minutes after that). And no, you're not expected to know what you're doing: a professional pilot guides you down. It's a little like skydiving in a thin metal tube. And as terrified as you may be, in our experience, it's also strangely addictive: you'll most likely head back up the mountain for another go.

TRYSIL AND THE GREAT OUTDOORS

Tucked away in a quiet corner along the Norway–Sweden border, rarely visited by international tourists (unless you count other Scandinavians), Trysil is the epicentre for one of Norway's most underrated adventure destinations. Winter skiing is the main event here: Trysil lies at the base of Norway's largest collection of ski slopes. But when the snows melt, canyoning, canoeing and horse riding keep people active.

Perhaps the most rewarding activity in summer is cycling (with mountain biking also gaining some traction). Fanning out from the town are at least six cycle routes, ranging from 6km to 38km. Route maps are available from the tourist office. Bikes can be hired from most hotels and campsites.

BEST FESTIVALS IN LILLEHAMMER

Lillehammer Jazz Festival
Four days of jazz in October make this a fun time to be in town.

Middle Ages Festival
Hamar locals dress up in period costume; enjoy Gregorian chants in the glass cathedral in June.

Hamar Beer Festival
Hamar Ølfestival means beer, music, more beer, then repeat. It's held in June, a celebratory time.

PEER GYNT VEGEN

When it comes to soulful Norwegian back roads, few compare to Peer Gynt Vegen. This road traces the mythical journey of one Peer Gynt, perhaps the best-loved character created by Norway's favourite literary son, Henrik Ibsen. Peer Gynt Vegen begins in Skei (north of Lillehammer, via the E6, and the Rv254) and meanders 60km to Espedalen, climbing to an altitude of 1053m along the way. It passes the Solbrå Seter farm where Gudbrandsdal cheese was first made in 1863. It also skirts Gålåvatn lake, where a concert performance is held in late August, and promises special views of the Jotunheimen and Rondane massifs at regular intervals. Read the book before you go, or better still, take it with you and follow the ill-fated hero's journey into literary immortality.

Journey into Central Norway's Past

LIVING HISTORY AT MAIHAUGEN

If you want to imagine how rural Norway once looked, spend a few hours at the open-air **Maihaugen Folk Museum**, on a hill above Lillehammer and 1.5km from Olympiaparken. You'll wander amid 180 wooden buildings, collected from across the country and gathered together to form a charming Norwegian village from the early 1900s. Like any such Norwegian settlement worth its salt, there's a 13th-century stave church, traditional turf-topped houses and shops, a post office, a schoolroom, fishing cabins and barns. Interpretative history volunteers, like wandering minstrels and storytellers, bring a fun ring of authenticity to the whole experience.

Lillehammer's position as protector of historical and cultural treasures takes on an added dimension across the road from Olympiaparken at **Bjerkebæk**, the memorabilia-filled former home of Sigrid Undset, who won the Nobel Prize for Literature in 1928. A little further away, 18km northwest of Lillehammer, **Aulestad** celebrates the life of Bjørnstjerne Bjørnson, winner of the 1903 Nobel Prize for Literature. Like Maihaugen, they're windows on a very different Norway than the one you're travelling in. Back in town, the Snøhetta-designed **Lillehammer Kunstmuseum** is both architecturally striking and home to pieces by Edvard Munch.

Ride the World's Oldest Paddle Steamer

CRUISING LAKE MJØSA

Lillehammer is an expert at taking you back in time, and there's one last journey into the past for you to enjoy before you leave. Three days a week in summer, you can board *Skibladner,* the **world's oldest paddle steamer**, and travel slowly (almost four hours) along Lake Mjøsa between Hamar and Lillehammer (via Gjøvik). This grand old boat first came off the assembly line in Sweden in 1856, and despite later modifications, it remains true to the golden age of paddle-steamer travel. Pass low hills of deep green on your lake voyage; on clear days, you'll see higher massifs away in the distance. In an age where everything happens in a hurry, such a journey can feel like an antidote of sorts.

Jotunheimen National Park

Jotunheimen
National Park
OSLO

Welcome to the 'Home of the Giants'. Snowbound for much of the year, Jotunheimen National Park is a rarefied world of high peaks, glaciers, canyons, waterfalls and deep lakes. The park is home to more than 275 summits above 2000m in altitude. These include Galdhøpiggen (the highest peak in northern Europe at 2469m), shapely Glittertind (2452m) and Store Skagastølstind (2403m).

But for all their beauty, Jotunheimen's many singular attractions pale in comparison to the region as a whole. This is a landscape of true grandeur and unmistakable gravitas, a world that just feels like one of Norway's grandest natural spectacles. Despite a short summer season, it also packs a lot in, from summer skiing to some of Norway's most storied hiking trails and most scenic drive. And to cap it all off, most Jotunheimen adventures begin in charming Lom and end on the shores of the fjords.

Hike the High Passes
WALK BESSEGGEN, NORWAY'S PREMIER TRAIL

If you go on one hike in Norway, make it **Besseggen**. It's arguably the country's most celebrated hike, beloved by generations of Norwegians stretching back to literary giant, Henrik Ibsen, who wrote that Besseggen 'cuts along with an edge like a scythe for miles and miles...And scars and glaciers sheer down the precipice to the glassy lakes, 1600ft below on either side'.

In total, Besseggen involves a six-hour day hike from Memurubu Lodge to Gjendesheim. Along the way, you'll reach an altitude of 1743m. The hike also involves a ferry crossing aboard the M/S *Gjende*.

Almost as soon as you leave Memurubu, the well-signed trail begins to climb steeply, leading to a plateau where there's some respite from the climb. Meandering across the plateau, you'll pass **Bjørnbøltjørn**, a small glacial lake. From here, there are superb views down to the much larger lake **Gjende**; the lake's vivid colours come from the 20,000 tonnes of glacial silt that funnels into it every year.

GETTING AROUND

The road (Rv55) from Lom to Lustrafjorden (107km) climbs over the park. It's usually open from May/June through September/October. Having a vehicle is essential for making the most of the park.

There are two public transport options by road. From mid-June to late August, a daily bus runs along the Rv55 between Lom and Sogndal (3½ hours). Covering roughly the same period, a Valdresekspressen bus connects Lom with various areas in the park, including Gjendesheim.

If you're hiking Besseggen, the M/S *Gjende* ferry crosses the lake between Gjendesheim and Memurubu, the hike's starting point.

☑ **TOP TIP**

Although the Sognefjellet Road is usually open from May to September, the snows sometimes don't melt until early July. Even when it opens, the road can be narrow and snow is often piled metres high on either side. Plan your visit for the height of summer.

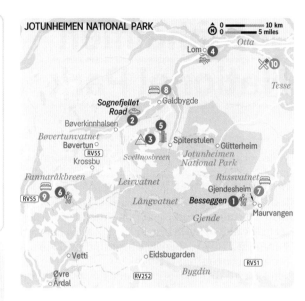

JOTUNHEIMEN NATIONAL PARK

WONDERS OF ICE

For an entirely different perspective on ice, **Mímisbrunnr Klimapark 2469**, close to Galdhøpiggen, takes you deep within the earth. A guide leads 60m through a carefully constructed tunnel of ice, pointing out along the way the subtleties of colour and structure that trace 6000 years of changing conditions. At once eerie, hauntingly beautiful and bathed in ringing silence, it's a strangely moving experience. It all begins at the mountain cabin of Juvasshytta and is signposted off the Sognefjellet (Rv55), 19km after you leave Lom.

The trail continues to climb gradually; a couple of hours after reaching the plateau, you begin the steepest part of the hike. If you're tempted to turn back, don't: the best views lie just ahead. Gasping in the thin air, you'll suddenly find yourself on the **Besseggen** ridge. The walk along the ridge is what gives Besseggen its fame and it's not for the faint-hearted, although it looks worse than it is. Yes, you do need to do a lot of scrambling and have a head for heights. But it's wider (and less scary) than it looks.

On the ridge's gentle upward trajectory, the trail traverses scree slopes all the way up to **Veslefjellet Plateau**. From there, the trail's summit, you'll want to soak in the sheer magnificence of the views, before starting on the relatively easy walk back down to Gjendesheim.

Ski Norway's Highest Mountain
SUMMER SHREDDING

There's something special about skiing in a northern summer. One of just a handful of summer slopes in Norway, the high-altitude **Galdhøpiggen Skisenter** is 1850m above sea level on the Veslejuv Glacier; the road to get here ends at

 WHERE TO STAY IN LOM

Nordal Turistsenter
This busy complex in the town centre has motel-style rooms, cabins, a campground and a cafeteria. €€

Brimi Bue
Norway's best restaurant now has rooms upstairs; they're among the best in town. €€€

Fossheim Turisthotell
Rooms 401 and 402 have great views at this historic family hotel; luxurious log cabins, too. €€€

1841m, which is the highest point you can reach by road in the country. The season runs from June until mid-November; once the road here closes, you'll need to ski or snowmobile in. The runs themselves are nothing special: it's more about skiing at this time of year in such a special place.

Stones and Stave Church
GET TO KNOW LOVELY LOM

Before you head up the Sognefjellet Road and through Jotunheimen, it's worth lingering for a short while in **Lom**, a charming little creek-side town surrounded by high mountains.

Start with **Lom Stavkyrkje**, which dates back to 1170 (with some 17th- and 18th-century modifications). Unusual for having two naves, it's still the local parish church. As with most of Norway's stave churches, you're free to wander the grounds but you must pay to enter and see the muted frescoes. If you're in Lom at night, stay in room 401 or 402 of the **Fossheim Turisthotell**: from the balconies, the ethereal church seems to hover in mid-air before darkened mountain silhouettes.

Another glittering Lom attraction is the **Fossheim Steinsenter**, a remarkable collection of rare and beautiful rocks, minerals and fossils from some of the most remote corners of the globe. It's a paradise for fossickers and collectors alike. Look for thulite, Norway's national stone, which was first unearthed in 1820 and is still mined in Lom.

And if you're heading towards Jotunheimen, don't miss **Norsk Fjellmuseum**, which is equal parts museum – dedicated to Norway's mountains – and visitor centre for Jotunheimen National Park.

Lom's Master Chefs
SAMPLE CENTRAL NORWAY'S BEST COOKING

At first glance, Lom makes for an unlikely culinary heavyweight. But Norwegians and foodies in the know have turned the town into a gourmet destination. Arne Brimi, Norway's long-standing celebrity chef, lives in **Vågåmo**, 30km from Lom, and has made the area central to his culinary vision, which he's dubbed 'Brimiland'. In the hills above Lom, Brimi's mountain lodge **Brimi Fjellstugu** is the chef's home kitchen, with a cafe, deli and nightly grills that show off his amazing talents.

(Continues on p126)

OTHER JOTUNHEIMEN HIKES

Hurrungane
The Hurrungane massif is mostly for mountaineers and skilled scramblers, but head east from Turtagrø Hotel to Norway's highest hut, Fannaråki (7.6km, four hours), for a doable day hike to the summit of Fannaråken (2068m).

Galdhøpiggen
The climb up Galdhøpiggen (2469m), Norway's highest peak, is a challenging eight-hour out-and-back trek with 1470m of ascent. It starts from Spiterstulen; you'll need a map and compass.

Øvre Årdal
From Øvre Årdal, head 12km up the Utladalen valley to Vettisfossen, Norway's highest free-falling waterfall (275m). This is an alternative access route to longer Jotunheimen hikes.

 WHERE TO STAY IN JOTUNHEIMEN

Bessheim
Super-slick mountain lodge and restaurant; it's the best place to stay near Besseggen ridge. €€

Turtagrø Hotel
Mountain heritage meets contemporary cool at this alpine hotel. Great base for outdoor pursuits. €€€

Røisheim Hotel
Combines 1858 charm with modern comforts and first-class meals by renowned chef Ingrid Hov Lunde. €€€

Scenic Sognefjellet

In a country blessed with countless scenic driving routes, it takes something special to stand out. Rising from Lom up and over mainland Norway's highest peaks, summer-only Sognefjellet enters the mountain realm of Jotunheimen, 'Home of the Giants', on its way between the deep valleys of central Norway with the exquisite fjord country of western Norway. If you only drive one road in Norway, make it this one.

1 Lom

With its stave church, geological show-rooms, pretty location and excellent dining scene, Lom is more than just the southern gateway to Jotunheimen National Park. Linger here for a few days before setting out to climb into the clouds.

The Drive: Follow signs out of Lom to Jotunheimen, heading southwest along the Rv55. From Galdesand, take the narrow mountain road that runs to Galdhøpiggen.

2 Galdhøpiggen Skisenter

This is both a summer ski centre and the trailhead to climb Norway's highest moun-tain. But we love it just as much for its set-ting. This is the highest point (1841m) you can reach by road in Norway and the views are simply superb.

The Drive: Return to Galdesand on the Rv55, then continue southwest as the road climbs further into Bøverdalen with its lakes, glacial rivers, grass-roofed huts and patches of pine forest.

3 Elvesæter Hotell

Surrounded by steeply forested hillsides, this hotel has been in the Elvesæter fam-ily for six generations. Apart from the lo-cation, the main sight is the Sagasøyla, a

ENIL/ALAMY STOCK PHOTO ©

Galdhøpiggen Skisenter

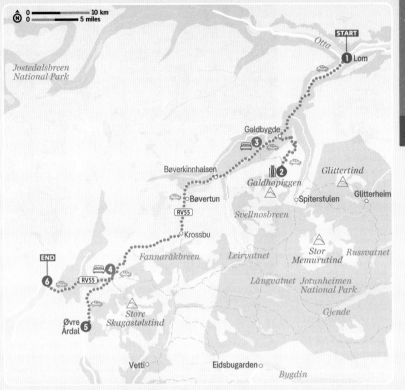

32m-high carved wooden pillar that tells the story of Norwegian history from unification in 872 to the 1814 constitution.

The Drive: Sognefjellet weaves its way between mountains, Nufshaug Scenic Viewpoint and relentlessly beautiful views before descending to Turtagrø.

4 Turtagrø Hotel

A hub for outdoor activities, Turtagrø is the kind of place you'll want to postpone your descent to the fjords just a little while longer. More beautiful views, and even more enticing exploration possibilities, surround you whichever way you look. The hotel itself has perfected the fireplace-and-woolsweater atmosphere.

The Drive: Drive south along the quiet road known as Tindevegen, which ascends between cleared snowdrifts all the way to Øvre Årdal.

5 Øvre Årdal

Øvre Årdal is little more than a name on a map; it's the getting here that's special. As you twist, turn and climb from Turtagrø, you'll take in astonishing views, almost cinematic in scope and beauty, of some of Norway's highest mountains, including Fannaråken (2069m), Skagastølstindane (2405m) and Austabotntindane (2203m). Beyond Øvre Årdal, the road continues down to Sognefjorden.

The Drive: Return to Turtagrø, then take the Rv55 as it drops steeply down through a series of hairpin bends, with superb views of the Skagastølstindane mountains on your left.

6 Skjolden

The quiet shores of Lustrafjord are a suitably picturesque place to end your journey. Skjolden has a pretty medieval church at the northeastern tip of the fjord. Roads from here hug the shoreline en route to the many fjords that lie just beyond.

125

JAN/ALAMY STOCK PHOTO ©

Traditional Norwegian pastries

Tina Brimi, one of Norway's most celebrated restaurateurs and part-owner of Brimi Bue, shares her recommendations for central Norway's signature ingredients.

Local beef and mountain trout
We dry-age local beef ourselves and serve it as carpaccio; we also love to use fresh-caught trout from nearby ponds and rivers.

Fresh berries
Norwegian berries are the best in the world, because we have up to 20 hours a day of sunlight and cold nights.

Reindeer
If you want a taste of Jotunheimen, you should try reindeer. The reindeer are the main reason why people moved here thousands of years ago.

(Continued from p123)

(Continued from p123)

You can also sample a simpler version at **Brimi Sæter**, a reinvention of a rural mountain farm with evening meals. The Brimi connection continues in Lom itself at **Brimi Bue**, which is swathed in glass and wood in the best Scandi style. Here, Dan-Robin Leirvåg and Tina Brimi, Arne's daughter, run a highly regarded restaurant serving innovative takes on Norwegian classics that change with the seasons.

But there's more to Lom's reputation for excellence than the Brimi family. Master baker Morten Schakenda has opened **Lom Bakery**, which is known for natural breads, wood-fired pizzas and, of course, superb pastries, freshly baked baguettes and sandwiches. We would, without exaggeration, drive across Norway and wait hours in a queue just to taste the cinnamon twists again.

Beyond Jotunheimen National Park

Rauma Railway •

• Dovrefjell-Sunndalsfjella National Park

• Rondane National Park

Sjoa River

• Ringebu

• Jotunheimen National Park

The spectacular landscapes of Jotunheimen ripple out across central Norway, with adventures at every turn.

Admiring the view is one way to experience the Jotunheimen hinterland. The other is to dive right in. Fortunately, the natural drama of these soul-stirring landscapes finds its perfect complement in the first-rate outdoor adventures on offer. Hike through Rondane National Park, a landscape that Henrik Ibsen once described as 'palace piled upon palace'. Go looking for the otherworldly musk ox in wild high country. Ride the rails of Romsdalen, a journey of unrivalled, unfurling beauty. Or get soaked on a whitewater rafting descent of the Sjoa River. Anything's possible within a couple of hours' drive from Jotunheimen. And while you don't have to do it all, if you have the time, why wouldn't you?

Hike Superb Rondane National Park

MOUNTAIN PERFECTION

The mountains of **Rondane National Park** are some of the shapeliest peaks in Norway. It's a world of pristine mountain streams, snow-domed mountains, deep valleys filled with pines and a ringing silence at altitude. Best of all, the summer hiking trails here get a fraction of the number of hikers you'll find in Jotunheimen.

Begin in Spranghaugen car park, around 13km by road from Otta, then hike the easy 6.2km trail (1½ hours) to Rondvassbu, where there's a popular staffed Den Norske Turistforening (DNT) hut. Some hikers return from here, but after an overnight stay, we strongly recommend the five-hour return climb to the summit of Storronden (2138m). Better still, tackle the strenuous six-hour-return trek to the summit of Vinjeronden (2044m), then follow the narrow ridge to neighbouring Rondslottet.

Some of the trails even open for mountain bikers, while the trails become cross-country ski trails the rest of the year.

GETTING AROUND

Most attractions in this region east of Jotunheimen National Park lie on (or just off) the north–south E6. A major thoroughfare in the region, it's reasonably well-served by buses. Many of these stop in Otta and Dombås, which make good bases for the national parks and other attractions in the area. That said, having your own vehicle will make it much easier to get around and see some of the more scenic areas.

☑ TOP TIP

To maximise your time and reach places you couldn't otherwise go, forsake public transport and rent a car.

Whitewater rafting, Sjoa River

SCENIC RONDANE DRIVE

Hiking takes you places you can't reach in a car, but the combined **Rv27** is officially recognised as one of Norway's most scenic roads. Running for 75km from Folldal to Venabygdsfjellet (Rv27) and from Sollia Church to Enden (Rvl29), the roads stay above 700m for most of the way and bring you to some of the best views of the Rondane Massif. Our favourite moments among many along this road include the tiered, wooden church at Sollia and the views from Sohlbergplassen.

Go Whitewater Rafting near Sjoa
NORWAY'S BEST RAPIDS

There's always the sensation as you drive through central Norway that a whole world of wildness and wilderness lies just beyond the treeline. Take the Sjoa River, for example. Barely visible from the E6 between Lillehammer and Dombås, it cascades down between deeply forested hills and steep-walled canyons.

Sjoa is the best kind of **whitewater rafting experience**. For a start, it has a variety of offerings that can suit all levels of experience and inclination. If your idea of fun is a gentle paddle on relatively calm waters, or you're travelling with small children, there are sedate Class I runs and operators who know them intimately. If you're concerned

WHERE TO STAY AROUND RONDANE

Rondvassbu DNT
Built in 1903, this fine old mountain hostel is 6km up a track from Spranghaugen; dorm beds. €

Otta Camping
Riverside Otta Camping is convenient, popular and well-placed; many of the sites have views. €

Thon Hotel Otta
This modern hotel in the centre of Otta, on the cusp of Rondane, has wood floors and a restaurant. €€

about whether you're up for churning waters, this can be a good place to start and get a feel for the whole experience.

Others prefer to dive right in. At the other end of the thrill-seeking spectrum, tempestuous Class V runs will have you clinging on for dear life as crazy rapids provide the only way through; the latter might include the roiling waters of fabled Åsengjuvet canyon that often looms from the mist, adding to its fearful allure. When it comes to the latter, you'll be travelling with professionals who know their stuff and for whom your safety is paramount, but it can still be dangerous: there were four fatalities on the river in 2010 and three in 2007.

Set out for a couple of hours or a couple of days; kayaking the same routes might also be possible. And if you have your heart set on a river journey, make sure your visit coincides with the season: rafting excursions only happen from the middle of May until early October, but the main season runs from mid-June to mid-September.

Discover Ringebu Stave Church

ENJOY QUIET MAGIC

You could easily drive through Ringebu and miss one of central Norway's most enchanted buildings. Inhabiting a meadow high above the road, **Ringebu Stave Church** has been here since 1220 – although an earlier version of the church occupied the site after the arrival of Christianity in the 11th century. The current version of the church dates back to the 17th century; that's when the red tower was attached.

The beauty of Ringebu Stave Church derives less from the curlicue flourishes of other stave churches elsewhere in Norway. Here, it's the sense of perfect proportions and deep earth colours of red and brown silhouetted against the piercing blue sky and deep greens of the surrounding forest that provide its charm.

Wander the manicured grounds with stone gravestones for free and admire the church's exterior from every angle. Then purchase a ticket to step into the almost claustrophobic gloom of the interior and see if you can make out the **statue of St Laurence** (c 1250) and the crude runic inscriptions on the walls. Concerts of Norwegian folk music are sometimes staged here in summer; check ringebu.com for dates.

BEST FOR RAFTING THE SJOA RIVER

Sjoa Rafting
Probably the pick of the rafting companies (sjoarafting.com) thanks to its location right beside the Sjoa River. It's 7.5km upstream from Sjoa along Rv257.

Go Rafting
A well-run company (sjoa.no) that organises half-, full- and multiday trips. It's based 8km west of Sjoa along Rv257.

Heidal Rafting
Longstanding rafting company (raftingisjoa. no) with a good reputation, a couple of kilometres west of Sjoa.

Sjoa Familierafting
This respected outfit (sjoafamilierafting. no) specialises in family-friendly descents of the river.

MORE SCENIC RAIL
The Dombås-to-Åndalsnes rail route is a candidate for Norway's most scenic rail trip. Another is the route between **Oslo and Bergen** (p22) that rises up and over Hardangervidda and down magnificently to the fjords.

WHERE TO STAY AROUND RONDANE

Rondetunet
This mountain hostel has basic huts and fabulous camping on the southeastern edge of Rondane National Park. €

Smuksjøseter Fjellstue
Simple rooms and apartments occupy this historic farmstay in Høvringen. Breakfast and dinner included. €€

Rondane Høyfjellshotell
One of the few upmarket options with spa facilities and pine-tinged rooms and a good restaurant. €€

HIGHLIGHTS OF DOVREFJELL-SUNNDALSFJELLA NATIONAL PARK

Fokstumyra Marshes
Much loved by birders, these wild marshes have 87 nesting species and 162 species overall. Take the 7km-long trail near the Dombås end of the reserve.

Mt Snøhetta
Snøhetta (2286m), the park's highest point, features in many Norsk myths and legends. Climb it in six hours from Snøheim (summer only).

Viewpoint Snøhetta
If you just want to look, this timber-and-mirrored-glass viewpoint has jaw-dropping views to Mt Snøhetta. It's signed off the E6 by Hjerkinn.

Just a few hundred metres up the hill from the church is another treasured historical building, the **Ringebu Samlingene**, which was built in 1743 and served as the vicarage until as recently as 1991. It's a lovely traditional complement to the church, and getting both in shot with the forested hillsides in the background makes for the perfect photo, especially when the sun is shining.

Ride the Rauma Railway
ALL ABOARD

Norway's list of scenic drives and train rides is one of northern Europe's most extensive, but of all the choices, the 114km-long **Rauma Railway**, from Åndalsnes and Dombås, is one of the best.

Snaking and climbing through **Romsdalen**, tracing the route of the picturesque Rauma River, this journey is achingly scenic. Almost as soon as you leave Dombås, the climb begins and the scenery unfurls in a procession of forests, valleys, lakes and mountains, all punctuated by isolated farms and small hamlets with narrow church spires and colourful wooden homes – if you're heading west, the best views are from the left side of the train. Along the way, you'll pass through six tunnels and over 32 bridges. Moody in the low clouds of winter, spectacular on a clear summer's day, the Rauma Railway is always worth the trip.

In addition to the regular train route, twice a day from June to August there's a shorter summer-only tourist train with onboard commentary from Åndalsnes' lakeside station up to **Bjorli**, at 600m. But we reckon this is one journey best taken all the way, when the landscape can speak for itself.

Not far past Borli, enjoy the multi-arched **Kyllingbrua bridge**. It's a stunning, stone span over a deep valley, and mark it as one to return to in a vehicle; a walking trail leads up from near the bridge to a viewpoint with glorious views.

Go on a Musk Ox Safari
PREHISTORIC GIANTS

You never forget the first time you look in wonder upon a musk ox. Looking for all the world like a relic of some bygone ancient era, the forgotten love-child of a bison and a woolly mammoth – in North America, the Inuit word for the musk ox is *oomingmaq,* which means 'the animal with skin like a beard' – these formidable creatures rank among the most charismatic standard-bearers for the Norwegian wild.

WHERE TO STAY AROUND DOMBÅS

Trolltun Gjestegård & Dombås Vandrerhjem
This good-value place has a lovely setting, decent meals and tidy rooms. €€

Hjerkinn Fjellstue
Whitewashed inn promises a warm welcome, spotless rooms, a nightly buffet and Icelandic horses. €€€

Kongsvold Fjeldstue
A charming place of early-18th-century timber buildings with warm, cosy and character-filled rooms. €€€

Musk oxen, Dovrefjell-Sunndalsfjella National Park

Safaris by Furuhaugli Fjellhytter out of Dombås operate into **Dovrefjell-Sunndalsfjella National Park**. The safaris leave at about dawn, climbing to the high plateau where these great shaggy beasts roam in herds. You'll be taken as close as your guide dares: musk oxen are surprisingly quick and agile when in attack mode. More often, they form a protective phalanx, like an ancient army, so effectively that they can appear to be a single entity. But catch one grazing out in the open, the morning sun glinting on its Viking-esque horns, and you'll capture a sense of the dark magic these strange animals project.

And when you know their story of survival, each musk-ox sighting can seem even more precious. *Moskus-okse* (musk oxen) disappeared from the Norwegian wild around 2000 years ago, hunted to death for their fur and meat. The species clung on in Canada, Alaska and sparsely populated Greenland. In the 1940s, conservationists reintroduced Greenlandic

WHY I LOVE RONDANE

Anthony Ham, writer

On my first journey to Norway many years ago, I fell in love with Rondane. It was the crystalline streams cutting through deep canyons, the quiet back roads, the mountains that seemed more beautiful than any mountains I had ever seen. As one view unfolded after another, and I found myself pulling over to the side of the road for yet more pictures, Rondane felt like an evocation of Norway's high-country charm, its perfect impression of an unspoiled mountain realm yet to be sullied by the degradations of overtourism. Remarkably, many years later, it still feels that way.

 WHERE TO BOOK ACTIVITIES AROUND JOTUNHEIMEN NP

Oppdal Safari
This experienced company runs safaris in search of musk ox and other wild inhabitants of Dovrefjell-Sunndalsfjella.

Opplev Oppdal
This multi-activity company specialises in whitewater rafting on the Driva River, as well as canyoning and ziplining.

Moskusopplevelse
Based at Furuhaugli Touristhytter, this guiding company offers daily musk-ox safaris.

IMAGEBROKER.COM/SHUTTERSTOCK ©

THE GUIDE

BEYOND JOTUNHEIMEN NATIONAL PARK CENTRAL NORWAY

Reinheimen National Park

NEARBY NATIONAL PARKS

Breiheimen National Park
Covering 1691 sq km and sitting between Jotunheimen and Jostedalsbreen National Parks, Breiheimen has excellent backcountry hiking and unstaffed mountain huts.

Dovre National Park
North of Rondane National Park, this 289-sq-km protected area is a popular playground for budding botanists: it contains almost every Norwegian flora type within its borders.

Reinheimen National Park
This mountainous 1969-sq-km park fills the landscape between Lom and Åndalsnes and gets few visitors. Watch for wild reindeer, wolverines and golden eagles.

musk oxen to Dovrefjell-Sunndalsfjella National Park and Femundsmarka National Park close to Røros. Today, only an estimated 100 survive in Norway.

Most operators offering musk-ox safaris can also send you out looking for elk (*elg* in Norwegian, or moose in the USA), either on the same safari or, more likely, on a different day. Europe's largest deer species is much more common than the musk ox, and is found across Norway, from the forests of the far south to the far north. Some of the best places for an elk safari are out of Oppdal or Dombås. Ask at the tourist offices in each town.

Hardangervidda National Park

Hardangervidda
National Park • •OSLO

The high plateau of Hardangervidda is unlike anywhere else in Norway. Its stats tell a story, to be sure: Norway's largest national park (3430 sq km) is also the country's least densely populated area and home to its largest herd of wild reindeer.

But Hardangervidda's specs can only tell part of what makes this such a special place. Where the mountains of Rondane and Jotunheimen inspire awe for their shapeliness, Hardangervidda is all about the scale of an endless horizon, the unpredictable weather that can change in an instant and the austerely beautiful country across which reindeer roam. Hardangervidda is Norway's wild heartland, where nature holds sway and marks a geographical and psychological frontier between the verdant south, the deep blue of the fjords and the icebound north. Hike for days. Walk across glaciers. And go looking for wildlife. It's all possible in this astonishing place.

Hike the Hardangervidda
EXPLORE THE WILD PLATEAU

Hardangervidda is the best kind of hiking destination: wide-ranging, wild and filled with possibilities. On a clear summer's day, it can seem as if Hardangervidda's horizon goes on forever. When the weather closes in and the low mists swirl and close in around you, it can be a strangely claustrophobic experience. At its best, it's a world of unrivalled beauty. At other times, nature's raw power weighs down upon the land.

Numerous trails cross Hardangervidda in all directions. As a general rule, most well-marked routes begin at either Vøringfoss, Finse or Geilo. One of our favourites is the two-day route from **Finse to Vøringfoss** that skirts Hardangerjøkulen glacier and will have you bedding down in Rembesdalsseter. Either end of the trail can be busy with day-trippers. Everywhere in between will feel like you've fallen off the map. If you're really energetic, add a day to your hike and make a four- to five-hour (one-way) detour to Kjeåsen Farm (p160).

Another option is the three-day trek from **Vøringfoss to Kinsarvik**. Again, you'll be blissfully alone for much of this

GETTING AROUND

The Rv7 is the only road across the heart of Hardangervidda. It connects eastern and western Norway, from Hønefoss (87km northwest of Oslo) to Hardangerfjord. Along the way, it passes through Gol, Geilo and Eidfjord. Although the road is usually kept open year-round, conditions can be difficult due to poor weather and heavy snowfalls.

In the nearly 10 months of the year when hiking is not possible on Hardangervidda, locals get around on cross-country skis, although this is strictly for experienced skiers who understand the local conditions.

☑ **TOP TIP**

Never set out on a trip here without a detailed weather forecast and emergency supplies. Even if the sun is shining, take wet-weather gear, extra food and water, and an emergency beacon. Always make sure someone knows where you're going.

DNT HUTS FOR HIKERS

Den Norske Turistforening (DNT) maintains a network of 460 mountain huts or cabins located a day's hike apart along Norway's 20,000km of wilderness hiking routes. Of these, more than 400 have beds for sleeping, with the remainder reserved for eating, rest stops or emergency shelter. DNT huts range from unstaffed huts with two beds to large staffed lodges with more than 100 beds and renowned standards of service. At both types of huts, DNT members receive significant discounts. Most DNT huts are open from 16 February to 14 October. DNT can provide lists of opening dates for each hut.

Use this QR code to pre-book a DNT cabin.

HARDANGERVIDDA NATIONAL PARK

walk. Highlights include having the strangely compelling Harteigen (1690m) dominate your horizon for much of the way, the panoramic views of the plateau from Harteigen once you arrive and the impossibly steep, old pilgrim way of the Monk's Stairway down off the plateau to the fjord-side village of Kinsarvik.

Making the most of Hardangervidda means planning ahead. If you can, before setting out try and stop by the **Norsk Natursenter** in Øvre Eidfjord. In addition to advice on hikes, it sells the Turkart series of maps of the park, at a scale of 1:100,000. Remember that hiking is only possible in July and August and that sudden changes in weather conditions (and unexpected, heavy snowfalls) can occur at any time of year.

Go on a Glacier Hike

WALK UPON THE ICE

Many glacier walks promise more than they deliver, but **Jøklagutane Glacier Walks**, operating out of Finse, offers a genuinely thrilling experience. You get to rope up and not only

WHERE TO STAY ON HARDANGERVIDDA

Finsehytta
This staffed DNT hut is close to Finse station, with dorms, meals and lots of hikers. €

Finse 1222
This high-altitude Finse hotel has a strong mountain vibe and outrageous views. €€€

Dr Holms Hotel
Century-old Dr Holms in Geilo has an air of undeniable grandeur with loads of antiques. €€€

step onto the slightly grubby ice fringes, but also cross onto the glacier in all its complexity. Of the seven hours you'll be on the excursion, two of these take place on the deeply textured ice sheet as you peer down into crevices that appear to drop down to the very centre of the earth. You'll also explore an ice cave and even summit a large ice dome for superlative views. It's an essential, perhaps even the defining, experience of wild Hardangervidda.

It all begins at Finse station. The Blåisen glacier tip of **Hardangerjøkulen** is a three- to four-hour hike from town, and the views en route are superb. And if the area around the glacier tip looks familiar, you must be a *Star Wars* fan: scenes set on the planet Hoth in *The Empire Strikes Back* were filmed around here.

Hardangerjøkulen

AMANDA MOHLER/SHUTTERSTOCK ©

NORWAY'S LARGEST REINDEER HERD

Contrary to popular belief, most of Norway's reindeer aren't wild. The large reindeer herds in the north belong to the Sami, who move the herds with the seasons in search of pasture. Truly wild herds are largely restricted to Svalbard (p302), Reinheimen National Park (p132) and Hardangervidda, which is home to the largest population.

A 1990s ban on hunting saw Hardangervidda's reindeer numbers reach unsustainable levels, and by 1998 there were 19,000. Despite the plateau's size, reindeer require large grazing areas, and many starved to death in winter. The park's authorities have since undertaken a program of resource management to keep the winter park's reindeer numbers at around 10,000. The two-day hike from Halne to Dyranut (via Rauhelleren) is excellent for encountering reindeer herds.

Bergen & the Southwestern Fjords

CAPTIVATING CITIES AND STUNNING NATURE

Breathtaking fjords, thundering waterfalls and history galore make southwestern Norway a must-visit destination.

If you're trying to choose a single area of the country to visit, one that captures the unique Norwegian combination of spirit and staggering natural beauty, look no further than the southwest. For much of the nation's history, it was this region – not Oslo – that was the seat of kings and the centre for seafaring and trade. Many Viking expeditions left from here, reshaping Europe, and it was near Stavanger that Harald Fairhair defeated his rivals at the 9th-century Battle of Hafrsfjord, bringing much of Norway under unified control. Later in the Middle Ages, the powerful Hanseatic League established its northernmost trading post in Bergen and made the city its own.

The southwest has also had an important influence on Norway's culture. Bergen's favourite native son, Edvard Grieg, is a giant of classical music, and Norwegian folk music wouldn't be the same without the Hardanger fiddle, created in the region of the same name. Bergen and Stavanger are at the forefront of Norway's creative food scene, which is based on fresh ingredients from the region's farms and water.

Beyond all this, southwestern Norway is simply stunning. From waterfalls tumbling dramatically down mountainsides and hundreds of blooming fruit trees on the slopes of the Hardangerfjord to the vast Folgefonna glacier and the adventure capital of Voss, southwestern Norway is filled with magic.

KJERSTI JOERGENSEN/SHUTTERSTOCK ©

THE MAIN AREAS

BERGEN	VOSS	HARDANGERFJORD	HAUGESUND	STAVANGER
Norway's vibrant second city. **p142**	Norway's thrill-seeking adventure capital. **p154**	Gorgeous scenery and fruit orchards. **p158**	Viking history and windswept shores. **p166**	Lively and historic port city. **p171**

Left: Hardangerfjord (p158) ; above: Kjeragbolten (p181)

Find Your Way

Southwestern Norway is a region of deep fjords, islands and rugged mountains. Separated from eastern Norway by geography, this region can take a little time to get around as you negotiate the mountains and waters.

BUS & TRAIN

Efficient bus service connects cities and towns throughout the region. Kystbussen and Vy offer frequent service between the major cities, while Skyss and Kolumbus operate local and regional services. Bergen and Voss have excellent rail connections.

CAR

Outside the major cities, a car is the most convenient way to get around because you'll be able to pause for photos whenever you like. The spectacular scenery pretty much guarantees you'll be stopping often.

Voss, p154

By a beautiful lake and equidistant between Bergen and the fjords, Voss trades on its good looks with a range of adrenaline-fuelled activities.

Bergen, p142

A lively, beautiful maritime city with a deep history, vibrant cultural institutions and a thriving culinary scene, Bergen has easy access to nature including mountain hikes within city limits.

Total

O Røldal

Suldalsvatnet

Utla

Blåsjøen

Botsvatn

Sauda O

Skånevik O

Utbjoa O

Valevåg O

Åfjord

FERRY

Passenger ferries are a convenient and scenic way to get around the fjords. Norled runs a daily passenger service between Norheimsund and Eidfjord, stopping at other villages around the Hardangerfjord. Ferries also connect Bergen with other destinations along the coast.

North Sea

Avaldsnes O

Kopervik O

Haugesund

Skudeneshavn

Utstein Kloster

ROGALAND

Ombo

Lysebotn O

O Årdal

Pulpit Rock

Tau *Lysefjord*

Jørpeland O

O Oanes

O Forsand

Lauvik

Stavanger

Sola O

Sandnes

Ørsdalsvatn

Sirdalsvatnet

Egersund O

Lundevatnet

O Sogndalsstrand

Flekkefjord O

Flekkefjord

N

0
0

50 km
25 miles

Hardangerfjord, p158

Often called the 'queen of the fjords', Hardangerfjord is known for its many waterfalls, great hiking and fruit orchards that burst into bloom in spring.

Haugesund, p166

This pretty, rarely visited harbour city is at the heart of a region steeped in Viking history, surrounded by scenic islands and other natural attractions.

Stavanger, p171

Norway's bustling oil capital has an attractive waterfront, excellent restaurants, and fascinating museums and historic sites.

Plan Your Time

You could spend weeks (months! years!) exploring southwestern Norway without running out of things to see and do, but even if your time is limited, you can see and do plenty if you plan carefully.

WIRESTOCK CREATORS/SHUTTERSTOCK ©

Fløibanen funicular (p151)

A Quick City Break

● **Bergen** (p142) is one of Norway's most attractive and historic cities, so if your time is limited, spend it here. Explore the colourful historic wharf, **Bryggen** (p142), popping into **Bryggens Museum** (p143) to learn more about the area's history through artefacts discovered here.

● Spend some time perusing the art collections at **KODE** (p147) and then take the **Fløibanen funicular** (p151) up **Mt Fløyen** (p151) for panoramic views of the city.

● Pay a visit to **Troldhaugen** (p148), home of Bergen's most beloved native son, Edvard Grieg, and then set off on a sightseeing cruise to **Mostraumen** (p152) for a look at some of Norway's famous fjord scenery.

Seasonal Highlights

Mid-June to mid-September is the best time for festivals, getting outdoors and finding everything open. Hardangerfjord is glorious in autumn and spring. Most roads remain open year-round.

FEBRUARY

February is one of the quietest (and coldest) months to visit southwestern Norway. Stick to the cities and **feel like a local**.

MAY

Bergen has one of Norway's largest **National Day** celebrations on 17 May. Fruit trees blossom in Hardanger.

JUNE

Ekstremsportveko, in Voss, is the world's biggest extreme sports festival, with everything from kayaking to BASE jumping.

WESTEND61/GETTY IMAGES ©, LISA STRACHAN/SHUTTERSTOCK ©, AQUATARKUS/SHUTTERSTOCK ©

Three Intense Days

● After a day in **Bergen** (p142), including hiking in the surrounding high country and meals at **Torget Fish Market** (p150) and **Pingvinen** (p150), drive or catch a ferry to **Stavanger** (p171), another vibrant city set around a busy harbour.

● Stay in town long enough to visit the **Norsk Oljemuseum** (Oil Museum; p175) and wander the charming old quarter of **Gamle Stavanger** (p175).

● Come mealtime, take your pick of **Restaurant SÖL** (p176), **Tango** (p176) or **RE-NAA** (p177) for Stavanger's best culinary experiences.

● On day three, head to **Preikestolen** (p179), one of Norway's best hikes and the amazing lookout over Lysefjord.

More Time to Explore

● With five to seven days, you can spend two or three days in **Bergen** (p142), a day in **Voss** (p154) and a few days exploring **Hardangerfjord** (p158).

● Base yourself in one of the lovely fjordside villages where you can immerse yourself in the region's spectacular scenery, hike to waterfalls and scenic overlooks, sample local cider, and take to the water on a kayaking tour, RIB boat safari or even just a quick ferry ride. Hiring a car gives you the most freedom to explore, but you can also go far using buses and ferries.

AUGUST	**SEPTEMBER**	**OCTOBER**	**DECEMBER**
Norway has a real spring in its step, with the short summer season for **outdoor activities** at its peak and lots of festivals.	This is usually your last chance to hike in Norway's higher altitudes, while Bergen gets tipsy during its **beer festival**.	**Brilliant colours** cloak hills and mountainsides, while Hardangerfjord farmers harvest fruit to make cider and juice.	**Christmas markets** bring light and warmth to major cities, and snow adds a new layer of beauty to fjord landscapes.

Bergen

Bergen
OSLO

Bergen ranks among Scandinavia's most beautiful cities. Surrounded by seven hills and seven fjords, the city has gorgeous wooden architecture that radiates from its compact historic centre, much of which dates from medieval times when the city was one of Europe's busiest trading ports. With storied Bryggen as its centrepiece, the area around Bergen's inner harbour hums with people, energy and a feel-good atmosphere that draws return visitors from across Europe and further afield. The city is known for its excellent culinary scene, and it has its own musical soundtrack. The hills that surround Bergen are crisscrossed with cable cars and hiking trails.

You could easily spend a week in Bergen getting to know its charms and hidden corners. In this sense, Bergen is very much a worthy destination in its own right. At the same time, the city is Norway's premier gateway to the country's fjords. Yes, Bergen really does have it all.

Explore Bryggen, Bergen's Historic Hub
MEDIEVAL HARBOURFRONT

Bergen's old city wharf, **Bryggen**, is a UNESCO World Heritage Site and has been the city's beating heart since the Middle Ages, when it was a major trading centre and the site of one of the powerful Hanseatic League's four foreign stations. These days, Bryggen's 58 buildings (some say 61) cover 13,000 sq metres (just 25% of the original). Most date from after the great fire of 1702. Nowadays, the brightly coloured, sometimes leaning buildings house everything from restaurants to galleries, clothing stores and souvenir shops, but the mercantile spirit and Bryggen's central role in Bergen life remain constant. Wandering through the narrow alleys is a pleasure, at least if you can avoid the crowds that descend when cruise ships are in port.

At **Finnegården** at Bryggen's southern end, two connected merchant houses from the early 18th century are preserved as the **Hanseatic Museum**. Unfortunately, after centuries

Bryggen

SAVING BRYGGEN

Fire has destroyed Bryggen at least seven times, most recently in 1955, when one-third of Bryggen was burnt down. In 1944, a Dutch munitions ship exploded in the harbour, blowing off roofs and shifting pilings, causing the tilt seen today.

After that fire, there were calls to tear down what many called 'the rats' nest' and a fire hazard. Plans were proposed to redevelop the site with modern, eight-storey buildings, a bus station, a shopping centre and a car park. Thankfully, Bryggen was saved. Nevertheless, it remains at risk as foundations rot, causing buildings to settle. To ensure their long-term survival, the Hanseatic Museum's two houses are undergoing extensive restoration, including replacing foundations, stabilising groundwater and raising the buildings by about 1m. Reopening is planned for 2026.

of decay, these buildings are in dire need of restoration and are closed until 2026. Luckily, you can still get a sense of what life was like for Hanseatic merchants by visiting **Schøtstuene**, a set of former assembly rooms near the 12th-century **Mariakirken** (St Mary's Church), Bergen's oldest building. *Schøtstuene* were the only buildings on Bryggen where open fires were permitted, making them popular gathering places during the cold, dark winters. The merchants dined and hosted parties, meetings and important discussions.

At **Bryggens Museum**, which incorporates ruins from the 12th century, you can see many artefacts revealed by the fire of 1955, from clothing and household objects to tools, utensils and fragments of letters that provide glimpses of what life and work were like here centuries ago.

A Thousand Years of History at Bergenhus
INSPECT THE CITY'S ANCIENT DEFENCES

Dominating the north side of Vågen Harbour, the fortress of **Bergenhus** represents nearly 1000 years of Norwegian history, incorporating three sites from different time periods merged into a single large military complex. The oldest

 WHERE TO STAY IN BERGEN

Thon Hotel Bristol
Bright modern hotel on Bergen's main square, close to restaurants, shopping and attractions. €€

Radisson Blu Royal Bergen
Conveniently located on Bryggen with a vast breakfast buffet. Can get busy with tour groups. €€€

Opus Hotel XVI
Classy city centre hotel with 65 rooms, run by relatives of Edvard Grieg. €€€

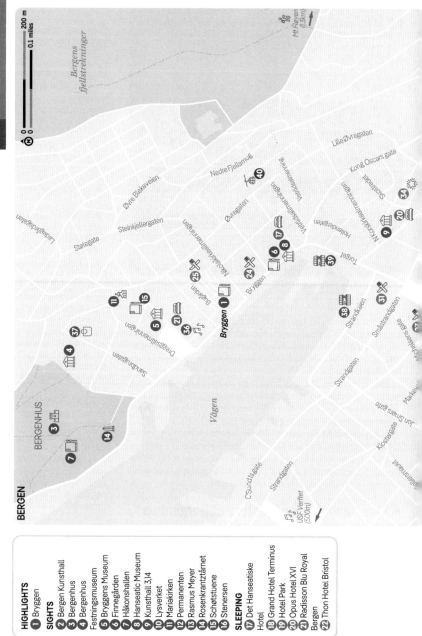

BERGEN

200 m
0.1 miles

HIGHLIGHTS
1 Bryggen

SIGHTS
2 Bergen Kunsthall
3 Bergenhus
4 Bergenhus
Festningsmuseum
5 Bryggens Museum
6 Finnegården
7 Håkonshallen
8 Hanseatic Museum
9 Kunsthall 3,4
10 Lysverket
11 Mariakirken
12 Permanenten
13 Rasmus Meyer
14 Rosenkrantztårnet
15 Schøtstuene
16 Stenersen

SLEEPING
17 Det Hanseatiske
Hotel
18 Grand Hotel Terminus
19 Hotel Park
20 Opus Hotel XVI
21 Radisson Blu Royal
Bergen
22 Thon Hotel Bristol

EATING
23 Allmuen
24 Bryggeloftet
25 Bryggen Tracteursted
26 Colonialen Matbar
see 53 Fjellskål
27 Hoggorm
28 Pingvinen
29 Råvarene
30 Smakeriet Bistrobar
51 Søstrene Hagelin

DRINKING & NIGHTLIFE
52 Cafe Opera
53 Hulen
54 Østre
see 18 Terminus Bar

ENTERTAINMENT
55 Café Sanaa
56 Madam Felle

SHOPPING
57 Arven
58 Fisketorget Mathallen
59 Torget Fish Market

TRANSPORT
60 Fløibanen

ARVEN SILVER FACTORY

If you're a fan of high-quality silver or artisan traditions, stop by **Arven**, a silver factory on Sandbrogaten opposite Bergenhus Festningsmuseum. This venerable company has been around since 1868, when Bergen was the most important silversmithing city in Norway.

Through a 40m-long glass wall that runs the length of the showroom, you can watch silver- and goldsmiths at work shaping the jewellery, cutlery, candleholders and other finely crafted products for which the company is known. If you'd like an even closer look at the production process, guided tours of the factory floor are available with advance booking.

KODE's Permanenten (p148)

part dates from about 1070, when King Olav Kyrre, Bergen's founder, built a cathedral, Christ Church, and other religious buildings here. They no longer exist, but Bergenhus became one of the principal seats of the Norwegian kings, including Håkon Håkonsson, who was crowned in Christ Church in 1247 and proceeded to build the impressive stone banquet hall **Håkonshallen**. Norway's largest extant building from the Middle Ages, the hall is open to the public when not being used for special events. When Håkonshallen is closed, you can still visit **Rosenkrantztårnet**, a stone tower built by King Magnus Lagabøte around 1270 and expanded 250 years later.

Even after Norway's political centre shifted east, Bergenhus continued to serve as an important administrative and military centre. The only time it saw battle was in 1665 when a large Dutch fleet, pursued by English warships, sought safe

WHERE TO STAY IN BERGEN

Det Hanseatiske Hotel
Combines period architecture with luxe contemporary fittings in original Bryggen timber buildings. €€€

Grand Hotel Terminus
Fine hotel dating from 1928. Opposite the train station, it harks back to the heyday of rail travel. €€€

Hotel Park
Two 19th-century houses packed with curios and antiques comprise this family-run treasure. €€€

harbour in Bergen. The English attacked, but the Bergenhus garrison intervened on the side of the Dutch, forcing the English to flee.

During WWII, German occupation forces used Bergenhus as their headquarters. At the free **Bergenhus Festningsmuseum**, exhibits trace the history of the fortress, including an excellent in-depth look at the Norwegian resistance movement during the war.

Step Back in Time in Old Bergen
LIVING HISTORY AT GAMLE BERGE

The great fire that destroyed much of Bryggen in 1702 also tore through other parts of Bergen, wiping out 80% of the city. As a result, Bergen doesn't have a whole lot of wooden buildings from before the 1700s, but after the fire, a flurry of rebuilding ensued, with many new buildings erected throughout the 18th and 19th centuries. **Gamle Bergen Museum** consists of 55 wooden buildings, dating from 1700 to the early 20th century, that have been moved to Sandviken, north of the city centre, mostly from downtown Bergen.

The houses are arranged as a reconstructed town, with different buildings illustrating various aspects of the city's history. Step inside a sea captain's house from 1758, a plumber's shop from the 1860s and a photographer's studio from around 1900. Look into the old schoolhouse, stop by the barbershop and visit the dentist's office – you'll be glad you aren't living in a time of no anaesthesia and indifferent hygiene. In some of the houses, actors in period costume play characters based on historical sources, giving a sense of what life was like for different types of people, including a civil servant, a merchant family, a seaman's family and a colonial trader in a shop selling goods that people could buy in 1926. Theatre performances take place in the main square approximately every hour.

The museum is open from late May to mid-September, but the grounds are open all year.

Explore Bergen's Art Museums
EDVARD MUNCH AND MUCH MORE

Collectively Bergen's top destination for art lovers, the four museums that make up **KODE** sit more or less side by side along the small lake of Lille Lungegårdsvann in the city centre. Start at **Rasmus Meyer**, named for the local businessman whose top-notch collection of works by Norwegian artists was donated to the city by his children after his death in 1916.

MORE BERGEN COMPOSERS

Edvard Grieg is not the only classical music luminary to come out of Bergen. One of his mentors was the composer and violin virtuoso Ole Bull, described by German composer Robert Schumann as 'the greatest of them all'. Bull had a summer home at **Lysøen** south of Bergen. The villa was closed for extensive restoration at the time of writing, but the beautiful island on which it is located is reachable by a 10-minute boat ride from Buena Pier.

One of Norway's most notable 20th-century composers, Harald Sæverud, was also a Bergen native. His home, **Siljustøl**, on Bergen's southern outskirts, is surrounded by beautiful nature and many walking trails. The house is open on Sundays in summer and for special concerts.

 WHERE TO EAT IN BERGEN

Søstrene Hagelin
Venerable casual seafood cafe serving moderately priced traditional fish soup, fish cakes and salmon wraps. €€

Hoggorm
Thin-crust pizza with creative toppings such as chicken with green curry, and mushroom with fish sauce. €€

Allmuen
Bistro menu structured around small dishes for sampling and sharing, with an emphasis on seasonal local ingredients. €€

Its pride and joy is an extensive collection of works by Edvard Munch that rivals that of the Munch Museum in Oslo. But there are also many fine works by other renowned artists from Norway's so-called golden age of painting (1880–1905), as well as some historic interiors.

Next door, **Lysverket** exhibits international and Norwegian art from the 15th to 20th centuries, while **Permanenten**, housed in a nearby Renaissance Revival mansion, focuses on decorative arts, including handicrafts and design. At the time of research, both Lysverket and Permanenten were undergoing renovation and were showing changing exhibits rather than the full collection. The fourth KODE museum, **Stenersen**, hosts temporary exhibits of contemporary art, architecture, handicrafts and graphic arts, with an average of six to eight new exhibits per year.

If contemporary art is your thing, **Bergen Kunsthall**, located between Rasmus Meyer and Stenersen, is the city's top venue showcasing contemporary exhibits by international artists working in a variety of media. Also worth a look is the smaller **Kunsthall 3,14** overlooking Vågsallmenningen, across the street from the Fish Market. It exhibits works by international artists that examine the world through a political or sociocultural lens.

Immerse Yourself in the World of Edvard Grieg
BERGEN'S MASTER COMPOSER

Norway's best-known composer, Edvard Grieg, wrote some of Scandinavia's most enduring pieces of classical music, including his two *Peer Gynt* suites written at the request of playwright Henrik Ibsen. Born in Bergen in 1843, Grieg is the city's most famous native son, honoured with everything from statues and the annual summer **Grieg in Bergen** festivalto a city square, a concert hall and a music academy bearing his name.

To immerse yourself in all things Grieg, head to **Troldhaugen**, where the composer lived with his wife, singer Nina (Hagerup) Grieg. Learn about the composer's life and work at the small **Edvard Grieg Museum** and then take a tour of his villa, where highlights include memorabilia from important events in the composer's life, the family dining room with original furnishings and Grieg's own Steinway piano, still perfectly tuned and used for special concerts.

Peer through the windows of Grieg's composer's hut on the shore of Lake Nordås below the house. Inspired by the view and serenity, he wrote many of his most famous compositions

BERGEN'S BEST OLD STREETS

Jørgen Jørgensen is a retired teacher. His family has lived in Sandviken, Bergen, for nearly 250 years. Here he highlights the must-see historic streets of Bergen.

'Start at the lower Fløybanenstation and follow **Øvregaten** north. This is Bergen's (and probably Norway's) oldest street. Turn right up the steep **Nicolaikirkeallmenningen** and continue up the **Steinkjellergaten**. Undisturbed by cars, you can walk the cobblestones and enjoy small local shops. From here, turn right up **Øvre Blekeveien** and walk to the historical **Skansen fire station**, offering a good view of the city. One more hill and you can stroll through **Fjellveien**, walking north towards **Sandviken**, the loveliest part of Bergen.'

 WHERE TO EAT IN BERGEN

Smakeriet Bistrobar
Popular downtown joint serving tasty fish and chips, truffle burgers, shrimp sandwiches and more. €€

Bryggeloftet
Century-old restaurant specialising in Norwegian classics, including fish soup and reindeer fillets. €€€

Fjellskål
Casual seafood restaurant serving high-quality fish and shellfish overlooking Vågen Harbour and Bryggen. €€€

Troldsalen concert hall

BERGEN FLAVOURS

Amanda Bahl, food journalist and project manager for Norway's largest culinary network, Smak of Kysten, shares her tips for sampling Bergen's flavours.

'One must-try local delicacy is *persetorsk* (sugar-salted pressed cod), celebrated annually on 28 January but available year-round at places like Bien Basar. Other traditional dishes include *plukkfisk* (cooked cod with creamy mashed potatoes) and fish soup, a Bergen staple. Treat yourself to fresh shrimp at the fish market and sample local cheeses, cured ham and traditional pastries. Don't miss the local cinnamon bun called *skillingsbolle*. You can even savour *skillingsbolle*-flavoured ice cream at Hallaisen in Skostredet. Fish Me at the fish market offers ice cream with the distinct flavour of local brown cheese.'

here. Edvard and Nina are buried in a rock tomb in another part of the Troldhaugen property, in a spot Grieg chose himself. Though the tomb is quite high above the ground, you can just make out the couple's names in rune-like writing on the stone face.

If you're visiting during the summer, book tickets for a daily lunchtime piano concert at **Troldsalen**, a gorgeous chamber music concert hall built into the hillside overlooking the composer's hut. Concerts include admission to the villa and museum.

 WHERE TO DRINK IN BERGEN ────────

Terminus Bar
A superb whisky bar, this wood-panelled den in the Grand Hotel Terminus has more than 500 peaty tastes.

Cafe Opera
A long-standing mainstay of the Bergen night, Cafe Opera has cocktails, craft beer and a folk-music soundtrack.

Bryggeriet
Downtown microbrewery overlooking the harbour with creative beers, mostly brewed in the Germanic tradition.

MUSICAL BERGEN

Bergen has music in its soul. The 'Bergen Wave' was largely responsible for putting Norway on the world electronica circuit in the first years of the 21st century. **Østre** is the city's home for cutting-edge Norwegian electronica.

Hulen is an almost mythic venue among European heavy metal and indie rock fans. Around since 1968, it's suitably dark and occupies a converted bomb shelter.

Fab little **Café Sanaa** thrums to a mix of live and DJ-spun jazz, blues and West African beats. **Madam Felle** in Bryggen is another fine little genre-busting venue, and there's no lovelier place for live music on a summer's evening than the waterfront **USF Verftet**. For classical music, the Bergen Philharmonic Orchestra takes to the stage at Grieghallen from August to June.

Ulriken

Culinary Bergen
NORWAY'S FOODIE CAPITAL

Bergen has everything from atmospheric dining halls in Bryggen that date from Hanseatic times to cutting-edge temples to New Nordic cuisine and bastions of home cooking. Ask the tourist office about food-themed tours.

At **Pingvinen**, locals come for the meals their parents and grandparents used to cook. These might include *kjøttkaker* (meatballs with mushy peas and lingonberries), *plukkfisk* (cod with mashed potatoes, bacon and flatbread) or *lapskaus* (salted lamb stew).

Torget Fish Market has casual red tents on the harbourfront, where it serves ready-to-eat salmon, calamari, fish and chips, prawn baguettes and seafood salads. Far slicker, **Fisketorget Mathallen** offers permanent stands, each with its

 BEST BERGEN FESTIVALS

Bergen International Festival	**Nattjazz**	**Bergen Beer Festival**
Bergen's 14-day cultural classic kick-starts the summer in late May; a great time to visit.	Also spanning the end of May and often spilling over into June, 'Night Jazz' takes to the stage mostly at USF Verftet.	Toast the end of summer like the Vikings of old with brews from across the globe over two September days.

own menu, from sit-down meals to traditional, creamy bowls of fish soup, oysters and caviar.

One of Norway's best eat streets, **Marken** runs from the train station to just in from the harbour and is filled with multicultural options and fun cafes. Try the uber-cool **Råvarene**, Bergen's first zero-waste cafe, with sandwiches (open and otherwise), salads and snacks made using locally sourced and sustainable ingredients.

Historic Bryggen dining rooms don't come any more authentic than **Bryggen Tracteursted**. It inhabits a 1708 building that ranges across the former stables, kitchen (note the stone floor, which meant it was the only Bryggen building permitted to have a fire) and Bergen's only extant *schøtstuene*. The restaurant serves traditional Norwegian dishes that change regularly.

For artfully conceived and expertly executed New Nordic cooking (or New Fjordic as it's occasionally called), plan to have a meal at **Colonialen Matbar** or **Lysverket**.

Climb Seven Mountains (or Just One)

VIEWS AND HIKING TRAILS

Rome may have seven hills, but Bergen goes one better, boasting seven mountains. To be completely accurate, there are actually more than seven peaks surrounding the city, but the most commonly counted are Sandviksfjellet, Fløyfjellet (Fløyen), Rundemanen, Ulriken, Løvstakken, Damsgårdsfjellet and Lyderhorn. Together they provide abundant possibilities for recreation, as well as magnificent views in all directions.

The most accessible is **Mt Fløyen**, whose summit is just a few minutes' ride on the **Fløibanen funicular** from a station near Bryggen. The panoramic view from the top encompasses the city centre, the harbour and the surrounding islands and mountains. If you want to walk back down, trails lead to the city centre; the walk takes about 40 minutes.

Southeast of Fløyen is **Ulriken**, the highest of Bergen's mountains at 643m. Its summit is rugged, with rocky outcroppings and few trees, unlike Fløyen's gentler, forested heights. Ascending Ulriken on foot is demanding, involving a 750m-long staircase with some 1400 stone steps. If you want to admire the view without exertion, take the Ulriksbanen cable car – officially named **Ulriken643** – from Haukelandsbakken, which can be reached by bus or light rail from downtown.

Every year, the Bergen Hiking Club organises the **Seven Mountains Hike**, which tackles all the peaks in a single Sunday, usually in mid-May. The total distance is about 35km, with a total elevation change of about 2300m. For those who want slightly less of a challenge, there's a four-mountain version.

BEST BERGEN HIKES

Linn Kjos Falkenberg, communication manager at Visit Bergen, shares tips for local hikes.

Mt Fløyen
This is my go-to hike. I start the ascent through hairpin bends surrounded by mighty trees, with glimpses of the city in between. At the top, reward yourself with refreshments or continue to Blåmanen or Rundemanen.

Vidden
I really enjoy the hike on this mountain plateau between Ulriken and Fløyen. It offers 360-degree views towards the city and ocean on one side and untouched nature on the other.

Stoltzekleiven
If you want to push yourself, the hike up Stoltzekleiven is a local favourite, with around 800 stone steps going straight up the mountainside.

Beyond Bergen

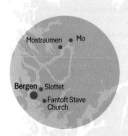

Mostraumen • Mo

Bergen • Slottet
• Fantoft Stave
Church

GETTING AROUND

You could digest bus, ferry and train timetables or trust in the wisdom of Google Maps. But to explore Osterfjord, Mostraumen and Mo, your best option is to take the ferry that leaves from Zachariasbryggen alongside the Fish Market. Check with the tourist office or buy your ticket on the boat.

☑ **TOP TIP**

Consider the Norway in a Nutshell tour (norwaynutshell.com): on a day out from Bergen, you'll go further than you think is possible.

Bergen's setting is as exciting as the city itself, and exploring its hinterland is a genuine treat.

Thanks to the clockwork-like precision of Norway's rail, bus and ferry system, much of southwestern Norway is within day-tripping distance of Bergen. Even Voss is just an hour from Bergen, and networks of fjords aren't a whole lot further away. Even closer to town, the hills, valleys, and watery fjords and inlets are fabulous places to explore, sheltering tiny villages, pretty shorelines and fine viewpoints that few travellers see.

It would take careful planning and days to see it all under your own steam. But this being Norway, they've already thought of it all for you: there's a tour that makes it all happen in just three hours.

Half-Day Cruise to Mostraumen
A TASTE OF THE FJORDS

If you want to see some fjords but don't have time for heavy hitters like Sognefjord, Hardangerfjord or Geirangerfjord, the roughly three-hour cruise from Bergen to **Mostraumen** is an excellent option. Departing from Zachariasbryggen next to the Fish Market, the cruise provides good views of Bryggen, Mt Fløyen and other parts of downtown Bergen as you head out of the harbour.

After skirting the mainland north of downtown, the boat turns eastward, sailing between several large islands as it sails up **Osterfjord**, passing forested islands dotted with houses and the occasional country church, sheer cliffs with trees clinging to tiny ledges, and green fields with red farm buildings and white cottages. Eventually, the boat slows down to pass through the narrow straits known as Mostraumen. As the channel widens again, you pass close to glistening waterfalls tumbling down the mountainsides as the boat approaches the innermost part of the fjord and the brightly painted little village of **Mo**.

LINGBEEK/GETTY IMAGES ©

Osterfjord

FANTOFT STAVE CHURCH

Although technically part of Bergen, the **Fantoft Stave Church**, in the suitably named southern suburb of Paradis, is a fair hike on the light rail from the city centre. But it's worth it, in part also because of its chequered history. Built in 1150 in Sognefjord, the church was moved here in 1883. It survived until the early 1990s when members of a black-metal music band, whose lyrics promote an anti-Christian, Satanist philosophy, burned the church to the ground. What you see today is a faithful replica. What remains original is the nearby stone cross, which dates from 1050.

If you'd like to add a hike to your cruise, book the combination tour that includes both the fjord cruise and a guided hike to **Slottet** (the Castle), about an hour each way. The trail leads through forest and marshland and past rivers and moors as it gradually climbs about 200m to a plateau with fine views of the fjord. Enjoy the panorama before heading back down to Mo, where you can look around the village while waiting for the boat to take you back to Bergen.

Voss

Voss ● ✪ OSLO

GETTING AROUND

Voss is compact and easy to get around on foot. The city is only 1¼ hours from Bergen by train on the Bergen–Oslo rail line, which has frequent departures daily. From Hardangerfjord, buses run several times a day from Norheimsund to Voss. The trip takes about 1¾ hours from Norheimsund. Buses between Voss and destinations on Sognefjord stop at Myrkdalen, Stalheim and Skulestadmo (near Tvindefossen).

☑ TOP TIP

Voss (also known as Vossevangen) offers plenty of organised activities, but one of the best things you can do is go for a walk around the eastern end of the town's lake, Vangsvatnet. You quickly leave the crowds of visitors behind, and the views looking back towards Voss are superb.

Voss is an experience as much as it is a place. Beautifully sited between the magic of the fjords and the charms of Bergen, this compact town has a personality to go with its good looks.

Every summer, adrenaline-seekers from all over the world come to experience a uniquely Vossian offering of high-octane thrills. Whether up high or down in the water, there's almost nothing you can't do in Voss. But as you wander along its main street, dip into one of its cafes or visit the local craft brewery, you'll also see that Voss has retained a strong Norwegian personality.

A stay here doesn't necessarily have to just be about the town itself, and Voss also makes an excellent base for exploring the entire region. All manner of fjords lie just beyond the hills, and Voss is a lovely, quiet place to return in the evening when the day-tripping crowds have moved on.

Get Your Thrills in Voss
NORWAY'S EXTREME SPORTS CAPITAL

Adventure seekers from around the world flock to Voss, a small town that's earned a well-deserved reputation as a paradise for adrenaline junkies. Situated between two lakes, surrounded by mountains and within easy reach of Bergen and Norway's two longest fjords (Sognefjord and Hardangerfjord), Voss offers just about every type of outdoor activity you can imagine.

Lace up your hiking boots or cycling shoes – or strap on skis and snowshoes in winter – to hit the trails. Tours are run by top-notch operators such as **Voss Active** (vossactive. no), **Wild Voss** (wildvoss.no) and **Outdoor Norway** (outdoor norway.com). Hiking, mountaineering, rock climbing and mountain biking are all on the menu, as are water-based activities such as river canoeing, sea kayaking, stand-up paddleboarding, riverboarding, canyoning and whitewater rafting on the Class III Raundalselva. Most sea kayaking trips take

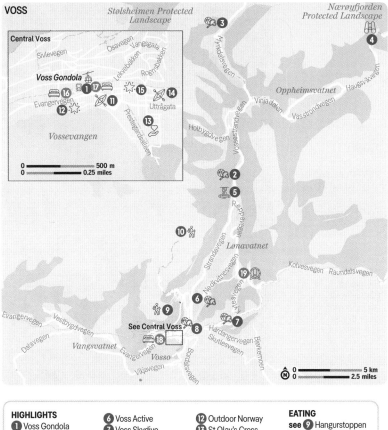

HIGHLIGHTS
1 Voss Gondola

SIGHTS
2 High Rope and Zipline Park
3 Myrkdalen
4 Stalheim
5 Tvindefossen

6 Voss Active
7 Voss Skydive
8 Voss Vind

ACTIVITIES, COURSES & TOURS
9 Hangurstoppen
10 Lønahorgi
11 Nordic Ventures

12 Outdoor Norway
13 St Olav's Cross
14 Vått & Vilt
15 Wild Voss

SLEEPING
16 Fleischer's Hotel
17 Scandic Hotel Voss
18 Voss Hostel

EATING
see 9 Hangurstoppen Restaurant

DRINKING & NIGHTLIFE
see 15 Tre Brør
19 Voss Bryggeri

place on nearby fjords, but you can also paddle right in Voss on lakes Vangsvatnet and Lønavatnet with **Nordic Ventures** (nordic ventures.com). For anyone serious about improving their paddling technique, **Vått & Vilt** (vaattogvilt.no) offers half- and two-day courses in sea and river kayaking.

For a different kind of adrenaline rush, head to Voss Active's **High Rope and Zipline Park**. If that's not exciting enough, how about parachuting or tandem skydiving with **Voss Skydive** or indoor flying in the wind tunnel at **Voss Vind**?

RAYINTS/SHUTTERSTOCK ©

BEST PLACES TO VISIT NEAR VOSS

Tvindefossen
This gorgeous roadside waterfall tumbles 110m over staircase-like rocks 12km north of Voss.

Myrkdalen
Family-friendly ski resort known for long, snowy winters, as well as excellent summer hiking and mountain biking.

Stalheim
Panoramic views of the Nærøy Valley from Stalheim Hotel. The winding Stalheimskleiva road is open to foot traffic.

Skjervefossen
Large two-tier waterfall with a 150m total drop, located along the old road between Voss and Granvin.

Tvindefossen

The last week of June is **Ekstremsportveko**, the world's largest extreme sports festival, with an exhilarating programme of adrenaline-fuelled activities for all ages and levels of experience. Plan well ahead if you want to visit Voss at this time.

 WHERE TO STAY IN VOSS

Voss Hostel
Waterfront hostel with mixed dorm rooms that can be reserved for private groups and a small shared kitchen. €

Fleischer's Hotel
Historic hotel with classic rooms as well as self-catering apartments in a separate motel building. €€

Scandic Hotel Voss
Modern hotel overlooking Vangsvatnet lake close to Voss Station and downtown restaurants. €€€

Head for the Mountaintop

VOSS GONDOLA TO HANGURSTOPPEN

The state-of-the-art **Voss Gondola** whisks passengers from Voss Station to 820m above sea level on **Hangurstoppen** in less than nine minutes. At the top are kilometres of hiking trails and fantastic views of the town and Vangsvatnet lake. There is also **Voss Resort**, one of western Norway's largest ski resorts, with 18 lifts to 24 downhill pistes, as well as 18km of groomed cross-country trails. In warmer months, you can bring a mountain bike on the gondola (rentals are available at the base). The clear alpine lake Valbergstjørni has a swimming dock, so bring your swimsuit to take a dip.

At the upper station, **Hangurstoppen Restaurant** serves seasonal menus of dishes based on ingredients from local farms. Prebooking a table for the evening à la carte service – recommended during the summer and other busy times – gets you a discount on gondola tickets.

Several hiking routes lead back down to Voss, while other trails climb further into the mountains. The most ambitious is the trail to **Lønahorgi**, which ascends to an altitude of 1410m. At the other end of the spectrum, there's a wheelchair-accessible 1km loop with panoramic views of Voss. Along this path, the **Hangurshusko swing** is popular for its sweeping views that almost tempt you to fly off into the scenery. Try it yourself or just watch the gliders as they soar down into the valley.

MORE THRILLS

Voss isn't Norway's only adrenaline hub. **Åndalsnes** (p203) is a magnet for mountaineers, and in the far north, **Tromsø** (p278) is ideal for a variety of Arctic adventures. Down south, **Rjukan** (p94) has lots to get you active.

MORE VOSS HIGHLIGHTS

Vangskyrkja
Voss' Gothic-style church is one of Norway's loveliest stone churches.

St Olav's Cross
This simple yet beautiful weathered stone cross has stood since 1023.

Tre Brør
The heart of Voss' social scene, with super coffee and a great range of microbrews.

Voss Bryggeri
This much-respected brewery has Oregonian pale ale, Natabjødn ('nut beer'), an English-style brown beer and traditional Vossaøl, which is brewed with juniper tea. It's 6km north of Voss.

Hardangerfjord

Hardangerfjord ● ✪ OSLO

GETTING AROUND

A car is necessary if you want complete freedom to explore all the nooks and crannies of Hardangerfjord, but if your time is flexible, you can reach many of the region's top attractions using a combination of different forms of public transport. In summer, the Norled passenger ferry connects villages along the fjord. There are also car ferries between Kvandal, Utne and Kinsarvik, as well as Jondal and Tørvikbygd. Buses also run between villages along the shores of the fjord.

☑ **TOP TIP**

Most of Hardangerfjord's tourist offices are staffed by volunteers, and they may have restricted hours outside the summer months, when some open only at weekends. When you find one open, most have excellent resources, including hiking maps. Hardanger Hiking Highlights (30kr) is outstanding.

Among Norway's largest fjord systems, Hardangerfjord is the heart and soul of Norwegian fjord country. Villages cling improbably to narrow footholds between the water's edge and steep hillsides, while cliffs soar high into snow and cloud. Perhaps more than the world-famous Sognefjord and Geirangerfjord, Hardangerfjord retains its Norwegian character, and locals often outnumber foreign visitors, even at the height of summer. Across the fjord network, there are plenty of opportunities to escape the crowds.

Hardangerfjord's natural beauty is reason enough to visit, especially for its iconic lookouts and splendid waterfalls. But it's the interplay between human beings and their near-impossible surrounds that gives Hardangerfjord its gravitas, from apple orchards to Viking echoes and from historically inaccessible Kjeåsen Farm (still a challenge to reach today) to glacier hikes across one of the largest ice sheets in northern Europe. It's a remarkable place that's worth as much time as you can give it.

The Nature of Hardanger
FROM FJORD TO FALLS

Eidfjord, 153km by road east of Bergen, makes an ideal gateway to the Hardangervidda plateau, the largest mountain plateau in northern Europe. It's possible to reach Eidfjord by bus, but having your own vehicle really opens up possibilities once you're here. From Eidfjord, the Rv7 twists upwards through Måbødalen before climbing onto the plateau. Along the way are some stirring attractions.

In Øvre Eidfjord, 7km from Eidfjord, stop in the fabulous **Norway Natursenter**. Interactive exhibits explore the region's flora and fauna, and staff have information on activities. There's an outstanding 20-minute film to inspire you, which makes you feel as though you are flying over the region's fjords, mountains, waterfalls and glaciers. Continuing further up the valley through a series of remarkable corkscrewing tunnels brings you to the stunning 182m-high **Vøringsfossen**,

HARDANGERFJORD

HIGHLIGHTS
1. Norway Natursenter
2. Skytjefossen
3. Vøringsfossen

SIGHTS
4. Hardanger Folk Museum

ACTIVITIES, COURSES & TOURS
5. Best Adventures
6. Hardanger Fjordsafari
7. Kjeåsen Farm
8. Mt Vikanuten
9. Trolltunga Active

SLEEPING
10. Eidfjord Gjestgiveri
11. Sandven Hotel
12. Utne Hotel

THE HARDANGER FIDDLE

The Hardanger fiddle is a variant of the violin used in Norwegian folk music. It differs from a regular violin in that it has a flatter bridge and six secondary strings. Many are richly decorated.

The oldest Hardanger fiddle in existence was made in 1651 and is now at the Bergen University Museum. The instrument was originally played in people's houses, but after the well-known violinist Ole Bull helped bring it to broader attention, it became more widespread. Edvard Grieg was just one of the composers who incorporated the Hardanger fiddle in his works.

The **Ole Bull Academy** in Voss is dedicated to preserving and developing traditional Norwegian folk music and dance, and it has a workshop specifically for making and repairing Hardanger fiddles.

View from Kjeåsen Farm

where waters plunge over the plateau's rim and down into Måbødalen, some with a vertiginous drop of 145m. Trails lead to overlooks on both sides and across a dramatic footbridge with 99 steps suspended 50m over the rushing Bjoreio river.

Another option is to head for **Skytjefossen**, which lies 12km north of Eidfjord in the Simadalen valley. Cascading almost 300m off the Hardangervidda plateau to the valley floor below, these falls are among Norway's highest. Drive as far as Tveit and park just after the last house. The hike to the falls is about 3km and takes 1½ hours there and back.

Enjoy the View from Kjeåsen

SURVEY THE SCENE

Nothing says Norway quite like **Kjeåsen Farm**. In a country where carving out a space to live and farm is often a back-breaking task, Kjeåsen takes things to a whole new level.

On a steep, cleared slope between forest and a precipitous drop 600m above Eidfjord are two farms that look out over spectacular views. Occupied since at least the mid-19th century, the farms were accessible only via a steep hiking path until a road was built in 1975. Until then, all building materials had to be carried on people's backs. (It's said that one of the structures took 30 years to build.) The last permanent

WHERE TO STAY AROUND HARDANGERFJORD

Eidfjord Gjestgiveri
A classic Norwegian guesthouse with whitewashed wood, period furnishings and its own pancake cafe. €€

Energihotellet
This boutique hotel and fusion restaurant occupies a repurposed 1960s-era power station in Nesflaten. €€

Hardanger Gjestegard
This 19th-century wooden guesthouse is like sleeping in a Hans Christian Andersen fairy tale. €€

resident, Bjørg Wiik, who lived here alone for four decades, left in 2019, although she still returns in summer.

Getting up here is half the fun. You could reach Eidfjord by bus, but you'd still need a vehicle to get to Kjeåsen, so it's best to make the entire journey in your own vehicle. To reach Kjeåsen, drive 8km north of Eidfjord along the Rv7. From the signposted turnoff to the farm, the road leads steeply up for 2.5km and then a further 2.5km through a steep tunnel. Because the road is so narrow, traffic is allowed to travel in each direction only once an hour: going up on the hour and coming down on the half-hour. The road is usually closed for much of winter.

Follow Hardanger Folk Traditions in Utne
FROM FIDDLES TO FARMSTEADS

Just a few minutes' walk from the Utne ferry dock, the **Hardanger Folk Museum** is the place to go to learn about the cultural heritage of the Hardanger region. The informative exhibits cover everything from regional folk costumes and wedding traditions to furniture, handicrafts, embroidery and folk music. On the hill behind the main museum building is a collection of historic wooden buildings from around the region including houses, farm buildings, workshops and a school. The oldest was built around 1220, but most date from the 18th and 19th centuries and are furnished as they would have been while in use. The views of Utne, the fjord and the surrounding mountains are glorious.

Hardangerfjord by Boat
FERRIES, KAYAKS AND MORE

It would be a shame to visit the Hardangerfjord area without getting out on the water at least once. **Hardanger Fjordsafari** operates RIB-boat safaris from Eidfjord, including some with cider tasting at a local fruit farm. For a more leisurely exploration, **Best Adventures** offers three-hour, half-day and full-day kayaking tours on the Simadalsfjord, the secluded innermost arm of the Hardangerfjord, departing from the centre of Eidfjord. **Trolltunga Active** runs two-day kayaking tours from Uskedalen on the western arm of Hardangerfjord, as well as five-hour trips from Lofthus.

The **Norled passenger ferry** runs daily from Norheimsund to Eidfjord and back again, with stops in key villages along the way. Alternatively, you can walk aboard **Fjord1 car ferries** for free for a quick trip across the fjord between Utne and Kvanndal or Kinsarvik, or Jondal and Tørvikbygd.

VIKINGS OF HARDANGER

The fjords were very much part of the Viking realm. From the 8th to the 11th centuries, Kinsarvik was one of the region's largest Viking settlements. The small U-shaped patch of greenery opposite the Kinsarvik tourist office was the former Viking port. **Kinsarvik Church** also marks a clear break with the Viking past. Built around 1180 by Scottish invaders, it serves as a reminder of how quickly Viking dominance waned once the glory days were over.

Just 30km up the road in Eidfjord, 350 Viking burial mounds, dating from 400 to 1000 CE, mark the largest Iron Age site in western Norway. The tourist office has a map with a marked 5.3km walking trail (allow 1½ hours).

 WHERE TO STAY AROUND HARDANGERFJORD

Sandven Hotel
Right by the fjord in Norheimsund, charming Sandven dates back nearly 170 years. €€

Utne Hotel
Norway's oldest hotel (1722) rises by the fjord and has some contemporary interiors and nightly cider tastings. €€€

Hardanger Panorama Lodge
High above Ulvik, this beauty feels like a luxury treehouse experience, swathed in glass and Norwegian pine. €€€

THE GUIDE

HARDANGERFJORD BERGEN & THE SOUTHWESTERN FJORDS

Like many roads around Hardangerfjord, this route hugs the coastline but heads to a lesser-known corner of Hardanger. This journey begins in quiet little **1 Norheimsund**, a useful gateway to the region if you're coming from Bergen. It was once a popular weekend escape for Bergenites, and it's a pretty little fjord-side town. Just 6km by road around a few fjord corners to the northeast, **2 Øystese** has been transformed from a nondescript Hardanger town to one of Norway's leading contemporary art centres. Kunsthuset Kabuso draws international artists that have included Damien Hirst and Matthew Barney.

Tracking northeast along the Fv7 for 34km takes you to **3 Kvanndal**, from where regular ferries leave for **4 Utne**. Fruit orchards surround this charming hamlet, which is known for its wonderfully preserved traditional streets and the excellent Hardanger Folk

Museum. From Utne, the 36km Rv550 road to **5 Jondal** is a quietly beautiful route, especially in late spring or early summer. The road hugs the fjord the whole way, passing through orchards and by fishing shacks and tiny beaches. In Hereiane, smooth rock rises straight up from the fjord to the peaks above, while the boat-shed kiosk in Jondal serves waffles.

Continuing in a roughly southerly direction, you reach **6 Rosendal** 54km after leaving Jondal. Although it's separated from the rest of Hardangerfjord by high mountains and the ice cap of Folgefonna National Park (p164), Rosendal gets more visitors than you might imagine thanks to its regular ferry connections with Stavanger and Bergen. Rosendal has a good national park centre and Baroniet Rosendal (1665), Norway's only baronial mansion, which sits on a gentle rise above the town and has a stunning rose garden.

Beyond Hardangerfjord

Hardangerfjord
• Norwegian Museum
of Hydropower
and Industry
• Trolltunga
• Folgefonna
National Park
Røldal Stave
Church

You don't have to go far beyond Hardangerfjord to see that it's just the start of a soul-stirring adventure.

Hardangerfjord might be the worthy centrepiece of your trip through southwestern Norway, and its tentacles reach out inexorably into the surrounding country. But it's also just a starting point.

The high ridges and summits that look down on the fjord's waters have, not surprisingly, some high-altitude thrills in store. Extending away to the north, east and south are glorious uplands that provide a spectacular wild counterpoint to the manicured beauty of the fjord and its villages. Hike the Troll's Tongue (Trolltunga) to one of Norway's signature viewpoints or venture out onto the glaciers of Folgefonna. Deep down below, valleys shelter stave churches alongside roads that meander through scenery of rare and exceptional beauty.

Hike Up High to Trolltunga
GO TO THE EDGE OF THE PRECIPICE

Jutting out from the mountainside 700m above Ringedalsvatnet lake like the troll's tongue it's named for, **Trolltunga** is quite possibly Norway's most spectacular rock formation. Shaped by the ice that once covered most of Scandinavia, it's part of a plateau that forms the western edge of Hardangervidda.

Getting to Trolltunga involves a demanding hike through alpine landscapes – 27km round-trip from Skjeggedal, with an elevation change of almost 800m – and takes between eight and 12 hours. Alternatively, you can start from Mågelitopp, which shaves off 7km and reduces the elevation gain to about 320m. Shuttle buses run from Odda via Tyssedal to Skjeggedal and on to Mågelitopp.

The trail is generally good, with decent signage, but hikers should be in good physical condition and carry the proper equipment for wilderness hiking. The ascent is brutally steep in places. En route, look out for the **Tyssestrengene waterfall** (646m). Once you reach the top, the challenging nature of the hike fades away: the views are extraordinary and worth every aching muscle. Walking out to the tip of the tongue takes considerable nerve.

GETTING AROUND

To make the most of your time, plan on having your own wheels. The E13 from Stavanger runs through Odda and hugs the eastern shore of Hardangerfjord on its way north. Access to many attractions in the Hardangerfjord hinterland lies off this road. One of these roads is the Fv551, which links Rosendal and Folgefonna to Hardangerfjord. The Fv551 includes the 11.15km-long Folgefonna Tunnel, which runs beneath the ice cap.

☑ TOP TIP

Allocate at least a day each for Folgefonna and Trolltunga, plus an extra day to relax and get between the two.

If you have any energy left, continue to **Preikesto-len** (Pulpit Rock), a smaller version of the much more famous perch of the same name overlooking Lysefjord, near Stavanger.

The hike is usually doable from late May to early September, and it's recommended to start early in the morning and pay close attention to weather conditions. Unless you have experience in the Norwegian mountains, consider joining a guided trek, especially if you are hiking outside the summer months. **Trolltunga Active** and **Trolltunga Adventures** are two reputable operators that offer hikes. They might also be able to organise sunrise or sunset versions of the hike, as well as bungee jumping and ziplining.

For a different approach to Trolltunga, try the **Trolltunga Via Ferrata**, which combines hiking with climbing on fixed cables and ladders. Whichever way you get to the top, you're rewarded with views that will take your breath away – if you have any left, that is!

MORE LOOKOUTS

Overlooking Lysefjord west of Stavanger, **Preikestolen** (p179) is the granddaddy of Norway's death-defying lookouts. It's reached by a glorious hike in Norway's southwestern fjord country.

Glacier Trekking in Folgefonna
ON THE HIGH ICE

Mainland Norway's third-largest icefield, **Folgefonna National Park**, covers 168 sq km. The icefield has numerous access points, from Jondal in the west to Odda in the east. These access points lie within 120km and 190km from Bergen and are best reached by car (with the Tørvikbygd–Jondal ferry thrown in).

In some parts, the ice at Folgefonna is 400m thick. It is a dramatic, beautiful place, with glaciers snaking down into nearby valleys. From a distance, the icecap glistens in the sun and turns charcoal grey whenever clouds swirl around it. Up close, an otherworldly swatch of ice colours – glacier blue to the purest white – and deep crevasses characterise this richly textured landscape.

Hiking in such a place is no ordinary undertaking. At one level, this means you'll enjoy the privilege of an up-close encounter with a glacier, a signature landscape of Europe's far north. But it also means that, aside from a few walks around the glacier fringes, you should set out on a true glacier hike only in the company of a professional guide. One option is the timeless Folgefonna traverse, a multiday expedition from Sundal to Odda, but much shorter day hikes are options as well. The six-hour 'Blue Ice' trip to **Juklavassbreen** is especially

---

HARDANGER'S APPLES

Hardangerfjord and the surrounding area is Norway's orchard. Apples are the speciality, and roads are dotted with signs offering *Bær salg* (fruit for sale) from little roadside boxes. For more information see siderlandet.no/en.

Lofthus Ekspedisjon
Has its own cider brewery and fjord-side restaurant, and can organise tastings.

Hardanger Saft og Siderfabrikk
A traditional fruit farm with apple and plum orchards, and juice- and cider-production facilities.

Ulvik Frukt & Cideri
Sample homemade apple juices and ciders, plus fresh apples and cherries.

WHERE TO STAY BEYOND HARDANGERFJORD

Hordatun Hotel	Energihotellet	Tyssedal Hotel
This concrete curve overlooking a lake has loads of personality, great views and a good restaurant. €€	In a disused 1960s power station, this boutique belle is minimalist chic with a great restaurant. €€€	Built in 1913, Odda's art deco Tyssedal Hotel has terrific rooms with their own ghosts. €€€

Folgefonna icefield

good. Most hikes are suitable for anyone in good physical condition. Wear warm clothing and sturdy footwear.

Folgefonni Glacier Team (folgefonni.no), based in Jondal, and **Best Adventures** (bestadventures.no) in Øvre Eidfjord are two excellent operators.

A Place of Pilgrimage
CHURCH OF THE SWEATY CROSS

The **Røldal Stave Church** lacks the size and distinctive dragon carvings of some of the more famous stave churches, but it's worth a stop if you're passing through the area. Built between 1200 and 1250, it has been modified multiple times but retains many of its original features, including a crucifix that's said to sweat on the night of 6 and 7 July annually. These sweat droplets were believed to have healing powers, making Røldal a popular pilgrimage destination for centuries. It still receives lots of visitors at the appointed time every year, just in case.

Røldal Stave Church is richly decorated on the inside, with elaborate rosemaling paintings from the first half of the 17th century covering the walls, pulpit and other surfaces.

TYSSEDAL HYDROELECTRIC POWER STATION

Just off the southernmost end of Hardangerfjord, close to Odda, the **Norwegian Museum of Hydropower and Industry** is a rare confluence of energy production plant and architectural innovation.

Built in the early 20th century by Thorvald Astrup, the Tyss 1 power plant blends classical European architecture with austere, functionalist lines. A student of the era's functionalist movement and a passionate lover of Italian cathedrals, Astrup believed that even industrial sites could be beautiful. Tyssedal is his masterpiece, and it certainly more resembles an abbey than a power plant. Take the guided tour to learn more.

WHERE TO STAY BEYOND HARDANGERFJORD

Sundal Camping
Pleasant campsites and cabins in Sundal, 28km northeast of Rosendal. €

Baroniet Rosendal
This rambling farmhouse has attractive rooms and three-course dinner menus. €€

Rosendal Turisthotell
Opposite the quay, this handsome house dates from 1887 and has a fine restaurant. €€

Haugesund

Haugesund OSLO

GETTING AROUND

Haugesund's city centre is compact and easily walked, but you need a car to make the most of the surrounding area. Kolumbus (kolumbus. no) is the operator for bus routes within Haugesund and Haugalandet, as well as to destinations further afield in Rogaland.

☑ **TOP TIP**

Don't miss the **Marilyn Monroe Memorial** along the town's waterfront. Somewhat bizarrely, Haugesund claims to be the ancestral home of Marilyn Monroe, whose father, a local baker, emigrated from here to the USA. This statue, next to the Scandic Maritim Hotel, is suitably coquettish, if not a great likeness.

The area around Haugesund is considered by many to be the birthplace of Norway. It's known especially as the place where Harald Fairhair united western Norway in the 9th century.

However, the city itself is relatively young by Norwegian standards. Its origins lie in the local traditions of fishing and salting herring in the mid-19th century. As fishing communities settled along the bay and boat traffic grew, Haugesund became known as *sildabyen* (the herring city) and developed into a commercial centre for the industry.

The city's origins are still reflected in the distinctive character of the buildings alongside Smedasundet, the channel that divides the mainland from the islands of Risøy and Hasseløy. It's a lively, appealing place with a strong local character, and few tourists make it out here. Haugesund has good restaurants, numerous annual festivals and easy access to beautiful islands, including Karmøy with its beaches, idyllic villages and historic sites.

In the Footsteps of Harald Fairhair
THE FOUNDER OF UNITED NORWAY

Harald Fairhair is one of Norway's most legendary kings, credited with uniting Norway into one kingdom following his victory at the Battle of Hafrsfjord in the late 9th century. According to the Norse sagas, he was a handsome man, known for his long, flowing hair and his strong, wise leadership. A statue of Harald with flowing locks stands atop a rocky outcrop at the end of **Haraldsgata**, the short street in Haugesund bearing his name. Harald holds his helmet and shield as he surveys the view of **Smedasundet** – a view you, too, can admire from the overlook just below the sculpture.

Harald had his royal seat at Avaldsnes on Karmøy (p168). According to the Icelandic saga bearing his name, he died of illness in about 930 CE and is buried in a mound at Haugar

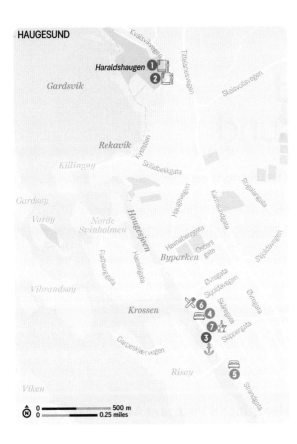

HAUGESUND

HIGHLIGHTS
1 Haraldshaugen

SIGHTS
2 Krosshaugen
3 Smedasundet

SLEEPING
4 Clarion Collection Hotel Banken
5 Scandic Maritim Hotel

EATING
6 To Glass

DRINKING & NIGHTLIFE
7 Brasserie Brakstad

BEST PLACES TO STAY & EAT IN HAUGESUND

Clarion Collection Hotel Banken
Haugesund's best hotel occupies a grand turn-of-the-century stone building with elegant rooms and super views. €€

Scandic Maritim Hotel
This sprawling Scandic has the best harbourside location in town and appealing rooms. €€

Brasserie Brakstad
The pick of the places to eat, this groovy gastropub serves big pepper steaks, bowls of mussels and baked salmon. €€

To Glass
This small upstairs and upscale restaurant is away from the harbour but serves good sharing plates. €€€

overlooking the Karmsund strait. When Snorre Sturlason, the author of the sagas, visited the area in 1220, he was shown a burial mound that was said to be Harald's. Scholars now question this identification; however, it was fully accepted in 1873, when an imposing monument, **Haraldshaugen**, was erected on the site in honour of the 1000th anniversary of the Battle of Hafrsfjord and the unification of Norway. There are good views of the coast from the monument.

Nearby is **Krosshaugen**, a smaller mound topped with a stone cross from the early days of Christianity in Norway, around 1000 CE.

Beyond Haugesund

Åkrafjorden

Haugesund

Utsira

Avaldsnes

GETTING AROUND

The E134 runs straight from Haugesund to Karmøy. Buses run every 30 minutes between Avaldsnes and downtown Haugesund. The island's southernmost town, Skudeneshavn, is 28km south of Avaldsnes and can be reached via either Rv47 on the west coast or Rv511 on the east. The less frequent bus 210 connects Avaldsnes with Skudeneshavn, so having your own wheels increases your options.

☑️ **TOP TIP**

Check the stone obelisk at St Olav's Church in Avaldsnes. Legend suggests that when it touches the wall, Judgment Day is at hand.

Occupying a near-mythic status in Norwegian history, Haugalandet (the area around Haugesund) is a fascinating detour.

Buffeted by North Atlantic winds and far enough west of well-travelled routes to feel like an adventure, the island of Karmøy feels like nowhere else in this part of the country. Its historical significance is difficult to overstate – the idea of Norway as a single, united country began here.

But it's also a lovely landscape, one that resembles the highlands of Scotland or windswept Irish moors more than it does the fjord country not far to the east. Karmøy is arguably more interesting than Haugesund itself, so if you've made it that far, you'd be crazy not to carry on just a little further. The rewards are an experience that few visitors to Norway even know exists.

Meet Kings & Vikings at Avaldsnes

ROYAL HISTORY AND ARCHAEOLOGY

The site of Harald Fairhair's principal residence, **Avaldsnes** is considered Norway's oldest royal seat. Yet this site on north-eastern Karmøy actually dates back much earlier than Harald's 9th-century reign. When Harald established his base at Avaldsnes, it had already been a seat of power for roughly 1700 years. The site was strategic because it allowed rulers at Avaldsnes to control Karmsundet, the narrow strait that all ships passed through along Nordvegen (the way north), the route that gave Norway its name. For Harald, Avaldsnes became the place from which he could most easily control his kingdom, and his successors continued to maintain a royal manor at Avaldsnes for centuries.

Arriving at Avaldsnes, the first thing you'll see is **Olavs-kirken**, a stone church built around 1250 in honour of King Olav II Haraldsson (St Olaf), who is credited with bringing Christianity to Norway. Because of this association, Avaldsnes was once an important stop along the pilgrim route to Nidaros. Near the church, but set mostly underground to minimise its impact on the surrounding landscape, the excellent **Nordvegen Historiesenter** tells the fascinating story of Avaldsnes through artefacts and multimedia displays.

BPFOTO/SHUTTERSTOCK ©

Utsira lighthouse

From the museum, a trail leads through a landscape dotted with remnants of old burial mounds, building stones and other ancient signs of human habitation to the **Viking Farm**, where you can experience what daily life was like during the Viking Age. Built in as authentic a manner as possible based on archaeological discoveries, the farm is open during the summer, with a variety of hands-on activities, as well as a popular annual **Viking Festival** in early June.

Soak Up Island Life on Utsira

BIRDS, FISH AND ART

About 20km west of Haugesund, **Utsira** is a small dot in the vast North Sea, on the outer edge of southwestern Norway. The lighthouse on the island has been in operation since 1844 and originally consisted of a pair of twin towers. Only one is still in use as Norway's oldest still-functioning weather station.

The country's smallest municipality, Utsira measures only about 6 sq km. It has just over 200 human inhabitants but an abundance of birdlife – 330 recorded species, including some never seen elsewhere in Norway – making it a magnet for ornithologists during the migration season.

TRAILS AROUND HAUGESUND

Haugesund is located along a branch of **Kyststien**, the coastal trail that runs from Skillebekkgata at Killingøy north to Kvalsvik. Here, the sculpture *The Rising Tide* by Jason DeCaires Taylor stands in the sea, portraying riders atop four horses with oil pumps instead of heads, commentary on humanity's ambivalent attitude towards climate change. Along the way, there are wonderful ocean views as you walk through mixed terrain including heather-covered hills, rocky shores and pastures where sheep graze. Another favourite local hiking spot is **Steinsfjellet**, the rocky 227m summit just east of Haugesund, with fine views of the city and the ocean beyond. There's a road to the top and a variety of trails to choose from once you're there.

WHERE TO GET INFO IN HAUGALANDET

Nornehuset
This friendly B&B occupies a converted Karmøy warehouse, and the friendly owners have information about the region.

Avaldsnes Tourist Office
Part of the Nordvegen Historiesenter, this summer-only office has good information about the region's sites.

Skudeneshavn Tourist Office
This is the place for information if you're exploring the southern reaches of Karmøy.

ÅKRAFJORDEN

Stretching along the south side of the Folgefonna Peninsula, northeast of Haugesund, **Åkrafjorden** is one of southwestern Norway's lesser-known gems. Its star attraction is **Langfoss**, Norway's fifth-highest waterfall, which thunders over several steps and under the E134 road as it cascades 612m into the fjord. It's a four-hour round-trip hike along a winding hillside path to the top of the falls, where you're rewarded with panoramic views of the fjord, mountains and the Folgefonna glacier.

If you're driving, take the old road, Gamle Åkrafjordvegen, between Kyrping and Langfoss rather than the long tunnel on the E134. **Åkrafjordtunet** in Teigland is worth a stop for information about the area and the opportunity to buy locally produced food products.

NICHT ALICIA/SHUTTERSTOCK ©

Langfoss

Another reason to visit Utsira is the art. Scattered throughout the island are murals, sculptures and other installations: some whimsical, some political and some drawn from everyday life, but all interesting and distinctive. Many are by internationally known street artists.

To get to Utsira, take the ferry from Haugesund, which runs three or four times daily and takes 70 minutes. It takes about 20 minutes to walk across the island between the northern and southern harbours. There are a few different dining options, as well as self-catering accommodation at the light station and other spots along the shore.

Stavanger

Stavanger ● ✪OSLO

In the contest for western Norway's coolest city, Stavanger flies a little under the radar – especially when compared with Bergen – but it has no reason to envy its neighbour to the north. Stavanger has plenty of substance, including great restaurants and museums, to go with its good looks.

Stavanger has attitude and confidence, combining its role as Norway's oil city with a pretty harbourside setting, an impressive portfolio of historical sites and a delightful old quarter. The compact town centre is best explored on foot. Fuelled by oil money, Stavanger has an embarrassment of riches when it comes to restaurants. Yes, it can be expensive, even by Norwegian standards. But it's also the archetype for a prosperous Scandinavian city that knows how to have a good time.

More than that, Stavanger is the gateway to the spectacular experiences of Lysefjord, all of which are possible on a day trip.

Dive into Stavhaugesund's Distant Past
FROM PREHISTORY TO THE VIKINGS

The University of Stavanger's excellent **Museum of Archaeology** is the ideal place to learn about thousands of years of human and natural history in Stavanger and the surrounding region. Its treasures include the well-preserved Stone Age skeleton of a young boy, as well as 3000-year-old bronze *lurs* (a kind of musical instrument), cult axes from the Bronze Age, a runestone from the end of the Viking Age, and various well-preserved jewels and coins from different periods. Another highlight is the well-preserved skeleton of a polar bear that lived 12,400 years ago on nearby Finnøy. It's a fascinating collection.

Presiding over the city from a hill above the innermost (southern) point of the harbour, the stone-built **Stavanger Domkirke** (Stavanger Cathedral) is Norway's oldest medieval cathedral still in its original form. Stavanger dates its founding from the completion of the cathedral. First built in 1125, the cathedral is a fascinating blend of Gothic, baroque, Romanesque and Anglo-Norman influences. It's undergoing restoration and is expected to reopen in 2024.

GETTING AROUND

Downtown Stavanger is walkable, with most top attractions within easy reach of one another, the harbour and the train station. An efficient network of buses and passenger ferries connects downtown with other parts of the city and beyond.

☑ TOP TIP
If you're driving to Stavanger, try to find a hotel with private parking. The city's parking stations cost at least 240kr per day. Unless you're on a day excursion to Lysefjord, you're unlikely to need your car while you're in town, so you can leave it for the duration.

171

Tastagata

Øvre Strandgate

Vågen

GAMLE
STAVANGER

4

Strandkaien

1 Gamle
   Stavanger 10

Møllegata

Løkkeveien

Øvre Strandgate

Lars Hertervigs gate

Stokkaveien

Steingate

Møllegata

Niels Juelsgate

Løvdahls gate

9

Nedre Strandgate

Haumeringen

20

26

Valbergata

Nedre Holmegate

Øvre Holmegate

Skagenkaien

2
25

11

27 18

Breigata

Kirkegata

19

Skagen

Rosenkildetorget

17

23

Domkirkeplassen

Byparke

Breiavan

Håkon

Olav Vs gate

Peder Claussens gate

12

Klinkenberggata

Løkkeveien

Eiganesveien

Olavskleiv

Engelsm gate

Jernbanev

Musegate

5

3

Prinsens gate

Dronningens gate

13

Kannikgata

Musegate

Kannikgata

Madlaveien

Peder Klows gate

Stavanger
Kunstmuseum (1.7km);
Sverd i Fjell (4.9km)

Storgata

2 Museum of
   Archaeology

CATHEDRAL ARCHITECTURE & RESTORATION

Norway's oldest cathedral still in use, Stavanger Domkirke was completed in 1125 and extensively rebuilt after a fire in 1272, with a Gothic choir added to the original Romanesque nave. The large portal at the western end and the distinctive twin towers on the east side also date from this time. The impressive interior has massive stone columns, high vaults resembling the hulls of ships, an elaborate baroque pulpit, five large epitaphs and stained glass by Norwegian artist Victor Sparre installed in 1957.

After centuries of continuous use, Stavanger Cathedral was closed in 2020 for extensive restoration. At the time of research, it was scheduled to be reopened in August 2024 in anticipation of its – and the city's – 900th anniversary celebrations in 2025.

SAIKO3P/SHUTTERSTOCK ©

Norsk Oljemuseum

One of the most important battles of the Viking Age took place just outside Stavanger in the late 9th century. Traditionally dated to 872 CE but now believed to have taken place somewhat later, the Battle of Hafrsfjord saw Harald Fairhair defeat his rivals to unite western Norway under his control, a pivotal event that eventually led to the establishment of a single kingdom. The impressive **Sverd i Fjell** monument at Møllebukta commemorates the battle with three giant stone swords stuck into a rocky headland overlooking Hafrsfjord.

Experience Harald Fairhair's story through virtual reality at **Viking House** on the Stavanger harbourfront. Though a tad pricey for a 25-minute experience, it's a fun way to get a different perspective on Norway's dramatic past. Booking ahead is recommended (vikinghouse.no).

 WHERE TO STAY IN STAVANGER

Thompsons B&B	Darby's Inn	Stavanger B&B
Cosy B&B occupying a 1910 villa, with an intimate, welcoming atmosphere and fine breakfasts. €	Opulent vintage interiors in a historic home plush with antique furnishings, Persian rugs and a baby grand. €€	This reasonably priced mini hotel is simple; some rooms are small, but rates include breakfast. €€

Wander Through Gamle Stavanger

COBBLESTONE STREETS AND WHITE-WOOD HOUSES

There's something charming, even magical, about **Gamle Stavanger** (Old Stavanger), the city's intimate historic quarter, which runs above and behind the modern buildings along the western shore of the harbour. Dating from the late 18th century, the whitewashed wooden houses, all immaculately kept and adorned with cheerful, well-tended flower boxes, crowd the cobblestone laneways. Most are residential buildings, but you'll also find silversmiths and potters, even the occasional cafe with a photogenic cat. There are some stunning photo opportunities between the buildings and through the trees at the old quarter's northern end. It's all a contemplative counterpoint to the occasional brashness of Stavanger, the prosperous modern oil city.

There's little to anchor your stay other than the quiet charm of your surroundings. But don't miss a stop at the **Canning Museum**. If Piers Crocker, who has overseen this museum for decades, is around to act as a guide, then even better. Before Stavanger had oil, it was all about sardines, and this thoroughly entertaining museum, housed in an old cannery, tells the story of these humble fish and their effect on Stavanger. Stavanger was once home to more than half of Norway's canning factories. By 1922, the city's canneries provided a remarkable 50% of the town's employment. The exhibits take you through the whole 12-stage process from salting to threading, smoking, decapitating and packing. An adjoining building houses a touchingly restored workers' cottage furnished in 1920s (downstairs) and 1960s (upstairs) styles. Souvenirs and even sardines are sold here as well.

Explore Norway's Oil City

BLACK GOLD

Stavanger is the home port of Equinor (formerly Statoil), Norway's largest oil company. It's also where, when each shift ends, an ever-rotating cast of oil workers returns to the mainland every few weeks for some R&R and to spend their earnings.

Norway's oil story is told in fascinating detail at the **Norsk Oljemuseum**, one of the country's best museums. Highlights include the world's largest drill bit, simulated rigs, a vast hall of oil-platform models and coverage of the Alexander L Kielland drilling-rig tragedy in 1980 when 123 oil workers were killed.

Norway is the world's 11th-largest oil producer, and the museum doesn't shrink from the implications of that. Exhibits are devoted to climate change, and the understated, thoughtful

BEST STAVANGER MUSEUMS

Canning Museum
Stavanger's best small museum is all about the humble sardine.

Museum of Archaeology
Learn everything there is to know about the Vikings (and perhaps even meet a few).

Stavanger Kunstmuseum
Norwegian art from the 18th century to the present, with a fine little sculpture garden.

Stavanger Maritime Museum
Two centuries of seafaring history with some harrowing shipwreck tales.

Norwegian Children's Museum
Childhood through the ages, with antique train sets, giant dolls and Meccano kits.

 WHERE TO STAY IN STAVANGER

Comfort Hotel Square
Just above Gamle Stavanger, this swish place offers more individuality than most. Check out at 6pm Sundays. €€

Clarion Collection Hotel Skagen Brygge
Quietly luxurious and right on the harbour, with a free evening meal thrown in. €€€

Myhregaarden Hotel
Boutique exteriors and slightly dated black-and-purple interiors with wooden beams and fireplaces. €€€

A STREET OF MANY COLOURS

Once upon a time, Øvre Holmgate was a nondescript street bisecting the neighbourhood east of Stavanger's Vågen Harbour. That changed when a local hair stylist, Tom Kjørvik, proposed something radical. Why not liven up the area by adding a bit of bright colour?

In consultation with artist Craig Flannagan, Kjørvik set about convincing local leaders and business owners to approve his plan. Fortunately, they did, and **Fargegaten** – the Street of Colours – is now one of the most vibrant spots in Stavanger. Along the pedestrian street are cafes, bars and shops with facades painted every colour of the rainbow. Whether you settle in for a drink and some people-watching or simply stroll through, a visit to Fargegaten is sure to add some colour to your day.

14-minute film *Oljeunge* (Oil Kid) provides a human face to Norway's struggle to reconcile the contradictions between the prosperity the oil industry has brought to Norway and towns like Stavanger, and the growing awareness of the industry's negative environmental impact. Count on spending at least a couple of hours in the museum.

Visit Old Stavanger Mansions
OPULENT ARCHITECTURE

On a lovely estate west of the town centre, **Breidablikk**, a grand late-19th-century manor house, is well worth a detour. From the city centre, the walk is about 750m and is interesting in itself, taking you from a touristy area out into the city's residential streets. Built by the merchant shipowner Lars Berentsen, Breidablikk is a rare surviving example from the period, and a visit is like opening a window onto a little-known period of the city's history (although its colour scheme and gables make it look more like it belongs in the fairy tale forests of Telemark in southern Norway). Its faithfully preserved, authentic late-19th-century interiors include old farming implements, books and decorative objects.

Just to the north of Breidablikk and occupying the heart of Ledaalsparken, **Ledaal**, another period manor house, dates back even further. Also built by a wealthy merchant shipowner (in this case Gabriel Schanche Kielland), the empire-style Ledaal was built over four years between 1799 and 1803. Later restorations remain faithful to the original home and interiors, which include unusual antique furniture. These days, Ledaal serves as the local residence and summer home for Norway's royal family.

Sample Culinary Stavanger
FRUITS OF THE SEA AND LAND

Stavanger is one of the best places to eat in Norway. **Torget Fish Market** has a deli section where you can pick up ready-to-eat shrimp or smoked salmon, as well as an upmarket dine-in restaurant next door.

Stavanger's most exciting (and sustainable) dining experience is **Restaurant SÖL**, which offers natural wines, local and seasonal produce, and expert cooking. Like all New Nordic restaurants, SÖL is at its best when it takes traditional Norwegian recipes and riffs by taking them in new directions. **Tango**, above the southern end of the harbour, is another brilliant choice in a similar vein.

 WHERE TO EAT IN STAVANGER

Torget Fish Market
Stavanger's fish market has fresh catches and a good sit-down restaurant. €€

Moo Goo
Stavanger's best ice cream experience, with dozens of flavours. €

Døgnvill
This slinky burger joint does artisan buns, cheeses, salads and locally sourced meats. €€

Gladmat food festival

RE-NAA, the flagship restaurant of Michelin-lauded chef Sven Erik Renaa, has just a handful of tables. Renaa takes his cue from both place and season. Fish, seafood, meat and game are combined with microgreens, foraged ingredients and edible flowers. You can also enjoy Renaa's food at a lower price point at cafe-style **Sirkus Renaa Sølvberget**.

The flourishing interest in plant-based eating hasn't gone unnoticed here either. Though many restaurants of the fine-dining persuasion don't cater to strict vegan diets, industrial-chic **Bellies** offers a full plant-based tasting menu that showcases seasonal vegetables and legumes in its contemporary dishes.

Stavanger's role as one of Norway's foremost culinary spaces is confirmed every June and into July when it hosts **Gladmat**, one of Scandinavia's biggest food festivals. Expect cooking demonstrations and lots of special menus in restaurants.

HEAD FOR THE BEACH

Stavanger may not be known internationally for its beaches, but that's because locals like to keep the best spots for themselves. The bracing weather doesn't help either. In summer, take a 20-minute drive south of Stavanger to the series of soft sand beaches that stretch down the coast. Backed by sea grass-spiked dunes and dotted with wooden holiday shacks, they're incredibly atmospheric, although some are a little exposed if the wind picks up. **Sola** sits right near the airport and has parking and a kiosk, along with the historic **Sola Strand Hotel**, which dates from 1914. A little further south, **Hellestø** and **Bybergsanden** are quiet and picturesque, perfect for a long barefoot walk and a frolic in the shallows.

WHERE TO EAT IN STAVANGER

Thai Street Food
Norwegian Thai can be some of the best in Europe, and this place has a more creative menu than most. €€

Bølgen & Moi
Attached to the Oil Museum, this reliable chain has good views, international dishes and a fine fish soup. €€€

NB Sørensen's Damskibsexpedition
Dine beneath nautical memorabilia and enjoy a menu of international dishes. €€€

177

BEST STAVANGER FESTIVALS

Gladmat
Food from local eats to international dishes takes over the city, with public events and special restaurant menus.

Stavanger Vinfest
This wine celebration invades the city's best restaurants for a week in March.

May Jazz Festival
An established part of Norway's excellent jazz festival circuit, drawing a handful of well-known international performers in May.

International Chamber Music Festival
Internationally respected classical music festival, with innovative programming and venues.

Bøker og Børst

A Night Out in Stavanger
HAVE A DRINK AFTER DARK

Like all port cities, Stavanger's nights are lively, fuelled by cashed-up oil workers on rotation back on shore. Most of the action, which can be fairly generic and usually rather rowdy, centres on the eastern shore of **Skagenkaien** (Skagen Quay), the narrow, U-shaped harbour in the heart of town. A handful of nightclubs sit just behind the row of restaurants.

For something more discerning, **Broremann Bar**, a little further to the north along Skansen Quay, has been a classy Stavanger wine bar for the over-30s for as long as we can remember. Apart from the slick, downtempo soundtrack, it whips up the city's best cocktails.

Just up the hill and another good choice if you want to avoid the clamour around the harbour, **Café Sting** has live jazz, art exhibitions and a fab roof terrace.

Things get lively on nights along Holmegate, and **Bøker og Børst** is a favourite stop. With craft beers on tap, books on the shelves, retro furnishings and a covered courtyard, what more could you need?

Beyond Stavanger

Balance above the abyss at either end of Lysefjord or take a boat cruise along the fjord's length. Better yet, do it all.

Lysefjord is by far the most picturesque fjord in the southern reaches of western Norway's fjord country. Hidden in the interior northwest of Stavanger, Lysefjord offers three of Norway's best-loved fjord experiences.

The pick of these is the hike to Preikestolen (Pulpit Rock), a fine trail and the precursor to an utterly unforgettable view. You can also see it down below, from the deck of a boat dwarfed by vertiginous rock walls as you cruise along the fjord. If you're brave, foolhardy or both, you can hike to the chockstone of Kjeragbolten for an iconic Norway snap of yourself standing atop the rock (possibly the least scary part of the experience).

Hike to Preikestolen
STUNNING VIEWS FROM PULPIT ROCK

An almost perfectly flat-topped plateau, **Preikestolen** rises 604m directly from the Lysefjord, providing panoramic views. One of Norway's best-known rock formations, it's an irresistible magnet for hikers and Instagrammers.

The hike is moderately challenging but possible for anyone of reasonable fitness. The 2019 addition of stone steps along the steepest sections of the trail (which are near the start and around the midpoint) has made the climb a little easier. There are few clues to the drama up ahead until right near the end. A few hundred metres before Preikestolen, a sheer drop suddenly opens up on your left, hundreds of metres above the fjord. Even on a cloudy day, the light can have an ethereal quality unique to this fjord.

The cliff has even had its moment of movie fame in a scene in *Mission: Impossible – Fallout,* in which Tom Cruise climbs the sheer rock face. The 8km hike starts from the Preikestolen

GETTING AROUND

With the opening of the Stavanger–Tau tunnels, including the world's longest subsea tunnel, Ryfast (14.3km) in 2019, getting to Preikestolen became much easier. You can now drive the Rv13 from downtown Stavanger to Tau and on to the trailhead at Preikestolhytta in a little under an hour. If you don't have a car, Pulpit Rock Tours runs at least four daily buses (50 minutes) from Stavanger's main bus terminal to the trailhead from March to November.

Rødne Fjord Cruises runs year-round 3½-hour boat cruises to Lysefjord from Stavanger. From mid-June to the end of September, Go Fjords offers day-long bus trips from Stavanger to Kjeragbolten, with time allowed for the five-hour hike.

☑ TOP TIP

At Preikestolen, climb the rocky hillside above the main platform for the best views of Pulpit Rock and beyond.

HESSEL HAKER/SHUTTERSTOCK ©

Hengjane waterfall

NORDSJØVEGEN

The long-distance **Nordsjøvegen** (North Sea Route, northsearoute.com) hugs the North Sea coast of southwestern Norway, covering just over 300km from Kristiansand to Haugesund. Along the way, it cuts through numerous destinations covered in this chapter, including Sola, Stavanger, Karmøy, Utsira and Haugesund. The website lists many possible itineraries suitable for driving and cycling, as well as accommodation suggestions, detailed route descriptions, worthy detours and lots of inspirational photos.

Fjellstue mountain lodge and takes about four hours round-trip. Guided hikes are available. The website preikestolen365.com is a useful resource to gauge likely hiking conditions and crowds.

Easy to reach by car (40 minutes) or bus (one hour), the Preikestolen trailhead lies well within Stavanger's orbit.

WHERE TO STAY AROUND LYSEFJORD

Preikestolen Fjellstue
Hostel, lodge and cottage rooms at the start of the Preikestolen hike; ideal for beating the crowds. €

Preikestolen Camping
Set 5km from the Preikestolen trailhead, with a shop-restaurant and a lovely forest setting. €

Lysefjorden Lodge
Simple DNT hut-style accommodation by the fjord in Lysebotn; convenient base for Kjeragbolten. €

Cruise to Scenic Lysefjord
DAY TRIP TO THE FJORD OF LIGHT

Lovely **Lysefjord** takes its name from the word *lys,* meaning light – a reference to the pale rock faces of the mountains that line the fjord. It's a perfect day trip destination from Stavanger, with three-hour sightseeing cruises departing from Strandkaien in Stavanger year-round.

Heading out of the harbour, the boat passes under the Stavanger City Bridge and past islands and coastal villages as you travel east and then southeast to the mouth of the Lysefjord. Entering the fjord, you sail under another dramatic bridge, **Lysefjordbrua**, and alongside steep, rocky shores with gravity-defying trees and bushes clinging for dear life. Here and there, the captain navigates the boat into narrow inlets, close to tumbling waterfalls and right up to the rock face beneath high cliffs, including the iconic Preikestolen (Pulpit Rock), which juts out directly above the fjord. You also draw near to **Vagabonds' Cave** and the **Hengjane waterfall**.

If you prefer a faster ride, **RIB boat safaris** also depart from Strandkaien and last approximately two hours. For more leisurely exploration, **Nordic Paddling** runs half-day and multiday kayaking trips departing near Forsand.

Stand Atop the Kjeragbolten Boulder
DEFY GRAVITY ON THE CHOCKSTONE

One of southwestern Norway's most iconic images, **Kjeragbolten** is a massive boulder wedged between two towering rock walls, 984m above Lysefjord. Standing atop Kjeragbolten is a thrill and not for the fainthearted.

To reach the site it's a tough 10km round-trip hike from Øygardsstølen Cafe high above Lysebotn (allow at least five hours) or around 2½ hours by road from Stavanger. The road to the trailhead is open from late May through October. En route, there are three steep ascents and a total elevation gain of 750m. Once there, you need to negotiate an exposed ledge on a 1000m-high cliff and then crawl down onto the rock itself for the ultimate photo.

WHY I LOVE LYSEFJORD

Anthony Ham, writer

Lysefjord was the first fjord I ever saw, and I was spellbound. There is a rare quality to the light here, and the views of the fjord from Preikestolen in any season – on a clear summer's day, in winter when the surrounding summits are icebound, whenever there's a storm brewing – are still my favourite in Norway.

Unlike many other fjords across western Norway, you can look at Lysefjord from every angle, from a boat upon its waters or from high above atop Preikestolen and Kjeragbolten. Because it's a little south of Norway's main tourist axis, it's still possible to explore without feeling like you need to take a number and wait in line.

GIEDRIUS AKELIS/SHUTTERSTOCK ©

Above: Atlanterhavsveien (p217); right: Nigardsbreen (p195)

THE MAIN AREAS

SOGNEFJORDEN
A spectacular 203km-long adventure. **p188**

JOSTEDALSBREEN NATIONAL PARK
Glaciers and glorious scenery. **p195**

THE FJORD COAST
Rarely visited Atlantic shore. **p200**

The Western Fjords

NORWAY'S FJORD HEARTLAND

When you think of Norway and its astonishing natural beauty, you're most likely thinking of the country's western fjords.

Norway's western fjords are filled with so many thrilling places to visit that it can be difficult to figure out where to begin.

Perhaps the best place to start is with a scenic drive. Atlanterhavsveien (Atlantic Rd) showcases edge-of-the-world beauty, or there's the miraculous steepness of Trollstigen (Trolls Ladder) and the high-country wonder of the Gamle Strynefjellsvegen.

Then again, it would also make sense to start with a favourite fjord, from the chocolate-box perfection of Geirangerfjord and the inner reaches of Sognefjorden to the unrelenting wonder of Nærøyfjord and the quieter pleasures of Lustrafjord. No discussion of the region's natural drama would be complete without mention of its glacier tongues snaking down off the heights

from Jostedalsbreen, mainland Europe's largest icefield.

As ever in Norway, there are many places where the human presence complements or adds its own drama to the staggering beauty of the surroundings. Art nouveau Ålesund is one of Norway's prettier larger towns, while fjord-side villages provide charming counterpoints to this world where nature reigns supreme.

The western fjords are one of Norway's most popular areas to visit, but there are opportunities to escape the crowds. Runde has many more birds than people, for example, while the Fjord coast around Florø is filled with little-known treasures. Even in the heart of the fjords, there are places where you can have it all to yourself.

STEFANO ZACCARIA/SHUTTERSTOCK ©

ÅNDALSNES
Pretty town with endless activities. **p203**

GEIRANGERFJORD
Norway's king of fjords. **p208**

ÅLESUND
Art nouveau–styled fjord gateway. **p211**

Find Your Way

Perhaps more than anywhere else, Norway's western fjords region highlights that high mountains and big bodies of water are no barrier for Norwegians to get around. It's all made possible through roads, tunnels and ferries.

FERRY

With so many fjords penetrating hundreds of kilometres into Norway's coastal hinterland, drive-on, drive-off ferries cut journey times by hours. They're always on time but can have long queues in summer. Most have a small cafeteria and toilets.

AIR

Western Norway is much larger than it appears. If time is tight, base yourself in a city and fly around the area, hiring a car for short periods. Florø, Ålesund and Kristiansund have direct flights from Oslo, Bergen and elsewhere.

CAR

Driving is the best way to get around western Norway. Having your own wheels means that there are few places you can't reach – just expect that it will take a while to get there.

Åndalsnes, p203

This picturesque mountain town is surrounded by impossibly sheer rock walls, beautiful valleys and iconic drives begging to be explored.

Ålesund, p211

Reimagined in art nouveau splendour from the ashes of a 1904 fire, this impossibly pretty city leads the way to the fjords of the north.

ATLANTIC
OCEAN

Stadhavet

Runde

Godøy

Ålesund

Møre og
Romsdal

Ona

Aukra

Budo

Hustadvika

Dyrnesvågen

Smøla

Grip

Kristiansund

Kvernes

Bremsnes

Vevang

Averøya

Sylte

Molde

Funnefjord

Langfjorden

Romsdalsfjorden

Åndalsnes

Rauma

Isfjorden

Trollvegen

MØRE OG
ROMSDAL

Eikesdalsvatnet

Tingvollfjorden

Driva

Storfjorden

Geirangerfjord, p208

Norway's most photographed fjord never disappoints, no matter how many pictures you've seen. Explore by boat or look down from above.

Jostedalsbreen National Park, p195

With glaciers up on the heights and post-card-pretty villages down below, this western Norwegian heartland promises a world of adventure.

The Fjord Coast, p200

See a side of Norway that few visitors en-counter in this world of islands in thrall to a wild Atlantic beauty.

Sognefjorden, p188

It's one of Norway's most popular natural attractions, but you can still find a quiet slice of paradise along the world's second-longest fjord.

NORWAY

Norwegian Sea

North Sea

50 km
30 miles

Plan Your Time

In western Norway, sinuous mountain roads connect the world's most beautiful fjords, tiny villages and graceful towns. Planning your route through them is one of life's more pleasurable pastimes.

Nærøyfjord (p190)

KARN YOSTHORNSAWASD/SHUTTERSTOCK ©

Pressed for Time

● If you only have three or four days – a long weekend, perhaps – focus your visit on exploring **Nærøyfjord** (p190) for the first couple of days. Take one of the popular boat cruises or the **Flåmsbana Railway** (p190), but make sure that you stay overnight in **Undredal** (p191) to experience the fjords in all their quiet magic.

● Drive around **Sognefjorden** (p188) to enjoy the many **stave churches** (p192). With a further foray away to the north, take a glacier hike on **Nigardsbreen** (p195) or one of the glacier tongues in the valleys around pretty little **Fjærland** (p197).

Seasonal Highlights

The summer months are best for weather, but expect crowds. Visiting at quieter times can be wonderful, but some roads may be closed.

JANUARY
It's busy around Christmas and **New Year**, but with extremely cold weather. On clear days, the scenery has a crisp, crystalline quality.

APRIL
The weather's improving, and services, such as **boat tours** on Geiranger, are starting up again after the winter hiatus.

MAY
Tourist facilities begin to reopen, from fjord boat services and summer ski seasons to the reopening of **Trollstigen** mid-month.

UNIQUE STOCK/SHUTTERSTOCK ©, TRPHOTOS/SHUTTERSTOCK ©, AVIJIT NANDY/GETTY IMAGES ©

A Week to Explore

● You're spoilt for choice when it comes to choosing a fjord in this part of the country, but **Geirangerfjord** (p208) is a favourite of many visitors. Spend a couple of days here, taking the Hellesylt–Geiranger ferry, kayaking and climbing to the world-famous lookouts. **Åndalsnes** (p203) and the surrounding country are worth another couple of days.

● Include a drive down **Trollstigen** (p206) and back up again.

● Drive away to the west for two more days in stunning art nouveau **Ålesund** (p211), with a drive along the peerless **Atlanterhavsveien** (p217) to finish your Norwegian sojourn on a wildly beautiful high.

Ten Wonderful Days

● You can have it all if you are able to devote 10 days to exploring the region. Build your itinerary with the big highlights: plan for a couple of days around **Nærøyfjord** (p190), a couple more around **Fjærland** (p197) and **Jostedalsbreen** (p195), and then a day driving **Trollstigen** (p206) and a boat trip on **Geirangerfjord** (p208) en route to **Ålesund** (p211) for two days more.

● On one of those days, take a day trip along the **Atlanterhavsveien** (p217) to **Kristiansund** (p215) before finishing with two days exploring the wonderful **Fjord Coast** (p200), including **Selja Monastery** (p202).

JULY

High tourist season is in full swing. It's your last chance to see puffins on Runde. Enjoy the **Ålesund Boat Festival**.

AUGUST

It's the height of the **summer season**. Queues are long for ferry crossings, and most boat trips require advance bookings.

SEPTEMBER

This month is a great time to visit, with decent weather and **smaller crowds**. Most roads and services are open until mid-September.

NOVEMBER

Many tourist operators go into hibernation, and the weather turns icy, but you can still drive the **Atlanterhavsveien** and explore the fjords.

Sognefjorden

Sognerfjorden
★ OSLO

GETTING AROUND

Getting to and around Sognefjorden involves a combination of road (car, motorcycle and bus), train and boat. Most connections run like clockwork. The main road through the Aurlandsfjord and Nærøyfjord arms of Sognefjorden is the E16, which connects Oslo with Bergen on Norway's west coast.

TOP TIP

The year-round Norway in a Nutshell tour (norwaynutshell.com) is a fabulous option. These itineraries (taken in whole or in part) combine the Bergen or Oslo train to Myrdal, the Flåmsbana line to Flåm, a cruise along Nærøyfjord to Gudvangen, a bus to Voss, and a final leg to Bergen or Oslo by train.

If you only have time to visit one Norwegian fjord, make it Sognefjorden. At 203km, it's the world's second-longest fjord (after 350km-long Scoresby Sund in Greenland). The views are simply extraordinary, an elemental combination of vertiginous rock, winter snow and ice, and waters that take on every shade of blue. Add some achingly pretty fjord-side villages and the iconic, near-vertical Flåmsbana Railway, and it's little wonder that the Sognefjord arms of Nærøyfjord and Aurlandsfjorden are popular with visitors.

Opportunities to escape the crowds and find your own little corner of this paradise are many, whether you're cycling up the mountains or kayaking with the seals. For every pretty-but-busy village and traveller hub like Flåm or Aurland, there's an Undredal or Otternes that feels like a fjord-side village unchanged by time. Many travellers miss these spots altogether because they're so busy admiring the views.

High Above Aurlandsfjord
LOOK DOWN IN WONDER

Deep and narrow **Aurlandsfjord** runs for a glorious 29km, branching away from the main Sognefjord in a water-filled chasm barely 2km wide in places. Climbing up above Aurlandsfjord yields some of the country's best vantage points and some brilliant journeys to reach them.

The 45km, summer-only **Aurlandsfjellet** – or Snøvegen (the Snow Rd), as it's known locally – is among the most dramatic mountain roads in a country of many. This sinuous, narrow route climbs from sea level to the desolate, boulder-strewn high plateau that separates Aurland and Lærdalsøyri (Lærdal) and then back down again. Along the way, you can stop at **Stegastein**, an observation point that juts out above the abyss 630m above Aurlandsfjord. Clad in pine and balancing on worryingly slender steel legs, it's a sleek, daringly designed platform that offers nothing but a glass rail between

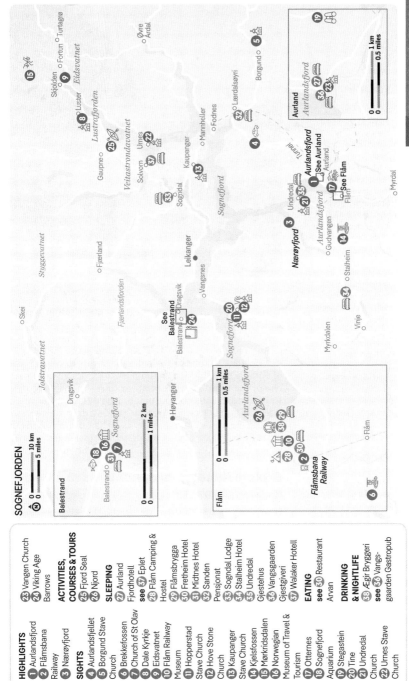

SOGNEFJORDEN

HIGHLIGHTS
1 Aurlandsfjord
2 Flåmsbana Railway
3 Nærøyfjord

SIGHTS
4 Aurlandsfjellet
5 Borgund Stave Church
6 Brekkefossen
7 Church of St Olav
8 Dale Kyrkje
9 Eidsvatnet
10 Flåm Railway Museum
11 Hopperstad Stave Church
12 Hove Stone Church
13 Kaupanger Stave Church
14 Kjelsfossen
15 Mørkridsdalen
16 Norwegian Museum of Travel & Tourism
17 Otternes
18 Sognefjord Aquarium
19 Stegastein
20 Tine
21 Undredal
22 Urnes Stave Church
23 Vangen Church
24 Viking Age Barrows

ACTIVITIES, COURSES & TOURS
25 Fjord Seal
26 Njord

SLEEPING
27 Aurland Fjordhotell
see 57 Eplet
28 Flåm Camping & Hostel
29 Flåmsbrygga
30 Fretheim Hotel
31 Midtnes Hotel
32 Sanden Pensjonat
33 Sogndal Lodge
34 Stalheim Hotel
35 Undredal Gjestehus
36 Vangsgaarden Gjestgiveri
37 Walaker Hotell

EATING
see 50 Restaurant Arvan

DRINKING & NIGHTLIFE
50 Ægir Bryggeri
see 36 Vangs-gaarden Gastropub

189

STALHEIM

Sitting halfway between Voss and Nærøyfjord, Stalheim offers one of the most famous views in Norway from half of the rooms and the terrace at the **Stalheim Hotel**. From 1647 until 1909, it was a stopping-off place along the Royal Mail route between Copenhagen, Christiania (Oslo) and Bergen, and it was here that the mail deliverers and their horses rested from the climb up from the valley floor.

These days, there's a one-way road (with an 18% gradient!) through the Stalheimskleiva gorge, flanked by the thundering **Stalheim** and **Sivle waterfalls**. There's also a small **folk museum** and two brilliant hikes: **Husmannsplassen Nåli** (along a ledge to an old farm worker's cabin) and **Brekkedalen** (which climbs up above Stalheim).

THOMBAL/SHUTTERSTOCK ©

Undredal Church

you and a long, long drop. Even if you don't travel the full Aurlandsfjellet road, you can still reach Stegastein along a winding 8km road from Aurland.

Anything Aurland can do, Flåm, in the deep, inner reaches of Aurlandsfjord, can do, too. The **Flåmsbana Railway** is a 20km-long engineering wonder that hauls itself up 866m of altitude gain through 20 tunnels. At a gradient of 1:18, it's one of the world's steepest railway lines. The vintage-style train takes 45 minutes to climb to **Myrdal**, atop the bleak, treeless Hardangervidda plateau, passing deep ravines and thundering waterfalls along the way. The railway links both timetable and location to the dramatic Oslo–Bergen railway, which wonderfully increases your options for onward travel.

Explore Nærøyfjord by Boat

MAXIMUM FJORD DRAMA

If you were to design the perfect fjord, it would look something like the deep and lovely **Nærøyfjord**. Yes, it's one of the most visited of all Norwegian fjords, but its deeply textured cliffs with waters plunging from the heights is a good reason for that. Only Geirangerfjord can compete with Nærøyfjord's sheer cliffs, and its meadows and mountain cabins cling to impossible ledges high above.

 WHERE TO STAY NEAR NÆROYFJORD

Flåm Camping & Hostel
One of Sognefjorden's best campsites with hostel accommodation, cabins and grassy camping areas. €

Undredal Gjestehus
Charming little B&B and the ideal base for its namesake enchanted waterside hamlet. €€

Vangsgaarden Gjestgiveri
Whitewashed Aurland guesthouse with simple rooms behind an 18th-century facade, plus fjord-side cabins. €€

The best way to see Nærøyfjord in all its glory is on a **Nærøy-fjord cruise**, which usually means taking one of the regular summer-only boats from Flåm to Gudvangen. These can get busy in summer, so book the earliest departure you can to avoid the worst of the crowds. You can also board the boat in Aurland and hop your way up the fjord, starting in Flåm and getting off for a wander in Aurland and Undredal on your way to Gudvangen. Get up on the top deck, where you'll be able to appreciate the scale and also zero in on the detail.

One waterfall to watch for is **Kjelsfossen**, which tumbles from the southern wall of Nærøydalen valley above **Gudvangen** village. So steep are the valley walls that an avalanche would have a force of 12 tonnes per sq metre, move at 50m a second and, according to local legend, carry a herd of goats all the way across the fjord. In the absence of floating goats, watch for seals sunning themselves on the rocks, imagining themselves unseen.

Escape the Crowds
FIND YOUR OWN FJORD CORNER

Take the boat cruise in Nærøyfjord and climb to Myrdal by train from Flåm, by all means. But silence reigns a short distance away.

Reached via a narrow dirt road (or by hiking from Flåm), **Otternes** was abandoned in the 1990s. The views here are astonishing. If you come early in the day when no one else is around, the 27 restored farm buildings (some dating from the 17th century) swirling in morning cloud can feel like a film set. Otternes has summer guided tours that include locally made organic ice cream, fresh apple juice or pancakes.

Undredal is one of the loveliest, quietest villages in all of Norway's fjord country. Most boats stop here, but few passengers disembark. If you drive the narrow mountain road down to Undredal off the Flåm–Gudvangen road, you may have this charming little place to yourself. Turn off the engine, park the car and walk. Better still, stay overnight: there's magic in the air as darkness falls and silence descends. Barely 60 people live here year-round, and although it gets busy whenever a tour boat pulls in, quietness quickly settles upon the village once again.

Try the local (and locally famous) Undredal goat cheese (available at the jetty or in one of the village cheese shops). The jetty cafe also has a small exhibition on Undredal's cheesemaking traditions. Climb up through the village to the cute-as-a-postcard 12th-century **Undredal Church**, mainland Scandinavia's smallest still-operational house of worship.

AN EPIC HIKE

To leave the crowds behind in summer, embark on the classic four-day trek down **Aurlandsdalen**, from Geiteryggen to Aurland. Downhill most of the way (it follows a stream), it's an ancient trading trail that once connected eastern and western Norway.

Open only in summer, the trail begins at **Finse** (a stop on the Oslo–Bergen rail line). Most people break up the journey with overnight stops in Geiterygghytta, Steinbergdalen and Østerbø. If you don't want to walk the whole way, take the bus (one hour) from Aurland to Østerbø (820m) and hike down to Vassbygdi (95m), which is 15 minutes by bus from Aurland. It's an incredibly scenic six- to seven-hour day hike.

 WHERE TO STAY NEAR NÆRØYFJORD

Flåmsbrygga
Beside the dock in Flåm, with balconies, superb fjord views, and an excellent pub and restaurant. €€€

Aurland Fjordhotell
Swathed in white wood and topped with a gabled roof, this summer-only hotel has motel-style rooms. €€€

Fretheim Hotel
In an 1870s building, handsome Fretheim has a mix of historic and contemporary rooms. €€€

THINGS TO DO IN BALESTRAND

Viking Age Barrows
This pair of barrows once housed a boat, two skeletons, jewellery and several weapons.

Church of St Olav
Wooden St Olav's was built in 1897 in a stave-church style; the owner of Midtnes Hotel has the key.

Sognefjord Aquarium
Visit this rather dated aquarium for tanks filled with Sognefjord's saltwater inhabitants.

Norwegian Museum of Travel & Tourism
This museum tells the story of travel and tourism through the fjords and beyond.

Even in winter, Undredal escapes the worst of the cold: the village has something of its own microclimate with the high mountains storing the day's warmth from any sun.

Linger in Flåm & Aurland
PRETTY FJORD-SIDE VILLAGES

Living in Flåm must be a strange experience. On a winter's night, an almost sepulchral silence seems to envelop the town, sometimes with an accompanying mist. Yet at the height of summer, the village's population of around 400 can be over-run by boatloads and busloads of visitors. Few linger longer than it takes to switch modes of transport and enjoy a quick browse in the souvenir shops.

But the village rewards those who stick around. Pop into the free **Flåm Railway Museum**, which tells the dramatic story of how Flåmsbana, one of the world's steepest railways, was built. Also worth a quick look is **Flåm Church**. Built in 1667, this small brown wooden church has decorative elements dating from several different centuries. You've already seen more than most visitors, but to replace the waterside clamour with soaring natural beauty, go a little further by making the beautiful 5km hike up the Flåm Valley to the impressive waterfall of **Brekkefossen**. The hike takes about 2½ hours round-trip.

From Flåm's **Njord** kayaking centre, you can get out on the water and let the quiet lapping of paddles replace the sometimes over-bright bonhomie of the captains on the boat tours. All signs of mass tourism evaporate, too, along the 12km-long, fjord-side **Flåm to Aurland Walking Path**. Ask at Flåm's tourist office about hiring a bicycle to make the same trip.

There's not a whole lot to see in **Aurland**, except the view, of course. The view from the village's waterfront is the best of any of the Nærøyfjord villages. It's worth stopping by the town's striking white **Vangen Church**. Dating from 1202 (though restored several times over the centuries), it's the largest of Sognefjorden's churches and is often called the 'Sogn Cathedral' by locals.

Follow the Sognefjorden Stave Church Trail
MEDIEVAL HOUSES OF WORSHIP

If Norway's stave churches and other medieval religious buildings have captured your imagination, Sognefjorden offers an especially rich portfolio. They're spread out across the fjord network, so you can let the churches guide your route around Sognefjorden's shore.

 WHERE TO EAT NEAR NÆRØYFJORD

Vangsgaarden Gastropub	**Ægir Bryggeri**	**Restaurant Arvan**
Well-priced summer-only international cooking with fabulous views in Aurland. Fish dishes are best. €€	Craft beers and Norwegian comfort food in a building that's all wood, flagstones and sheepskins. €€€	Upstairs in Flåm's Fretheim Hotel, Arvan focuses on local ingredients and seasonal produce with a few twists. €€€

ZOROASTO/SHUTTERSTOCK ©

Brekkefossen

Established in the 12th century alongside the major overland trade route between eastern and western Norway, **Borgund Stave Church** now lies around 30km southeast of Lærdalsøyri along the E16. In an excellent state of repair, the church is dedicated to St Andrew and has a wonderfully simple and darkly suggestive interior, a superb hand-carved altar and Norway's only extant free-standing medieval wooden bell tower.

Along sinuous fjord-hugging roads to the north, overlooking Lustrafjord, UNESCO World Heritage-listed **Urnes Stave Church** is Borgund's rival as Sognefjord's most impressive church. Dating from 1170 and built on the site of a previous chapel, Urnes is Norway's oldest church. Apart from its special location, it's defined by intricate wooden carvings, including exquisite vines and mythic creatures, and it looks like a forgotten set from *Lord of the Rings*.

Not every old Norwegian church is a stave church, and **Dale Kyrkje** in Skjolden in the innermost reaches of Lustrafjord is a fine example of the wider genre. Built from stone in 1250, it sports a predominantly Gothic style and has a wooden tower and vivid early-17th-century paintings around the entrance. Both the crucifix and the main arch are originals.

Back on the main Sognefjorden arm, **Kaupanger Stave Church** is one of Norway's tallest stave churches. It's also

GAMALOST

A few blocks straight up the road from the ferry pier in Vik, the **Tine** dairy preserves a long cheesemaking tradition. It's the only place in the world that still produces Gamalost, literally 'old cheese', a unique type of brown cheese that dates from the Viking Age, more than 1000 years ago.

What makes Gamalost unique is that it contains 50% protein and just 1% fat. It's a crusty cheese with a strong, robust flavour and a sharp, pungent aroma. The dairy recommends eating it on flatbread with sour cream, butter and lingonberries with a side of fresh fruit. If you'd like to try it for yourself, head to Tine's cheese bar, **Ostebaren**, for samples.

WHERE TO STAY AROUND SOGNEFJORDEN

Midtnes Hotel
This old family house in Balestrand has a pretty white exterior, lovely rooms and great meals. €€

Sanden Pensjonat
A guesthouse for almost 100 years, this gem has lovely details and personal service in Lærdal. €€

Sogndal Lodge
Sogndal's excellent hostel has four funky rooms that are Scandi-simple with vintage overlays. €€

EXPLORING AROUND LUSTRAFJORD

Eidsvatnet
The Rv55 runs east alongside the glacial lake Eidsvatnet, which is a magical shade of blue.

Mørkridsdalen
This valley cuts north of Skjolden; great hiking country with fine views down the fjord.

Fjord Seal
Kayak the fjord's calm waters, including among a colony of seals.

Mollandsmorki Circuit
Go mountain biking along this 25km circuit from Solvern, with stunning views.

Jotunheimen
The Rv55 runs past Skjolden and up onto epic Sognefjellet Rd (p124).

NIKKRAD/SHUTTERSTOCK ©

Hopperstad Stave Church

known for its Celtic-style chancel arch, something you won't find in Norway's other stave churches. Raised in 1184 but much restored and recast in the 17th century, the church has some superb wall paintings with vines, flowers and musical annotations.

Way out to the west, a long drive and the odd ferry crossing away, Vik is another important site on the church trail. Perhaps more than any other similar structure, **Hopperstad Stave Church**, on the southern edge of Vik, feels like it was handcrafted by medieval artisans and then pieced together; it consists of 2000 different parts. It was built in 1130, making it the second-oldest in the country, and has the usual mix of fairy-tale-style carvings on the outside and colourful mural paintings within.

Also dating from the 12th century in Vik, **Hove Stone Church** is a stirring medieval structure, with intriguing paintings. Look especially for the wooden figures from Norse legend in the roof beams and the external gables.

MORE SOGNEFJORDEN CHURCHES
Extend your church-focused explorations of the area with a stop in **Undredal** (p191), home to Norway's smallest still-operational church, and the **Vangen Church** (p192) in Aurland, which is sometimes referred to as 'Sogn Cathedral'.

WHERE TO STAY AROUND SOGNEFJORDEN

Eplet
Amid a Solvorn fruit orchard, this hostel has rooms in two rustic wooden buildings and garden campsites. €€€

Walaker Hotell
The oldest family-run hotel in Norway (1640) with antiques, old-fashioned beds and clawfoot baths in Solvorn. €€€

Stalheim Hotel
Ask for room 324 or one of its neighbours for the ultimate view down Nærøydalen. €€€

Jostedalsbreen National Park

Jostedalsbreen
National Park

OSLO

Where the fjords end, the high mountains and their glaciers begin. This geography comes as no surprise. Much of Norway was once a giant icefield with mountains higher than the Himalayas, and it was the weight of ancient glaciers that gouged out the fjords. Of all the icefields and their glaciers that remain, Jostedalsbreen is the most impressive, not to mention the largest, anywhere on mainland Europe.

For years, Jostedalsbreen and its many glaciers bucked the trend of retreat caused by climate change. Sadly, that tide has now turned, but even so, Jostedalsbreen remains a staggering force of nature. The icefield continues to gouge out 400,000 tonnes of rock every year across an area of more than 450 sq km and with a thickness of up to 600m. Getting up close to these glaciers and the towns that surround them is a fantastic complement to the fjords.

Experience the Glacier from Every Angle
EXPLORE NIGARDSBREEN

At the head of Jostedalen, the long valley that climbs towards the mountains north of Lustrafjord, **Nigardsbreen** might be your best bet for an all-round glacier experience, especially on the southern shore of the icefield. Apart from anything else, Nigardsbreen has that lonely end-of-the-valley gravitas where the tongue of the towering glacier rises before you.

You'll come to understand both the scale and the intimacy of the whole glacier experience on a single trip when you take a tour with **Ice Troll**. Contemplate the majesty of Nigardsbreen as you kayak towards it across the lake; you can also cross in a dinghy. Feel the crunch of ice under your boots as you leave the kayak and walk out onto the glacier itself. Both leave you spellbound. Other companies also offer glacier walks, while Ice Troll also offers all manner of alternatives: ice climbing, snowshoeing, sleeping out on the glacier (and listening to it moan in the night) or even whitewater rafting down the glacial river.

GETTING AROUND

The northern and southern sides of the national park are some distance apart, so they need to be visited separately. To access the southern side of the park, the towns of Solvorn, Sogndal and Fjærland are the main gateways. On the northern side, Stryn, Loen and Olden are the best bases.

☑ **TOP TIP**

Each glacier or glacier tongue offers a different experience, so plan carefully. Nigardsbreen is good for the range of activities on offer, including getting out on the glacier. Briksdalsbreen and Kjenndalsbreen are reached by scenic drives, but the latter is quieter. Bøyabreen allows you to get the closest by car.

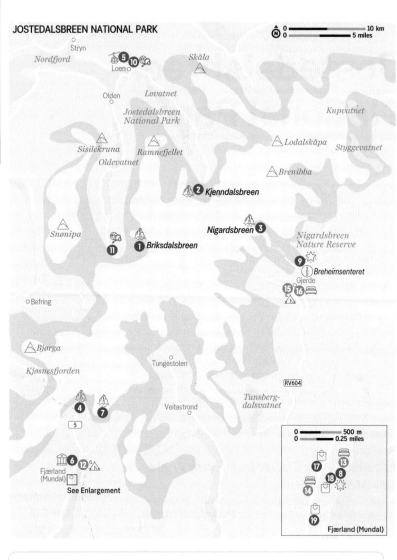

JOSTEDALSBREEN NATIONAL PARK

0 — 10 km
0 — 5 miles

Stryn
Nordfjord
Loen
5 10
Skåla
Olden
Lovatnet
Jostedalsbreen
National Park
Kupvatnet
Sisilekruna Ramnefjellet
Oldevatnet
Lodalskåpa Styggevatnet
Brenibba
2 Kjenndalsbreen
Snønipa
Nigardsbreen 3
11 1 Briksdalsbreen
Nigardsbreen
Nature Reserve
9
Breheimsenteret
Gjerde
15 16
Befring
Bjørga
Kjøsnesfjorden
Tungestolen
RV604
Tunsberg-
dalsvatnet
4
7
5
Veitastrond
0 — 500 m
0 — 0.25 miles
6 12
Fjærland
(Mundal)
See Enlargement
17 13
14 18 8
19
Fjærland (Mundal)

HIGHLIGHTS
1 Briksdalsbreen
2 Kjenndalsbreen
3 Nigardsbreen

SIGHTS
4 Bøyabreen
5 Loen Skylift

6 Norwegian Glacier
Museum
7 Supphellebreen

**ACTIVITIES, COURSES
& TOURS**
8 Fjærland Guiding
9 Ice Troll

10 Loen Activ
11 Oldedalen Skyss

SLEEPING
12 Bøyum Camping
13 Fjærland Fjordstove
Hotel
14 Hotel Mundal

15 Jostedal Camping
16 Jostedal Hotel

SHOPPING
17 Bok og Bilde
18 Gamleposten
19 Tusund og Ei Natt

Discover the Northern Glaciers

VISIT BRIKSDALSBREEN AND KJENNDALSBREEN

These two glaciers on the northern side of the icefield nicely combine the sheer grandeur of the glaciers with a quieter experience away from the crowds.

Getting to **Briksdalsbreen** can be half the fun. This splendid wall of slow-moving ice is reached along an achingly pretty 23km drive from Olden. Even if you turn back where the road ends, it's still worth the drive. For the full experience, park the car and climb the steep 5km track to the face of the glacier. There's also a longer, less challenging cart track, where golf-cart-like buggies (known locally as – what else? – troll cars) operated by **Oldedalen Skyss** run most of the way to the glacier face. Book in advance at the **Briksdalsbreen visitor centre**. Where the paths come together is where you stand in awe before this magnificent natural structure.

As with all glaciers, every now and then, you'll hear a groan, creak or crack, and everyone looks up nervously. For safety reasons, glacier hikes are not allowed but ask at the visitor centre about RIB boat tours on the glacier-fed lake.

Another scenic drive lies ahead if you choose to reach for **Kjenndalsbreen**, which lies 21km up Lodalen valley, close to Briksdalsbreen but separated from it by high mountains. For reasons that we aren't fully clear about, this glacier tongue receives the fewest number of visitors – not that we're complaining. Along the way, you pass **Lovatnet**, an ice-blue glacial lake, before passing through a toll gate. It's a further 5km to a lookout that ranks among our favourite Norway views.

Fan Out from Fjærland

WESTERN FJORD'S COOLEST VILLAGE

If you're driving through the region and can't decide where to find the perfect small village, look no further than **Fjærland**. It has incredibly good looks and sits at the end of its own fjord, **Fjærlandsfjorden**. It also has that classic Norwegian look of perfectly manicured, colourfully painted wooden homes at the base of some very high cliffs. The village itself is reason enough to linger.

Among Fjærland's many charms is its fidelity to the ebb and flow of the seasons. It almost hibernates as the days shorten into October and then rouses itself again to life at the start of May when the ferry returns to the water. Not a single road reached Fjærland as late as 1985. Until then, you could get to the town only by boat. Interestingly, former US Vice President

LOEN HIGHLIGHTS

The tiny fjord-side village of Loen is more than just another gateway to Jostedalsbreen and the Bødalen and Kjenndalen glacial tongues.

Loen Skylift is one of the world's steepest cable cars. When you board, you're by the fjord, but five minutes later, you're 1km higher, atop Mt Høven. From the top, you can enjoy epic views and go back down, hike the many high-country trails, strap on your skis (in winter) or just enjoy a meal with an incredible view at the restaurant.

From the top cable car station, **Loen Activ** runs a vertigo-defying via ferrata, where you clamber along and up ropes and ladders bolted into the sheer rock face of Mt Høven.

WHERE TO STAY & EAT AROUND JOSTEDALSBREEN

Jostedal Camping
One of Norway's most gloriously sited campsites with great facilities and a super-helpful owner. €

Jostedal Hotel
One of few hotels in the main valley, this family-run place has good rooms and a farm-to-table restaurant. €€

Briksdalsbre Fjellstove
Rooms and a restaurant close to Briksdalsbreen visitor centre; wonderfully quiet once the tour buses leave. €€

BOOK TOWN

Fjærland is famous around Norway as the country's favourite 'book town'. At last count, it had 10 bookshops, with more than 150,000 secondhand books among them. Most are in Norwegian, but there's plenty for English-language visitors to enjoy. Most shops open from May to mid-September. At the height of summer, **Boknatts** is the village's summer solstice festival when the main (read: only) street is taken over by pop-up bookshops that remain open all night, with plenty of musical accompaniment.

Close to the ferry jetty, **Tusund og Ei Natt** (Thousand and One Nights) has a 15m-long row, stacked seven shelves high, of novels in English. **Gamleposten** also has a good English-language selection, while **Bok og Bilde**, at the tourist office, is good for thrillers.

Bøyabreen

Walter F Mondale officially opened the road here from Skei as his family originated in these parts.

While you're here, don't miss the **Norwegian Glacier Museum**, an essential stop on your glacier tour of the area. Hunkered down in a striking concrete wedge-shaped building, the museum teaches you everything you need to know about glaciers and the wildlife that calls them home. You can even enjoy a simulated ice tunnel, admire the woolly mammoth models and ponder the tusk of a mammoth that roamed the earth 30,000 years ago.

Thus inspired, it's time to head out into the landscape that is such a presence wherever you are in Fjærland. Stop by the **tourist office** to pick up the *Escape the Asphalt* guide that lists 12 local hikes. Most of the walks follow routes the local shepherds used until quite recently to lead their flocks to higher summer pastures.

You can also visit the accessible local glacier tongues, **Supphellebreen** and **Bøyabreen**. The latter is the most spectacular of the two, with astonishing views from the glacial lake, while ice blocks from Supphellebreen were used as podiums at the 1994 Winter Olympics in Lillehammer. If you want to do more than just look, **Fjærland Guiding** arranges spectacular guided hikes and glacier walks.

WHERE TO STAY & EAT IN FJÆRLAND

Bøyum Camping
Camping and cabins 3km from the Fjærland ferry landing with superb Bøyabreen glacier views. €

Hotel Mundal
This historic place oozes late-19th-century grandeur, with period interiors, a tower suite and fjord views. €€€

Fjærland Fjordstove Hotel
This delightfully old-fashioned guesthouse is swathed in white wood and sits right by the fjord. €€€

BY-STUDIO/SHUTTERSTOCK ©

This spectacular 130km route is an inspirational drive with mountain views as impressive as anywhere in the country. It took a team of local and immigrant Swedish navvies more than 10 years to lay the Gamle Strynefjellsvegen (Old Stryn Mountain Rd) over the mountain, and it opened in 1894. Allow at least four hours. The Gamle Strynefjellsvegen is normally free of snow from June to October.

Head east from **1 Stryn** along the Rv15 as it runs alongside the river that descends from **2 Strynevatnet** lake and then follows the lakeshore itself. After 20km, stop to visit the **3 Jostedalsbreen National Park Centre** in the village of Oppstryn. At an interpretive panel 17km beyond the national park centre, turn right to take the Rv258. The climb to the high plateau is spectacular, enhanced by thin threads of water tumbling from the heights and a trio of roaring roadside torrents carrying glacial melt. Savour the view from the platform above **4 Videfossen**. Some 9km along the Gamle Strynefjellsvegen, you reach **5 Stryn Summer Ski Centre**, a bleak place outside the short late-May-to-July season. With the steep ascent behind you, continue along a good quality, unsurfaced, single-track road that runs above a necklace of milky turquoise tarns overlooked by bare, boulder-strewn rock. On this upland plateau, the sparse vegetation hugs the ground close. After crossing the watershed 10km beyond the ski centre, begin a much more gentle descent to rejoin the Rv15. Turn left for a fast, smooth, two-lane run beside **6 Breidalsvatn** lake before diving into the first of three long tunnels that bring you back to the national park centre and onward, retracing your steps to Stryn.

The Fjord Coast

The Fjord
Coast
OSLO

Most people visit
the Fjord Coast by
sea. Ferries shuttle
from Bergen, and
the Hurtigruten ferry
stops on its regular
route along the
coast. There's also an
airport in Florø.

To explore beyond
the main towns, hire a
car. Otherwise, you'll
miss out on some
of the experiences
that make a visit
here such a special
thing. Most towns are
accessible only by
road, and there's no
public transport to
most of them.

TOP TIP

A visit to the Fjord Coast
offers the opportunity to
slow down your journey, so
plan on spending at least
three days exploring the
region. It might not look far,
but the Fjord Coast can take
a while to get to by road, and
it takes longer than you may
expect to get around.

Look at a map of Norway's coastline and try for a moment to ignore the fjords that penetrate deep into the Norwegian interior. And then look where those fjords begin. Out on Norway's far western shore, far beyond where most tourists go, the country's fractured, fissured Fjord Coast is waiting to be discovered. Similar to Scotland's highlands, Norway's Fjord Coast is a world of wind-scoured coastal plains, lighthouses, picturesque fishing villages, near-perfect beaches and famous (if unlikely) surf swells.

When it comes to Norway's history, it's all here, from timeworn fishing villages and Viking ships to oil-powered prosperity and a medieval monastery somewhere just beyond mainland Norway's outermost edge. It all serves as an antidote to Norway's summer crowds, offering respite from busy roads and well-worn travel itineraries that lead to the same place. All it takes is a decision to drive out west and then keep on going.

Travel Along Norway's Quiet Atlantic Shore
COASTAL CULTURE AND LANDSCAPES

To get a flavour of this little-known region way out beyond the tour itineraries along the west coast, begin with a little context at Florø's **Coast Museum**. It covers everything from the hard-won – and often impoverished – fishing past (the model of the 1900 fishing family's home is a highlight) to the Snorreankeret display that brings to life the North Sea oilfields that have transformed life along the coast.

Afterwards, take a boat trip to **Kinn Island** to explore on a guided excursion; book through the tourist office in Florø. The island's stunning stone church dates from the 12th century, and it's a backdrop to the obligatory guide's picaresque tales of the island from the distant past. Before boarding the boat for the return journey, climb the hill called **Kinnaklova** for views over the whole island. On a windy day, imagine trying to eke a living from this wild coast.

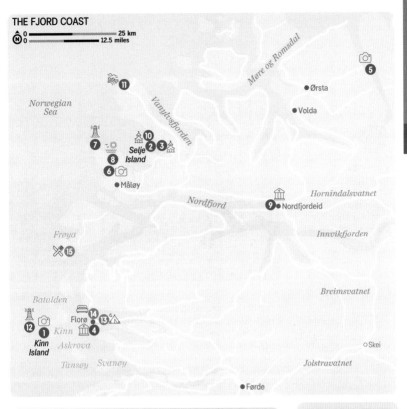

THE FJORD COAST

0 — 25 km
0 — 12.5 miles

Møre og Romsdal

Norwegian Sea

Vanylvsfjorden

● Ørsta

● Volda

11

7 **10** **2** **3**
8 Selje Island
6

● Måløy

Nordfjord

Hornindalsvatnet

9● Nordfjordeid

Frøya

15

Innvikfjorden

Breimsvatnet

Batalden

Florø **14** **13**
12 **1**
Kinn **4**
Kinn Island

Askrova

Tansøy   Svanøy

○ Skei

Jolstravatnet

● Førde

HIGHLIGHTS
1 Kinn Island
2 Selje Island

SIGHTS
3 Church of St Sunniva
4 Coast Museum
5 Hjørundfjorden

6 Kannesteinen
7 Kråkenes Lighthouse
8 Refviksanden
9 Sagastad
10 Selja Monastery
11 Vestkapp

12 Ytterøyane Lighthouse

SLEEPING
13 Efinor Camping Krokane
14 Quality Hotel Florø

EATING
15 Knutholmen

KRÅKENES LIGHTHOUSE

If you want to experience the power of the collision between the Atlantic and the Norwegian shore, drive to Kråkenes Lighthouse, a wildly beautiful place. The main house is also a B&B (with five double rooms).

It's a 42km round-trip along the Rv617 from Måløy, following the signs for Kråkenes Fyr (Kråkenes Lighthouse). The road unfurls over grassland, offering jaw-dropping views of steep cliffs.

Try to get a glimpse of another important local landmark, **Ytterøyane Lighthouse**, built in 1881. On a remote island about 20km west of Florø, you can see it from Kinn Island (or from the Bergen or Hurtigruten ferries). In a wild winter storm, the optics of watching it get battered by high seas are epic.

Journey to Norway's Wild West
WAY OUT THERE

All along the Fjord Coast, you'll catch glimpses of Norway's outermost reaches: the landscape laid bare by incessant winds, the tumultuous seas and the small villages clinging to the

View from Vestkapp

EXPLORE FURTHER

Hjørundfjorden
Halfway between the Fjord Coast and Ålesund, this little-known but utterly magnificent fjord remains one of Norway's best-kept secrets.

Sagastad
This excellent museum celebrates Viking history with the 30m-long replica Myklebust Ship.

Refviksanden
Voted Norway's best beach in a 2010 online poll, 1.5km-long Refviksanden is a white-sand gem just off the road to Kråkenes Lighthouse.

Kannesteinen
A 10km drive west of Måløy brings you to this much Instagrammed rock formation, rising from the sea like the tail of a whale.

edge of the continent. But to experience the true essence of this wild shore, take a trip to **Selje Island**.

You won't see many other tourists out here, which is, of course, a significant part of Selje's charm. Selje may not be blessed by everyone's idea of the perfect climate, but it has a gorgeous beach that would be much celebrated if it lay on a tropical island. Selje and its coast offer proof that not everyone is cut from the same cloth. Europe's hardcore cold-water surfers have turned this stretch of coast into one of their favourite playgrounds. They rave about the experience, but we'll take their word for it.

On rocky Selje Island lie the haunting ruins of the 11th-century **Selja Monastery** and the 12th-century **Church of St Sunniva**. They have been drawing pilgrims for more than 1000 years. Climb the 40m-high tower for the best views along this stretch of coast, but hang on tight, as the winds rarely abate. To reach the island, take a boat from the quay in Selje. It takes around 15 minutes to reach the island; don't miss the boat back. For more information, visit the town's tourist office alongside the harbour.

If Selje feels like the end of the road, then drive a further 32km to **Vestkapp**. Despite the name, it's not quite mainland Norway's westernmost point. The ocean views from Vestkapp are stunning.

WHERE TO STAY & EAT ALONG THE FJORD COAST

Efinor Camping Krokane
Camp on a secluded peninsula east of Florø; cabins and boat hire are also part of the deal. €

Quality Hotel Florø
This waterfront place has harbour views with excellent rooms and an in-house seafood restaurant. €€

Knutholmen
One of the best spots for fresh fish. Try the seafood platter within sight of the fishing fleet. €€€

Åndalsnes

Åndalsnes

OSLO

It doesn't matter which way you approach the town of Åndalsnes: it's difficult not to imagine that you're on your way somewhere special. From the east and southeast, you pass through the splendour of Romsdalen. From the south, you take Trollstigen, one of Norway's most dramatic mountain roads.

Perhaps because the city was badly bombed during WWII, leaving a memory of tragedy and destruction, an awareness of beautiful places not far away runs through every fibre of Åndalsnes. Everything from hotel rooms to public spaces seems designed to take in the view. Wander around the water's edge and linger in lovely cafes to find a welcoming community just getting about its business.

Once you've been suitably impressed by the views, you'll find plenty of locals who love to get out and explore, and many of them are experts in taking you out there with them.

Climb Åndalsnes' Biggest Cliff

ON THE SHEER ROCK WALLS

Åndalsnes may be a small town, but it looms large in the mountaineering world, with an abundance of climbing routes in the surrounding mountains and valleys. Most famous is **Trollveggen**, a sheer cliff face that rises 1100m straight from the floor of Raumadalen valley. For context, that's nearly twice the height of the famous Preikestolen (Pulpit Rock; p179).

Europe's highest vertical mountain wall, first climbed in 1965, Trollveggen featured in the 2023 film *Mission: Impossible – Dead Reckoning Part One,* starring Tom Cruise. The echoes from famous films start even before you get there. The section of Romsdalen just outside of Åndalsnes appears in *Harry Potter and the Half-Blood Prince.*

Obviously, the rock-climbing part is not to be undertaken lightly. Regardless of your level of experience, you'd be crazy not to tap into the ready-to-hand local knowledge and experience at **Norsk Tindesenter** (Norwegian Mountaineering

GETTING AROUND

Åndalsnes is small and easy to walk around. But for most things worth doing in the area, you need your own wheels. If you have a car, there's nowhere you can't go.

☑ **TOP TIP**

Rather than try to piece together an itinerary through the region, come and go from Åndalsnes. Travelling Trollstigen or on the Rauma Railway in both directions is well worth doing. By returning over and again to Åndalsnes, you get a delightful sense of small-town Norway to go with the world-class attractions nearby.

BEST PLACES TO EAT & DRINK

Sødahl-Huset
If only other Norwegian towns had a Sødahl-Huset. This fabulous small-town cafe has eclectic furniture, beer tastings, live music and house-made dishes of local produce. It's run by three lovely women.

John Kofoed Fishing Trips
John Kofoed runs three-hour fishing tours on Romsdals-fjorden in search of any of the 68 different fish species. Afterwards, cook your turbot, cod or coalfish over a campfire.

Kjellar'n
The Grand Hotel Bellevue's cellar bar, backlit in startlingly kitschy pink and lime green, is the place to be on Saturday nights.

Centre). It's the place to go in town for all things climbing and more. Assuming you have the requisite experience, if you're planning on climbing Trollveggen, contact Norsk Tindesenter in advance of your visit to discuss routes, timing and equipment. Located at the base of the Romsdal Gondola, this mountain activity centre also has Norway's highest climbing wall (21m), with 60 different ascents, and offers beginners' climbing courses as well as private climbing instruction and guided excursions. Serious climbers should also track down *Klatring i Romsdal* (300kr), which includes rock- and ice-climbing information in Norwegian and English.

Hike the Spectacular Åndalsnes Hinterland
KEEP YOUR FEET ON THE GROUND

You don't have to be a climber to enjoy Åndalsnes. Hiking trails fan out from the town, which means you could stay here for days and take a different path each morning. For the most part, the hikes are serious trails, not for the unfit, and often with steep altitude gains as part of the experience.

If you're looking for something a little easier on the knees and calf muscles, go for a walk around the lake at Åndalsnes. Consider also **Kløvstien**, which begins in Isterdalen along the Rv63 and follows the valley in the form of a gentle walk through the forest. If you're up to it, resist the urge to turn around where the trail starts to climb; instead, test your fitness levels with the ascent to **Stigfossen**.

One of the most dramatic hikes in the area is along **Romsdalseggen**, a rugged ridge with spectacular views of Åndalsnes, the Trolltinder mountains, Trollveggen, the Rauma river valley and beyond. It's a challenging 10km hike with an elevation gain of 970m and takes about eight hours. Another classic climb is the 1550m-high **Romsdalshorn**, just across the valley from Trollveggen. If you're looking for an exhilarating experience with less risk, the **Romsdalsstigen Via Ferrata** offers the perfect combination of adrenaline and safety, with both introductory and advanced routes.

Right next to downtown Åndalsnes, **Mt Nesaksla** rises 715m above sea level. The hike to the top takes about two hours and includes a section of steep stone steps made by Nepalese sherpas. The 360-degree views from the top are your reward.

SKIING

Hiking and climbing might get all the attention around Åndalsnes, but skiers also know it as a favourite spot because it offers untouched powder and unrelenting fjord views. Remember, however, that skiing here is usually of the wilder kind and involves ski-up, ski-down challenges.

Kirketaket (1439m) is a Romsdalen classic. It takes three to five hours to ascend, but from the top, you have more than 1000 vertical metres of steep downhill slopes. In one of Norway's great skiing experiences, you can ski right down to the fjord. Spring and early summer skiing is possible once the Trollstigen road opens as well.

See romsdal.com and fjords.com/isfjorden for more information. For ski guides, check skiromsdal.no or contact Hotel Aak.

A. ALEKSANDRAVICIUS/SHUTTERSTOCK ©

Romsdalseggen

🛏 WHERE TO STAY IN ÅNDALSNES

Åndalsnes Vandrerhjem
Great hostel with simple rooms surrounded by greenery and providing satisfying breakfasts. €

Grand Hotel Bellevue
Historic but lovingly recast, this mountain place has views from every room. €€€

Hotel Aak
This historic mountain hotel is a fab place to stay, with knockout mountain views and a focus on activities. €€€

Beyond Åndalsnes

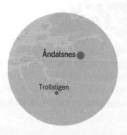

Åndalsnes

Trollstigen

Åndalsnes draws thrill-seeking adventurers, but its superb setting means travellers of all types can find activities to their liking.

GETTING AROUND

There's only one way to experience Trollstigen, and that's with your own set of wheels. There's no public transport, although the occasional (or, in summer, not-so-occasional) tour bus makes the trip. A car is also useful to get elsewhere in the area, although consider the Rauma Railway if you're heading east; it's shadowed by the E136 if you're driving.

☑ TOP TIP

The website nasjonaleturistveger .no/en/routes/geiranger -trollstigen is a fantastic resource for driving Trollstigen, with inspiring photos, practical information and things to watch out for.

Åndalsnes lies in the heart of spectacular countryside, including some of the most dramatic landscapes anywhere in Norway's northern fjords. Vertiginous upthrusts of sheer rock create an astonishing world of vertical cliff walls, more of them perhaps than anywhere else in the country. Nowhere is this more evident than in Trollstigen, one of Norway's most celebrated and unlikely drives.

To the east, Romsdalen funnels down off the high summits and deep into the very different and more intimate world of central Norway. With so much happening at a scenic and geological level, it should come as no surprise that Åndalsnes and its surroundings draw visitors with an explorer's spirit.

Drive the Troll's Ladder
ON THE ROAD AT TROLLSTIGEN

Trollstigen, a twisting, sky-topping corkscrew of a road, might be the most famous stretch of tarmac in Norway. Completed in 1936 after eight years of labour, the Troll's Ladder (Fv63) is a stunning feat of road building, spiralling up the mountainside through 11 hairpin bends and a 1:12 gradient. After heavy rain, waterfalls cascade down the mountainside, drenching cars as they pass and adding to the overall sense of an elemental Norwegian experience. To add to the thrill, much of it is effectively a single lane, meaning traffic jams and passing vehicles are part of the hair-raising experience.

At the crest of the pass, a gravity-defying platform and a series of viewpoints have been built out of rusting steel and concrete, a striking artificial counterpoint to the bare rock and natural scenery all around. Teetering precipitously over the plunging cliff and allowing stomach-churning views right down the mountain, the site was designed by architect Reiulf Ramstad and has become one of the most famous locations on the National Tourist Route network. Don't miss it.

Despite its length – just 55km – we recommend taking at least half a day to experience the road. This route is understandably slow going, but it's also all about pulling over at

Trollstigen

NATIONAL TOURIST ROUTES

Trollstigen belongs to an elite portfolio of Norway's 18 most scenic road trips, designated by Norway's road and tourism authorities. Covering 1850km and known as **National Tourist Routes** (nasjonaleturistveger. no/en), the roads are a fabulous planning tool. If you were to drive them all, you'd have seen Norway at its most varied and spectacular.

As part of the designation, architects built daring, contemporary structures that have transformed lookouts in the most remarkable places. Other recognised routes include Sognefjellet Rd in central Norway, two routes through Hardangerfjord, the island of Senja, the Atlanterhavsveien (Atlantic Rd) near Kristiansund, the Lofoten Islands, and the Gamle Strynefjellsvegen between Grotli in Oppland and Videseter in Sogn og Fjordane.

every opportunity, visiting every lookout and taking your time without rushing. We recommend that you drive the road in both directions; this route never loses its ability to surprise.

The road is usually open from mid-May to October. There is no public transport to or along Trollstigen.

MORE EPIC SCENERY
Rauma Railway (p130) between Dombås and Åndalsnes is a superb echo of Åndalsnes and its surrounds. This train route is a fine way to enjoy the scenery and let someone else do the hard work.

Geirangerfjord

Geirangerfjord

★OSLO

GETTING AROUND

Buses meet the ferry at either end – Geiranger or Hellesylt – but services can be irregular outside the summer months. As with so much of Norway's fjord country, your best choice is to have your own car, allowing you to meander along beautiful byways.

If you've seen a picture of a Norwegian fjord, it was probably Geirangerfjord. Norway's king among fjords, this UNESCO-listed spot is a natural feature without peer, an unrivalled concentration of huge cliffs, plunging waterfalls and deep-blue water. Yes, it's popular in summer, and yes, you might have to queue at a lookout or to board a busy boat. But that can't take away from the sheer, jaw-dropping beauty of this place.

The key is finding the right angles from which to view its perfection. With so much natural magnificence to take in, Geiranger is unique in Norway's fjord country for the range of activities on offer. You can take a boat cruise, kayak away from the crowds, hike in just about every direction, explore on a mountain bike and more. Choose as many of these as you can; each gives a different and enduring perspective on this most remarkable of fjords.

☑ TOP TIP

Avoid visiting Geirangerfjord at the height of summer when queues for boat tours are long and the general clamour at every turn can be overwhelming. Late spring or early autumn are usually excellent, combining fewer visitors with generally good visibility, even if the weather is a little less predictable.

Geirangerfjord from the Water

THE WORLD'S MOST FAMOUS BOAT TRIP

First established as a common ferry, an alternative for local people taking long road trips to travel the relatively short distance between Hellesylt and Geiranger, the **Hellesylt–Geiranger ferry** long ago achieved celebrity status. As a ferry, it's cheaper than taking a boat tour. Because it runs the length of the fjord, you have the perfect vantage point from which to enjoy Geirangerfjord in all its glory.

It all begins from the pretty former Viking port of **Hellesylt**, which is bisected by a thundering waterfall. The tourist office is a mine of useful information.

As the boat trip begins, the scenery is striking, though on par with other fjords you may have seen. But barely half an hour into the trip, the route turns east into the narrowing arm of **Geirangerfjord**. From this moment on, you travel

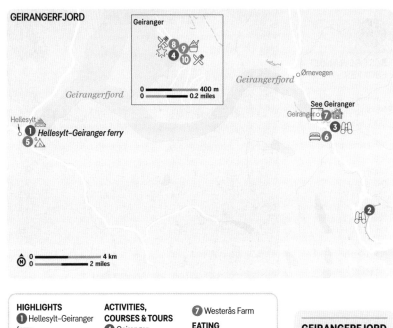

GEIRANGERFJORD

HIGHLIGHTS
① Hellesylt–Geiranger ferry

SIGHTS
② Dalsnibba Lookout
③ Flydalsjuvet

ACTIVITIES, COURSES & TOURS
④ Geiranger Fjordservice

SLEEPING
⑤ Hellesylt Camping
⑥ Hotel Utsikten

⑦ Westerås Farm

EATING
⑧ Brasserie Posten
⑨ Geiranger Sjokolade
⑩ Olebuda & Cafe Olé

past one extraordinary view after another. You're in for an hour of craning your neck upwards, mouth open, and wondering all the while whether you have enough memory for all the photos you're taking. Greatest hits include the waterfalls known as Seven Sisters, the Suitor and the Bridal Veil. The ferry's captain points out various features and tells a little of their stories, and the commentary is as informative as it is delightfully avuncular. The captain may also tell of the more sobering 1934 disaster when a chunk of the mountain slid into the fjord, creating a tsunami that swallowed Geiranger.

Especially in summer, we strongly recommend getting here as early as possible. By lunchtime, queues can be long, and you may have to wait a few hours to board.

Another option – either as an extension of your ferry experience or a more in-depth alternative – is the sightseeing boat trip run by the experienced **Geiranger Fjordservice**. Its standard 1½-hour trip runs up to five times daily in mid-summer, just once daily in April and October, and not at all from November to March. These tours are pricier than the ferry, but they also give you longer on the fjord.

GEIRANGERFJORD FOR FOODIES

Geiranger Sjokolade
One of the great sensory highlights of Geiranger is following the scent of chocolate to Bengt Dahlberg's chocolate-making workshop in the basement of an old boathouse.

Brasserie Posten
Everything on the simple menu uses fresh local ingredients and recipes. The setting is superb, and the Geiranger Platter is *the* order.

Olebuda & Cafe Olé
In Geiranger's old general store, this pretty place does house-smoked goat and local salmon upstairs and has a casual cafe below.

BEST GEIRANGER ESCAPES

Kayaking
Geiranger Fjordservice runs sea-kayaking excursions from Geiranger.

Hiking from Geiranger
There are 18 signposted walks from Geiranger, ranging from 1.5km to 5km; the tourist office has a map (10kr).

Hiking to Skageflå
Take the Geiranger Fjordservice sightseeing boat and then make a steep 45-minute ascent to this incredible perch from the Skagehola landing.

Mountain Biking or Hiking above Hellesylt
Savour great views high above Hellesylt, where the tourist office has maps.

RPBAJAO/SHUTTERSTOCK ©

Flydalsjuvet

Find Your Favourite Lookout

GEIRANGERFJORD FROM ABOVE

Once you've experienced the fjord from below, it's time to get up high for that postcard shot. The **Dalsnibba lookout** (1500m) is easily the most spectacular of all Geiranger lookouts, especially from **Geiranger Skywalk**, with its see-through floor and glass rails. To get here, take the signposted 5km road (150kr per car) that climbs from the Rv63.

But the view that you'll see promoting Geirangerfjord everywhere was taken elsewhere: from the overhanging rock **Flydalsjuvet**. Flydalsjuvet is about 5km up a steep and winding hill from Geiranger on the Stryn road and offers amazing views. The full version of the famous view is accessible only 150m down a fenced-off, slippery and rather indistinct track over the edge. We strongly recommend that you enjoy the extraordinary view from the fence, but that doesn't stop carloads of visitors from making the perilous descent.

 WHERE TO STAY AROUND GEIRANGERFJORD

Hellesylt Camping
If you're planning to catch the first ferry out of Hellesylt, stay at this fjord-side campground. €

Westerås Farm
This high-altitude working farm has apartments, pine-clad cabins and a great restaurant in the 17th-century barn. €€

Hotel Utsikten
Around since 1893, the Utsikten has stunning views over the town and fjord and decent rooms. €€€

Ålesund

Bathed in the ethereal, subarctic light of Norway's mid-north and arrayed across a series of peninsulas and islands that reach out into the Atlantic, Ålesund is a beautiful small city that exudes a beguiling, end-of-the-road feel.

The place you see today rose from the ashes of a fire that destroyed the town in 1904. With a compact, uniformly pretty centre clustered around small, interconnected harbours and set against a backdrop of high hills, Ålesund has superb examples of Jugendstil (art nouveau) architecture. It also has an intimacy lacking in other large Norwegian cities, and it's an easy city to explore on foot. From above, it's a glorious tableau of urban perfection set against a backdrop of wild seas, snow-crowned mountains and an ocean that seems to go on forever.

As the home base for Norway's largest cod-fishing fleet, it's also a fine place to sample the freshest local seafood.

The View from Above
NORWAY'S PRETTIEST ROOFSCAPE

The view of Ålesund from the **Kniven Viewpoint** (on Askla Hill, immediately east of the centre) is the quintessential image of the town. Norway's tourism authorities frequently put it front and centre in their campaigns to lure visitors to the country. It's not difficult to understand why.

Seen from above, Ålesund has a magical, too-pretty-to-be-true aspect. On a clear summer's day, the city's tiered gables and muted colours have the quality of an idealised painting of a Scandinavian harbour town. Capturing an altogether different mood, a sunny interlude between autumn storms adds drama and texture to the backdrop, with dark ocean waters and distant islands and summits swirling through anvil-shaped clouds. On a dark winter's day, with the city blanketed in snow, or at twilight, Ålesund can appear like a magical urban fairy tale lit by a thousand winking lanterns.

GETTING AROUND

Ålesund has great air links to the rest of Norway, with frequent flights to Bergen, Oslo, Trondheim and Stavanger. European destinations include Amsterdam, Copenhagen and London.

On its northbound run, the Hurtigruten ferry makes a popular detour from mid-April to mid-October to Geiranger town. It departs from Ålesund's Hurtigruten ferry terminal.

Bus journeys to and from Ålesund can seem like they last forever. If you're travelling by road, do so by car. Once you're in town, park your car and walk. Everything worth seeing in the town itself is within walking distance of the city centre.

☑ **TOP TIP**

Ålesund is a long way from anywhere, and that's a big part of its charm. If you're just visiting Ålesund and have no plans to explore the hinterland, visit the city as a stop on a Hurtigruten coastal ferry instead of taking the long drive or an expensive flight to get here.

ÅLESUND

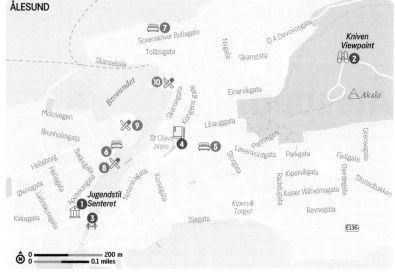

HIGHLIGHTS
1 Jugendstil Senteret
2 Kniven Viewpoint

SIGHTS
3 Hellebroa
4 St Olavs plass

SLEEPING
5 Hotel 1904
6 Hotel Brosundet
7 Quality Hotel Ålesund

EATING
8 Restaurant Apotekergata No 5
9 Sjøbua
10 XL Diner

BEST SEAFOOD IN ÅLESUND

Restaurant Apotekergata No 5
In Hotel Brosundet, this place does fermented trout, *lutefisk* (stockfish cooked with lye) and more in a refined setting enhanced by fine service. €€€

XL Diner
It's all about the cod (think salt cod and pan-fried cod tongue) at this waterfront spot. XL Diner claims to serve the best fish soup in town, and it's right. €€€

Sjøbua
A harbourside beauty, Sjøbua serves a divine lobster soup, as well as a mean lye fish with bacon and almond potatoes. €€€

There are two ways to reach the viewpoint. The best is to take the 418 steps to the top, a steep but infinitely reward-ing climb. Follow Lihauggata from the pedestrian shopping street of Kongens gate, pass the Rollon statue and begin the 15- to 30-minute puff to the top of the hill. It doesn't matter how long you take as long as you turn around often and take in the changing view.

There's also a road to the crest. Take Røysegata east from the centre and then follow the 'Askla' signposts up the hill.

Art Nouveau Ålesund
A LIVING ARCHITECTURAL MUSEUM

No city in Norway radiates a uniform architectural style quite like Ålesund. When the city burned to the ground in 1904, the Jugendstil (art nouveau) movement was sweeping Europe. The fire destroyed 850 buildings in 24 hours, and Jugendstil came to define the city when it was rebuilt. Jugendstil drew on nature for its inspiration, which resulted in its defining organic shapes and flower-inspired ornamental flourishes. More muted in Ålesund than elsewhere (such as Barcelona in Spain), art nouveau made abundant use of archways and asymmetrical and curved forms. The widespread use of stone-work drew on the American branch of Art Nouveau design.

To begin your journey through Ålesund's architectural riches, visit the **Jugendstil Senteret**. This former pharmacy is a fine example of the art nouveau genre, especially its exquisite and almost entirely original interior, including a sinuous staircase and a richly patterned dining room. Don't miss the museum's excellent 14-minute multimedia story *From Ashes to Art Nouveau*.

To get a broader sense of Ålesund's style, wander along **Kongens gate** – Nos 19 and 25 are notable examples – and stone-built Kongens gate 10b is Ålesund's narrowest home. **St Olavs plass** is another good place to stop and look upwards at the decorative flourishes typical of the period. The views from **Hellebroa** showcase some fine stone buildings and the lovely facades of Ålesundet sound's former waterfront warehouses.

BEST SUMMER FESTIVALS

Ålesund Boat Festival
Watercraft fill Ålesund's harbours in July, and the view at ground level and from on high is incredible.

Jugendfest
Western Norway's biggest music festival has performances by local and international bands in the second half of August.

Norwegian Food Festival
Street food, special menus in restaurants, celebrity chefs and kids' cooking classes are all happening in late August (matfestivalen.no).

KONSTANTIN YOLSHIN/SHUTTERSTOCK ©

Ålesund

 WHERE TO STAY IN ÅLESUND

Hotel 1904
Ålesund's oldest hotel blends period structural design with clean, contemporary lines. €€

Quality Hotel Ålesund
Next to the Hurtigruten port, this slick modern hotel is at its best in the rooms that look out over the ocean. €€€

Hotel Brosundet
Architect-designed waterfront belle with wooden beams, exposed brickwork and brown velvet. €€€

213

Grip •
Kristiansund •
•
Kvernes Stave
Church
Ålesund
Runde •—• Sunnmøre
• Museum

Beyond Ålesund

Out where Norway's west meets the windswept
Atlantic, the big horizons beyond Ålesund are the
wild antithesis of the inland fjords.

GETTING AROUND

Unless you have
endless time, make
sure you have your
own set of wheels to
explore the region.
There are car hire
agencies in Ålesund,
including at the
airport.

☑ TOP TIP

It takes a long time to get
around. The combination of
ferry crossings and winding
roads means that relatively
short distances can take
hours.

Ålesund sits so far out on its own peninsula that it's easy to
imagine it's a world unto itself. While that's part of its appeal,
Ålesund is also a gateway to attractions that are, in some cas-
es, even more remote.

Sinuous roads buck and weave across the contours of a landscape stippled with high hills and deep fjords, with islands
offshore adding to the sense of a land on the outer edge of
Norway's Atlantic shore. Runde Island is one of Europe's premier birding destinations, while Kristiansund, the island of
Averøy and the wild and windswept Atlanterhavsveien (Atlantic Rd) make it worthwhile to spend at least a couple of
days exploring the region.

Take Your Binoculars to the Island of Birds

RUNDE'S SEABIRDS, SCENERY AND LOST TREASURE

As you cross the long, curving bridge to **Runde**, a green, almost treeless speck of land on Norway's outer edge, you enter a world shaped by wind and waves and bound by rocky
beaches and towering cliffs. The large colonies of seabirds
that spend time here far outnumber Runde's slightly more
than 100 human inhabitants. Most famous are the Atlantic
puffins, and an estimated 60,000 nest here from April to July.
Watch also for northern gannets (March to October), common murre (April to August) and the island's recovering population of sea eagles.

Seabird numbers have declined substantially in recent
decades, but if you come during the right season, it's still an
experience of a lifetime to hike up to Norway's southernmost
bird cliffs and watch large numbers of puffins coming and going as evening approaches. **Runde Environmental Centre**
offers guided evening tours to the bird cliffs that include a
supper of fish soup, a screening of the centre's documentary
film and a tour of the centre's exhibits. It's also possible to observe the seabird activity on boat tours to the base of the cliffs.

ANDREI ARMIAGOV/SHUTTERSTOCK ©

Puffins, Runde

To make the most of your visit, stay overnight on Runde. There's a campground near the start of the hike to the bird cliffs, or for more comfort, book one of Runde Environmental Centre's spacious self-catering apartments. Be sure to buy groceries before arriving on the island.

Explore Norway's Most Traditional Port Town

GET TO KNOW KRISTIANSUND

Spread across three islands, **Kristiansund** is a classic Norwegian port town. Once a cod-fishing port, the city now services the oil industry but retains much of its original character. Because it's off the main roads between the western fjords, central Norway and Trøndelag, it doesn't see many tourists.

Before exploring the pretty old quarter, begin at **Mellemværftet**, the scruffy, gritty old waterfront that still functions as a working boatyard. It has echoes of a 19th-century shipyard, with a forge, workshop and workers' quarters. All across town, you'll see racks of cod salting and drying. A significant proportion of the world's *klippfisk* (salted cod) is cured around Kristiansund.

SUNNMØRE MUSEUM

You don't have to go too far from Ålesund – just 4km to be precise – to see one of Norway's best folk museums. **Sunnmøre Museum** occupies the site of a trading crossroads that was hugely important to the economy of western Norway from the 11th to 16th centuries.

Wander around more than 50 traditional buildings and 40 historic boat replicas, among them copies of Viking-era ships and a trading ship that plied these waters around 1000 CE. Also on the site is the **Medieval Age Museum**, with its relics and recreations of the trading centre that once drew merchants from across Norway and further afield.

 WHERE TO STAY BEYOND ÅLESUND

Skjerneset Bryggecamping
These converted *rorbuer* (fishing huts) on the island of Ekkilsøy are endearingly old-fashioned. €

Sveggvika
This guesthouse has stylish, simple rooms in an updated 1920s salted cod warehouse. €€€

Håholmen Havstuer
A former fishing village that occupies its own islet with rooms in 18th- and 19th-century cottages. €€€

KELIFAMILY/SHUTTERSTOCK ©

Walking path, Eldhusøya

EXCURSIONS FROM KRISTIANSUND

If you're based in Kristiansund for any length of time, consider a detour 26km south to **Kvernes Stave Church**. Built in 1300, the church's interior dazzles. There's an unusual model ship carving and an eye-catching 15th-century altarpiece.

Another possible excursion is to the island of **Grip**, 14km across the water from Kristiansund. Once home to a 1000-strong cod-fishing community, Grip's last residents left in 1974. The pretty pastel-hued houses, 15th-century stave church and late-19th-century Bratthårskollen lighthouse remain, making for a haunting experience. A boat leaves from Kristiansund's Piren pier daily from late May to late August. You spend 1½ hours on the island, with an hour getting there and another hour back.

Much of central Kristiansund was bombed during WWII, and rebuilding was done with little inspiration – concrete rules. One example that bucks the trend while remaining true to the new functionalist aesthetic is **Kirkelandet Church**. Designed by Odd Østbye and built in 1964, it's an arresting showpiece of copper and concrete on the outside and bathed in the spectral light from 320 stained-glass windows inside.

And yet, old Kristiansund survives. **Gamle Byen**, the picturesque old town on the island of **Innlandent**, is a world of 17th-century clapboard buildings. **Lossiusgården**, at the eastern end, is a standout structure that belonged to a wealthy 18th-century merchant. The 300-year-old **Dødeladen Café** is another favourite haunt. To get to Gamle Byen, take the Sundbåten Ferry from Piren pier or walk across Heinsgata bridge.

Unfurling across a storm-lashed Atlantic coast, defying most rules of road-building along the way, the Atlanterhavsveien (Atlantic Rd) really does have to be seen to be believed. In places, it seems to float above the water. The heart of the route (Vevang to Averøya) is just 8km, but there are plenty more scenic sections.

Most trips begin in **1 Bud**. While you're in this sleepy village, note the WWII-era Ergan Coastal Fort and the marvellous Drågen Smokehouse; the latter is where Petter Aune smokes freshly caught Aukra salmon with local wood and herbs. Come to see the process, sample and buy. Just 10km north of Bud, pull into the glass-fronted viewing platform at **2 Askevågen**.

Hug the shore as you pass one-lane side roads that head off into tiny harbours and continue along a gloriously moody and windswept stretch of road that's spectacular when buffeted by an autumn or winter storm and just as magnificent in the summer sunshine. The road passes through quiet **3 Farstad** and then to **4 Vevang**, where it's easy to see how this road is an engineering miracle. Of the eight bridges that connect the 17 islets between Vevang and Averøya, the most impressive is **5 Storseisundet**, a gravity-defying serpentine marvel that curls and twists from Eide to Averøya island. This bridge in particular, and the road in general, has featured in countless luxury car advertisements, and it played a starring role in the 2021 James Bond thriller *No Time to Die*. Several scenic overlooks beckon along the way, among them the rest area and walking path at **6 Eldhusøya**, an island off the southwest of Averøya. Afterwards, it's a short final hop into **7 Kristiansund**.

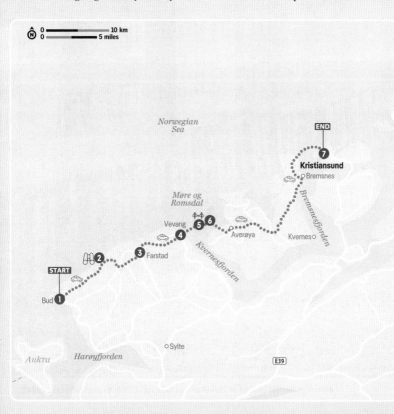

Above: colourful houses of Trondheim (p222); right: rock formations, Leka (p243)

Trøndelag

PAGE-TURNING HISTORY AND REGIONAL FLAVOURS

Prehistoric geology, an ancient battleground, industrial heritage and flavour-packed local produce: head to Trøndelag to discover its past and get a taste of the present.

Halfway up the country, just as it begins to narrow, Trøndelag is Norway in miniature, with its fjord-slashed coastline, snow-dusted mountains and bucolic farmland.

Standing proud as the region's capital, 1000-year-old Trondheim leads the way with its arresting Gothic cathedral. Yet it has a thoroughly modern story to tell too, with a student population enlivening the after-dark scene and fresh Nordic menus in its Michelin-lauded restaurants.

Speaking of the culinary arts, in 2022 Trøndelag cooked up a storm as the European Region of Gastronomy, recognised for the wealth of small-scale food producers across this area known as 'Norway's larder'. You'll just as easily find quality cooking and the freshest local produce in a laid-back restaurant as you will in a starred establishment. Going straight to the source is possible too, with farm shops on the Inderøy peninsula making for a flavour-packed detour off the E6 motorway.

The region could also rightfully have the moniker 'Norway's birthplace': a nation became possible at Stiklestad, the site of Norway's most consequential battle and a turning point in the country's history, while up the coast on the tiny island of Leka, 60-million-year-old rock formations tell of continents separating.

Meanwhile, tales of the industries that once powered Norway's economy are still told all over Trøndelag, from the heyday of cod fishing on the Namdalen coast to the copper-mining boom at Røros, a UNESCO World Heritage Site.

SASHA ALTERANT/SHUTTERSTOCK ©

THE MAIN AREAS

TRONDHEIM
Historic city with photogenic wharves. **p222**

RØROS
UNESCO-protected historic mining town. **p234**

NAMSOS
Rocking gateway to coastal treasures. **p238**

Find Your Way

Trøndelag sits between the dramatic western fjords and the alluring Arctic. Travelling between major towns is doable on public transport, but a car is more convenient for reaching remote places.

FERRY
Trondheim and Rørvik are scheduled stops on the Hurtigruten coastal ferry. Reliable but infrequent passenger boats run between Namsos, Rørvik and Leka, while a regular car ferry connects Leka to Gutvik on the mainland.

CAR
The E6 blazes a trail through the region and flirts with the coastline between Trondheim and Steinkjer. The Kystriksveien coastal route starts at Steinkjer and links coastal towns further north.

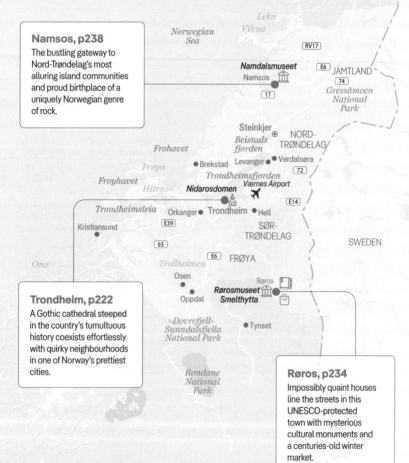

Namsos, p238
The bustling gateway to Nord-Trøndelag's most alluring island communities and proud birthplace of a uniquely Norwegian genre of rock.

Trondheim, p222
A Gothic cathedral steeped in the country's tumultuous history coexists effortlessly with quirky neighbourhoods in one of Norway's prettiest cities.

Røros, p234
Impossibly quaint houses line the streets in this UNESCO-protected town with mysterious cultural monuments and a centuries-old winter market.

Leka
Vikna
Norwegian Sea
RV17
Namdalsmuseet
Namsos
E6
JÄMTLAND
74
Gressåmoen National Park
17
Steinkjer
NORD-TRØNDELAG
Beistadsfjorden
Frohavet
Brekstad
Levanger
Verdalsøra
Frøya
Trondheimsfjorden
72
Froyhavet
Hitra
Nidarosdomen
Værnes Airport
Trondheimsleia
Orkanger
Trondheim
Hell
E14
Kristiansund
SØR-TRØNDELAG
SWEDEN
E39
65
Ona
Trollheimen
E6
FRØYA
Osen
Røros
Rørosmuseet
Smelthytta
Oppdal
Dovrefjell-Sunndalsfjella National Park
Tynset
Rondane National Park

Bakklandet (p225)

Plan Your Time

Trondheim, the big-ticket city in Trøndelag, has plenty to keep you occupied, but the region's story unfolds as you explore its coastal treasures, taste its local produce and visit its nationally important historic sites.

A Weekend Trip

- In **Trondheim** (p222), marvel at the monumental west front of Gothic cathedral **Nidarosdomen** (p222), stroll over the Old Town Bridge to the cobbled streets of **Bakklandet** (p225), then devour a seasonal menu at acclaimed **Fagn** (p229). Take the train to **Røros** (p234) to peep into pretty, wooden houses and hear about the town's 333-year copper-mining history at **Rørosmuseet Smelthytta** (p234).

A Week to Explore

- After you've explored Trondheim, make your way to **Stiklestad** (p231) to understand the famous battle that martyred King Olav and transformed Norway. Head to **Namsos** (p238) for a rocking pit stop and then take the express boat to wild little **Leka** (p243). Cycle around the island and see the rare 60-million-year-old rock formations that led to it becoming Norway's Geological National Monument.

Seasonal Highlights

SPRING	SUMMER	AUTUMN	WINTER
Flowers bloom, and late spring sees Norwegian flags fly for **Constitution Day** on 17 May, with the biggest regional celebration taking place in Trondheim.	Seasonal attractions open, music and cultural festivals abound, and locals take advantage of longer days to enjoy the *friluftsliv* (life in the fresh air).	Cooler temperatures and warm colours are perfect for scenic hikes. Local lamb, game, mushrooms and root vegetables make appearances on seasonal menus.	Nights lengthen, temperatures plummet and UNESCO-protected Røros is transformed with stalls, dancing and traditional music as the **Rørosmartnan winter market** comes to town.

Trondheim

Trondheim

OSLO

GETTING AROUND

Trondheim S is the main station for buses and trains, and is a 35-minute train ride from the airport.

City buses stop at or near the corner of Munkegata and Dronningens gate. The Gråkallbanen tram line runs west from St Olavsgata to Lian. Download the AtB app (atb.no/en/app-atb) to buy tickets.

You can pick up and drop off bikes throughout the city. Download the Trondheim Bysykkel app.

Driving in Trondheim, comes with toll charges when you enter and leave the city centre and steep parking charges. Visit trondheimparkering.no for full details on electric vehicle charging points and parking spaces.

☑ **TOP TIP**

You'll find Trondheim S station in Midtbyen, as well as most sights, shops, restaurants and bars. To the south is cobbled Bakklandet, and to the west is the Bymarka hiking area. Stylish Solsiden is to the east.

Trondheim is, without doubt, one of Norway's most photogenic cities. Colourfully painted wooden wharves line the banks of the Nidelva as it meanders out to the yawning Trondheimsfjord, and the spire of its sculpture-laden Gothic cathedral stands in contrast to the city's pleasingly low profile. The country's historical capital is now its third-largest city, and the grandeur of some of its buildings still hints at its affluent past – a story told across its museums and galleries.

Today, this ancient city maintains a youthful visage courtesy of stylish cafes and bars, a cutting-edge cuisine scene and forward-thinking arts venues. The huge student population helps too: almost a fifth of the city's residents attend its highly regarded universities.

But this city isn't a place that tries too hard. Trondheim is simply a pleasure to wander or cycle around, whether through quaint neighbourhoods with quirky shops or alongside the river on a sunny summer's day.

Archbishops, Saints & Royalty

TRONDHEIM TELLS THE STORY OF NORWAY

The historical significance of the city once known as Nidaros is etched into its ancient ecclesiastical buildings, and you'll discover the story of Norway itself when you visit them.

In 1035, a humble wooden chapel was built on the burial site of St Olav, the king, martyred at Stiklestad in 1030, who led Norway into Christendom. Almost 1000 years and several extensions later, **Nidarosdomen** (Nidaros Cathedral) is the world's most northerly Gothic church. Its towering west front features 76 sculptures of historical figures and a 10,000-piece stained-glass rose window. No longer the 'dark cathedral', Nidarosdomen's Gothic interior is now accented by an award-winning lighting system, completed in 2020.

RESTORING NIDAROSDOMEN

After 132 years, the restoration of Nidaros Cathedral was officially completed in 2001, but its ongoing maintenance still employs a team of about 60 people in its Restoration Workshop, around 25 of them artisans such as stonemasons and blacksmiths. Plasterers also play a vital role: the team is making casts of all the cathedral's decorative elements, such as figures and heads, so that exact copies can be carved in the future should they become damaged. With 5000 elements to document, it's a daunting task, and it looks like their jobs will be safe for some time to come – it's taken 25 years to cast just a fifth of them.

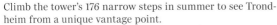

Gamle Bybro (p225)

Climb the tower's 176 narrow steps in summer to see Trondheim from a unique vantage point.

In the adjacent 12th-century **Erkebispegården** (Archbishop's Palace), you'll find the **Archbishop's Palace Museum**, which houses finds discovered during excavations in the 1990s, including original sculptures from Nidarosdomen, eroded by time, weather and fire. Don't miss the fascinating film celebrating the master craftspeople involved in the cathedral's restoration. The **Riksregaliene** (Crown Regalia), created in 1818 after Norway separated from Denmark, is displayed in an atmospherically lit, vaulted cellar space in the palace's west wing. The collection includes several priceless items, including gold crowns burdened by the weight of precious gems, and an astonishing red-velvet, ermine-lined embroidered robe.

The king's official residence in Trondheim, **Stiftsgården** is an 18th-century house on Munkegata. More than 100 rooms are spread over 4000 sq metres at this grand abode, the largest wooden palace in Scandinavia. Visit on a 45-minute guided tour in summer, and access the peaceful garden from Dronningens gate.

 WHERE TO STAY IN TRONDHEIM

Trondheim Vandrerhjem	City Living Sentrum	Nidaros Pilegrimsgård
Around 2km uphill from Midtbyen, this modern hostel has helpful staff, clean facilities and great views. €	Trade frills for simple, clean rooms, a large guest kitchen and a city-centre location. €	A quiet guesthouse resting between Nidarosdomen and the Nidelva. Open to non-pilgrims too. €€

TRONDHEIM

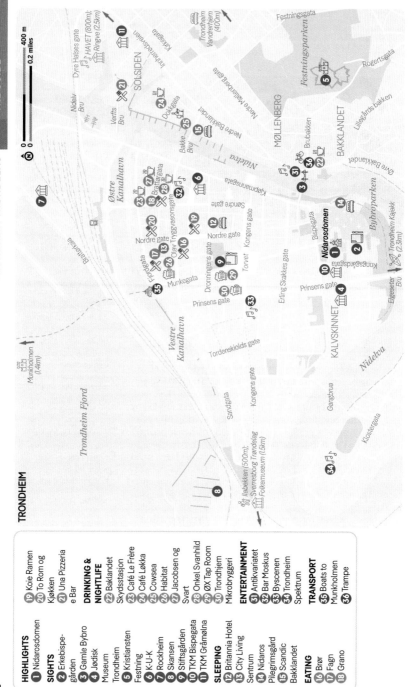

HIGHLIGHTS
1 Nidarosdomen

SIGHTS
2 Erkebispe-gården
3 Gamle Bybro
4 Jødisk Museum Trondheim
5 Kristiansten Festning
6 K-U-K
7 Rockheim
8 Skansen
9 Stiftsgården
10 TKM Bispegata
11 TKM Gråmølna

SLEEPING
12 Britannia Hotel
13 City Living Sentrum
14 Nidaros Pilegrimsgård
15 Scandic Bakklandet

EATING
16 Brør
17 Fagn
18 Grano

19 Koie Ramen
20 To Rom og Kjøkken
21 Una Pizzeria e Bar

DRINKING & NIGHTLIFE
22 Baklandet Skydsstasjon
23 Café Le Frère
24 Café Løkka
25 Cowsea
26 Habitat
27 Jacobsen og Svart
28 Onkel Svanhild
29 ØX Tap Room
30 Trondhjem Mikrobryggeri

ENTERTAINMENT
31 Antikvariatet
32 Bar Moskus
33 Byscenen
34 Trondheim Spektrum

TRANSPORT
35 Boats to Munkholmen
36 Trampe

Bakklandet & the Top of Trondheim
COBBLESTONE STREETS AND FJORD VIEWS

Strolling alongside the pastel-hued wooden buildings on the cobbled streets of **Bakklandet** is a true pleasure of any trip to Trondheim.

From Nidarosdomen, it's a short walk towards the river and **Gamle Bybro**, the Old Town Bridge redesigned by Carl Adolf Dahl in 1861. Walk through the red-painted, wrought-iron archways towards Bakklandet and snap that essential photo of the brightly painted wharves on either side of the Nidelva. Once over the bridge, while away some time in the cafes, boutiques and restaurants of this pretty neighbour-hood. Highlights include homely **Baklandet Skydsstasjon** (p225) and live music cafe-bar **Antikvariatet** (p227) – there's a viewpoint framing the wharves a bit further along from this bar on the left.

At the foot of Brubakken, just up from the *Radio Otto* sculpture dedicated to Trondheim composer Otto Nielsen, watch steely-nerved locals ascend the hill on **Trampe**, the world's only bicycle lift. Feeling brave? There's a Trondheim Bysyk-kel station right next to it to try for yourself.

For unrivalled views over Trondheim, head up Brubakken and follow the road around to the right until you reach **Kris-tiansten Festning**. The white 17th-century fortress has a summer-only museum, but you can take in the expansive views year-round.

Trondheim from the River
KAYAKING DOWN THE NIDELVA

Paddle down the Nidelva in a kayak to get a river's-eye view of the city. Depending on the time of year, you might see an-glers catching salmon from the river's rich pickings and, as you near the city centre, you'll pass the mighty Ni-darosdomen on the left, as Kristiansten Festning surveys the city high up to your right. The high-light is passing under the Old Town Bridge, pad-dling between the brightly painted wharves to the sound of chattering riverside pub-goers on the terrace above. You'll finish at Skansen guest harbour, west of the city centre.

Trondheim Kajakk offers a variety of trips, either self-guided or with an instructor; the clas-sic trip takes about two hours. The meeting point is hidden behind some football pitches, and your

BEST PLACES FOR ART

TKM Bispegata
Trondheim Kunstmuseum's main venue houses a permanent collection spanning 150 years, plus changing contemporary exhibitions.

TKM Gråmølna
TKM's Solsiden outpost hosts temporary exhibitions and works by influential Norwegian artist Håkon Bleken.

K-U-K (Kjøpmannsgata Ung Kunst)
Young artists fill the ever-changing roster at this independent gallery. The excellent shop sells original pieces too.

THE PILGRIMS' WAY
Since his canonisation in 1031, St Olav has inspired pilgrims to make the journey to his burial site at Nidaros Cathedral on *Pilegrimsleden* (the Pilgrims Way). Pilgrims and non-pilgrims can learn more about his fatal battle at **Stiklestad** (p231).

WHERE TO STAY IN TRONDHEIM

Quality Hotel Prinsen
Sink into the pillowy beds at this large Kongens gate hotel with a subtle, botanical-themed design. €€

Scandic Bakklandet
The most central Trondheim Scandic has smart rooms with quirky artwork, plus a satisfying breakfast buffet. €€€

Britannia Hotel
Understated opulence, from the five-star front-desk service to the cushion-laden beds and waterfall showers. €€€

TRONDHEIM'S TOP FESTIVALS

Trondheim Jazz Festival
This annual four-day-long celebration of jazz takes place at venues across the city each May and has been running for more than 40 years.

Olavsfest
Norway's favourite saint inspires a week-long cultural festival around Nidarosdomen with concerts, talks and exhibitions.

Trøndersk Matfestival
August sees the Trøndelag Food Festival presenting the region's best local food and drink in the streets around Torvet.

Pstereo
A city-centre pop, rock and electronic music festival held in Marinen park over two days in August.

JELENA SAFRONOVA/SHUTTERSTOCK ©

Kayaking on the Nidelva (p225)

map app might lead you on a merry dance – take bus 1, 2 or 10 from Prinsens gate to Valøyvegen and walk via Bostadvegen.

An Islet Adventure

PICNICKING ON MUNKHOLMEN

It's been a Viking-era execution ground, a Benedictine monastery, a prison and a fortress, and you can take a summertime boat trip out to the mysterious little island fortress of **Munkholmen**, 1.5km from the shore, to wander, swim and while away an afternoon with a picnic.

Join one of the hourly guided tours to hear about Munkholmen's varied history, dare to enter its dank dungeon and see military installations from the days of occupation during WWII. Its small beach trails out into the fjord, and there's a large grassy area to relax and look back towards the city. If you haven't brought a picnic, there's a cafe serving light lunch fare. Boats depart from **Ravnkloa**, at the end of Munkegata, and run between May and September. It's about a 15-minute trip, and you can buy your ticket from the kiosk.

WHERE TO GO FOR HOT DRINKS IN TRONDHEIM

Jacobsen og Svart
Expertly crafted coffee drinks made by true aficionados in stylish but unpretentious premises.

Onkel Svanhild
This quirky cafe and bakery has coffee drinks, Palais des Thés teas and indulgent pastries.

Café Le Frère
The coffee is strong, and the picture windows are perfect for people-watching at this corner cafe.

The Story of Trøndelag

FOLK HISTORY AT SVERRESBORG

Set around the ruins of King Sverres' 12th-century hilltop castle, **Sverresborg Trøndelag Folkemuseum** is, for our money, the best museum of its kind in Norway.

The vast 'Images of Life' exhibition chronicles life in the region via displays of toys, clothes and vintage vehicles. Outside, peek into buildings transported from across Trøndelag, from Sami homes to the windowless **Haltdalen Stave Church**, dating from 1170. The lively town section has time capsules that include shops and a toothache-inducing dentist's office. Ramble up towards the castle ruins for Trondheim-wide views.

Take bus 11 in the direction of Stavset from Kongens gate and alight at the Trøndelag Folkemuseum stop.

Sounds in the City

MUSIC-THEMED MUSEUMS AND LIVE GIGS

For the backstory to Norway's popular music scene, drop into **Rockheim**, an interactive romp with instruments, listening stations and the Rockheim Hall of Fame. Start on the 6th floor and work your way down. Norway's national music museum **Ringve** is more traditional, with historical instruments from its 2000-strong collection on display, from the familiar to the long forgotten. It's in Lade, reachable on bus 20.

If the museums inspire you to hear some live sounds, Trondheim has you covered. Book ahead for **Trondheim Spektrum** arena gigs, which headlines big-name touring acts such as 50 Cent and Röyksopp. **Byscenen** is a popular venue on Kongens gate, and artists including Mayhem and Sigrid have played to its 1500-capacity crowd. You can catch intimate sets at much smaller venues too. **Antikvariatet** has regular jazz and acoustic gigs in its book-lined back bar, while **Bar Moskus** puts on a varied program with blues, Americana and jazz on the lineup. Genres from hip-hop to funk are staged at **HAVET**. Download the Broadcast app for listings, look out for the free paper or visit the website broadcast.events.

INSPIRING TRONDHEIM

Edith Serine Thomassen (pottemaker.no) is a Trondheim-based ceramicist who works from her gallery-workshop in Sverresborg Trøndelag Folkemuseum. Her work is inspired by the coast and the sea. Here she shares her tips for inspiring places in and around Trondheim.

Skansen
There are sailboats and possibilities to pause for a beer or coffee, swim and walk by the seaside at this guest harbour.

K-U-K
This city-centre art gallery opened in 2021 and is a space for young artists. I take inspiration from the regularly changing exhibitions here.

Museet Kystens Arv
It's situated an hour outside Trondheim, but this museum is set in beautiful surroundings and focuses on traditional boat building.

 WHERE TO EAT IN TRONDHEIM

Koie Ramen
Perch on a high stool around one of the communal tables for hearty ramen bowls and gyoza. €

Brør
Lively bar-restaurant with a slimline menu of tasty burgers, flavourful tacos and substantial sides. €

Baklandet Skydsstasjon
In an 18th-century wooden house, Trondheim's famously cosy cafe has comforting classics like fish soup. €€

The western neighbourhood of Ila was the focus of Trondheim's Gatekunst (Street Art) Festival in 2018, and several of the original murals remain. To see some of them, start at **1 Skansen Station** and walk through Ila Park towards Mellomila. You'll pass a mixture of colourful wooden houses and modern apartments before reaching the brightly coloured **2 Bird in Kaos** by Pablito Zago on your left. Take the little cut-through directly opposite the mural (between the yellow and red houses) and walk down towards the fence line. Turn left and you'll see Millo's 600-sq-metre **3 What You Don't See/ Quello Che Non Vedi** (nicknamed 'Ilapia') across the carriageway. To the left is **4 Galleri Dropsfabrikken**, showing contemporary Norwegian art in a former candy factory. Follow the lane around to the left and then turn right. Soon after, up to the left behind

a small allotment garden (Ilens Hage), you'll see Ivan Blažetić Šumski's dreamlike **5 Seeds of Future**. Continue back on Mellomila and take the first right, with the stream to your left, and head for the passage between two buildings on the right. This **6 Open Street Art Gallery** still has some of the original murals from the festival, including pieces by Skurktur and Birgers Oterutleie. Walk back to the stream, stroll over the little bridge and pass tiny, sandy **7 Ila Beach**. Wander past the quaint cottages of **8 Ilsvikøra** before retracing your steps back along Mellomila. Weave your way to Kleists gate. Tucked away in a lane on the right, you'll find Ståle Gerhardsen's heartwarming **9 Ta Vare På De Rundt Deg** (Take Care of Those Around You). Head for Ilevollen to continue back to Skansen, passing a **10 statue of King Sverre Sigurdsson**, a 12th-century ruler, along the way.

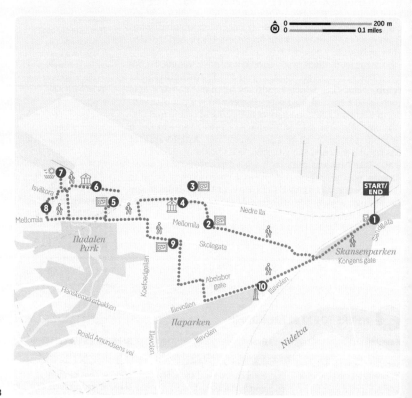

Ilabekken City Hike

A RIVERSIDE RAMBLE

Take a short but hilly hike up **Ilabekken**, a small river with a wooded path running alongside it that leads towards the **Bymarka forest reserve**. From Ilaparken, you can reach the 1.5km-long trail via Hanskemakerbakken. The path is signposted on the left for Bymarka, not far past the little parade of shops and restaurants. You'll walk up past rushing waterfalls, climb Insta-worthy wooden steps and continue into a wilder forest section, remaining close to the stream until you reach Theisendammen reservoir. You can swim here in summer or continue your walk around the lake, an additional 2km round trip. If you don't fancy walking the whole way back, hop on bus 11 to return to the city centre from Schiøtz' vei.

Uncovering Jewish Trondheim

REMEMBERING THE PAST, LOOKING TO THE FUTURE

Trondheim is home to one of only two synagogues in Norway, and although it's still in use for celebrations and meetings, it now forms part of the **Jødisk Museum Trondheim** (Trondheim Jewish Museum) on Arkitekt Christies gate. The exhibition in the basement (mostly in Norwegian) covers the lives and traditions of Jewish families in Trondheim through photographs and personal belongings. Upstairs, 'Home. Gone. Holocaust in Trondheim' shares the personal stories of some of the Jews who were murdered during the Holocaust. A poignant film shows interviews with survivors. Outside, there's an uplifting exhibition about Norwegian Jews' sporting achievements. Around the city, look out for several **Stolperstine**, brass blocks in the ground placed to remember victims of Nazi ideology.

An Evening in Solsiden

EAT, DRINK AND BE MERRY

Translating as 'the sunny side', the former shipyard warehouses of **Solsiden** now invite an evening of merriment. Solsiden sits to the east of Bakklandet and, starting at Bakke bru (Bakke Bridge), there are several places to grab a drink and a bite. **Cowsea** has sushi, burgers and killer cocktails, plus a DJ until the wee hours on Saturdays. Mustard-yellow **Café Løkka** is a veritable Trondheim institution and

WHY I LOVE TRONDHEIM

Gemma Graham, writer

Walkable, welcoming and dripping with Norwegian history, Trondheim is my favourite city in Norway. From the imposing but reachable hilltop fortress of Kristiansten Festning to craft beer in the friendly basement bar ØX Tap Room, Trondheim has a top-to-bottom easygoing charm that draws you in to discover more about its nation-defining backstory while feeling like a home away from home.

And nothing drew me into Trondheim's fold quite like turning out to cheer the parades along the city's streets on Constitution Day. Though the wind howled and the rain pelted down on the revellers – most wearing a *bunad,* the national dress – I was warmly welcomed to join the celebrations as we all defied the elements with ice cream and shouts of *'hipp hipp hurra!'*.

 WHERE TO EAT IN TRONDHEIM

Grano
Outstanding Italian pizza in a busy corner spot close to the train station. €€

To Rom og Kjøkken
Impeccable service and dishes crafted with locally sourced ingredients. Choose three, five or seven courses. €€€

Fagn
Stellar chefs conjure magical meals in the Michelin-starred restaurant and the Bib Gourmand-rated bistro upstairs. €€€

BEST CRAFT BEER BARS

Habitat
A foliage-festooned bar that pulls craft beer by Trondheim's own Monkey Brew and more from its 26 taps. Great pizza too.

ØX Tap Room
A subterranean beer den that thrums with an eclectic mix of patrons keen to taste the vast selection of house brews.

Trondhjem Mikrobryggeri
There's a beer hall vibe at this Trondheim favourite with up to eight of its own tipples on tap.

NOWACZYK/SHUTTERSTOCK ©

Waterfall, Ilabekken (p229)

has burgers, salads and sandwiches, plus milkshakes and cocktails. Further on in Solsiden proper, there are several so-so chain restaurants around the dock. Instead, make a bee-line for **Una Pizzeria e Bar** for *deliziosa* Italian favourites.

Sweat It Out in a Floating Sauna
SAUNAS, SWIMMING AND MUSIC

To the east of the city, **HAVET** is a fun four-in-one venue, with saunas, bathing, events and a bar. Book in for a 2½-hour sauna session (either shared or private) in one of the five ARK saunas, which have sea pools, an outdoor shower and a jetty to jump in the harbour and cool off. For a different sort of evening, join a weekend DJ sauna session in the 100-person Árdna sauna. There's also a bathing jetty with a diving tower. The aesthetic here is very much 'industrial cool' (the venue overlooks a scrap yard), but you'll be too busy getting a sweat on to care.

Beyond Trondheim

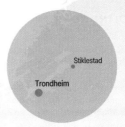

Stiklestad

Trondheim

In the fertile farmland around Trondheim, you'll taste the region's abundant flavours and uncover a defining moment in Norway's history.

Not far from Trøndelag's capital lies Stiklestad. The location would still be best known for the lush surrounding farmland were it not for an 11th-century clash that would steer Norway out of the Viking Age, into the Middle Ages and towards the monarchy we know it as today. Indeed, many historians tout this as the place where modern Norway became possible.

Further north, the region's farms really are the main event. The Inderøy peninsula in the Innherred district is the perfect place to ease off the gas and meander along the Golden Road (Den Gyldne Omvei). This scenic route guides you to local food producers, farm shops, art galleries and picturesque churches, and its forgiving topography makes it perfect for cycling.

A Pilgrimage to Stiklestad
NORWAY'S MOST FAMOUS BATTLEGROUND

Few places are more significant to the story of Norway's creation than **Stiklestad**. The battle that took place here in 1030, in which King Olav II was slain, set events in motion that would lead to the end of the Viking Age and the Christianisation of the country under one king. The **Stiklestad National Culture Centre** has an indoor exhibition, 'Stiklestad 1030', which puts the events leading up to the battle and soon afterwards in context, with Viking-era finds, life-size dioramas and a sinister soundtrack.

Outside, the site unfolds like an open-air museum. **Stiklestad Church** was built in the 12th century over the spot where Olav was killed (as legend has it). Inside, frescoes by Norwegian artist Alf Rolfsen depict the battle story. The buildings in the **Stiklestadir** area – including a replica Viking longhouse and a guest loft – illustrate the transition from the Viking Age to the Middle Ages. The **folk museum** has an assemblage of buildings from the 1600s to the 1800s, including Molåna, an 18th-century *trønderloan* (long, narrow house) open as a cafe in the summer months.
(Continues on p233)

GETTING AROUND

For the Inderøy peninsula and the Golden Road, leave the E6 at Røra (signposted 'Den Gyldne Omvei') from the south. From the north, the turnoff is about 6km outside Steinkjer at Vist. The whole route around the peninsula covers about 50km. Røra is the closest train station, and there's a patchy bus service between Røra and Straumen; it's only slightly less patchy from Steinkjer. Download the AtB app for journeys and tickets.

Stiklestad is about 5km off the E6 at Verdal. By public transport, you can get as far as Verdal on the train from Trondheim or Steinkjer and then it's a straightforward but uninspiring 4.5km walk. (The sporadic bus service isn't helpful.) In a pinch, you can arrange a taxi at Verdal station, but it's a pricey option (150kr to 200kr).

☑ TOP TIP

Trains from Trondheim stop near, but not directly at, Stiklestad and Inderøy. Plan your route so you don't get stranded.

A detour off the E6 between Levanger and Steinkjer, the Golden Road (Den Gyldne Omvei) runs around the Inderøy peninsula, which has quality local food producers, farm shops, galleries and a gentle, pastoral landscape. Start off at **1 Røra Station**, having prearranged bike rental with Visit Innherred (en. visitinnherred.com). Cycle 8km partly alongside Borgenfjorden to Straumen, and stop in at **2 Nils Aas Kunstverksted**, a gallery sharing the story and works of one of Norway's most famous sculptors. Stroll around to **3 Muustrøparken**, a sculpture park with 10 of Aas' works (look out for *Ringkatta*). Afterwards, get back on your bike, heading north on the Rv761. After 4.5km, you'll reach **4 Gulburet**. This farm shop sells local produce such as cheese, honey and freshly baked bread, and the farm cafe has homely seating in the creaky-floored loft. Back on the Rv761, continue 7km to

5 Gangstad Gårdsysteri, a charming dairy with award-winning cheeses in the shop and rich creamy ice cream (try the chocolate dream flavour). For a tree-lined detour, cycle up to 12th-century **6 Hustad Church**; otherwise, continue for 11.5km on Nessetveien around to **7 Kjerknesvågen Kai**, a scenic marina that's home to the historic *jekt Pauline*. Cycle onwards for 2.5km to **8 Berg Gård**. This outstanding farm has a shop filled with local products, an Aquavit distillery (pick up a bottle here as a special souvenir), farm animals and elevated fjord views. For a special dinner, it's a steep climb up to **9 Øyna Kulturlandskapshotell**, which serves a seasonal menu showcasing the flavours of Inderøy in a dining room with unparalleled views across the fjord. Overnight in one of their luxurious rooms built into the hillside before travelling back to your start point in the morning.

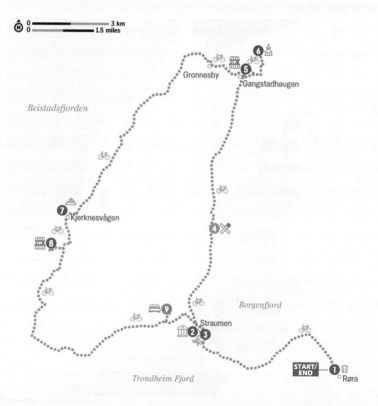

Gulburet

FROM KING TO SAINT

After setting out on a Viking voyage at age 12, Olav Haraldsson returned determined to Christianise Norway and become king. Olav succeeded, but opposition from his enemies forced him to flee in 1028. When he returned to win back power in 1030, his men were outnumbered at Stiklestad two to one by a peasant army allied to the Danish king. After Olav was slain, his body was carried to Nidaros (now Trondheim), and people soon began to report miracles wherever he had been. Upon opening his coffin a year after his death, it was reported that Olav's body hadn't deteriorated. He was canonised, and from then on, he was known as St Olav.

(Continued from p231)

Throughout the year, you can wander around outside for free, but June to August is the liveliest time to visit, with crafts and family activities during 'Viking Summer', and **Olsokdagene** (Olsok Days), a cultural festival in July. If you need accommodation, you can stay at the **Scandic Stiklestad**, which forms most of the National Culture Centre building.

Røros

● Røros
✪ OSLO

GETTING AROUND

It's possible to fly from Oslo in under an hour, but Røros is a scenic 2½-hour train journey from Trondheim (a little longer but similarly picturesque by bus), which makes it feasible to visit on a day trip. The drive from Trondheim is around two hours.

Set against bleak, partially forested fells around 150km southeast of Trondheim, enchanting Røros is a UNESCO World Heritage Site with uniquely unusual monuments.

For more than three centuries, it was the epicentre for copper mining in Norway, and the riches afforded to the mine owners were ploughed into the town in the form of attractive wood-clad homes and an incongruously large church. As you wander past the immaculate 18th-century houses secreting cafes, galleries and artists' workshops, you'd be forgiven for thinking it was an open-air museum.

Its pretty buildings stand in sharp relief against the protected slag heap of the former copperworks, now part of a fascinating museum telling the story of the back-breaking graft on which the town's fortunes were built. Røros may be pretty, but you'll need sturdy shoes – in common with its industrial origins, some of its streets are fairly rugged.

☑ TOP TIP

Røros' main sights are concentrated over only a few streets (Kjerkgata and Mørkstugata are the two main ones), and they're very easy to walk between, but there's quite an incline to get up to Smelthytta from the train and buses, which arrive at the foot of the hill.

Unearthing the History of Røros' Copperworks

MINING HERITAGE AT RØROSMUSEET SMELTHYTTA

You won't have to look far to find traces of Røros' industrial heritage. At the top of Mørkstugata is **Hyttklokka** (the shift clock), the bell that once pealed to signal the start and end of the work day at the smeltery. Head over the road and across the open area known as **Malmplassen** (Ore Place) to **Rørosmuseet Smelthytta**, a cavernous museum and itself a former copper-smelting works that presents the 333-year-long history of copper mining in the town. Animated scale models and live demonstrations illustrate the arduous mining and smelting processes in detail.

Behind the museum building, cross a wooden bridge to reach the protected **Slegghaugan** (slag heap). The hulking, charcoal-grey dunes of smelting waste make for a bizarre heritage monument, but the climb to the top affords views over

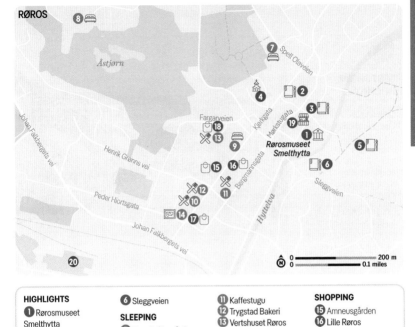

HIGHLIGHTS

1 Rørosmuseet
Smelthytta

SIGHTS

2 Hyttklokka
3 Malmplassen
4 Røros Kirke
5 Slegghaugan

6 Sleggveien

SLEEPING

7 Erzscheidergården
8 Røros Hotell
9 Vertshuset Røros

EATING

10 Grillhuset Røros

11 Kaffestugu
12 Trygstad Bakeri
13 Vertshuset Røros

**DRINKING &
NIGHTLIFE**

14 Røros
Kunstformidling

SHOPPING

15 Amneusgården
16 Lille Røros
17 Lysgaard Keramikk
18 Potteriet Røros
19 Røros Brukt & Antik

TRANSPORT

20 Røros Skysstasjon

the town. The track running between the river and slag heap
leads to **Sleggveien** (Slag Rd), a short lane of turf-roofed miners' cottages. Some are open to visitors on selected days during
the summer (check rorosmuseet.no for details), but their rustic facades present a glimpse of the past even on days when
they aren't open to the public.

A Mountain Church: Bergstadens Ziir

INSIDE A SYMBOL OF RØROS' RICHES

The 50m-high white and black tower of 1600-seat **Røros
Kirke** (Røros Church) stands tall as a symbol of the town's
fortunes in the 18th century. Completed in 1784, the church,
also known as Bergstadens Ziir ('mountain church'), is open
for a few hours each Saturday when you can see its white
and powder-blue interior. There are portraits of notable figures in the town's history and two organs (a baroque organ
dating from 1742 and a 2012 Berg and Ryde instrument). The

BEST SHOPS IN RØROS

Lille Røros
Cosy shop brimming with colourful homewares, gifts, paintings and accessories up wooden steps on Kjerkgata.

Lysgaard Keramikk
A rainbow of trippy ceramic plates, cups, candleholders, vases and ornaments in an unexpectedly large shop.

Røros Brukt & Antik
A treasury of antique and secondhand curios, ceramics, glassware and furniture inside a 19th-century Røros house.

Amneusgården
Gifts and trifles, some Røros themed, as well as toys and local history books in the former premises of venerable bookshop Amnéus' Boghandel.

ADELHEID SMITT/ALAMY STOCK PHOTO ©

Røros

mining company's logo features on the royal box, making it one of the few churches in the country to advertise its sponsor.

Outside to the left of the church is the **family vault** of Peder Hiort, a wealthy managing director of Røros Copper Works in the 18th century and a major donor towards the church's construction.

A Winter Market by Royal Decree

SHOPPING AND CULTURE AT RØROSMARTNAN

Travel to Røros in late February and you'll be joining 70,000 others for five days of trade, good food, storytelling, folk dancing and hearty revelry. The **Rørosmartnan** winter market has taken place since 1854, following a royal decree by King Oscar I. Between the second-last Tuesday in February until the following Saturday (originally Friday), more than 200 stallholders line Kjerkgata, Mørkstugata and the surrounding streets. Some revellers still arrive from far and wide by sleigh, just as traders did in the early days.

 WHERE TO STAY IN RØROS

Erzscheidergården
Exceptional service and a break-feast of local produce in a tastefully rustic 17th-century hotel. €€

Vertshuset Røros
Individually styled period rooms over two buildings (one a former wool factory) halfway up Kjerkgata. €€

Røros Hotell
Comfortable rooms, swimming pools and a playground make this large hotel a great choice for families. €€€

Predictably, beds in this little town are like gold dust during the market. If you can't find a place to stay, visit on a day trip by train or bus from Trondheim.

Drawing Inspiration in Røros

WORKSHOPS AND ART GALLERIES

Some notable Norwegian artists – most famously Harald Sohlberg – have captured picturesque Røros in their artworks. Though not an artists' community in the traditional sense, the town has a strong artistic tradition, with many galleries and workshops crammed into its narrow streets.

Occupying part of the former Brødrene Krogs Ullvarefabrikk (woollen factory), **Potteriet Røros** crafts artisan tableware inspired by traditional designs from the region, with more modern pieces glazed in weathered-copper green. **Lysgaard Keramikk** is owned by Per Lysgaard, whose ceramic creations range from brightly coloured tableware to alien-like forms, ceramic hats, mosaics and underwater-themed pieces.

Røros Kunstformidling is a traditional gallery in a huge corner spot at the foot of Kjerkgata that sells works by established and local artists, blankets by Røros Tweed and other local textiles. **Kunst og Kaos**, a smaller gallery on Mørkstugata, showcases works by contemporary artists such as Julie Ebbing.

BEST PLACES TO EAT IN RØROS

Trygstad Bakeri
Satisfy your sweet tooth with a wedge of cake or fill up from the selection of pizzas. €

Kaffestugu
Eat tasty staples such as *smørbrød* (an open sandwich) and hearty soups in a charming muralled dining room. €€

Vertshuset Røros
An elegant restaurant serving locally sourced produce, such as reindeer entrecote with Røros mushrooms. €€€

Grillhuset Røros
In a former butcher shop, this esteemed restaurant serves a seasonal three-course menu using quality local meats. €€€

Trygstad Bakeri

DAVE AND SIGRUN TOLLERTON/ALAMY STOCK PHOTO ©

Namsos

Namsos

OSLO

GETTING AROUND

Namsos Airport, 4km east of the centre, is served by Widerøe flights (30 minutes) from Trondheim Værnes Airport. Regular bus service runs from Steinkjer (1¼ hours), with train connections to Trondheim S (two hours). Check atb.no for times. Namsos is on the Fv17, which branches off the E6 about 14km north of Steinkjer.

Namsos is generally flat and easy to walk around, but it's strung out along the water's edge, so you might want to get a bus to and from the museums. Bus 609 stops at or near each of them. Download the AtB app to plan your journey and buy tickets.

☑ TOP TIP

Namsos stretches out along approximately 5km of the Namsenfjord's shoreline, but the main centre is clustered around the Namsos Storsenter shopping mall to the east, with the express boat quay, bus station, hotels, shops and restaurants in the surrounding streets. The airport and campground are to the west.

With a population of about 15,000, Namsos is a diminutive city, but because it was founded in 1845, it has played a prodigious role in the timber industry and, perhaps surprisingly for its size, Norway's rock music scene. In its short lifespan, Namsos has suffered two devastating fires, in the late 19th century and a bombing campaign during WWII. As a result, the city's architecture isn't conventionally inspiring, but its position at the mouth of the Namsen River, with the Namsenfjord stretching out beyond, is far more easy on the eye.

Namsos is the primary hub for the surrounding towns and villages in the Namdalen district. It's well stocked with shops, and there's a cultural centre, a contemporary art gallery and a few small museums. For visitors, it makes a good base to explore the further reaches of the beguiling Namdalen coastline and its surrounding nature.

Folk Tales & Timber

LOCAL HISTORY IN NAMSOS' MUSEUMS

Uncover Namdalen's history at Namsos' local museums. **Namdalsmuseet** is an open-air collection of 24 houses from around the region, including a schoolhouse and a blacksmith's forge. For a few weeks in summer, there are guides, open houses and family activities. The site is open and strollable year-round, but you'll have to book ahead if you'd like a tour out of season.

Hop on the 609 bus to Buret and then walk for about 850m to reach the niche **Norsk Sagbruksmuseum** (Norwegian Sawmill Museum). Before WWII, there were seven sawmills around Namsos; this one, Spillum Dampsag & Høvler, had its own joinery and was the first in Norway to make prefabricated houses. Outside, you can see the drying building and sawmill. The visitor centre has displays about the industry, the sawmill's founder and how the timber was floated down the river to be processed before being shipped off for sale to northern Norway, for a time by the *jekt Anna Karoline*. Wander around on your own, or join one of the guided tours.

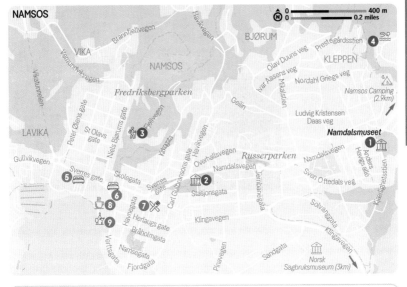

NAMSOS

0 — 400 m
0 — 0.2 miles

HIGHLIGHTS
① Namdalsmuseet

SIGHTS
② Kunstmuseet Nord-Trøndelag

ACTIVITIES
③ Bjørumsklompen
④ Oasen

SLEEPING
⑤ Scandic Rock City

⑥ Tinos Hotell

EATING
⑦ Mintage Sushi
see ⑥ Tinos Restaurant

DRINKING & NIGHTLIFE
⑧ Hamstad Bakericafe
⑨ Onkel Oskar

Culture on the Coast

CONTEMPORARY ART AT KUNSTMUSEET NORD-TRØNDELAG

A stark white vaulted space inside Kulturhus i Namsos (Namsos Cultural Centre), **Kunstmuseet Nord-Trøndelag** (Nord-Trøndelag Art Museum) shows rotating exhibitions from its collection and hosts shows by contemporary artists such as Anja Carr. It has an excellent shop with prints, postcards and books, and the stylish drinkery **Barrique Vinbar** opens in conjunction with events. Kulturhus also has a theatre and a library where staff can offer basic tourist information. It's near the AMFI shopping mall about 1km from Namsos Storsenter.

Namsos from Above

A SHORT CITY HIKE

For big Namsos views, take a short but sweet hike up mid-city mountain **Bjørumsklompen** (114m). There are a couple of ways to summit, and both routes take about 20 to 30 minutes. The first route is signposted with red Den Norske Turistforening (DNT) 'T's, starting at the Scandic Rock City and heading via Skolegata to a wooded trail and then veering up some precarious, rocky steps. The other route is up a tree-lined asphalt

BEST PLACES TO EAT & DRINK

Hamstad Bakericafe
Oven-fresh bread and heavenly buns, pastries and cakes from this long-established bakery. €

Mintage Sushi
A busy Nordic-Asian fusion restaurant serving tasty sushi in a pared-back monochrome dining room. €€

Tinos Restaurant
Italian favourites such as pizza, lasagne al forno and tiramisu downstairs at Tinos Hotell. €€

Onkel Oskar
Inviting Ye Olde English–style pub with leather seating inside and a breezy outdoor terrace.

NAMSOS: ROCK CITY

Around Namsos, you'll see intriguing allusions to rock music: the Scandic Rock City, a sculpture of a guitar player on Kirkegata and even a mural on the REMA1000 supermarket that declares, 'We built this city on rock and roll'. After WWII, many young men left to find work as sailors. Influenced by rock-and-roll artists such as Elvis and Little Richard, they returned and created a new sound: *Trønderrock*. Namsos produced several successful acts, and bands like Prudence became icons in Norway in the 1970s. The city's reputation as a hotbed for music has subsided, but you can learn more at **Trønderrockmuseet** inside Rock City (next to the Scandic) during summer.

Scandic Rock City

road with looming rocky cliffs at points – take the left fork up Fjellvegen from Kirkegata.

At the top, benches look out over the spread-out city, across the inky Namsenfjorden and towards the brooding distant mountains. There's a visitor logbook, boards with historic photos and a smart 2016-built glass-fronted pavilion with static binoculars to zoom in on the streets below. If you bring supplies, you can use a barbecue too.

Great Lengths
SWIM INSIDE A MOUNTAIN

While 'oasis' is stretching the bounds of reality a little, **Oasen** swimming pool is certainly one of the quirkiest places you'll take a dip. Built into an escarpment, this pool gives Bond-villain-lair vibes, and you can stare up at the bare mountain rock while you're doing a few lengths of backstroke. There's a 50m pool, diving tower, sauna, hot tub and a smaller heated pool for children. Book ahead for set 90-minute sessions through the Namsos Kommune website (namsos.kommune.no; search for Oasen Namsos), but it's an ideal rainy-day activity or a place to stretch out after a long journey.

 WHERE TO STAY IN NAMSOS

Namsos Camping	Tinos Hotell	Scandic Rock City
A basic but well-kept campsite with cabins next to a small swimming lake 4.5km from the town centre. €	A traditional, family-run hotel with spacious rooms and welcoming staff who go above and beyond. €€	Standard Scandic comforts with some understated rock-themed decor in a gleaming white cube by the mall. €€

Beyond Namsos

Leka
Rørvik
Sør-Gjæslingan
Namsos

Travel to centuries-old coastal communities and see the Earth's crust on a picturesque island formed 60 million years ago.

The prettiest parts of the Namdalen coastline lie beyond Namsos. The little port town of Rørvik was once a hub for trading in the late 19th and early 20th centuries. It's remained on the map in recent years thanks to its coastal museum in an incongruously modern building. It's also the gateway to the windswept protected fishing village of Sør-Gjæslingan.

Further up the coast is tiny but geologically outstanding Leka. Part of the Trollfjell UNESCO Global Geopark, Leka has 50 marked trails and Stone Age cave paintings. Because of the way it was tilted upwards when the European and North American continents separated 60 million years ago, it's possible to see the Earth's crust and mantle in places.

Namdalen's Coastal History
EXPLORING KYSTMUSEET NORVEG IN RØRVIK

Encompassing a collection of sites in and around **Rørvik**, **Kystmuseet Norveg** (Norwegian Coastal Museum) brings to life the history and culture of the Namdalen coast. The main site, **Norveg**, is a striking building jutting out into the harbour, its design reminiscent of gigantic sails. Inside, you'll find mixed exhibits covering 10,000 years of coastal history, a gallery with rotating exhibitions and a 2023-opened exhibition about salmon fishing.

Over the bridge from the main museum is **Berggården**, an elegant whitewashed 19th-century trading post and shop. A few of the rooms inside have been restored, and you can see them on a summertime guided tour – it's included with your ticket to Norveg.

Day-Tripping to Sør-Gjæslingan
A REMOTE PROTECTED FISHING VILLAGE

Now under the care of Kystmuseet Norveg, the protected former fishing village of **Sør-Gjæslingan** is a cluster of islands and skerries exposed to the whims of the Norwegian Sea about 50km southwest of Rørvik. Huddled together on the remote little archipelago is a collection of traditional

GETTING AROUND

By road, it takes around two hours on the Fv769 from Namsos to Rørvik including a hop on the Hofles–Lund ferry. It's about 2¾ hours from Namsos to Leka via Gutvik for the ferry.

Reliable Hurtigbåt (express boat) services running the Namsos–Rørvik–Leka (Skei) route are operated by Vidar Hop Skyssbåter (vidarhop.no) with at least one service a day in each direction. This route also stops at Sør-Gjæslingan on selected journeys during the summer – you need to phone the day before to confirm. Also phone in advance if you want to travel as far as Leka on weekends outside of high season.

There are no taxis or buses from the express boat quay on Leka, so if you don't have your own wheels you'll need to walk. You can hire bikes at hotel-restaurant Leka Brygge even if you're not staying there.

☑ TOP TIP

If you're visiting Leka for longer than a day, take supplies (especially in low season) because eating options are limited.

SASHA ALTERANT/SHUTTERSTOCK ©

Leka

BEST PLACES TO EAT & DRINK BEYOND NAMSOS

Kafé Norveg, Rørvik
Stop by the airy cafe at Kystmuseet Norveg for sandwiches, luxurious house-baked cakes and coffee. €

64° Nord, Rørvik
Filling pub fare such as juicy burgers and fish and chips in a stylish bar-restaurant inside Havnesenteret. €€

Café Flora, Leka
A little gem serving sandwiches and stone-baked pizzas in a pretty setting surrounded by farmland. €€

white-, yellow- and red-painted wooden buildings. Many of these were once packed with the fishers (up to 6000 of them), who gathered here in winter to take advantage of the rich pickings during bountiful seasons more than a century ago.

As well as guided boat trips run by Kystmuseet Norveg (which also stop at a fish farm), public boat schedules align to make day trips possible on weekends between late June and mid-August (either from Rørvik on Saturdays or Namsos on Sundays). You can wander around the rocky sea-soaked village at leisure, but its story is really brought to life on the 30-minute guided tour. Buy tickets in the period-styled shop, which also sells souvenirs and snacks. Several of the rustic *rorbuer* (fishers' cabins) are available to rent for short stays in summer. Book online at kystmuseetnorveg.no.

 WHERE TO STAY BEYOND NAMSOS

Kysthotellet Rørvik
Simple rooms, some with nature-themed feature walls, a five-minute walk from the express boat quay. €€

Leka Motell og Camping
Options include tent pitches, apartments, family cabins and stone cottages. Motorhome spots have top views. €

Leka Brygge
Bright, modern apartments and slick, glass-fronted cabins on a private quay with boat and bike rental. €€

Leka on Two Wheels

CYCLING THE ISLAND

With a diverse but relatively flat landscape, little **Leka** is perfect for exploring on two wheels. From the port, a 28km gently undulating, circular route takes you past all of the island's highlights, plus many trailheads for a short hike along the way. It's best done clockwise.

Drop into **Leka Steinsenter** (Leka Stone Centre; at Leka Motell og Camping), which has a small free museum with information about the island's formation and geology. Further on, you can take a detour to **Årdalssand**, a secluded sweep of sand hidden down a farm track. You'll pass **Solsemhula** (Solsem Cave), which conceals a collection of Stone Age cave paintings, the first to be discovered in northern Europe. You can see them on a guided tour during July and August with **Leka Opplevelser**.

Continuing around the east side of the island, the terrain becomes more wild and prehistoric, a landscape of extraordinary red and yellow rocks that were once part of the Earth's interior. At the site of the **Ørnerovet** (eagle kidnapping), there's a marker high up on the mountain where, as the story goes, 3½-year-old Svanhild Hansen was deposited after being snatched by an eagle in 1932. Carry on along the road through the mountain-backed green pastureland. At Husby, hang a left to reach **Herlaugshaugen**, Norway's third-largest Viking burial mound. Continue and you'll reach **Skeisnesset** cultural landscape, an expanse of rocky, heather moorland crisscrossed with trails and grazed by sheep, with 6th-century burial mounds.

THE MIGHTY JEKT

For 400 years, Norway's coastal trade – mostly stockfish – was powered by speedy ships called *jekts*. You can see the world's only preserved Nordlandsjekt, *jekt Anna Karoline*, and learn about her predecessors at **Jektefartsmuseet** (p248) in Bodø.

BEST HIKES ON LEKA

Familieloypa
A family-friendly 1.5km circular route across Skeisnesset's heather moorland.

Løva on Solsem
A short, steep climb (just under 1km) through forest and up over bare rock for western Leka views.

MOHO
A fascinating, demanding 3km to-and-fro hike to see the Earth's mantle and crust.

Lekamøya from Haug
Reach the legend-inspiring mountain landmark on this varied, moderately tough 2km out-and-back route.

Herlaugsløypa
The big one on Leka: a challenging 11km circular route across the open mountain landscape.

THE GUIDE

BEYOND NAMSOS TRØNDELAG

Nordland

NORWAY'S GREATEST HITS

Nordland has the perfect mix of scenic drives, remote
islands, exciting wildlife and timeless coastal villages.

Nordland is where Norway narrows and
heads for the Arctic. In doing so, it relies on
two of northern Europe's most remarkable
roads. The Kystriksveien Coastal Route
unfurls along Norway's deeply textured
coastline, a triumph of human
imagination and engineer-
ing, with meandering coastal roads and ferries taking
you from one exquisite
North Sea view to the
next. The Arctic High-
way serves a similar
purpose, forging a path
across the Arctic Circle
and through a magical
landscape. Running be-
tween the two is one of Norway's largest icecaps, the wild
and glacier-filled Saltfjellet-Svartisen
National Park.

But so much of what makes Nordland
special happens along the coast. It begins
down south in the hinterland of Brøn-

nøysund, with charming Træna and Vega,
archipelagos better known to locals than
international travellers. Further north, the
Lofoten Islands rise into the sky in scenes
of astonishing natural grandeur, with idyllic villages perched upon the shore.
Put simply, Lofoten is extraor-
dinarily beautiful.
Vesterålen is at times a
match for the beauty of
its near neighbour, but
with many added ben-
efits: wildlife safaris, a
virtual rocket ride, dog-
sledding, a brilliant coastal hike and, at the end of
a road that once fell quiet,
there's lovely little Nyksund.
Nyksund is a quintessential star
of the Norwegian coast: beautifully
built, set in a magnificent landscape and
animated by a story of remarkable human
resilience and inspiration.

PETR SALINGER/SHUTTERSTOCK ©

THE MAIN AREAS

BODØ	**LOFOTEN ISLANDS**	**VESTERÅLEN**	**SALTFJELLET-SVARTISEN NATIONAL PARK**	**BRØNNØYSUND**
Culture and wild nature. p248	A magnificent archipelago. p251	Whale-watching and other adventures. p257	Glaciers at every turn. p264	Charming small-town Norway. p269

LAURI LOHI/SHUTTERSTOCK ©

Left: puffins (p258); above: Lofoten Islands (p251)

Find Your Way

Nordland occupies a long, narrow strip of land between the North Sea and the Swedish border. All routes between northern and southern Norway pass through Nordland.

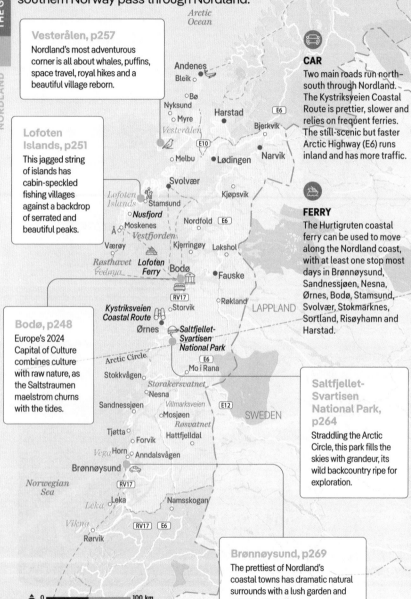

Vesterålen, p257
Nordland's most adventurous corner is all about whales, puffins, space travel, royal hikes and a beautiful village reborn.

Lofoten Islands, p251
This jagged string of islands has cabin-speckled fishing villages against a backdrop of serrated and beautiful peaks.

Bodø, p248
Europe's 2024 Capital of Culture combines culture with raw nature, as the Saltstraumen maelstrom churns with the tides.

CAR
Two main roads run north–south through Nordland. The Kystriksveien Coastal Route is prettier, slower and relies on frequent ferries. The still-scenic but faster Arctic Highway (E6) runs inland and has more traffic.

FERRY
The Hurtigruten coastal ferry can be used to move along the Nordland coast, with at least one stop most days in Brønnøysund, Sandnessjøen, Nesna, Ørnes, Bodø, Stamsund, Svolvær, Stokmarknes, Sortland, Risøyhamn and Harstad.

Saltfjellet-Svartisen National Park, p264
Straddling the Arctic Circle, this park fills the skies with grandeur, its wild backcountry ripe for exploration.

Brønnøysund, p269
The prettiest of Nordland's coastal towns has dramatic natural surrounds with a lush garden and restaurant nearby.

0 — 100 km
0 — 50 miles

Saltfjellet-Svartisen National Park (p264)

Plan Your Time

The linear nature of Nordland makes it easy to maintain momentum and cover a lot of ground in a short space of time.

Five Glorious Days

● Begin down south in **Brønnøysund** (p269), drive north along the **Kystriksveien Coastal Route** (p266), timing your arrival to coincide with the maelstrom at **Saltstraumen** (p249) on your way to **Bodø** (p248). From here, take the ferry to **Lofoten** (p251) and spend a couple of days driving to beautiful villages like Henningsvær, Nusfjord and Å, with a stop at Reine for Norway's best view.

Leave the Crowds Behind

● Stay overnight in **Brønnøysund** (p269), then spend a couple of days out in the soulful **Vega archipelago** (p271). Meander along the **Kystriksveien** (p266) for a couple of days, factoring in detours to **Saltfjellet-Svartisen National Park** (p264) and **Lovund** (p273). From **Bodø** (p248), drive to **Vesterålen** (p257) to look for **whales** (p257) and **puffins** (p258), before falling off the map at **Nyksund** (p260).

Seasonal Highlights

SPRING	SUMMER	AUTUMN	WINTER
A glorious time in northern Norway. Days are getting warmer, and locals have a real spring in their step with summer on the way.	The best time to travel in Nordland, with (usually) mild temperatures. Everything's open and it's your best chance for fine Lofoten days.	The last colour leaves the landscape as winter draws nearer. Quieter roads and clear days early in the season can be a winning combination.	Bad weather is never far away, but clear winter days can be superb. Most roads remain open, but whale-watching is less frequent in Vesterålen.

Bodø

Bodø

OSLO

GETTING AROUND

The train station, ferry quay and Hurtigruten terminal are at the eastern end of the harbour, while Svolvær-bound express boats leave from Sentrumsterminalen, close to the Scandic Havet hotel.

Local buses serve Bodø's airport, about 3.5km from the city centre, as well as the area's main attractions; download the Billett Nordland app to buy bus tickets. If you're heading to Saltstraumen, public buses 200 and 300 will take you there in about 40 minutes, but it can be tricky to time these with the tides. Having a car means you're less at the mercy of infrequent or delayed public transport.

☑ TOP TIP

It can be fiendishly windy in and around Bodø, especially between October and March. If you're visiting Saltstraumen, it's worth keeping an eye on the wind forecast, as well as checking the tides, as both the bridge and the trail down to the waterside are very exposed.

From the waterfront at Bodø, the Lofoten Islands rise from the horizon like jagged ramparts from some mythical ocean kingdom. But there's more to Bodø than a gateway to lovely Lofoten.

Bathed in the clear light of the north, Bodø has a superb location at the end of many roads. This is as far north as Norway's rail network reaches, and it's the northernmost terminus of the Kystriksveien Coastal Route, surely one of Europe's most beautiful drives. Not far away lie both Lofoten and the the legendary Saltstraumen, the world's largest tidal maelstrom.

The city itself emerges from the shadow of its surroundings with an appeal all its own. Built in the aftermath of WWII, the town centre has in recent years acquired an award-winning concert house and library that will form the centrepiece of Bodø's time as European Capital of Culture 2024.

Fish and Flying Machines

JOURNEY INTO BODØ'S PAST

Close to Bodø's airport, you'll find two impressive museums that tell in-depth stories of trade, exploration and travel in northern Norway and beyond.

The newest, **Jektefartsmuseet** (Norwegian Jekt Trade Museum), opened in 2019. On the craggy shores of Saltfjorden at Bodøsjøen, the dark wooden building shields the *Anne Karoline*, the last of the trade *jekts* (wide wooden cargo vessels) in Nordland. For four centuries, these *jekts* carried stockfish (p253) from the north to Bergen. At the time, this cargo was worth more to the country's economy than oil is today. Transporting this precious commodity came at great risk: the museum tells some harrowing tales of lives lost at sea.

A kilometre closer to the centre, the **Norsk Luftfartsmuseum** (Norwegian Aviation Museum) is a vast propeller-shaped building that celebrates the history of civil and

BODØ

SIGHTS
1 Norsk Luftfartsmuseum

SLEEPING
2 Scandic Havet
3 Smarthotel
4 Thon Hotel Nordlys

EATING
5 Craig Alibone

DRINKING & NIGHTLIFE
6 Hundholmen Brygghus

BEST PLACES TO EAT IN BODØ

Craig Alibone
Patisserie by day and champagne bar by night, this chic cafe has decadent artisan cakes, truffles and macarons. €

Hundholmen Brygghus
Huge menu of beers at this inviting, dimly lit gastropub that serves classic pub meals and Norwegian dishes. €€

Kafe Kjelen
On a headland overlooking the maelstrom, this gorgeous cafe serves *møsbrømetse* (flatbread with brown cheese, sugar and melted butter) and more. €€€

military flight in Norway. The 10,000-sq-metre ode to aviation is strung with aircraft including the iconic Spitfire, and exhibits cover pioneering flights such as those undertaken by Hans Dons, Norway's first pilot, and Roald Amundsen's 1926 airship exploration of the North Pole. You can get to grips with the physics of flying, sit in a Cessna and climb a retired control tower to look for planes coming in to land at the airport.

Saltstraumen Whirlpools

THE WORLD'S MOST POWERFUL MAELSTROM

As you drive along the Fv17 through the farmlands and pine forests south of Bodø, there's nothing to suggest that the world's largest maelstrom lies just ahead at **Saltstraumen**. Even as you arrive at the 150m-wide strait that connects Saltenfjorden with Skjerstadfjorden, everything seems calm. But don't be fooled: this is one of Norway's most unlikely natural phenomena.

The **maelstrom** happens every six hours or so, whenever the tide turns. Before you travel here, pick up a table with tide timings from the tourist office in Bodø or check online. First impressions matter, so, assuming you've arrived at the right time, park the car, then climb Saltstraumbrua bridge on foot and wait.

 WHERE TO STAY IN BODØ

Smarthotel
Basic and compact rooms with chic, pared-back stylings in a budget hotel opposite the train station. €€

Thon Hotel Nordlys
Some of the comfortable rooms at this harbourside hotel have Northern-Lights-themed decor and Nespresso. €€

Scandic Havet
It's the standard Scandic offering in this snow-white tower, but the rooftop bar is perfect for sea-gazing. €€€

EUROPEAN CAPITAL OF CULTURE 2024

Bolstered by Stormen, the world-class culture house and library, plus an already packed annual program of cultural offerings including rock and classical music festivals, Bodø became the first European Capital of Culture north of the Arctic Circle in 2024. The year-long program, **ARCTIculation**, encompasses over 600 events, from Sami theatre and art to local foodie experiences and a festival of light in winter. You'll see pop-up art and culture in the city itself, while Nordland's unique scenery will form the backdrop for many other events. Organisers are keen to keep up the cultural offerings long after the curtain falls on Bodø 2024. Check bodo2024.no for updates.

Saltstraumen maelstrom (p249)

As the tide turns, you'll start to notice smaller eddies, then tiny whirlpools form and join. As momentum gathers, sometimes all of a sudden, the channel becomes a roiling, churning watery mass as 400 million cu metres of water cascade through the channel. As a natural occurrence, the intensity of the whirlpools varies. Should you be unlucky enough to hit an off day, the whole experience may recall little more than the water swirling around your bath plug. But at its best, it's a thrilling spectacle. When this happens, having seen the scale of the maelstrom, you should have time to head down to the shore for the more immediate thrill of a water-level view.

To really experience the sheer power of Saltstraumen, **Stella Polaris** (stella-polaris.no) and **Explore Salten** (explore salten.no) run RIB tours to the strait from Bodø, zipping past looming mountains and, if you're lucky, beneath a soaring sea eagle or two en route. These vessels' powerful motors enable the skipper to deftly dart around the churning water for the most adrenaline-pumping way to experience the phenomenon.

Lofoten Islands

Lofoten Islands

⬦OSLO

Welcome to one of the most beautiful places on earth. From the moment you first sight them across the water, Lofoten's craggy silhouettes seem too beautiful to be true. Like some mythical Tolkienesque natural fortress, the impossibly high mountains rise steeply from the shore like a series of mirages.

Steeped in the fishing traditions of Norway's storied coastal communities, Lofoten isn't just about astonishing natural grandeur. Clinging to the narrow shore and deep valleys are some of Norway's most beautiful hamlets, with Viking histories, hiking trails and a pretty harbour lined with colourful wooden buildings and great racks of cod, salted and dried, that lend a strange beauty to many already-spectacular scenes. And although the views are sometimes obscured by the dark storms of the Atlantic, Lofoten never loses its drama or its wild beauty. Spend as long here as you possibly can.

Take a Slow Boat to Lofoten

CROSS THE WATER TO PERFECTION

You could drive to the Lofoten Islands, but everyone should take the **boat** at least once in their lives. That's because the approach by water is one of the most beautiful you can imagine. The experience you have can depend on the route, but some things remain unchanged: on a clear day, the Lofoten Islands seem impossibly high and jagged, as if they're an apparition of a Norwegian Atlantis with spires and ramparts rising from the very ocean itself. When the sun is in the west, the shape of the islands is accentuated by their profile in silhouette. And when the sun is behind you in the east, it often picks out the detail of colourful houses clinging to the shore. Either way, it's one of the great boat journeys in Europe.

There are three main routes from the mainland to Lofoten. From Bodø, there's the foot-passenger express ferry to Svolvær (3½ hours), or a car ferry to Moskenes (3½ hours) via Røst and Værøy. Another option is the summer-only Skutvik–Svolvær car ferry (2½ hours). And, of course, the Hurtigruten coastal

GETTING AROUND

Lofoten's main islands are linked by bridges or tunnels. Remarkably, given the terrain, most roads stick to sea level without any scary sections. Having your own vehicle makes exploration so much easier as bus services anywhere off the E10 are infrequent at best.

Buses do run the entire E10 from Fiskebøl–Melbu ferry in the north to Å at the road's end in the southwest. The most useful service is the 23-760, which shuttles across the islands several times a day. Plan trips online at reisnordland.no/lofoten.

Tourist offices sell the *Hjulgleder*, an excellent Lofoten cycling guide, with handy pull-out maps.

☑ TOP TIP

For something really special, plan to be here when the midnight sun bathes Lofoten in perpetual daylight (28 May to 14 July), or the polar night when the Northern Lights are always a possibility (5 December to 7 January).

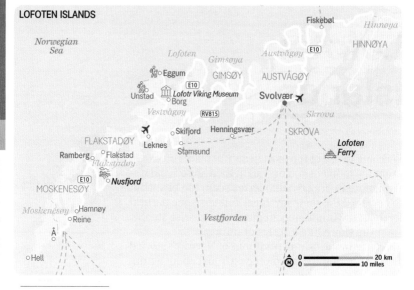

LOFOTEN ISLANDS

Norwegian Sea

Fiskebøl

Hinnøya

HINNØYA

Lofoten

Gimsøya

Austvågøy

E10

Eggum

GIMSØY

AUSTVÅGØY

Unstad

Lofotr Viking Museum

E10

Borg

Vestvågøy

RV815

Svolvær ✈

Skrova

Skifjord

Henningsvær

SKROVA

FLAKSTADØY

Leknes

Stamsund

Lofoten Ferry

Ramberg

Flakstad

Flakstadøy

MOSKENESØY

E10

Nusfjord

Moskenesøy

Hamnøy

Reine

Vestfjorden

Å

Hell

N

0 — 20 km
0 — 10 miles

BEST LOFOTEN FESTIVALS

Codstock
Henningsvær goes gaga for fish in mid-May, with three days of cooking, fishing and sea shanties by visiting musicians.

Constitution Day
The people of Lofoten are very proud of their unique identity, and on 17 May, locals dress in their traditional finery for parties and public celebrations.

World Cod Fishing Championships
Every year in March, Svolvær's best fisherfolk take to the water and you can enjoy fishy themed activities and meals around town.

ferry passes through Lofoten on its daily journeys, stopping at Bodø, Stamsund, Svolvær and Sortland (Vesterålen).

One final thing to note. If the weather's poor, it may not be worth making the journey. Storm clouds can make a spectacular photographic backdrop, but seas can be very rough on the crossing.

Scale Svolværgeita

SVOLVÆR'S BEST VANTAGE POINT

Most visitors to Svolvær are happy just to sip a coffee or cocktail and take in the view from a cafe overlooking the harbour. And there's nothing wrong with that. But if Lofoten's soaring backdrop inspires you to get high, then consider **Svolværgeita**.

Nicknamed 'The Goat' because its two granite spires resemble a goat's horns, Svolværgeita is visible from all over Svolvær and the view from up top adorns every second postcard on sale in town. In summer, you can enjoy the view yourself, as long as you have a head for heights and half a day to dedicate to the experience.

We strongly recommend taking a guide: try Kabelvåg-based **Northern Alpine Guides**. If you decide to go it alone, walk northeast along the E10 towards Narvik. After passing the marina, turn left on Nyveien, then double back on Øvreværveien,

 WHERE TO STAY IN SVOLVÆR

Fast Hotel Svolvær
Rooms are spartan, but you can't quibble with the quayside location for this self-check-in budget option. €

Svinøya Rorbuer
This collection of contemporary and traditional *rorbuer* across Svinøyabrua is some of Lofoten's best. €€€

Thon Hotel Lofoten
Encased in glass, this stylish harbourside hotel has fabulous views from the upper floors and binoculars in every room. €€€

then left on Blåtindveien. The trailhead is just beyond the kids' basketball court. It's a steep climb but well worth it to have Svolvær, the fjord and the distant mountains laid out at your feet. We can't recommend that you follow in the footsteps of many and leap between the two spires, but that doesn't stop people from ignoring this advice.

For even better views, you could climb beyond Svolvær-geita for another 30 minutes to the summit of Fløya (590m).

Drive from Village to Village

DISCOVER THE PERFECT LOFOTEN VIEWPOINT

Nothing whispers Lofoten quite like rows of vividly painted *rorbuer* (fishers' cabins) clustered around rocky shorelines and small harbours with boats bobbing down below. Whatever else you do while here, dedicate at least a couple of days to just driving every meandering road you can find, taking every detour available to find your favourite village view. What follows are our greatest hits, but this still leaves plenty for you to discover.

At the end of a road that barely seems to fit between the steep rock walls and the fjord, happening **Henningsvær** isn't just a pretty face, though it's certainly that too. Arranged more or less in a 'U' around its long, narrow harbour, the village tumbles with stylish boutiques and coffee shops and has plenty of spots to stop for a photo op. Beyond the harbour, though, lies what could be the most picturesque football pitch in the world. **Henningsvær Stadium** is at the end of Hellandsøya, its floodlit grounds completely open to the elements, with rocky islets providing an otherworldly view beyond the sidelines.

On the island of Flakstadøy, **Nusfjord** is another, albeit very different, Lofoten treasure. The road off the E10 takes in some superb scenery, and after 6km you'll arrive at Nusfjord, one of the loveliest villages in Norway's north. Sheltered from the sea and tucked away in the lee of high hills, nearly 40 oxblood-red wooden buildings – *rorbuer,* a cod-liver-oil factory, an old sawmill – encircle Nusfjord's tiny harbour. At the closed southwestern end of the harbour, climb the rocky slope for the classic Nusfjord vantage point. Back down in the village, stick your nose inside the century-old country store with its vintage cans, bottles and boxes.

Down south on Moskenesøy, the view from the E10 just south of **Reine** might just be one of the world's most spectacular: fantastical mountains, colourful fishing cabins, deeply textured rocks and ice-blue seas; there's a car park to enable safe stopping.

STOCKFISH 101

All across Lofoten, you'll see row upon row of huge wooden racks that are used to dry cod and create *tørrfisk* (stockfish). Once the lifeblood of the local economy, this staple is still produced using centuries-old methods. The cod is cut and hung out on the racks in February, where it's left exposed to Lofoten's salty winds for almost four months until May, when it's taken indoors to mature for a further two or three months before being sorted according to quality for various markets.

To see what all of the fuss is about, Svolvær's **Børsen** is an adapted stockfish warehouse turned fine-dining restaurant with stockfish on the menu. **Lofotomat**, in Henningsvær, is another fine option. In Å, there's also the **Lofoten Tørrfiskmuseum**.

WHERE TO STAY BEYOND SVOLVÆR

Moskenesstraumen Camping
This wonderful clifftop campground, just south of Å, has flat, grassy pitches between the rocks and cabins. €

Nusfjord Rorbuer
The simple *rorbuer* here are faithful representations of the traditional fishing cabin; they're all comfortable. €€

Eliassen Rorbuer
A terrific collection of 26 *rorbuer* in Hamnøy, close to Reine, with refurbished interiors; some have great views. €€

LUC KOHNEN/SHUTTERSTOCK ©

WHY I LOVE LOFOTEN

Anthony Ham, writer

Unlike Norway's world-famous fjords, Lofoten has a wild and untamed beauty about it. There's the brooding rock walls rising abruptly from the shore, the tempestuous sea encircling the archipelago, the quiet backcountry hikes. Glorious in perfect sunshine, Lofoten takes on a whole new character when a storm builds offshore, swirls to conceal an icebound summit or buffets the tight huddle of houses around any village harbour. Beyond Lofoten lies the North Sea, and the islands' inhabitants have always been at the mercy of the elements. To really understand Lofoten life, I'm so glad to have seen its many moods.

Lofoten Islands (p251)

And at the southernmost tip of Moskenesøy, **Å** (sometimes written as **Å i Lofoten**) is the kind of place that postcards were made for, with bleak, soaring rock faces looming over picturesque turf-topped cabins. There are many reasons to linger here, but the bakery, in a building dating back to 1844, serves utterly divine *kanelsnurr* (cinnamon scrolls) that taste every bit as good as their lovely name sounds.

Meet the Vikings of Lofoten

IMMERSE YOURSELF IN VIKING LORE

With its isolated harbours and fortress-like mountains, the Lofoten Islands seem custom-made for Viking sagas. Thankfully, there's a museum that tells that story wonderfully.

On a hilltop high above a bend in the E10 14km from Leknes on **Vesvågøy**, the **Lofotr Viking Museum** transports you a millennium back in time to the golden era of the Viking Age. Why here? Because in 1981, archaeologists discovered a remarkable, 83m-long chieftain's longhouse at nearby Borg. It was the largest of its kind ever discovered in Scandinavia.

The exhibition in the main museum building recounts the unexpected discovery and showcases some of the bejewelled

 WHERE TO STAY BEYOND SVOLVÆR

Henningsvær Bryggehotell
A top-notch heritage hotel overlooking the harbour, with cosy rooms and classy soft-grey decor. €€€

Nyvågar Rorbuhotell
At Storvågan, Nyvågar has snazzy seafront cottages. The *rorbuer* are attractive and fully equipped. €€€

The Tide
Well-furnished *rorbuer* with contemporary interiors and a small, ultra-stylish hotel in Sørvågen. €€€

treasures and artefacts that were discovered along with the building, among them gold-foil amulets, jewellery and ceramics. But the real highlight awaits you inside the replica long-house, where costumed guides bring the Viking era to life, demonstrating traditional techniques in weaving and knitting. There's a 1.5km trail on-site, leading past farm animals and down to the water's edge, where there's a replica Viking ship.

Email the museum in advance to book into a Viking-themed feast: an evening of food and storytelling inside the longhouse. Or time your visit for early August, when the museum hosts a Viking festival, with a market, concerts, games and more.

Hike from Unstad to Eggum

TREK A REMOTE HEADLAND

It's amazing how few vehicles deviate from the E10 path down through the heart of Lofoten. The road to **Unstad** is quiet, meandering along a gentle rise, past white wooden homes above the quiet fjord waters. And if the road is quiet, it's nothing compared to the splendid 9km one-way hike (figure on two hours).

Both Unstad and **Eggum** are tiny settlements that crouch along Lofoten's western Atlantic shore, unprotected from off-shore winds. It's a mostly flat trail, save for a slightly tricky section where you may want to use the metal chain handrail to keep your balance. The views are wild and windswept, winding past several headlands, a solitary lighthouse, superb seascapes and the ruins of a fortress by the ocean. Around 1.5km before you reach Eggum, watch for the *Head* sculpture by Swiss artist Markus Raetz. Part of the *Skulpturlandskap* series, this extraordinary piece changes shape and takes on 16 different forms as you walk around it.

If your car is parked at Unstad, walk back the way you came to enjoy it all over again.

Artistic Lofoten

GO ON A GALLERY CRAWL

There are times when Lofoten can feel like one big artist's colony. Svolvær is a real centre for established art galleries and museums highlighting Norwegian and international artists alike. Right on Torget (the main square), **Nordnorsk Kunstsenteret** showcases the work of the region's best contemporary artists and runs the biennial **Lofoten International Art Festival (LIAF)**. Another private Svolvær gallery to check out is **Galleri Dagfinn Bakke**. Over in Storvågen, **Gallery Espolin** celebrates the life and works of one of Norway's

NEXT-BEST LOFOTEN VIEWS

After Reine, Nusfjord and Svolværgeita, these are some of the best views and vantage point on the islands.

Ramberg
An arc of white sand fronting a sparkling blue-green bay against a backdrop of snowcapped Arctic peaks on the north coast of Flakstadøy.

Flakstad
Flakstad's 18th-century onion-domed church is magnificent, especially against the darkened backdrop of a storm-thrashed Atlantic.

South from Å
Fantastic view of Værøy island with, if you're lucky, the mighty maelstroms created by tidal flows between the two islands. If you can't see them, take a boat excursion.

 WHERE TO EAT AROUND SVOLVÆR

Bacalao
A casual bar-restaurant on Svolvær's harbour with sandwiches, burgers and a filling fish soup. €€

Børsen
The speciality is Lofoten stockfish at Svolvær's top table, served in the atmospheric dining room on Svinøya. €€€

Havet Restaurant & Bar
Book in advance for this smart Sørvågen restaurant, which has a seafood-focused menu in The Tide hotel. €€€

OTHER LOFOTEN HIKES

Glomtind

Accessible off the E10-to-Henningsvær road, the climb to Glomtind (419m) is a strenuous 1½-hour ascent to fabulous views. The final stretch to the summit is especially steep.

Festvågtind

Also close to Henningsvær, this three-hour return climb to Festvågtind (541m) has some steep sections with loose rocks, the lovely lake Heiavatnet where you can swim and fine Henningsvær-and-beyond views.

Kvalvika & Ryten

Beyond Ramberg on the road to Å, follow signs to Fredvang, then Torsfjorden. Take the clearly marked short trail to Kvalvika, then the tough, three-hour climb to Ryten (543m) and some of the best views in Lofoten.

greatest artists, Karre Espolin-Johnson, whose haunting etchings of everyday people are displayed alongside a documentary about his life and a library room filled with books featuring his illustrations.

There are fewer options beyond Svolvær, but Henningsvær, in particular, is home to a handful of galleries and workshops, of which the most outstanding is **KaviarFactory**. The 1950s building was indeed a factory for caviar paste production until the late 1990s, but it now serves as a contemporary exhibition space for acclaimed international creators. Recent exhibitions have featured Ai Weiwei and Olafur Eliasson. Its perch right next to the water makes the Lofoten scenes framed by the picture windows inside all the more dramatic.

Many double as galleries and showrooms with artworks for sale. At **Lofoten Glass** in Kabelvåg, you can even sign up for a workshop to learn the art of glassblowing yourself, or simply browse the gallery and boutique for souvenirs.

Heading down into the south of the archipelago, you can add some gallery-hopping to the general sightseeing. If glass is your thing, you'll want to detour to **Glasshytta**, in Flakstad on Flakstadøy, one of the longest-standing exhibitors in Lofoten. Not far away, in Reine, **Galleri Eva Harr** displays works by renowned Norwegian artist Eva Harr.

Hamsunsenteret

COMMEMORATING A NOBEL PRIZE WINNER

If you take the ferry from Skutvik to Svolvær (and even if you don't), make sure you visit the **Hamsunsenteret**, around halfway between the E6 and Skutvik, along the Rv81. Daringly designed, the centre commemorates the life of Knut Hamsun, who won the Nobel Prize for Literature in 1920 and was both a literary giant and a controversial figure, thanks to his support for Nazi Germany. The centre covers both in a stunning series of unflinching displays. Hamsun moved to Hamarøy with his family at age three and later returned for a number of his working years as a writer.

MORE LITERARY TRAVELS

To build an itinerary around Norway's past literary giants, begin with the **Petter Dass Museum** (p272) near Sandnessjøen. Near Lillehammer are Bjørnstjerne Bjørnson's house, **Aulestad** (p120), and Sigrid Undset's former home (p120); the latter two both won the Nobel Prize for Literature.

WHERE TO EAT ELSEWHERE IN LOFOTEN

Bakeri

An unmissable stop on any visit to Å, the historic village bakery sells divine *kanelsnurr*. €

Lorchstua Restaurant

This acclaimed Kabelvåg restaurant serves local specialities with subtle twists in a formal atmosphere. €€€

Fiskekrogen

An elegant Henningsvær restaurant with a hearty seafood soup and more delicate options. €€€

Vesterålen

Vesterålen

✪OSLO

The Lofoten Islands may get most of the attention, but Vesterålen, just to the north, is a similarly brilliant destination, with some world-class experiences on offer. It's also set against a beautiful backdrop that is wilder than its southern neighbour.

It's the breadth of experiences on offer that defines Vesterålen. Depending on the season, you could go whale-watching, hike in the footsteps of royalty, take a virtual journey into space, set out to sea in search of puffins, drive along a coastline of austere beauty or spend time in a once-deserted village that's at the mercy of the Atlantic, yet was brought back to life against all odds.

And it's just fine with us if people underestimate Vesterålen. That means the roads here are quieter, and in places there's a palpable sense of Norway before the tourists arrived. Visit Lofoten by all means. But on no account miss its alter ego, Vesterålen.

Watch Whales off Vesterålen

GO ON A WHALE SAFARI

There's a reason why everybody gasps whenever a sperm or humpback whale breaches nearby. There are few more thrilling sights in nature than getting up close to one of these gentle giants as its great tail emerges from the depths, then pauses, suspended above the water, before diving again. Perhaps it has something to do with the fact that whales were endangered for so long but still survive. Or it could just be their astonishing size, agility and grace. We've even pulled up along a sleeping whale in the waters of Andenes: it was many times longer than the boat and it was an experience of great beauty.

The main season for **whale safaris** is in summer (late May to September), when boats leave Andenes and Stø, on the Vesterålen island of Langøya, on an almost daily basis. Trips usually last between 1½ and three hours, although five-hour trips are also possible. Excursions in search of whales take place at other times of the year, but less frequently, and they're sometimes called off due to bad weather.

GETTING AROUND

Vesterålen's largest town is Harstad; it has air, sea and road connections to the rest of Norway. Ferries also connect Andenes with Senja (summer only) and Melbu with Fiskebøl (for Svolvær and the Lofoten). Andenes also has flight connections with Tromsø, via Narvik or Bodø.

Once you're here, you'll need your own vehicle to get around; bus services are infrequent.

☑ **TOP TIP**

If you can spare a week here, do so. There's lots to do but don't forget to stay the night: this is when you'll most appreciate being here. There's no need to backtrack at the end of your stay: take the little-used ferry from Andenes to glorious Senja.

VESTERÅLEN

20 km
10 miles

Andenes
Bleik Fiskenes
Skogvoll
Nature
Reserve Stave
Skogvollvatnet Nature Reserve Skogvoll Andfjorden
Nordmela Myrset
Myre
Andøya Meløyvær
Nøss
Anesvatnet
Bø Sundsvoll
Bjørnskinnfjellet
Bømyra
Nyksund Stø Bjarkøya
Strengelvåg Åknes Grøtavær Sandsøya
Risøyhamn
Myre Liltje Risøya Elgsnes Grytøya
Alsvåg Risøya
Alsvågvatnet Risøysundet Lundenes
Nature Finnsæter
Skogsøya Holm Reserve
Eikefjelldalen Gapøya Kasfjord Ervika
Langøya Protected Borkenes
Landscape Harstad-Hårstták
Hinnøya

PUFFIN SAFARI OPERATORS

Puffin Safari
Based in Bleik, a charming seaside village and the closest departure point for visits to Bleiksøya, this local operator (puffinsafari. no) is perhaps the pick of the bunch.

Whale 2 Sea
Based in Andenes, this outfit (whale2sea. no) used to run trips to snorkel with the puffins; ask if they've been restarted.

Wild Ocean
This small Andenes operator is run by passionate birders and the guides really know their stuff (wildocean.no).

In summer, you're most likely to see majestic sperm whales and possibly pilot whales. In winter, when herrings migrate to the seas off Andenes, orcas (killer whales), humpbacks and fin whales are all possible. Contact the operator in advance if you're coming in winter as they only have two sailings a week.

In summer, most operators are so confident that you'll see whales that they offer a free excursion the following day if you strike out the first time around.

Go on a Puffin Safari

ICONS OF THE ARCTIC

Everybody loves puffins. With their melancholy, clown-like faces, these small seabirds are some of the great survivors of Arctic waters, making long journeys from one inhospitable ocean to another. Seeing one flying alongside a boat or bobbing on rough Arctic swells, it's difficult not to smile: it's like looking at a cartoon come to life and thrust into one of the most unforgiving environments on the planet. But don't be fooled by their size: puffins are tougher than they look; the oldest-known puffin lived for 43 years.

Although it's possible to see puffins in many places, it's usually incidental to some other experience. The main exception

WHERE TO STAY IN ANDENES

Andenes Camping	Fargeklatten	Hotell Marena
This basic campground, 3.5km from town, is on a gorgeous seaside meadow. It has a common kitchen. €	Rooms in this restored 18th-century home have antique furniture; modern apartments elsewhere in town. €€	Filled with stunning nature photographs, the 12 rooms at this boutique hotel are the best in Andenes. €€

is to go on a dedicated puffin safari to **Bleiksøya**, a protected nature reserve, which is where you'll find one of the largest and most important puffin colonies in northern Europe: more than 80,000 pairs nest here in summer. Boats leave out of Andenes or Bleik; visiting Bleiksøya from Andenes involves a longer boat ride than if you visit from Bleik.

Trips from Bleik usually last around 1½ to two hours and although it's not possible to go ashore at Bleiksøya, you'll see thousands of puffins; sightings of sea eagles are also guaranteed. The island also has large populations of cormorants, black guillemots, razorbills and gannets, and these massed, noisy, guano-soaked colonies cling to cliffs in an amazing spectacle that's every bit as exciting as seeing the puffins.

Journey to Outer Space
A TRIP IN THE SPACESHIP AURORA

Who would have thought that in a quiet corner of northern Norway you could watch whales in the morning, then travel into outer space (albeit virtually) in the afternoon?

South of Andenes along the road to Bleik, with its back to a barren rocky mountain, Norway's best-loved space centre welcomes you to an experience you won't find elsewhere. From this centre, Norway's scientists send up rockets to study the aurora borealis (Northern Lights) and you can learn all about their endeavours during the 16-minute video presentation, as well as through the other exhibits, which all have excellent explanations in English.

If that were all, this would just be a museum. But the real highlight is boarding a virtual mission on the **Spaceship Aurora**, which lasts between one and two hours. Designed by those who've travelled beyond the Earth's atmosphere, it captures everything from safety briefings to the bewildering array of dials, gauges and buttons to the innate claustrophobia of travelling in a small metal can into the heavens. You even get to launch a virtual rocket of your own. You'll need to reserve your spot on board in advance.

Drive the Scenic Andøya Coast
DISCOVER THE WILD WEST COAST

The west coast of **Andøya** is one reason why you should never rush your visit to Vesterålen. If you have a spare half-day, definitely use it to drive along this Norwegian Scenic Route. The beauty of this drive ranks alongside anything that Lofoten has to offer.

WHALE-WATCHING OPERATORS

Whale Safari
Andenes-based Whale Safari (whalesafari.no) is the largest operator with up to three daily departures in summer. They guide you around their Whale Centre before setting out. The tour includes coffee, tea and soup.

Whale 2 Sea
This Andenes whale-watching outfit (whale2sea. no) uses smaller boats. They also offer shorter seal- and birdwatching trips, plus winter outings to look for orcas, humpbacks and fin whales. Ask about snorkelling with orcas in winter and puffins in summer.

Arctic Whale Tours
Operating out of Stø, Arctic Whale Tours (arcticwhaletours. com) runs all-day safaris to see whales and dolphins, as well as seabird colonies.

 WHERE TO STAY & EAT ON ANDØYA

Stave Camping
Fabulous campground in tiny Stave with glorious views, a beach sauna and outdoor 38°C hot tubs. €

Midnattsol Camping
A good campground at the northern entry to the village with fine views from most sites. €

Lysthuset
The best of Andenes' limited dining options with an OK cafe and excellent restaurant. €€

MORE PUFFINS
You'll find puffins all across the Arctic, but three excellent places to find them are **Svalbard** (p302), **Runde** (p214) and the island of **Lovund** (p273) off the Nordland coast, where around 200,000 puffins nest from mid-April to mid-August.

AURORA BOREALIS

The visible aurora borealis, or Northern Lights, are caused by streams of charged particles from the sun, called the solar wind, which are directed by the Earth's magnetic field towards the polar regions. Because the field curves downward in a halo surrounding the magnetic poles, the charged particles are drawn earthward. Their interaction with the electrons in nitrogen and oxygen atoms in the upper atmosphere releases energy, creating the visible aurora. During periods of high activity, a single auroral storm can produce a trillion watts of electricity with a current of 1 million amps.

Heading south from Andenes, leave the Rv82 and follow the signs to Bleik. From here, you might very well be on your own; except in the height of summer, kilometres will pass without ever seeing another car. The road follows the shore along a narrow strip of land between sea and rocky mountain. After turning south, the countryside opens out onto a thin coastal plain and lovely little Bleik; from the foreshore, you'll have a view of offshore Bleiksøya, beyond which lies nothing but ocean all the way to Greenland.

After Bleik, the road heads inland, past lakes and between mountains, before rejoining the coast near tiny **Stave**; take the detour to **Hestvika Viewpoint**. From Stave to the southernmost tip of the island, the road hugs the bare and beautiful coast; look for the cloudberry marshes in the far south.

If you return north from Risøyhamn to Andenes along the Rv82, you'll cross a moor-like landscape reminiscent of the Scottish Highlands. Note the giant hillocks of peat by the roadside, which have been extracted, dried and ready to be transported to garden centres around the world.

For an alternative take on all of this, hire a **bike** and make the mostly flat journey by pedal power. If you were to rent a bike at Fargeklatten in Andenes, you could go as far as Sortland, where you can send it back to Andenes by bus.

Nyksund and the Art of Coming Back to Life
AN ABANDONED VILLAGE REBORN

If you like your picturesque Norwegian villages to come with a story, you'll love **Nyksund**. Back in the 1960s, the village, like so many remote communities across Scandinavia, turned the corner towards extinction when its last businesses, the post office and bakery, closed. Occupying one of the most exposed stretches of Langøya's Atlantic coastline, it finally succumbed to a violent storm in 1975 and its last inhabitant, blacksmith Olav Larsen, left. The village fell silent. Sheep and vandals moved in.

End of story? Well, no. Unlike so many depopulated communities across Europe, over the decades that followed, artists and others began the process of rebuilding (and repopulating) the village. Derelict old homes and Nyksund's few commercial buildings were restored, and everything from guesthouses, art galleries, small shops and even a museum

 WHERE TO STAY IN NYKSUND & STØ

Holmvik Brygge	Expedisjonen	Gunnartangen Rorbuferie
This hugely welcoming guesthouse and cafe justifies the detour to Nyksund. *Everything* is sourced locally. €€	Nyksund restaurant and coffee bar, with a handful of prim wooden rooms with white-wood walls and fine views. €€	These five self-catering cabins overlook the quiet harbour at Stø, exuding warmth and personality. €€

INIGO CIA/500PX ©

Northern Lights, Nordland

VESTERÅLEN MUSEUMS

Nyksund Museum
Nyksund's small museum showcases local artefacts and before-and-after photos of the town.

Hvalsenteret
The whale centre has fun displays on these gentle giants, with whale skeletons a highlight.

Hurtigrutenmuseet
The Hurtigruten coastal ferry was founded in Stokmarknes in 1893; this museum tells the Hurtigruten's story.

Norwegian Fishing Industry Museum
In a country where fish is life, this abandoned herring-oil factory traces the life of a fish from the deep sea to the kitchen table.

preserving Nyksund's heritage and telling its story began to appear around the village's charming enclosed harbour.

One of those responsible for the transformation is Ssemjon Gerlitz, the German owner of the guesthouse **Holmvik Brygge** (nyksund.com). Gerlitz has lived in Nyksund year-round for over a decade, and he has made it his life's work to find the remnants of old Nyksund and incorporate any found relics into the guesthouse. Two things in particular keep him here. He speaks of the lure of silence, with nothing but the rhythm of wind and waves for most of the year. And he feels a sense of communion with long-gone fisherfolk ('Every rusty nail I pull out was hammered in by someone who lived and worked here').

Nyksund retains its small-town feel – just a handful of residents overwinter here, and even in summer, barely 40 live

WHERE TO STAY ELSEWHERE IN VESTERÅLEN

Sortland Camping og Motell
About 1.3km from the centre, with a campground, motel rooms and hearty northern Norwegian cooking. €

Hurtigrutens Hus Turistsenter
This friendly spot in Stokmarknes is over the bridge with cabins and rooms. €€

Sortland Hotell
A comfy place on the main road through town, Sortland has bright modern rooms with parquet floors. €€

OTHER VESTERÅLEN ACTIVITIES

Moose Safari
Andøy Friluftssenter (andoy-friluftssenter. no) runs moose (elk) safaris, wilderness walks and deep-sea fishing from its base at Buksnesfjord, 63km south of Andenes.

Dogsledding
Husky-Andøy (husky-andoy. com) organises dogsledding trips; in summer the sleds have wheels. It also arranges hiking and climbing.

Seal Safari
. Stø's Arctic Whale Tours (arcticwha-letours.com) takes you to a nearby seal colony, often as part of its birding and whale-watching trips.

Sea Kayaking
Every year in July, the six-day Arctic Sea Kayak Race is the ultimate challenge. Less-intensive sea-kayaking tours are also possible.

DAVE WILLIAMS/GETTY IMAGES ©

Moose, Lofoten Islands

in the village. And whenever a storm rolls in, Nyksund – a tight huddle of colourful buildings around an enclosed harbour, accessible only by a steep, narrow access road – can feel as if it's at the mercy of the wild Atlantic. But it's a special and hauntingly beautiful place.

Sample Culinary Excellence at Kvitnes Gård

ENJOY ONE OF NORWAY'S BEST RESTAURANTS

Halfway between Vesterålen and the Lofoten Islands, **Kvitnes Gård** is one of Norway's most remarkable culinary experiences. Tucked away by the shores of a minor fjord, surrounded by farming communities and set in a farm that has been in the same family since 1855, this wonderful place is not so much a restaurant as a destination. It's the work of Halvar Ellingsen, one of Norway's most decorated chefs and formerly of Michelin-starred Oslo restaurants. At Kvitnes Gård, Ellingsen has returned to his roots, but lost none of his adventurous, innovative spirit.

 BEST VESTERÅLEN FESTIVALS

Arctic Arts Festival
Harstad's Arctic Arts Festival is a full week of music, theatre and dance in June.

Sommer-Melbu Festival
This festival on Hadseløya is one of northern Norway's liveliest, with music, theatre and art exhibitions.

Sortland Jazz
Takes place over a couple of September weeks and is a worthy member of Norway's jazz festival circuit.

The building itself, steeped in history and swathed in white wood, is very much a part of the experience. The decor is classy and old-fashioned; this extends into the restaurant and the guesthouse rooms where you can stay overnight. And with its garden beds and animal pens, the sense of a working farm, and of a connection between the food and the land where it was grown, is strong and enduring.

If you're lucky enough to secure a table – advance reservations are required – you'll sit down for a multicourse set menu, one in which both ingredients and inspiration are sourced locally, sometimes from the farm itself, sometimes from not far away. Recipes draw on the deep traditions of Vesterålen, and change with the seasons and local availability of produce. The menu might include woodsmoked halibut or salmon, baby goat or cured lamb, cloudberries, jellied eels and salt-baked cod.

In summer, you'll need to make a reservation months in advance: Kvitnes Gård only opened to the public in 2020, but it's already gained an international reputation for excellence and charm. If you've been saving up for a special meal while in Norway, put this one on your shortlist.

TRAVELLING TO THE TOP OF EUROPE?

Harstad (p286), Vesterålen's largest town, lies near the border of Nordland and Troms, and is a good transition point for travelling between Vesterålen or Lofoten and the far north. It also has onward ferries to **Tromsø** (p278).

HIKE THE QUEEN'S ROUTE

To drive from Stø would require a 25km looping detour by road. Or you could walk. Depending on which route you take, the 12km to 15km (three- to six-hour) return hike is waymarked with red letter Ts. On the outward journey, make the considerable effort to summit Finngamheia (448m); the views from up there are incredible. There's also a relatively flat route that follows the coast. And if you were wondering about the name, it dates back to 1994 when Norway's Queen Sonja walked this way. Ask for a free guide-pamphlet from Sortland tourist office.

The Queen's Route

MICHAL I/SHUTTERSTOCK ©

Saltfjellet-Svartisen National Park

Saltfjellet-Svartisen National Park

❂ OSLO

GETTING AROUND

For the most part, you'll need your own vehicle to get really close to the park boundaries, especially from Mo i Rana. On the west side, any vehicle travelling the Rv17 can drop you at the boat port, north of the vehicle crossing at Forøy. Out east, access is via the E6 or Rv77 by road. By train, stop at Lønsdal on the Fauske–Trondheim line.

☑ **TOP TIP**

Unless you're an experienced and entirely self-sufficient cross-country skier, there is only a small window in July and August (depending on conditions) in which to explore the park. The rest of the year, you'll just have to enjoy the view from the road or ferry.

Brooding over the land with all the dark grandeur of an oncoming storm, Saltfjellet-Svartisen National Park, just north of the Arctic Circle, is a special place. The deep greys of a cloud-covered icy landscape can suddenly transform from forbidding to astonishing whenever the sun breaks through, revealing the jagged peaks and glacier tongues of the Svartisen icecap, Norway's second-largest glacier.

The park can be enjoyed simply as a looming, formidable view on a side excursion from the Hurtigruten coastal ferry, or along the Kystriksveien Coastal Route. You'll catch enticing glimpses at various points along the latter, but the views are best just north of the ferry crossing of Forøy. You can go further, detouring into the park to hike atop glaciers or look for wildlife. Doing so opens up the more remote eastern reaches of the park where bleak, high moorlands roll to the Swedish border.

Draw Near to a Glacier

WALK TO THE EDGE OF AN ICECAP

Sitting astride the Arctic Circle, the two **Svartisen icecaps** are epic natural formations. Most of these icefields are around 1500m above sea level, although gravity dictates that some glacier tongues drop to lower altitudes through narrow valleys; where they do this, they're the lowest-altitude glaciers in Europe. In places, the ice is over 600m thick. Remember that it was the sheer weight of glaciers that carved out the fjords over millions of years – one day, long after we've gone, this may go the same way.

You can visit either of the two icecaps, and each offers a different experience. The western side is more spectacular but you'll really only get a sighting from a distance along the Kystriksveien Coastal Route, especially just after the Kilboghamn–Jetvik ferry crossing heading north. Most visitors to either side do this as a quick hop by boat (look for signs advertising boat trips soon after you emerge from the

SALTFJELLET-SVARTISEN NATIONAL PARK

SIGHTS
1. Grønligrotta
2. Lønsdal
3. Mo i Rana
4. Saltfjellet-Svartisen National Park
   see 1 Setergrotta
5. Svartisen Lake

SLEEPING
6. DNT Blakkådalshytta Hut
7. Graddis Fjellstue og Camping

Straumdatunnelen), but hikers will find more joy approaching from the east.

You can reach **Østisen**, the eastern glacier, from **Mo i Rana**. From the airport, drive for 20km up the Svartisdalen road. Where the road ends, you have two choices. One is to take one of the ferries that cross **Svartisen Lake** (Svartisvatnet) four times a day in summer, then hike for 3km to the Austerdalsisen glacier tongue. There you'll discover that it's one thing to admire a glacier from afar, and quite another to stand beneath it in all its deeply textured, awe-inspiring glory.

The other option from the end of the road from Mo i Rana is to hike up to the **DNT Blakkådalshytta hut** close to the shore of the mountain lake Pikhaugsvatnet, which occupies a glorious spot surrounded by snowy peaks and ice. Taking this route opens up a whole world of possibilities, including day hikes up the Glomdal valley or to the Flatisen glacier.

Explore a Remote, Icebound Massif
THE SALTFJELLET PLATEAU

Saltfjellet-Svartisen National Park doesn't draw many visitors beyond its spectacular fringe, so if you set out to explore the broad upland plateaus of the **Saltfjellet Massif**, you'll feel like a genuine wilderness explorer.
(Continues on p268)

CROSSING THE ARCTIC CIRCLE

You could, in theory, cross the Arctic Circle (latitude 66°33' N) at any place along this latitude, but two places in particular allow you to mark the moment. On land, the Arctic Highway between Mo i Rana and Fauske crosses the line in a broad, snow-drowned valley where you'll find the rather commercial Polarsirkelsenteret (Arctic Circle Centre). If you're travelling along the Kystriksveien, you'll make the crossing while aboard the Kilboghamn–Jektvik ferry: look for the silver globe on a headland to the east, and listen for the captain's announcement.

Driving the Kystriksveien Coastal Route

Norway is so beautiful and so blessed that it takes something special to stand out. Meandering past inlets and islands on ferries, and bucking and weaving over a landscape that lives up to the billing of the world's most beautiful coast, the Kystriksveien Coastal Route (plan on taking two to four days) is the crowning glory of a country that is one spectacular road trip after another.

1 Brønnøysund

Lovely little Brønnøysund is what passes for a big town in these parts. But in truth, it's little more than a speck in this landscape of big horizons. This world of islands and water surrounds a pretty, quaint town of wooden buildings and green gardens. Visible from many places along the Kystriksveien, rocky Torghatten is one of the most recognisable natural landmarks in northern Norway.

The Drive: It isn't long on the drive north from Brønnøysund (92km) before you take Kystriksveien's first ferry, from Horn to Andalsvågen, with another from Forvik to Tjøtta.

2 Sandnessjøen

The final approach into Sandnessjøen is between the Syv Søstre (Seven Sisters) mountain range in the east and the offshore islands to the west. Apart from its pedestrianised main street, Sandnessjøen

EINAR/GETTY IMAGES©

Syv Søstre (Seven Sisters)

is all about the setting; it's a burgeoning oil town but it's still a pretty place.

The Drive: North of Sandnessjøen, the curving Helgelandsbrua spans the fjord. From here to the Levang–Nesna ferry is an easy drive across the hills. After the ferry, the road traces Ranafjord inland then back out to the west before turning north. It's 107km from Sandnessjøen to Stokkvågen.

3 Stokkvågen

Blink and you might miss Stokkvågen, but you won't care because it's along one of the most spectacular stretches of the route. Nearby are the ruins of the former Nazi fort at Grønsvik, as well as countless places to pull over and enjoy the view.

The Drive: From Stokkvågen, the spectacular views continue across the Kilboghamn–Jektvik ferry with its Arctic Circle crossing and glacier views of Saltfjellet-Svartisen National Park, with more fine views all the way to Storvik (149km).

4 Storvik

The town of Storvik is the last thing you expect to find in the Arctic: a pretty coastal town with a white-sand beach that wouldn't look out of place in the tropics. Go for a walk along the beach and swim if you dare.

The Drive: After Storvik, the road spends longer inland, passing pine forests, farmland and the Saltsraumen maelstrom, before the final push to Bodø (96km).

5 Bodø

By the time you reach Bodø, you'll be gasping for air. If you're not tempted to turn around and drive back down the Kystriksveien so you can enjoy it all again, then linger long enough to enjoy the big charms of Bodø, with its fine museums and pedigree as the 2024 European Capital of Culture. And the views of Lofoten from the waterfront should be inspiration enough for your next adventure.

ATTRACTIONS NEAR SALTFJELLET-SVARTISEN NP

Grønligrotta
Scandinavia's only illuminated tourist cave lies 22km north of Mo i Rana. Take the 30-minute tour along an underground river.

Setergrotta
This cave, 21km north of Mo i Rana and signposted off the E6, involves a couple of tight squeezes and a thrilling shuffle between rock walls while straddling a 15m-deep gorge.

Polarsirkelsenteret
Mostly a souvenir shop, the Arctic Circle Centre has a video presentation on Arctic regions and memorials to Slav forced labourers who constructed the Arctic Highway for the occupying Nazis.

Hiking trail, Saltfjellet Massif (p265)

(Continued from p265)

Out in the east of the park, the icy peaks of the massif rise above the high Saltfjellet Plateau. To reach the plateau's trailheads, take the Rv77, which follows the southern slope of the Junkerdalen Valley, or travel by train and request a stop at Lønsdal (between Fauske and Trondheim). Once you turn off the car engine, or the train continues on its way, you'll be struck by the superb, snowy silence of this special place.

There are numerous possibilities here, but most coalesce around the venerable **Graddis Fjellstue og Camping** (graddis-fjellstue.no), which has been in the same family for more than 150 years. Use it as a way station along the 15km walk from the trailhead to the Swedish border. On your way here, watch for signs to a handful of ancient Sami fences and sacrificial sites, some of which date back to the 9th century. Keep an eye out for the region's shy populations of wolverine, Eurasian lynx, elk and a breeding population of Arctic fox. Ask also for the way to **Methusaleh**, a nearby 1000-year-old pine tree.

Sleep overnight and ask the owner's advice on treks in the area: this is one of Norway's least-visited hiking destinations.

MORE GLACIERS
If glaciers are your thing, Norway has some excellent opportunities for more glacier hikes, including **Hardangervidda** (p133), **Folgefonna** (p164) and **Jostedalsbreen** (p195). Near the latter, at Fjærland, there's also the excellent **Norwegian Glacier Museum** (p198).

WHERE TO STAY NEAR SALTFJELLET-SVARTISEN NATIONAL PARK

Graddis Fjellstue og Camping
This cosy little guesthouse out on the Saltfjellet moors has simple, cosy rooms and camping. €

Fjordgaarden Mo
Handy for Mo i Rana's train station and rather stylish, Fjordgaarden Mo has simple rooms. €€

Meyergården Hotell
Mo's longest-established hotel is full of character, with slick, contemporary rooms. €€

Brønnøysund

Brønnøysund

✪OSLO

When it comes to the towns you'll drive through along the Kystriksveien Coastal Route, few live up to their surrounds. Brønnøysund is something of an exception, and it's the kind of place where you'll want to break up the journey.

From above, Norway's deeply fissured North Sea coast is filled with inlets, channels and so much water that there scarcely seems room for a settlement. Compact Brønnøysund, with its population of barely 5000 souls, clings to what little land there is, with a stunning backdrop of nearby rocky headlands and an island-studded sea. It's the quintessential Norwegian coastal town, reached via a series of bridges and with oxblood-red fishing warehouses hanging out over the water. Despite the apparent lack of available land, the town has made the most of what it has, with lots of greenery at every turn to complement the deep oceanic blues that prevail to the horizon.

Twenty-four Hours in Brønnøysund

SMALL-TOWN NORWAY

Try and time your arrival in **Brønnøysund** for late afternoon. One of the great pleasures of this delightful town is walking its main streets, especially late in the day when the day-trippers leave and car traffic stops. Colourful wooden cottages fronted by flowerbeds and small shops line the main street and side streets. On a summer's evening, find your way to the waterfront to admire the view to listen to the quiet beauty of sheltered waters lapping at the shore.

You'll have seen the dramatic rocky outcrop of **Torghatten** – which rises from Torget island, 15km south of Brønnøysund – almost as soon as you arrive in town. If you're staying overnight, and we recommend that you do, get an early start the next morning to drive out to Torghatten for a closer look. Before leaving, ask at the town's tourist office for maps and advice on how to climb to the top. One of Torghatten's more

GETTING AROUND

Most travellers arrive in Brønnøysund either in a rental car or on the Hurtigruten coastal ferry. You could get here aboard one of the daily buses from Mosjøen or Sandnessjøen, or on a Widerøe flight from Trondheim, Oslo and Bergen. But you'll still need a vehicle to get around once you arrive, and car rental options in Brønnøysund are practically nonexistent.

☑ TOP TIP

If you're travelling along the Kystriksveien in summer and plan to overnight in Brønnøysund, book ahead. There aren't many places to stay, and what there is often sells out weeks in advance during the summer, especially July and August.

A HURTIGRUTEN MINI CRUISE

For an alternative take on the Torghatten outcrop, the tourist office sells tickets for a spectacular mini-cruise on the Hurtigruten. Leaving Brønnøysund at 5pm, the coastal ferry passes Torghatten on its way south – the views from the boat are widely considered to be the best as it rounds the island. The cruise continues south to Rørvik in Trøndelag, allowing an hour to explore the town and visit its splendid **Norveg Centre for Coastal Culture and Industries**. To return, hop aboard the next northbound ferry to reach Brønnøysund again at 1am.

Torghatten (p269)

unusual features is that a hole – 160m long, 35m high and 20m wide – pierces the rock. Take the walking track to the summit (20 minutes) and enjoy superb views of the town and west towards the North Sea.

Having summited Torghatten, make your reward lunch at **Hilders Urterarium**, a gorgeous little spot 6km north of Brønnøysund. If you have to wait for a table, wander Hilde's herb garden with its 400 different types of herbs and a backdrop of some enchanted old farm buildings. Lunch itself is a delight of seasonal ingredients, locally grown products and expert cooking, served in a rustic dining room.

Beyond
Brønnøysund

Exploring beyond Brønnøysund takes you into one of coastal Norway's most fascinating corners, with natural beauty and stunning human outposts.

While enjoying the summer procession along the Kystriksveien Coastal Route, you won't see many Norwegians. That's because if they're visiting the area, they're likely here to visit UNESCO World Heritage-listed Vega, with its intriguing human history. Or perhaps they're climbing the Seven Sisters near Sandnessjøen. Or island-hopping from one tiny North Sea outpost to another. The destinations that lie within Brønnøysund's hinterland see very few international travellers, and, as such, they're custom-made for a very Norwegian holiday experience.

Consider this as a detour or, better still, a time-out from the Kystriksveien, rather than an extension of it. Chances are that by the end of your visit, you'll feel like you've stumbled upon a well-kept local secret of the best kind.

Travel to Europe's Outer Reaches in Vega

A UNIQUE UNESCO SITE

There's something special about **Vega**, but it's not anything you can easily put a finger on. Part of it comes from where you are: one look at a map tells a story of delicious isolation, with Vega perched on Europe's outer rim, a last outpost of the continent before the wild North Sea takes over. Another part of Vega's appeal derives from its people and their ability to survive sustainably in one of Europe's most inhospitable corners. It was this human story, stretching back 1500 years, that earned it the coveted UNESCO recognition. At the heart of that story is the Vega practice of eiderdown harvesting, undertaken mostly by women. For more on these special ducks and their down, visit verdensarvvega.no.

And then there's Vega's sheer beauty, with oxblood-red structures that turn magnificent with the setting sun, turf-roofed homes and the ocean's deep blues offset by a lovely landscape of deep green. Echoing out from the main island

GETTING AROUND

Having your own vehicle is essential for exploring Norway's Nordland coast around Brønnøysund and Sandnessjøen. To reach the islands of Vega, Træna and Lovund, you can take a car ferry from the mainland. Widerøe flies to both Brønnøysund and Sandnessjøen from Oslo, Trondheim, Bodø and elsewhere, while infrequent buses run up and down the coast through both towns. The Hurtigruten coastal ferry also stops in both Brønnøysund and Sandnessjøen. Check hurtigruten.no for timetables.

☑ TOP TIP

Allocate at least four days to the area. Too many visitors try and see everything in just one day.

In the map (top right): Træna, Lovund, Kystriksveien Coastal Route, Sandnessjøen, Vega, **Brønnøysund**

BEYOND BRØNNØYSUND NORDLAND

OTHER HIGHLIGHTS AROUND SANDNESSJØEN

Dønnmannen
If you need one more peak to climb, Dønnmannen (858m) is a challenging 8km hike (out and back) for serious hikers only. Trails start at Hagen, across the water from Sandnessjøen.

Petter Dass Museum
Don't miss this avant-garde architectural showpiece, dedicated to the Norwegian poet Petter Dass (1647–1707) at Alstahaug, south of Sandnessjøen.

Kulturbadet i Sandnessjøen
If you're travelling with children, don't drive past Sandnessjøen's swimming complex. It has heated indoor pools and a terrific water slide.

are the more than 6500 skerries (islets) and large rocks that make up the Vega archipelago. Birds love this wild landscape, too, with 228 species having been recorded here.

To get here, drive north from Brønnøysund to Horn for the car ferry (1½ to 2¾ hours) to Vega, or, if you're coming from the north, Tjøtta (2¼ hours). Express boats also make the trip to/from both Brønnøysund (45 minutes) and Sandnessjøen (1½ hours). Whichever boat you take, it's difficult not to escape the sensation that you're casting off into the vast ocean from some deserted shore. And the approach to the main island itself is like arriving at a magical place unchanged by the passing years. Every time we've travelled to Vega, we've been the only non-Norwegians on board.

Hike the High Hills near Sandnessjøen
THE SEVEN SISTERS

Hiking opportunities are surprisingly slim along the Kystriksveien Coastal Route, but Sandnessjøen more than makes up for the lack elsewhere.

Just south of town, the **Syv Søstre (Seven Sisters)** range is a dragon's-back string of bald peaks that shadows the shore. The summits range from 910m to 1072m in height, and, this being Norway, there's an extreme-sports competition every few years where hikers try to summit all seven in as little time as possible: the record stands at a remarkable three hours and 54 minutes.

Whether you're climbing all seven (which should take most hikers of reasonable fitness around 15 to 20 hours) or just one, drive or take a taxi down the Rv17 to Breimo or Sørra (around 4km south from Sandnessjøen), then follow the sign and drive a further 2km to the base of the mountains. Parking is easier back at Breimo or Sørra if you're in your own vehicle.

The climb to **Botnkrona** (1072m), the highest of the peaks, takes most hikers of reasonable fitness three to four hours one-way; count on two to three hours to climb each of the other peaks (also one-way). Remember that each of the climbs is pretty relentless: you're gaining almost one vertical kilometre climbing each peak and there are few flat sections to offer respite. Then again, there's nothing to stop you from resting every once in a while and enjoying the view.

Before setting out, pick up simple maps and basic route descriptions from the Sandnessjøen tourist office. Even better, buy the *Alstahaug* (1:50,000) map. Trails are blazed with red

 WHERE TO STAY ALONG THE NORDLAND COAST

Sandnessjøen Camping
Around 10km south of Sandnessjøen, this place has fab views, campsites and simple cabins. €

Torghatten Camping
This lovely option has a small lake beach and is close to Torghatten peak. €

Sandnessjøen Guesthouse
A guesthouse with simple, dated rooms, a friendly welcome and reasonable prices. €

dots, making it difficult to lose your way. Before you leave Sandnessjøen, tell the tourist office where you're going and when – it's an important safety precaution. Finally, carry more water than you think you'll need and keep an eye on the weather: things can change quickly out here. And when you're done, if you want to receive a diploma in the mail, sign your name in the book at each summit, fill in a control card and leave it at the tourist office.

Explore the Remote Archipelago of Træna

A FORGOTTEN ISLAND WORLD

If you liked Vega, you're going to love **Træna**. This archipelago sees even fewer visitors than Vega; only five out of 1000 small, flat skerries in the archipelago are inhabited.

Make the islet of **Husøy**, which has most of Træna's population and lodgings, your first stop, then head for neighbouring **Sanna**, the perfect purveyor of Træna's unique charms: it's barely 1km long, with a low mountain range crescendoing through the heart of the island. The crowning spire is **Trænstaven** (318m) in the north. Down at the other end of the island, there's the cathedral-like **Kirkehelleren Cave**. If you can, come here in July for the four-day **Trænafestivalen**, one of Europe's most remote music festivals.

Ferries to Husøy leave from Bodø, Sandnessjøen and Mo i Rana once or twice daily.

Spot Puffins on Lovund

A QUIET ISLAND RETREAT

The thing about Norway's islands is that they receive only a fraction of visitors compared to the mainland. Take Lovund, for example. Were it connected to the mainland by a bridge, it would be a crowded major attraction. Instead, it's accessible only by a two-hour ferry and remains a wonderfully well-kept secret. Covering just 47 hectares, **Lovund** (population 250) is a huddle of red wooden houses beneath a 623m-high rocky Atlantic outcrop. On 14 April every year, islanders celebrate **Lundkommardag**, marking the return of 200,000 puffins who come here to nest. Stay overnight at the excellent **Lovund RorbuHotell**.

MORE UNESCO SITES

Norway has eight UNESCO World Heritage Sites. Among them are the fjord-side **Urnes Stave Church** (p193), **Geirangerfjord** (p208), Bergen's waterfront **Bryggen district** (p142) and the former mining town of **Røros** (p234).

WHERE TO STAY IN VEGA & TRÆNA

Vega Camping
The waterside location makes this simple campground one of the prettiest in Norway; boat rentals too. €

Vega Havhotell
This isolated getaway is tranquillity itself, with tech-free, impeccable rooms and resident eider ducks. €€

Træna Rorbuferie
These ochre-hued *rorbuer* have fine views, simple furnishings and blissful isolation. €€€

 WHERE TO STAY ALONG THE NORDLAND COAST

Clarion Collection Hotel Kysten
A fine Sandnessjøen hotel overlooking the waterfront with stylish rooms and an evening buffet. €€

Scandic Syv Søstre
This large hotel has a cool contemporary style, excellent breakfasts and fine views from most rooms. €€

Thon Hotel Brønnøysund
Modern rooms, good breakfasts and sweeping views make this the best place to stay in Brønnøysund. €€

Above: Nordkapp (p290); right: humpback whale, Tromsø (p278)

The Far North

EMBRACE THE MAJESTIC NORTHLANDS

Venture into an untouched landscape, where rich cultural heritage and endless adventure await.

It's easy to think that the far north is a barren tundra – desolate, cold and devoid of life. And while it is the least populated part of Norway today, with fewer than 250,000 inhabitants, it is a region with a diverse landscape and heritage that can be traced back over 10,000 years.

The counties of Troms and Finnmark have always been home to travellers, from the early settlers and Vikings to the native Sami and Russian 'Pomor' traders.

Though much of the far north was burned down during the WWII under Adolf Hitler's Nero Decree, there are still pockets of old Norway to be found if you know where to look. Today, cultural heritage plays an important part for those who live here. The native Sami herd thousands of reindeer, the oceans are fished by locals, and the landscapes offer truly remote adventures, whether skiing under the Northern Lights or trekking under the midnight sun.

In the southern county of Troms, high mountain peaks surge out of the ocean and kiss the sky. In Finnmark, wide plateaus spread out as far as the eye can see, bordered by the turbulent Barents Sea and Russia to the east. Slightly larger than Ireland, this is a massive region that remains largely unexplored by travellers today.

MARCIN KADZIOLKA/SHUTTERSTOCK ©

THE MAIN AREAS

TROMSØ	**ALTA**	**VADSØ**
Capital of the north. **p278**	Landscapes and history. **p287**	Remoteness and wildlife. **p294**

Find Your Way

The long scenic roads here are best explored by car. Longer ferry routes offer good connections to the primary coastal towns and there are daily flights to the major towns. There are few buses and no trains.

CAR

The E6 is Norway's arterial road and is the best way to explore the far north. It's sometimes quicker to drive through northern Finland and/or Sweden if you're travelling to destinations further south in Norway.

FERRY

Norway's ferry system is comprehensive. The Hurtigruten ferry operates daily and can transport you to many of the major coastal communities. Travelling to the interior via ferry is much harder.

Tromsø, p278

A university town and centre of Arctic research, Tromsø is a springboard to remote mountains and fjords.

Alta, p287

The Northern Lights capital of Norway is the gateway to West Finnmark and Nordkapp, the northernmost point in Europe.

Vadsø, p294

On the Varanger Peninsula, this East Finnmark town has access to remote communities and wildlife.

Norwegian Sea · Barents Sea · Nordishavet · Østhavet · FINLAND · RUSSIA · SWEDEN

Tromsø · Alta · Hammerfest · Vadsø · Narvik · Vardø · Kirkenes

100 km
60 miles

Reindeer near Hamningberg (p297)

Plan Your Time

Time is your friend in the far north. Distances between towns are long, especially if you travel off the beaten path into the wilderness.

A Week to Spare

● Spend a few days exploring **Tromsø** (p278) before driving the stunning roads over Lyngen towards Alta. Stop by the **Alta Museum** (p287) to view ancient stone carvings, then travel along the dramatic coastal roads to the north of Magerøya, where you'll find **Nordkapp** (p290), Europe's northernmost point. From here, head south to **Kautokeino** (p293) and explore Finnmarksvidda's rich Sami culture and the magical Juhls Sølvsmie.

Multiweek Adventure

● Explore the entire region by travelling to **Vadsø** (p294). Drive the wild road to **Hamningberg** (p297) and keep an eye out for white-tailed eagles that fly along the coastline. Stop by **Vardø** (p296), Norway's easternmost town and a major fishing port. Drive the dirt road along the **Pasvikelva river** (p300), which separates Norway from Russia, and continue on to the Sami capital of **Karasjok** (p291).

Seasonal Highlights

SPRING
With the return of the sun after the polar night, this is a wonderful time to head to the mountains to ski. April is best.

SUMMER
Summer is ideal for a long road trip to drink in the dramatic landscapes and wildlife. June is the most crowded month.

AUTUMN
Autumn is short, but the colours are vibrant and the roads less busy. It's cooler but still wonderful for hiking and camping.

WINTER
December is peak **Northern Lights** season, with whale watching at its height in January and dogsledding in February.

Tromsø

Tromsø

⭑OSLO

GETTING AROUND

If you're driving to Tromsø, it's best to download the EasyPark app to pay for street parking. They are hot on ticketing here so be sure you pay. You can walk everywhere in town, but some of the side roads are steep. In winter, it's essential that you buy spikes for your shoes as the pavements are often icy.

☑ TOP TIP

For those eager to see the Northern Lights, the Fjellheisen cable car (295kr return after 5pm) is a must. At 421m above sea level, it has dazzling views over Tromsø. Head up after 6pm and check norway-lights. com for the most up-to-date forecasts.

In the 19th century, Tromsø was a haven for fashion, food and European culture, and garnered the title 'Paris of the north'. Like many coastal cities, it boomed as a fishing port and today is the hub of Arctic research, with a lively student population. Its proximity to the mountains makes it an adventure-seeker's paradise, and during the winter it attracts skiers from across the globe. On clear winter nights, you'll regularly see the Northern Lights flicker high above the city, and out in the fjords, you'll find orcas and humpbacks aplenty.

The centre itself is quaint. During the polar night, snow glistens under the warm streetlights and it exudes a fairy-tale quality. Year-round, the nightlife booms off the pedestrian-only high street Storgata and in the newly developed Vevert area beside the harbour. Chic bars serve cocktails and locally brewed beer, and restaurants prepare traditional cuisine, all within a 20-minute walking radius.

The Ocean's Magic

BREACHING WHALES, SOARING EAGLES

From November to January, humpbacks, orcas and minke whales spend time in the far north's fjords feasting on the rich stocks of migrating herring. **Whale-watching tours** are held in a variety of boats, and offer travellers an amazing opportunity to see these gentle giants up close and personal.

Several companies run tours daily from the ferry terminal near Nerstranda, a five-minute walk from the main harbour, and it's wise to clear the day as trips can take up to eight hours depending on where the whales are feeding. For the most intimate viewing, Brim Explorer uses hybrid boats that run on electricity when near the whales, which makes for a better experience for everyone.

(Continues on p280)

It's easy to explore the city centre on foot, but when walking in winter, it's best to buy snow spikes as the roads will be slippery. Buses 24, 40 and 42 from the airport run regularly from below the car park and take 15 to 20 minutes (get off at the at Wi-To stop, 41kr). There's ample paid parking in town for those arriving by car.

Walk along Storgata high street and step inside **1 Tromsø Domkirke** (Tromsø Church), which dates from 1861. Have a break at nearby **2 Risø** for the best coffee and cinnamon buns in town before walking the short distance to the **3 harbour**, where you'll see both fishing and expedition boats. This is the last stop before Svalbard for many sailors. Continue around the harbour to the **4 Polar Museum**. Built in a warehouse dating from the 1830s, this is the best place to discover more about the far north's polar history. The museum takes in everything from the history of trapping to the groundbreaking expeditions of Nansen and Amundsen. There are some fascinating artefacts and black-and-white archive photos. From here, walk by the traditional coloured wharf houses and through the recently developed **5 Vervet**.

Stroll over Tromsøbrua and you won't miss the modernist triangular **6 Ishavskatedralen** (Arctic Cathedral) built in 1965 and inspired by the surrounding mountains. The glowing stained-glass window that occupies the east end depicts Christ descending to earth, while the west end is filled by a futuristic organ and icicle-like chandeliers of Czech crystal. Head back to the harbour for a sauna session at **7 Sauna Pust** (book in advance), which lies at the end of the floating pontoon. Make sure you finish it with a bracing dip in the ocean.

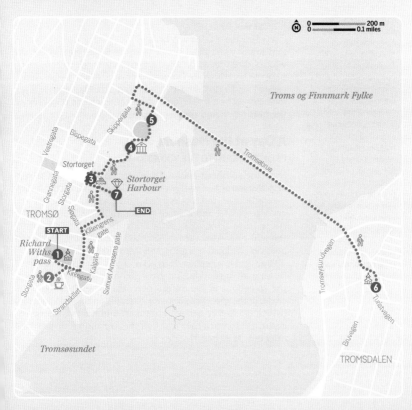

WHY I LOVE TROMSØ

Hugh Francis Anderson, writer

I moved to Tromsø for the mountains and stayed for the people. It might be the largest city in the far north, but it's full of small-town charm. I came here for the same reasons that many other people do – proximity to the wilderness, with endless ski-touring options during the winter, and hiking, camping and trail running in the summer. But what surprised me most was the vibrant and contemporary city life: world-class food, fantastic local beer, regular exhibitions in the local galleries, live music every week and an absolute treat every January when the **Tromsø International Film Festival** takes over.

Orcas (p278), Tromsø

(Continued from p278)
It is also an amazing way to enjoy the scenery around Tromsø, and many tours head north towards **Skjervøy**, where the whales often feed. On the two- to four-hour transit, you'll pass the breathtaking Lyngen Peninsula, where jagged snow-capped peaks rise almost 2000m right from the ocean. If you look closely, you'll also spot white-tailed eagles that prey on the fjords' fish and smaller seabirds.

A Day at the Museum
FROM THE SAMI TO THE VIKINGS

Near the southern end of Tromsøya, the **Tromsø University Museum** has well-presented and documented displays on traditional and modern Sami life, ecclesiastical art and accoutrements, and a small section on the Vikings. Downstairs, learn about rocks of the north and ponder a number of thought-provoking themes (such as the role of fire, the consequences of global warming and loss of wilderness).

There's also a replica 'Northern Lights machine', or terrella, an early invention that gives you in miniature a sense of the splendour of the aurora borealis. Other highlights include, in the garden, a *gammen,* or traditional Sami sod house (which offers free coffee in summer) and a set of hourglasses, turned to warn the vicar that their sermon time was running out. Take bus 37.

Beyond
Tromsø

The landscape around Tromsø is truly thrilling and a playground for those who want to embark on an adventure.

From Tromsø, it's easy to access remote fjords, high mountain peaks and dense forests. To the west, the island of Kvaløya is a hot spot for skiing and hiking. To the south is Senja. Though this is the country's second-largest island, it is a little-visited gem and is often dubbed Norway in miniature. To the west, you'll find the easily accessible Øvre Dividal National Park. With its old-growth birch and pine forests, lakes and rolling mountains, it's a year-round adventure destination. To the south, you'll find cultural history in Harstad, the gateway to Versterålen and Lofoten.

Always be aware of reindeer and moose, which often wander onto the roads. If you drive here in your own car in winter, consider spiked tyres.

A Drive around Whale Island
THE HOME OF ADVENTURE

The island of **Kvaløya** is accessed via Sandnessundbrua, the bridge on the west of Tromsøya. Drive south and turn right at Eidkjosen towards Kaldfjord. There are plenty of spaces to stop along the south of the fjord to embrace the wild views over **Kaldfjorden**, with the dorsal-fin-shaped peak of Store Blåmann, the island's highest mountain, easy to spot to the west.

For those looking for sublime summer hikes or phenomenal winter ski tours, turn left at Henrikvik for ample options along **Kattfjordeidet**. From here, you can enjoy the winding roads past Nordfjordbotn towards Sommarøy, which offers endless views over the North Atlantic, with a ferry to Senja accessed from nearby Brensholmen. Or drive on to beautiful **Ersfjord** for coffee and cake at the rustic interior design cafe Bryggejentene.

Head north and you'll feel the remoteness of Kvaløya as you skirt Kaldfjord and rise past Storvatnet to **Grøtfjord**. With its wide sand beach and westerly views, it's a perfect location for the Northern Lights and midnight sun.

Further still, you'll pass many hiking and ski-touring spots at the base of Grøtfjorden as you drive towards Tromvik. At

GETTING AROUND

There are brilliant ferry connections in Troms, and the Hurtigruten ferry from Harstad to Tromsø takes six hours and is a lovely way to see the coastline. This is a great option for those who are travelling without a car. However, for the best experience, it's best to hire a car so you can reach the magical locations off the beaten path.

☑ TOP TIP

In both summer and winter, it's essential that you travel by car to access these remote destinations.

SKIING IN TROMSØ

Avid ski tourers should always come prepared with the right skill set to be safe in the mountains. **Tromsø Ski Guides** offers guiding and training courses throughout the winter season, and for those looking to explore independently, Epsen Nordahl's *Ski Touring in Troms* is the definitive guidebook to the region.

To be safe in the mountains, it's imperative to have avalanche training and to download the Varsom app, which is updated daily and offers advance information about the snowpack and avalanche risk. In case of emergencies, call +47 113 or download the Hjelp 113 app, which sends your location to the emergency services once activated.

the junction, turn left onto the gravel road that leads to the quaint fishing village of **Rekvik**, where you'll find the trailhead for Skamtinden.

Ski-Touring in the Alps of the North
HIGH MOUNTAIN PEAKS

There are few places that have scenery as dramatic as the **Lyngen Peninsula**. If it's total immersion in nature you're after, this is the place to come. Its massive alpine peaks are formed from dark gabbro rock, one of the last remaining formations of the monumental Caledonian Range that once stretched from Svalbard to Scotland, and which has slowly worn down over the past 300 million years.

The mountains' magnificence first hits on the short ferry from Breivik to Svensby, which lies in the centre of the peninsula. Breivik is a 45-minute drive east from Tromsø. **Svensby** is a bucket-list destination for skiers, and today ranks as one of the most desirable places for ski-tourers.

The far north's tallest mountain, **Jiehkkevárri**, is found here and rises to 1834m. Capped by a massive glacier, it is often called the Mont Blanc of the north. There are plenty of mountains to ski here, from gentle faces to extreme descents, all of which offer sublime views.

During the summer, hiking and wild camping are a must around the peninsula's main town, **Lyngseidet**. Make sure to utilise norgeskart.no for detailed maps and trail options. On the east of the island, keep an eye out for whales that often feed in the north of Lyngenfjord, or join one of the local whale safaris or kayak tours.

Skiing and Hiking in Øvre Dividal National Park
WONDERLAND OF REINDEER

Øvre Dividal National Park is a beautiful two-hour drive southeast of Tromsø. Drive until you reach Frihetsli and continue to the end of the dirt road (there's a toll of 90kr), where you'll find ample parking and outdoor toilets. In winter, the dirt road is unmaintained, so you'll need to put your skis on here to reach the trailhead, which adds 1km to the trip.

The journey begins beside **Divielva**, the wide river that flows through the valley. There's a clear track that travels south up the valley. In summer, the old-growth pine and birch trees offer a magical backdrop to the sound of rushing water. In winter, silence fills the valley, and the river freezes over.

GETTING TO LOFOTEN
Harstad lies near the border of Nordland county and Lofoten to the west, making it a great spot from which to continue your journey. **Svolvær** (p252), the Lofoten Islands' largest town, takes just over two hours to reach by car.

TOP PICKS IN THE FAR NORTH

Aurora Spirit Distillery
Award-winning whisky from the world's northernmost distillery.

Blåivatnet
A gentle hike to a stunning bright-blue lake.

Lyngen Experience Lodge
A luxurious retreat on the banks of Ullsfjorden.

Lyngen Alps

Follow the red markers for 6km until the trail turns sharply north to **Dividalshytta**. A Den Norske Turistforening (DNT) cabin with 16 beds awaits. One person must be a member with a key; sign up in advance at dnt.no. If you prefer camping, there's ample space near the cabin to pitch your tent. The first day is gentle at just 8km.

Above the treeline, the trail continues into wide plateaus and high mountains. This is a native Sami herding area, and you'll see reindeer in both summer and winter. You'll push on over an unnamed mountain at 915m and see the magnificent Litle Jerta (1279m) to your left and Jerta (1428m) to your right. Continue through the valley between the mountains, around Stuora (1152m) and past the abundance of small lakes until you reach **Dærtahytta**. Stay in the cabin or camp nearby. This leg is 24km.

The final day is the longest at 26km and brings you back to Frihetsli over marsh and lakes and up 200m over a saddle to the north of Storfjellet (1045m). The descent is steep but well-marked as you pass back through the rich forests beside **Kvennelva** and onto the road. Make your way back to the parking spot.

WHERE TO SKI IN LYNGEN

Finn Hovem, ski guide, avalanche observer for Varsom.no and CEO of Hallo Lyngen, shares his thoughts on ski touring in the Lyngen Alps.

Backcountry Basics
While there are some simpler mountains in Lyngen, it's not an ideal location for beginners. Always check the avalanche forecast and consider hiring a guide.

Storgalten
This is a classic mountain on the northern end of the peninsula and accessible by car and sailboat. The panoramic double fjord views and various options for long descents to the sea make this a must-do!

Jiehkkevárri
The highest mountain in the Lyngen Alps, it means 'Glacier Mountain' in Sami. If you have the fitness and the right conditions, this massif is a joy to explore.

 BEST VIEWS IN TROMS

Grøtfjord
Easily accessible with ample parking, the beach here offers amazing views in both summer and winter.

Skamtind
This challenging hike brings you to 882m, with panoramic views over Kvaløya and the Atlantic.

Sommarøy
Charming fishing village with white-sand beaches overlooking minute islands and clear blue water.

A Multiday Hike across Norway in Miniature

Senja is two hours south of Tromsø and is Norway's second-largest island. Its name is unchanged from Old Norse and means to 'split apart'. As you travel from north to south, you'll uncover a land of alpine summits and enchanting lakes, and the best way to see it all is by hiking the 70km multiday Senja på Langs. It's best to drive to the remote trailhead and take a taxi back.

1 Bukkemoveien

When you begin the hike in the dense birch forests, you'll wonder where the mountains are. You'll hear rushing water from Lysvatnet as you head west into the luscious Nord-Heggedalen valley, a place plucked from a fairy tale. In the forests, deer and moose droppings litter the marked route, and the air is full of the sounds of birdlife.

The Hike: The path along the entire route is marked with red dots, and you'll see the first when you begin from the Lysbotn Kraftwork outbuilding at the end of the road. The path here is well trodden, but you still need to keep your eyes peeled for the red markers painted on trees and rocks. After 6.5km, you'll pass Heggedalshytta, an open cabin for campers. You can stop here or continue into Sør-Heggedalen to camp.

IMAGEBROKER.COM/SHUTTERSTOCK ©

Ånderdalen National Park

2 Heggedalshytta

As the journey continues, you emerge from the forests and begin climbing into Senja's dramatic mountains. Gradually gaining elevation, you'll soon see Istinden; it's worth leaving the path to hike to the summit (851m). Here, you'll have panoramic views over the fjords to the west and the valleys you'll soon walk through to the south.

The Hike: Continue west to Tromdalen before heading south. You'll be at 370m as you pass the long aquamarine Langdalsvatnet on the approach to Istinden. From the summit, continue down until the path cuts sharp east towards Kapervatnet. This descent is steep and if it's early in the season, you may have to wade across the river.

3 Ånderdalen National Park

The high mountains are behind you now and the national park is a wonder of old-growth pine forest, marshland and lakes. Camp beside the wide Åndervatnet or stay in the recently built Ånderbu cabin on the lake's eastern shore.

The Hike: The path circles Kapervatnet before descending towards Åndervatnet. From here, you rise again around the rocky Blåfjellet and follow the path southwest past Lutvatnet. There is ample fishing here and permits can be obtained in advance via inatur.no.

4 Olaheimen

The crossing of Senja is almost complete, and the luscious forests and marshland are abundant once again as you continue towards the end of the trail in the small village of Olaheimen. You will have walked 70km through Norway in miniature.

The Hike: The path is well marked as you continue down Olaheimen. Taxis aren't regular due to the island's remoteness, so it's best to call Senja Taxi on +47 48182010 well in advance.

THE FAR NORTH

BEYOND TROMSØ

FJELLVETT-REGLENE

A nation with a longstanding love for the wilderness, children learn the nine points of the Norwegian Mountain Code from a young age, and you should, too. To delve deeper, visit dnt.no.

1. Plan your trip and inform others about the route you have selected.
2. Adapt the planned routes according to ability and conditions.
3. Pay attention to the weather and the avalanche warnings.
4. Be prepared for bad weather and frost, even on short trips.
5. Bring the necessary equipment so you can help yourself and others.
6. Choose safe routes. Recognise avalanche terrain and unsafe ice.
7. Use a map and a compass. Always know where you are.
8. Don't be ashamed to turn around.
9. Conserve your energy and seek shelter if necessary.

A Town Steeped in History
VIKING SETTLEMENTS AND MEDIEVAL FARMS

In the south of Troms, you'll find **Harstad**, the second-largest town in the far north. Rich in history and the gateway to exploring Vesterålen and Lofoten, it's well worth stopping here. Bronze tools and weapons dated to 3000 years ago have been found on the Trondenes Peninsula near the city centre. This was an important settlement during the Viking Age where people gathered to meet and discuss, and it was a stronghold during the medieval period. The **Trondenes Historical Centre** showcases this diverse heritage, and the living **Medieval Farm** (24 June to 13 August) depicts how life would have been during the 12th century.

Ten minutes outside the city centre you'll find **Trondenes Church**, completed almost 600 years ago. It's the world's northernmost medieval stone structure and contains stunning Gothic paintings and an 18th-century organ.

For those travelling by ferry, the fast boat from Tromsø to Harstad runs twice a day (four times during the weekend) and takes just three hours. It's a wonderful way to experience the dramatic coastline of Troms from the sea itself.

The Adolf Gun
WORLD WAR II ERA GUNS

On the hill to the north of Trondenes Church, you'll find four surviving naval guns from WWII. With a barrel diameter of 16in, they are wide enough to fit an adult. These massive guns were a strategic defence against the Nazis and offered commanding views across the sea. Originally intended for battleships, they became part of the Atlantic Wall coastal fortifications, had a range of 56km and fired shells up to 1035kg. Today, only one gun remains in working order at **Trondenes Fortress**, which also serves as a memorial to the prisoners of war who built it. You can explore the fortress, witness the firing mechanism and even venture inside the 21m-long barrel. Guided tours cost 350kr per person and operate daily from June to September.

THE FERRY TO SENJA
The ferry from Brensholmen south to **Botnham** takes just 30 minutes and is a wonderful way to travel to **Senja** (p281). Timetables vary depending on the time of year, so make sure to check fylkestrafikk.no in advance.

 WHERE TO EAT & DRINK IN HARSTAD

Umami
This gourmet pick was voted northern Norway's best restaurant in 2017 and is a must for foodies. €€€

Bark
Come to the harbour in the centre of town for the best locally sourced ingredients and wines. €€€

Tapp Bar
A short walk from the harbour, enjoy beer brewed at Harstad Bryggeri, just 10 minutes away. €

286

Alta

 OSLO

With just over 20,000 people, Alta is the northern-most populated city in the world and your gateway to West Finnmark. Though the city itself is small, it has long been a meeting place for people and cultures of the north, including the Sami, Kvens and Norwegians. The Alta Museum showcases human origins in the region through the 7000-year-old UNESCO World Heritage rock carvings, and it was here in the late 1970s that the local Sami population petitioned against the creation of the Alta Dam, which disturbed swathes of native land. Though unsuccessful, it was this demonstration that brought global attention to Indigenous environmental rights in the north of Norway and a subsequent change in politics. Alta is not a beautiful city. It's really just a pit stop for nature lovers due to its proximity to Finnmarksvidda, Norway's largest plateau, with a plethora of activities during both summer and winter.

GETTING AROUND

You can get around Alta without a car, but you'll need your own wheels to explore the surrounding areas. If driving, park in the centre off Hesterkoen beside Biltema and walk from there.

Marvel at Stone Age Art
DEPICTIONS OF LIFE FROM THE LAST ICE AGE

The superb **Alta Museum** is in Hjemmeluft, at the western end of town, and features exhibits and displays on Sami culture, the copper-mining boom in nearby Kåfjord and the recent cultural and political struggles of the peoples who live in the north. The cliffs around it, a UNESCO World Heritage Site, are incised with around 6000 late–Stone Age carvings, dating from 7000 to 2000 years ago, and it's these petroglyphs that will live longest in the memory.

As the sea level decreased after the last Ice Age, carvings were made at progressively lower heights. Themes include hunting scenes, fertility symbols, bear, moose, reindeer and crowded boats. There are two walking routes to see the carvings. Many along the 1.2km boardwalk loop have been highlighted with red-ochre paint (thought to have been the original colour); the longer 3km loop includes many untouched carvings, and it requires sharp eyes to pick them out.

The Alta rock carvings were discovered by chance in the 1970s and added to UNESCO's World Heritage list in 1985.

☑ TOP TIP

The best time to visit Alta is in March when the annual **Borealis Winter Festival** takes place. Expect to see illuminated ice sculptures in the streets, live music and theatre, and be sure to watch the start of the famous ISSF World Championship Finnmarksløpet dogsledding race.

Sorrisniva Igloo Hotel

A SPECIAL STAY

At the **Sorrisniva Igloo Hotel**, all the bedrooms – and the beds too – are made entirely of ice, as are the chapel, bridal suite and the stunning ice bar with its weird and wonderful sculptures lit by fibre-optics. This is the world's northernmost igloo hotel, recreated by local artists and sculptors every year. Once the mercury drops, the hotel is built entirely from scratch using 250 tonnes of ice and 7000 cu metres of snow, harvested from the nearby lake Sierravann and the Alta River. Spanning 2500 sq metres in area, the Igloo is open to guests and day visitors (between noon and 8pm) from 20 December to 7 April. Sorrisniva is 17km south of Alta.

Dogsledding near Alta
YOUR CHANCE TO SHOUT 'MUSH!'

As the location of Europe's longest dogsled race, Alta is an ideal spot to experience what has been a form of transport in the Arctic since the 10th century BCE. The best time to go dogsledding is in the late winter and early spring months, although summertime seldding on wheels is also an option in many places.

Holmen Husky Lodge is a family-run business with tours ranging from 2½ to five hours in length. While dogsledding is traditionally thought of as a winter experience, the lodge also offers dryland mushing during non-winter months. A range of accommodation options are also available, including a *lavvu* (tepee; Sami tent dwelling) from which you can enjoy the Northern Lights above.

If you wish to combine a day of dogsledding with gastronomic delights in a fine-dining restaurant, head to **Trasti og Trine**, which focuses on local produce from the surrounding mountains, forest and sea. A variety of cooking courses are also available, starting at 152kr.

If you want to catch breathtaking views of the Northern Lights along the Alta River or experience the world's northernmost ice hotel, **Sorrisniva** has both a wilderness lodge and an igloo hotel. Arctic experiences from dogsledding to ice sculpting and snowshoeing can be organised here.

Beyond
Alta

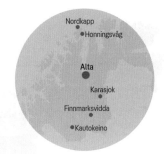

The wild northern coast is dotted with fishing villages and riven with grand fjords, while inland is a vast plateau.

The landscape changes almost beyond belief in West Finnmark. On the journey north, dense forests give way to Jurassic coastal roads until you reach the barren but breathtaking Nordkapp, with endless views over the North Atlantic. Birdwatching and fishing are found on Magerøya, and nearby Honningsvåg comes alive with regular concerts and festivals throughout the summer.

Below Alta lies Finnmarksvidda, one of Europe's largest plateaus, and a regular training ground for North and South Pole expeditions. It is also the homeland of the Sami and the stomping ground for thousands of reindeer. The Sami capital, Karasjok, lies to the southeast of the plateau, with nearby Kautokeino a hub for arts and culture.

History and Hikes in Honningsvåg
THE GATEWAY TO NORDKAPP

The quaint seaside town of **Honningsvåg** may be small, but it packs a lot of life into its charming streets. Like much of northern Norway, it was destroyed during WWII; the neogothic Honningsvåg Church built in 1885 was the only building to survive. After the war, the church became a refuge for the remaining inhabitants as they rebuilt the village, and the **Nordkappmuseet** by the quay documents the period in fascinating detail. If you're travelling on the Hurtigruten ferry, this is where you'll disembark.

The hike to the summit of **Storfjellet** (310m) provides fantastic views over the town and harbour. Though steep in places, the near-complete Nordkapptrappa steps make the journey much easier.

Off Sjøgata you'll find the rustic **Sjøgata Pub**, which serves beer from its own brewery. Above it is **Perleporten Kulturhus**, which comes alive during Our Northernmost Life theatre performance in June, the lively Oggasjakka music festival in August and the Nordkapp Film Festival in September.

GETTING AROUND

It's imperative to have a car to fully explore West Finnmark. Due to the vast distances and remote locations, it's very arduous to attempt this using the bus system, which has somewhat slowed since the COVID-19 pandemic. Wildlife rules the road here, so you do have to be very aware of wandering reindeer. And if driving in winter, anticipate harsh conditions and drive slowly.

☑ TOP TIP

From Alta, it's a stunning 3½-hour drive along Porsangerfjorden over to Magerøya and Nordkapp, Europe's northernmost point.

This spring and summer driving tour takes you on a journey all the way to Europe's northernmost point. While it can be done in one go, it's much nicer when spread over two or three days, or as part of a wider road trip across the far north. From **1 Alta**, follow the E6 across wide plains towards **2 Olderfjord**, where you peel left onto the E69 and are treated to 125km of twisting coastal roads. Take your time and enjoy the views over Porsangerfjorden to the east. You'll pass through the long **3 Nordkapptunnelen** (almost 7km) and then rise to Magerøya. At the fork, turn left and continue to **4 Nordkapp**. Europe's northernmost point is a popular and busy spot where the cliffs drop 307m into the Arctic Ocean, and you're closer to the North Pole than to Oslo. Until 1956, there was no road and visitors had to sail to Hornvika and hike 3km to reach Nordkapp. The small settlement can be reached on a short hike. On your way back, turn left towards **5 Skarsvåg**, Europe's northernmost fishing village. This is an ideal spot to fish for cod, halibut and king crab, with tours running daily. Stop by Daniels Hus for hearty homemade food. Drive 30 minutes west through rolling tundra, punctuated by dark pools and cropped by reindeer, to **6 Gjesvær**. Another beautiful fishing village, it's also the launch spot for the two-hour Bird Safari which sails out to **7 Gjesværstappan Nature Reserve** three times per day. It's home to one of the largest puffin colonies and a nice way to experience the northernmost point of Europe from the ocean. Now it's time to travel south and unwind in **8 Honningsvåg**, a small town that bustles with culture and life.

290

Cross Finnmarksvidda on Skis
NORWAY'S LARGEST PLATEAU

Ready to check another far-out experience off the bucket list? **Finnmarksvidda** is Norway's largest plateau, covering 22,000 sq km and sitting at an elevation of 300m to 500m, and accounts for a fifth of Norway's wild nature. The best way to see this wild expanse, of course, is on skis. There are several routes to take, but the most common is the four-day 85km **Finnmark på langs** from Stilla to Ássebákt. This is a trip that should be high on the list for any winter enthusiast and is best between January and May.

Begin in **Stilla**, a 25-minute taxi ride from Alta, and embark on the undulating 15km journey from Upper Stilla to Jotka Fjellstua. You can sleep and eat here, or camp nearby (bearing in mind that temperatures can drop below -30°C).

The second day is the longest, covering 30km to the Mollisjok Fjellstue. This path follows sections of the Finnmark cross-country course and includes a crossing of Lesjavri, the region's largest lake. Enjoy a hearty meal, followed by a sauna and deep sleep at **Mollisjok**, but be sure to book well in advance.

On the third day, you'll ski approximately 25km from Mollesjoka to **Ravnastua**. You'll gradually climb to beautiful but exposed terrain where conditions can be harsh. As you begin your descent, you'll see the forest begin to appear ahead, where you'll find **Ravnstua Fjellstua** and a warm meal and bed.

The fourth and final day involves skiing from Ravnastua to the Sami capital Karasjok, covering approximately 14km. The route passes through the dense birch forests of Karasjokdalen before dropping to **Ássebákt**, which lies on the 92 Hwy. From here, you can call a taxi or ski 15km along Karasjohka, the frozen river that flows towards Karasjok, where a bus (60, 63) will take you back to Alta.

Karasjok: Capital of the Sami
HOME OF THE SAMI PARLIAMENT

Kautokeino may have more Sami residents, but **Karasjok** (Kárásjohka in Sami) is Sami Norway's indisputable capital. The beautiful **Sami Parliament** (Sámediggi) is a great way to understand more about contemporary life. You'll first spot the summit-like silver-larch cladding through the treetops as you arrive. Inside is the **Vandrehallen**, a large foyer and library, which was inspired by the night sky and the

BEST PLACES TO STAY IN HONNINGSVÅG

Nordkapp Camping
This family-owned campsite just outside Honningsvåg is the perfect spot for those on a road trip. It also has cabins to rent if you're looking for something more comfortable. €

The View
A more luxurious option above town, come here for the advertised panoramas as well as access to a sauna and spa. €€€

Nordkappferrier Gjesvaer
Thirty minutes away in Gjesvær, the apartments here are far from the crowds and perfect if you're after a little solitude. €€€

OTHER PLACES TO EXPLORE BEYOND ALTA

Sørøya
On the west coast of Magerøya is the island of Sørøya, one of Norway's most tranquil spots.

Hammerfest
Become a member of the Royal and Ancient Polar Bear Society in this large town.

Havøysund
Experience dramatic landscapes on the drive to Havøysund on a longer road trip to Magerøya.

FINNMARKSLØPET

The Finnmarksløpet is Europe's longest dogsled race, covering 1200km across Finnmarksvidda over five to six days. With 160 teams and over 1500 dogs, it's an absolute spectacle to watch and a true feat of human and canine endurance. The race starts in Alta, crosses Finnmark to Kirkenes, then circles back to Alta. Mushers use up to 14 svelte and hardy Alaskan huskies, each of which requires 10,000 calories a day during the race. Held annually since 1981, the race takes place in early March and it is worth timing your trip north to coincide with the start.

MAURIZIO FABBRONI/SHUTTERSTOCK ©

Nordkapp (p290)

Northern Lights. The library houses Norway's largest collection of Sami-language books, and you'll discover interesting historical artefacts, including King Olav's signature on a reindeer hide when the first Sami parliament was opened in 1989. Along the corridors, you'll see portraits and artworks by Astrid Aasen, Kåre Kivijärvi and Synnøve Persen. The plenary hall's blue concrete slab reflects the Sami landscape, where there are 39 representatives of the local constituencies. Tours of the building begin at 1pm on Tuesdays, Wednesdays and Thursdays.

Culture and Livelihood at the Sami Museum
LEARN MORE ABOUT SAMI TRADITIONS

The **Sami Museum** (De Samiske Samlinger) in Karasjok offers wonderful insight into traditional Sami life. In the main building, exhibits include displays of Sami clothing, livelihoods, tools, *duodji* (arts) and music, including the joik (p294), one

 WHERE TO EAT IN HONNINGSVÅG

Honni Bakes
Come to this central French bakery for coffee, fresh bread, pastries, and homemade chocolate. €

Arctic Sans
This is the restaurant where the locals eat out, and it's one of the best in town. €€

Corner Spiseri
Corner is the oldest restaurant in town. If you're feeling brave, try the traditional cod tongues. €€

of the oldest forms of song, believed to be gifted to the Sami by the fairies and elves of the high Arctic.

Outside, several traditional buildings show how the Sami lived in this region before the advent of modern technology. Temperatures have been recorded as low as -51°C here, and it's truly amazing how resilient and ingenious the Sami were in the ways they lived with the land in order to survive in such extreme conditions. Entrance is 150kr per person.

Silversmithing and Reindeer in Kautokeino
THE SAMI'S WINTER HOMELANDS

Kautokeino, the traditional winter base of the reindeer Sami (as opposed to their coastal kin), remains more emphatically Sami than Karasjok, which has made concessions to Norwegian culture. For those who make it here, one spot not to miss is **Juhls Sølvsmie**: a magical silversmith, gallery and open house on a hilltop overlooking Kautokeinoelva, accessed off the arterial E45 that runs through the town. Danish artist Frank Juhls and his German wife Regina met in Kautokeino by chance in 1959. Inspired by Sami culture and the beauty of Finnmarksvidda, they built a small cabin here and began to restore prized Sami jewellery. Over the years, they added to the cabin; today, it is a striking art deco building that blends into the landscape. You enter through the silversmith, where local craftspeople create stunning jewellery. In the basement area, you'll discover a collection of Middle Eastern artefacts collected by the couple in the 1970s, and you may even spot Regina, now in her 80s, working on a vast mosaic that has formed her life's work. The staff, many of whom are local Sami, are incredibly knowledgeable and will gladly give you an unofficial tour.

Also here is the **Kautokeino Cultural Centre**, home to the only Sami language theatre in Norway, where performances run throughout the year. There's plenty of artwork and history here, but it's best to email or call ahead as opening hours vary, and all information is given in Sami. The centre is located on the outskirts of town towards Karasjok.

A BRIEF HISTORY OF NORDKAPP

At 71° N, Nordkapp has been a seafarers' landmark for centuries. Originally called Knyskanes by local Sami, it was named North Cape in 1553 by British navigator Richard Chancellor during an expedition to find a route through the Northeast Passage to Asia. With the onset of trade, it became a point of reference for sailors, and modern tourism began in 1873 when King Oscar II, Union King of Norway and Sweden, unveiled the king's monument here.

WHERE TO STAY IN KARASJOK

Karasjok Camping
Occupies a hillside site; perfect for those on a summer road trip. Cabins too. €

Engholm Husky Lodge
A luxurious cabin experience about 6km from town, with dogsledding tours. €€€

Jergul Astu
Outside of town with basic but rustic cabins that embrace the surrounding wilderness. €

Vadsø

Vadsø

✪OSLO

☑ TOP TIP

While the E6 is the arterial highway that runs through Norway, for the most magical experience peel off onto the Fv98 at Lakselv and rejoin the E6 at Tana. Once voted the most beautiful road in Norway, it should be on any road tripper's list.

A BRIEF HISTORY OF THE JOIK

Joiking is a traditional form of Sami singing that evokes or depicts a person, place or animal through song. Considered one of the oldest vocal traditions in Europe, joiks serve various purposes, including storytelling, honouring deceased loved ones, boosting self-esteem and expressing love. Joiking was suppressed during the Christianisation of the Sami and faced controversy due to its association with shamanism and pre-Christian rituals. Despite these challenges, joiking has persisted as an important aspect of Sami culture and is performed in both traditional and contemporary styles today.

Welcome to one of the most remote corners of Europe. On the northern shore of Vergangerfjorden lies the Varanger Peninsula, which extends into the Barents Sea. The northeasternmost part of Norway, its heart is Vadsø, a small but lively town with a population of just over 5000 and the gateway to East Finnmark. Like many coastal communities in the far north, it boomed as a fishing and trading port in the 19th century and was a hub for Kvens, a minority group descended from Finnish fishers and farmers. Due to its proximity to Russia, the entire peninsula was a strategic location for the Nazis during WWII, and Vadsø, like many other northern towns, was burned to the ground during the Nazi retreat. Following decades of modernisation, it is now the administrative centre for Finnmark, and the staging ground for festivals, events and outdoor experiences.

Steller's eider duck

RISTO RAUNIO/SHUTTERSTOCK ©

Strolling the Vadsø streets is the best way to get to know this far-flung town. Begin at the **1 Culture Park** on Store Vadsøya to learn about the region's early settlers. The remains of a medieval settlement can be found here, alongside numerous gun, bunker and trench sites, including the **2 Kokkenes Batteri** from WWII. Nearby, you'll also spot the oil-rig-shaped **3 Airship Mast**, built in the mid-1920s as an anchor and launch site for airborne expeditions to the polar regions. The expedition of Roald Amundsen, Umberto Nobile and Lincoln Ellsworth, which floated via the North Pole to Alaska in the airship *Norge N-1,* first used it in April 1926. Two years later it was the launch site for Nobile's airship *Italia,* which attempted to repeat the journey but crashed on Svalbard. Amundsen joined the rescue expedition and disappeared in the attempt, becoming a na-

tional martyr as well as a hero. The entirety of Varanger is a birdwatching paradise, and in early spring you'll likely see the rare Steller's eider duck here.

Across the bridge, turn right to learn more about Kven history at the **4 Esbensengården,** an opulent merchant's dwelling, complete with stable and servants' quarters, which was constructed in the mid-19th century. The nearby **5 Tuomainengården** is a historic Finnish farmhouse, built in 1840, with its own bakery, sauna and blacksmith. Both properties are a part of Varanger Museum and the only prewar buildings left in Vadsø. A 10-minute walk to the north of town brings you to the **6 Vadsø Museum,** the centre for Finnish and Kven history in Norway. Finish with a gentle stroll along the 2.5km **7 Kjærlighetsstien trail** to the west of town for stunning views over Vergangerfjord.

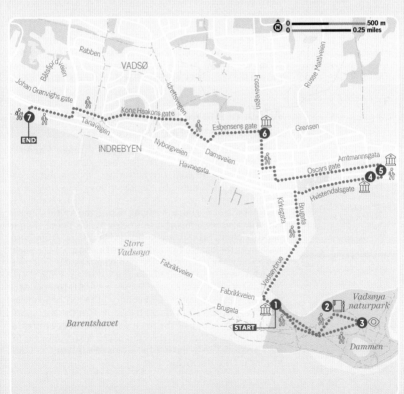

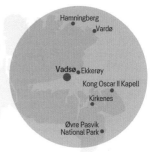

Beyond
Vadsø

Beyond Vadsø lies eastern Finnmark, a land of remote Arctic scenery and wildlife.

Along a single-track road dwarfed by jagged rocks is Hamningberg, one of the far north's only surviving prewar villages. Vardø is filled with colourful street art and polar history, and was the site of witch-burning during the 17th century. Reindeer line the sweeping coastal road while white-tailed eagles soar on the sea breeze. Inland, undulating mountains sweep across Varanger National Park, and white-sand beaches border clear blue water surrounding the bird sanctuary on Ekkerøy.

To the east, Kirkenes shows the close historical ties to Russia, and you can safely follow along Pasvikdalen, the river that forms the border, to the northeasternmost part of Norway or into the secluded Øvre Pasvik National Park to the south.

GETTING AROUND

Like the rest of Finnmark, it's difficult to get around without your own car. To make the most of this region, hire a vehicle first in Tromsø or Alta.

☑ **TOP TIP**

You're officially in the most remote part of Norway, where you'll need two things: a car and insect repellent.

A Tour of Norway's Easternmost Town
WITCHCRAFT, STREET ART AND MORE

Let yourself be surprised as you stroll through **Vardø**, a town where contemporary street art blends with a rich and varied history. Although this butterfly-shaped island is connected to the mainland by the 2.9km-long Ishavstunnelen (Arctic Ocean tunnel), locals maintain that theirs is the only 'mainland' Norwegian town lying within the Arctic climatic zone (its average temperature is below 10°C). There's ample parking along Strandgata beside the harbour. From here, walk over the bridge to the **Pomor Museum**, where you'll learn about the fascinating Russian Pomor fishers and traders who once frequented Vardø and Varanger. From there, it's a short walk to the powerful yet eerie **Steilneset Memorial**, which honours the memory of the 91 people executed for witchcraft in the 17th century. On the way there, you'll also pass one of the town's striking **street murals**. Artists painted these on the sides of old, abandoned buildings around Vardø during the Komafest in 2012 to commemorate the town's heritage.

Berlevåg (p299)

WITCHCRAFT IN VARDØ

The Steilneset Memorial honours the 91 victims of the Vardø witch trials, which were held between 1600 and 1692. Accusations were often made by neighbours, and the trials involved sins like poisoning, spellcasting and gatherings with the devil. Most victims were women, but some were men. On Domen, a hill about 2km south of town on the mainland, is the cave where they allegedly held their satanic rites and secret rendezvous with the devil.

As you walk through the memorial, you can read about each victim's crime and subsequent execution. All were burned. It's a powerful experience that sheds light on one of the darker aspects of human history.

The marked path then brings you to **Vardøhus Fest-ning**. The world's northernmost fortress, it was completed in 1738 and is free to visit. From the embankment you'll see the Russian peninsula of Rybachy across Varanger Fjord. It makes for an interesting tour, though much information is in Norwegian. A five-minute walk brings you to **Nordpol Kro**, northern Norway's oldest inn, where you can enjoy a bite to eat in the same place that Polar explorer Fridtjof Nansen stayed before his audacious FRAM 2 expedition to the North Pole in 1889.

A Wild Trip to Hamningberg

DRIVE TO FINNMARK'S OLDEST FISHING VILLAGE

The small village of **Hamningberg** lies at the very end of the Varanger Peninsula, where it braces against the might of the Barents Sea. The 45km mostly single-lane road is an absolute treat. Massive, gnarled cliffs cling to the coastline, the road cuts through enormous boulders and the wind drives in hard from the north. Look out for whales that often feed in the rich waters here as eagles soar above and reindeer wander freely.

In Hamningberg, park in the large car park at the town entrance and stroll past the traditional fishing houses, which escaped German destruction during the war. The oldest buildings have turf roofs and were used as trading houses with the Pomors.

THE UNIQUE ARCTIC CLIMATE

Varanger National Park is a wonder of wildlife-rich plateaus, marshlands and valleys. The Arctic landscape here formed before the last Ice Age and is unique to this region. In winter, you can ski across the park; in summer, it's a hot spot for hiking. However, if you head out alone you must have Arctic experience as most of the park is unmarked and you'll need to rely on compass and map-reading skills.

Visit Varanger partners with local companies to organise guided hikes for all abilities so that everyone can explore this remarkable place. Check out visitgreater arctic.com for more details.

PIOTR POZNAN/SHUTTERSTOCK ©

Arctic skua, Ekkerøy

Birdwatching in Ekkerøy
GENTLE HIKES AND DESERTED BEACHES

About 15km west of Vadsø on the E75 is a narrow isthmus leading to the fishing hamlet of **Ekkerøy**. Under the midnight sun, the white-sand beaches and clear blue bays feel more Mediterranean than Arctic. Past the village along the northern headlands of the former island are several marked hiking trails that lead through the nature reserve. This is one of the best places to watch rare birdlife in the region. Walk the gentle path to **Ekkerøy Fuglefjell** to observe more birds before continuing out to the easternmost tip for spectacular views over Varangerfjorden.

 BEST WINTER ADVENTURES BEYOND VADSØ

King Crab	Dogsledding	Snowmobile
Join a tour to catch and cook the enormous king crab, found in abundance around Kirkenes.	Snowhotel Kirkenes offers daily husky tours for those willing to brave the cold (October to April).	Drive your own snowmobile through the polar night in search of the Northern Lights.

Life on the Border in Kirkenes
A FUSION OF CULTURES AND HISTORY IN THE FAR NORTH

This is it: you're as far east as Cairo, further east than most of Finland, a mere 15km from the border with Russia – and at the end of the line for the Hurtigruten coastal ferry. It's also road's end for the E6, the highway that runs all the way down to Oslo.

Walking through the streets of **Kirkenes**, you'll likely hear people speaking Russian. And no wonder: the town is just 8km from the Russian border and has been a central hub for culture and trade for centuries. In fact, up until the war with Ukraine, Norwegian and Russian residents within 30km of the border used to be able to travel freely between the two countries, a policy that helped foster relations in the far north.

The **Borderland Museum** documents much of this history, including the role Russians and Norwegians played during WWII. The museum's Savio collection displays the distinctive woodblock prints of local Sami artist John A Savio (1902–38), whose works evoke the tension between Indigenous life and the forces of nature. Near the centre, you'll spot the **Soviet Liberation Monument**, in honour of the Russian forces that liberated the region in 1944. And around the corner you can go on a guided tour of **Andersgrotta**, the bomb shelter used during the 328 airstrikes that razed the city. Book tours in advance.

Kirkenes is the terminus of the Hurtigruten coastal ferry, which heads southwards daily. A bus meets the boat and runs into town and on to the airport.

The Siberian Taiga in Øvre Pasvik National Park
NORWAY'S MOST REMOTE NATIONAL PARK

Even when diabolical mosquito swarms make life hell for warm-blooded creatures, the remote lakes, wet tundra bogs and Norway's largest stand of virgin taiga forest lend appeal to little **Øvre Pasvik National Park**, in the far reaches of the Pasvik Valley.

Some 100km south of Kirkenes and 265km south of Vadsø is this last corner of Norway. Because of its remote location, it is rarely visited by tourists, even though it's one of the far north's most phenomenal landscapes. Home to the densest population of brown bears and the largest old-growth pine forests in the country, a journey here is truly off the beaten path. *(Continues on p301)*

WHERE TO EAT IN & AROUND KIRKENES

Silja Wara grew up in the Pasvik Valley near Kirkenes and now lives and works in the town centre. She shares her recommendations for food and drink in Kirkenes.

Aurora Restobar
This is *the* place to eat, with both local and international dishes. The atmosphere here makes you forget you're in a small town in northern Norway.

Boris Gleb Bar
In summer, book a boat trip with Barents Safari and float down the River Pasvik to Boris Gleb, an outdoor bar at the Russian border.

Bugøynes Bistro
Bugøynes is the perfect fishing village just 100km from Kirkenes; come for the views and local seafood dishes at Bugøynes Bistro.

WEST VARANGER HIGHLIGHTS BEYOND VADSØ

Båtsfjord
Norway's fishing capital, this is a lively working town with ample birdwatching opportunities.

Berlevåg
Feel the might of the Arctic Ocean at the northernmost town on mainland Norway.

Kongsfjord Gjestehus
Unwind with dramatic seascapes in a converted old farm in a truly remote location.

Nothing feels quite as remote as this road trip along the Russian border to Norway's easternmost point, which is only accessible by car in the summer months. From **1 Kirkenes**, head along the E105 until you see the Storskog Border Station leading to Russia. Turn left onto the Fv8860 that passes beside **2 Jarfjorden**. Take it easy and enjoy the Jurassic landscape and dense clouds that often hang low in the valleys as you continue east. After 40 minutes, the road becomes a heavily pitted gravel path that you'll need to drive carefully along. One kilometre further, stop beside the **3 Pasvikelva river**. The middle of the river is the border, and you'll see Russia's red-and-green marker pole on the other side. Do not approach or enter the river. As you continue along the gravel road, you'll spot Russian watchtowers above the forests until you reach **4 Kong Oscar II Kapell** after 8km. After numerous disputes, it was built in 1869 to help define the border and is a remarkable building to see in the middle of the wilderness. A few minutes further on you'll come to the end of the road. With ample parking, a firepit and toilets, it's a fantastic place to spend the night. Though much of the surrounding area is inaccessible due to military restrictions, it's worth stretching your legs on the sandy beach of **5 Sandstrand**, which offers commanding views of the Barents Sea. This is as far east as you can go within Norway and a thrilling highlight.

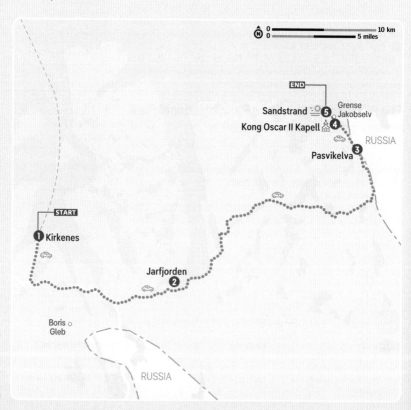

Jarfjorden

SAMI HERDING IN THE BORDER- LANDS

Sápmi, or Lapland, is an Indigenous Sami region that comprises the northern parts of Norway, Sweden, Finland and Russia. Descendants of northern Europe's nomadic peoples, the Sami trace their heritage back to the end of the last Ice Age, and reindeer herding has been a way of life for many communities for thousands of years.

Today, there are approximately 80,000 Indigenous Sami residing in Sápmi, and herders spend months guiding their reindeer across the harsh environment. These magnificent animals are not only a source of sustenance, but they also provide material for clothing and shelter. As such, they hold sacred importance in Sami culture. Reindeer meat is popular in the far north, and you'll find it in many supermarkets and restaurants in the region.

(Continued from p299)

Though you can visit year-round, this is a particularly magical place in summer. Begin by stopping at **Svanhovd Visitor Centre** to learn more about the park's conservation work and wildlife. There are many marked trails throughout the park, but the highlight is the manageable 5km hike to **Treriksrøysa**, the point at which the Norwegian, Finnish and Russian borders meet. You begin at Grensefossen and follow the undulating marked trail west. There are many planks across the boggy marshland, so it's best to wear waterproof hiking boots.

Another accessible route is off the poor road that turns southwest 1.5km south of Vaggatem and ends 9km later at a car park near the northeastern end of **Lake Sortbrysttjørna**. There, a marked track leads southwestward for 5km, passing several scenic lakes, marshes and bogs to end at the Ellenvannskoia hikers' hut, beside the large lake, **Ellenvatn**.

In the height of summer, midges and mosquitoes will be out in the millions – whatever you do, don't forget the insect repellent.

Svalbard

FROZEN LANDSCAPES AND MINING HERITAGE

A heart-stopping wilderness of snow and ice that calls the intrepid to venture further than they've been before.

Svalbard's raw, bleak beauty entices travellers seeking a taste of polar endeavour, walking where pioneering explorers, resilient miners and polar bears have gone before.

Lying between 74° N and 81° N, this icy archipelago was discovered in 1596 when a Dutch party, led by Willem Barentsz, was searching for the Northwest Passage. Tales of waters teeming with whales, walruses and seals soon spread. The race to win bragging rights over polar 'firsts' continued, and explorers such as Roald Amundsen used Svalbard as a jumping-off point to travel ever further north. Meanwhile, large-scale coal-mining operations began in the early 20th century. Today, Norway has only one remaining operational mine (Mine 7) and it's slated to close by 2025.

Scientific research and tourism now predominate here. Cruise ships and budget air links mean Svalbard is no longer the tantalisingly remote destination it once was, but it's still very much a place for the adventure-minded, with almost limitless options for tours, trips and expeditions into its soul-stirring, frozen wilderness. Tourism is managed more tightly here than on the mainland as protecting the fragile ecosystem, already at risk from climate change, requires constant vigilance – around 65% of Svalbard's landmass is protected and the imperative to 'leave no trace' is especially important. As the Sysselmesteren (Governor's Office) reminds visitors: 'It's not possible to be an invisible tourist – but we appreciate your trying'.

GINGER_POLINA_BUBLIK/SHUTTERSTOCK ©

THE MAIN AREAS

LONGYEARBYEN
Former mining town turned adventure capital.
p306

NY-ÅLESUND
Research station and the world's northernmost town. **p316**

FLORIDASTOCK/SHUTTERSTOCK ©

Left: Northern Lights above Longyearbyen (p306); above: polar bear, Svalbard

Find Your Way

Only a fraction of Svalbard's heavily protected, 61,000-sq-km expanse is accessible to casual visitors. You'll fly into Longyearbyen, the archipelago's largest settlement, and, to explore further, join the myriad guided day trips or tours available.

Ny-Ålesund, p316

A world-famous polar research station synonymous with pioneering expeditions and drama – and the furthest north you can send a postcard.

Longyearbyen, p306

Svalbard's 'big city', with cosy lodgings, good food, a smattering of cultural attractions and the relics of historic mining operations.

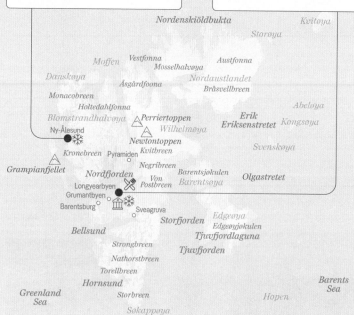

Nordenskiöldbukta

Kvitøya

Storøya

Moffen Vestfonna

Danskøya Mosselhalvøya Austfonna

Åsgårdfoona Nordaustlandet

Monacobreen Bråsvellbreen

Holtedahlfonna Abeløya

Blomstrandhalvøya Perriertoppen Erik

Ny-Ålesund Wilhelmøya Eriksenstretet Kongsøya

Kronebreen Pyramiden Kvitbreen Newtontoppen Svenskøya

Grampianfjellet Nordfjorden Negribreen Barentsjøkulen

Longyearbyen Von Barentsøya Olgastretet

Grumantbyen Postbreen

Barentsburg Sveagruva

Bellsund Storfjorden Edgeøya

Edgeøyjøkulen

Strongbreen Tjuvfjordlaguna

Nathorstbreen Tjuvfjorden

Torellbreen

Hornsund Barents

Greenland Storbreen Hopen Sea

Sea Søkappøya

BOAT

As there are no roads between settlements, travelling beyond Longyearbyen usually involves an organised boat trip. The season runs between May and September. Depending on weather conditions, journeys can be an adventure in their own right.

Norwegian
Sea

Bjørnøya

SNOWMOBILE

In winter the snowmobile (snøscooter) becomes a handy mode of transportation for locals. It's possible to zip to other settlements on one, and visitors can join various tours running until early May, snow conditions permitting.

0 ——— 100 km
0 ——— 50 miles

MARCIN KADZIOLKA/SHUTTERSTOCK ©

Global Seed Vault (p310)

Plan Your Time

Longyearbyen is an exciting base, but Svalbard's true beauty lies outside the town. The most popular excursions fill up quickly so book well in advance, especially during the peak seasons.

A Longyearbyen Pitstop

● Arriving in **Longyearbyen** (p306), head to **Svalbard Museum** (p306) for an introduction to the archipelago's nature and history. In winter, make like a musher on a **dogsledding experience** (p311); in summer, see Arctic giants on a **walrus safari** (p312). Year-round, experience life as a miner at **Gruve 3** (p308) and swap stories over a drink at **Karlsberger Pub** (p310).

Svalbard in Five Days

● After you've explored **Longyearbyen** (p306), set aside a day to visit **Ny-Ålesund** (p306) and follow in the footsteps of legendary explorer Roald Amundsen. For ultimate isolation, book an overnight trip to **Isfjord Radio** (p315) and swim in the Arctic Ocean between sauna sessions. For a last-night treat, make reservations at **Huset** (p310) for a tasting menu of Arctic delicacies.

Seasonal Highlights

SPRING
In March, locals celebrate the return of the sun over the horizon. Days grow longer but there's still snow.

POLAR SUMMER
From May to August the midnight sun brings 24-hour daylight. Boat trips offer the chance to see Svalbard's wildlife.

AUTUMN
The colours of autumn paint the Arctic tundra in September and early October. It's a good time to go sea fishing for cod.

POLAR NIGHTS
All-day darkness lasts from November to late January. It can be bleak, but if you're lucky, you'll see the **Northern Lights**.

Longyearbyen

Longyearbyen

✪ OSLO

GETTING AROUND

Daily flights from Oslo (three hours) and Tromsø (1½ hours) land 5km from town. Buses meet flights and shuttle passengers to every hotel and guesthouse.

The town is walkable and mostly flat but spread out. The 2km walk to a few lodgings (particularly Gjestehuset 102) can feel long in subzero conditions. If you need a ride, Svalbard Buss og Taxi and Longyearbyen Taxi are the two options.

You can wander freely around Longyearbyen (polar bears rarely venture into the centre) but don't go beyond the town boundary, clearly marked by polar bear signs, unless accompanied by a guide with a firearm. The risk of being attacked is tiny but the outcome could be a fine at best and death – for you and the bear – at worst.

☑ TOP TIP

Bring some slippers or cosy socks to wear indoors – the longstanding Svalbard tradition of taking off shoes at the door is upheld at every hotel (and in the museums too), recalling the days when miners wanted to keep their barracks coal-dust free.

Founded by American mining magnate John Monroe Longyear in 1906, Longyearbyen has come a long way since its beginnings as a company town on the shores of Adventfjorden. Though it's closer to the North Pole than to Oslo, Longyearbyen's lively international population lends it the feel of a European ski resort. About 2500 people from over 50 countries call Svalbard's biggest settlement home – a number that can almost double when a cruise ship docks and visitors disembark.

Longyearbyen's industrial waterfront and Arctic-hardy architecture can scarcely be described as attractive. But a varied selection of restaurants and bars and a few diverting museums make it an excellent base from which to venture into the surrounding mountains and valleys. Activity providers offer experiences close to town and deep into the archipelago's frozen reaches. Most trips depart from Longyearbyen and many can be booked through the tourist office.

Understanding the Archipelago
LONGYEARBYEN'S MUSEUMS

Start by exploring the archipelago from every angle at **Svalbard Museum**, in the same building as the University Centre. Hunting and trapping, whaling, wildlife, geology and the impact of climate change are all covered here, and there are temporary exhibitions too – recent topics include climate research and the history of democracy in Longyearbyen.

Towards the waterfront is the **North Pole Expedition Museum**. Over two floors, you'll uncover the background, drama and tragedy of North Pole exploration. Upstairs mainly covers the airship *Norge* expedition and the ill-fated airship *Italia* expedition; the disaster triggered the most intensive search and rescue effort the Arctic region had ever seen and claimed the lives of rescuers, including Roald Amundsen. (*Continues on p308*)

SIGNS OF THE PAST IN LONGYEARBYEN

Start outside **1 Lompensenteret** shopping centre and walk towards **2 Gruvearbeideren**, Tore Bjørn Skjølsvik's sculpture of a miner. The plaque reads 'We built Longyearbyen'. Walk straight ahead, turn right at the Tourist Office, then turn left. Take the second right, and follow the road around to the right until you reach the **3 Memorial to John Monroe Longyear**, the town's founder. Take a left, and ahead are the wooden **4 Sykehustrappa** (hospital steps) to your right, the remains of the original hospital and where locals celebrate the return of the sun each March. Continue towards welcoming **5 Svalbard Kirke**, open 24/7. Continue straight towards the **6 War Memorial** for the mine workers who died during WWII's Battle of Spitsbergen. Further on is the **7 Bell**, erected in 1949 and inspired by the Shift Bell in Røros, and the

8 Longyearbyen Sundial with its polar bear-shaped gnomon, readable by both sunlight and moonlight. There's more information in the green box on the railing. Retrace your steps back to Lompensenteret or, for a longer walk, keep left and continue for about 400m to the **9 Cemetery**. The white crosses a little way up from the road date to the early 20th century. Keep walking towards former miners' community centre **10 Huset** (now a restaurant) and take a selfie at the **11 Polar Bear Sign** up to the right. Outside Huset is the **12 Einar Sverdrup Memorial**, commemorating the CEO of Store Norske and WWII hero. Follow the road around to the left and look up towards the remains of **13 Mine 2** high up on the mountainside as you walk 2km back to Lompensenteret, keeping an eye out for wildlife, including reindeer, as you go.

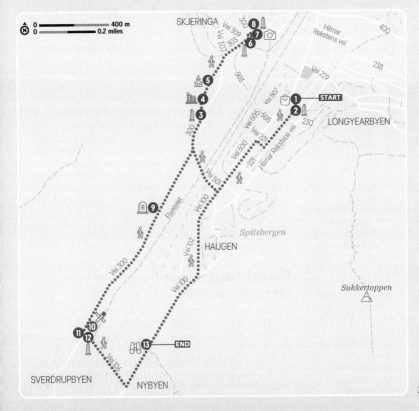

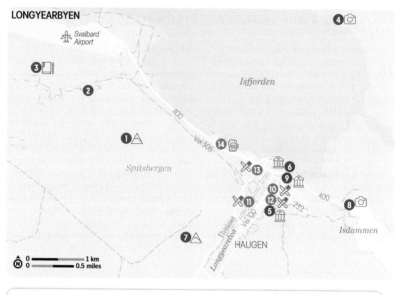

Svalbard Airport

Isfjorden

400

Vei 305

Spitsbergen

400

Isdammen

Elvesletta

Longyeardalen Vei 100

252

HAUGEN

0 — 1 km
0 — 0.5 miles

SIGHTS
1. Blomsterdalshøgda
2. Global Seed Vault
3. Gruve 3
4. Hiorthamn
5. Nordover
6. North Pole Expedition Museum
7. Platåfjellet
8. Polar Bear Sign
9. Svalbard Museum

EATING
10. Fruene
11. Nuga
12. Stationen
13. Vinterhagen

DRINKING & NIGHTLIFE
14. Svalbard Bryggeri

(Continued from p306)

There's a lot of material – much of it in Norwegian – so it's worth booking ahead to join a guided tour. Your ticket is valid for three days, so you can return if you'd like more time.

Opened in November 2022, the arts centre **Nordover** is part of the **Nordnorsk Kunstmuseum**, which also covers Nordland, Troms and Finnmark. The permanent exhibition is dedicated to the compelling works of Norwegian artist Kåre Tveter (1922–2012), who painted his stirring, atmospheric depictions of Svalbard's landscapes from memory. Rotating exhibitions fill the remainder of the calm, bright space. There's also a small cafe and a 32-seat cinema showing a mix of mainstream international and Nordic movies.

Going Underground
LIFE IN THE COAL MINES

Without coal, there would be no Longyearbyen. Take a trip to **Gruve 3** (Mine 3) to discover how the mining industry arrived in Svalbard, and to experience the working conditions of the men (and the few women) tasked with extracting this fossil fuel for the Store Norske Spitsbergen Kulkompani. From the clocking-in counter worn down over decades by miners banging to attract attention to the fossilised footprints of dinosaurs, the

BEST PLACES TO EAT

Stationen
Casual eatery serving classic Norwegian and pub fare. €

Fruene
Part cafe, part chocolatier, part knitting emporium, with sandwiches, daily specials and warming soups. €

Nuga
Flavourful sushi and noodle dishes inside Svalbard Hotell | The Vault. Book ahead. €

Vinterhagen
Local fare including reindeer and seal steak in the conservatory at Polarrigg. €€€

mine is etched with history. You'll visit the lunchroom before gearing up with heavy-duty overalls, gloves and a hard hat to walk just under 1km into the cold damp mine, all by the light of headlamps. Along the way, you'll pass workshops and hear tales of tragic accidents that occurred before the mine's closure in 1996. You can also crawl into one of the tight working spaces for a taster of the job and the risks involved – not for the claustrophobic.

Svalbard's Amber Nectar
VISIT LONGYEARBYEN'S HARD-WON BREWERY

A 1928 law once prohibited alcohol production and restricted sales on Svalbard, but Robert Johansen grew tired of making homebrew illegally and petitioned the Norwegian government every month for four years to change the law. Eventually, it relented and in 2011 **Svalbard Bryggeri** (Svalbard Brewery) was established, officially opening in 2015.

Book in for a brewery visit to hear Johansen's often comical story, learn about the alcohol regulations still in place and taste the fruits of his labour. You'll get to sup five craft brews, including Spitsbergen Pilsner, IPA and stout, and discuss the tasting notes of each. The walk to the brewery takes about 20 minutes from the centre of town. Enter through the door on the side of the building; the welcoming bar area is upstairs.

Half-Day Hikes
GUIDED TRAILS AROUND LONGYEARBYEN

If you don't have a lengthy polar expedition in your legs, there are several shorter guided hikes to choose from around Longyearbyen. One popular route leads you to the 424m-high summit of **Platåfjellet**, a peak overlooking the town with views across Adventfjorden from the top. Another will see you hike up **Blomsterdalshøgda**, 320m above sea level. The route takes you past mining relics from Gruve 3 (Mine 3) and on the descent you'll walk past the near-mythical Global Seed Vault (p310). If you want to go even further back into the mists of mining times, you can trek to the abandoned mining settlement at **Hiorthamn**, over the other side of the fjord from Longyearbyen.

Several routes are possible all year, but be aware that conditions can be brutal in winter, so it's essential to have appropriate clothing. You'll also need to be reasonably fit; hikes described as 'easy' may still involve steep sections or cover quite a distance. Note also that all of these hikes go outside of the town boundary, so polar-bear protection is required.

POLAR BEARS

From warning signs declaring 'Gjelder hele Svalbard' (applies to all of Svalbard) to the postcards on every souvenir stand, the polar bear is never far from your mind here. And for good reason: around 3000 of these powerful predators live on the archipelago, preying on ringed or bearded seals from the sea ice. But they're vulnerable to a changing climate and, as the ice sheet shrinks, so too does their territory and opportunity to hunt successfully.

It's illegal to hunt, chase or disturb polar bears. Your chances of encountering a live bear are slight. You will, however, see several historically stuffed ones in hotels around Longyearbyen, a reminder of how much attitudes have changed towards protecting this elusive marine mammal.

 WHERE TO STAY IN LONGYEARBYEN

Gjestehuset 102	Mary-Ann's Polarrigg	Svalbard Hotell	Polfareren
Dorms and private rooms with immaculate shared facilities, about 2.5km from the town centre. €	Snug rooms have shared facilities but the eccentric decor makes up for the lack of luxury. €€	Town-centre boutique hotel with rustic-chic rooms and an A-grade breakfast buffet. €€€

GLOBAL SEED VAULT

In daylight, the tall, narrow entrance to the **Global Seed Vault** doesn't look much, but its innocuous appearance betrays its international importance. This vast horticultural library contains around 900,000 seed types stored 100m into the permafrost and cooled to a steady -18°C. Inaugurated in 2008, the vault serves as an insurance policy against agricultural Armageddon and there's already been a withdrawal – to replant crops following the Syrian war. You can't enter, but several hikes and tours take you close enough to take photos from outside. It's at its most intriguing at night, when Dyveke Sanne's fibre-optic art installation *Perpetual Repercussion* illuminates the entrance with shimmering blue-green lights.

PÅL KLEVAN/ALAMY STOCK PHOTO ©

Huset

Fine Dining, Polar Style
TRY AN ARCTIC MENU

If Svalbard's remote location conjures images of foil-packed rations and basic survival staples you're in for a surprise. For a truly special meal book in for the tasting menu at **Huset**. 'The House' has been transformed since the days when it was a community hub for miners. Today, you'll be served Arctic staples such as Svalbard seal and rock ptarmigan. You can choose to pair your dishes with wine from Huset's *Wine Spectator*–award-winning cellar. The restaurant is close to Nybyen, around 2km from the town centre.

WHERE TO DRINK IN LONGYEARBYEN

Café Huskies
Coffees and teas in a homey place frequented by friendly hounds who mingle with patrons as they please.

Svalbar
Lively Svalbar has cocktails and a soundtrack that'll convince you to stay for just one more.

Karlsberger Pub
Popular with both locals and visitors, this comfortable, welcoming pub has a huge selection of whiskies.

Beyond Longyearbyen

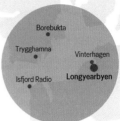

Borebukta

Trygghamna

Vinterhagen

Isfjord Radio   Longyearbyen

Longyearbyen's surrounding peaks, valleys and fjords are within reach on guided hikes and trips by snowmobile, dogsled and boat.

This is the Svalbard you've come to experience: the rush of driving your own team of sled dogs through a silent, snowy valley; the wonder of witnessing nature surviving in one of the most inhospitable places on Earth; and the joy of gazing out over the icy mountains from a boat leading you to ever more remote settlements. Many trips don't venture too far from Longyearbyen, while others whisk you out into the Isfjord to see wildlife such as walruses and seabird colonies. The opportunities to try thrilling activities are virtually limitless, whether you want to ski and camp, snowmobile for the thrills and spills, or simply enjoy the scenery and nature from the comfort of a boat.

Sled Dog Days
DOGSLEDDING ADVENTURES

Expectation: a thrilling glide over virgin snow, led by a pack of enthusiastic, athletic hounds. Reality: organised chaos that's more fun than you can possibly imagine.

There are several dog yards in Longyearbyen (p313) and they all offer similar taster sessions lasting a few hours. There are also several day-long trips and multiday expeditions to choose from, including Northern Lights chases, ice-cave visits and igloo overnighters. If you're opting for a short session, join one where you get to harness up the dogs and drive the sled yourself if you're physically able to – it's hard work but all the more rewarding. When there's not enough snow, there's also the option to go out in wheeled wagons. It's just as entertaining but the bumpy terrain makes this more physically demanding than sledding on snow, so bear that in mind if you don't have a lot of upper body strength.

With their piercing blue eyes and wolflike appearance, the sled dogs may look fearsome, but they're used to people and enjoy being fussed over when they're not working. Note that dog yards in Norway are subject to strict animal welfare standards. See mattilsynet.no for more information.

GETTING AROUND

All bookable tours and activities from Longyearbyen include transport to and from the start point. They'll usually pick you up from your accommodation so, depending where you're staying, you may have to wait up to 20 minutes after the stated start time to be collected.

Walrus safaris and trips to Isfjord Radio tend to be in closed RIB boats, which are warm and speedy, but the ride can be bumpy.

☑ TOP TIP

It's tempting to overload your schedule but planning a free day is helpful in case you need to rearrange weather-cancelled plans.

One-Tonne Wonders
SEE WALRUSES IN THE WILD

After being hunted extensively from the 17th to 19th centuries, the walrus population on Svalbard was decimated. But these massive mammals have made a comeback since they became a protected species in 1952. Estimates vary, but according to the Norwegian Polar Institute, around 2000 of the blubbery beasts now reside on Svalbard, so you'll have a good chance of seeing some in their natural habitat.

Walrus safaris commonly focus on **Borebukta** on the northwestern side of Isfjorden. The journey to get there takes around an hour, passing mesmerising snowy peaks before reaching the walruses' favoured spot. You'll have plenty of time to see them lolling sociably on the beach or ice, looking for molluscs in the shallows or hauling themselves up from the water. You'll be cosy inside the boat, but the Arctic wind can be biting when you're walrus-watching out on deck, so dress accordingly.

WALRUSES ON THE WAY

If you're travelling to **Ny-Ålesund** (p316), you may not need to book a separate walrus-watching trip. Poolepynten, a well-known walrus hauling-out place on Prins Karls Forland, is on the way and operators often pause the journey for a mini safari.

SVALBARD WILDLIFE

Polar Bears
This apex predator isn't easy to spot; on boat trips, keep your eyes focused on the shoreline.

Walruses
Weighing up to a tonne, walruses stick to shallow waters and hoover up molluscs, shrimps and soft-shell crabs.

Arctic Foxes
White in winter and brown in summer, Arctic foxes moult twice a year, May to July and September to December.

Eider Ducks
These clever migratory birds nest next to dog yards for extra protection against egg-stealing Arctic foxes.

Svalbard Reindeer
Seen across the archipelago, these reindeer are shorter than their mainland cousins.

Making Tracks
EXPLORE FURTHER WITH A SNOWMOBILE

Discover the most fun you can have on a motorised machine. After kitting up in a toasty snowsuit, balaclava and boots, you'll set off in convoy on an exhilarating journey to your destination of choice. Venturing deep into the valleys, you'll speed between mountains with the icy wind in your face. You could be zipping towards an ice cave, journeying further to Svalbard's eastern coast or travelling to spend the night in a wilderness lodge for true isolation. You'll need to provide a full current driver's licence that's recognised on Svalbard. Providers include **Hurtigruten Svalbard**, **Basecamp Explorer** and **Svalbard Adventures**; it helps to have some snowmobiling experience for the longer trips.

First-Time Flyers
WATCH GUILLEMOTS FLY THE NEST

You'll have a very short window – just a few days in July – to see the phenomenon of 'bird jumping'. Join a boat trip to the sheltered bay of **Trygghamna** and walk ashore to see Brünnich's guillemot fledglings take their first flight as they leap from their nests on the cliffs of Alkhornet mountain. It's an exciting watch but a heart-wrenching one too, as opportunistic Arctic foxes wait in the wings to snatch up stragglers. You'll also have the chance to see other bird species, such as kittiwakes and Arctic skuas, as well as other flora and fauna.

MARK SMITH/GETTY IMAGES ©

Arctic fox

Arctic Illuminations
NORTHERN LIGHTS SAFARIS

Catching a glimpse of the ethereal green, purple and red hues of the Northern Lights dancing high overhead is magical, and there are many different ways to go searching for them. Amateur photographer? You might like to capture the spirit of the lights under the expert guidance of small tour operator **Svalbard Photography**. Thrill seeker? You'd probably prefer to chase down the aurora on a snowmobile with **Better Moments** or on a dogsled with **Svalbard Husky**.

RUSSIAN SETTLEMENTS

Though officially a Norwegian territory, all signatories of the 1920 Spitsbergen Treaty – one of which is Russia – have the right to make use of Svalbard's natural resources. There are two primary Russian settlements on Svalbard, long popular with visitors.

Barentsburg, 60km southwest of Longyearbyen, still has an active coal mine and a hotel, while **Pyramiden** is a Soviet-era ghost town, its buildings abandoned when mining operations ceased in 1998.

At the time of research, Visit Svalbard was not promoting any tours to these settlements, or excursions run by Russian-owned tour companies, due to the war in Ukraine. Contact **Visit Svalbard** prior to travel to check the current situation if you plan to visit the Russian settlements.

SVALBARD DOGSLEDDING PROVIDERS

Svalbard Husky
Half- to full-day dogsled trips including family-friendly sightseeing tours and ice-cave experiences.

Green Dog Svalbard
Family-run dog yard offering short and multiday expeditions with husky–Greenland dog mixes.

Svalbard Villmarkssenter
Nature-focused provider offering short and multiday experiences including a week-long mushing adventure.

CAN I GO IT ALONE?

Many travellers prefer to get around independently and organised tours may seem unappealing. However, Svalbard is a unique destination, with unique risks. Anyone travelling outside of Longyearbyen's town boundary requires polar bear protection, namely a firearm. Though it's not impossible for suitably qualified visitors to acquire the appropriate firearms permissions, the process is lengthy and strict. Even then, travel on the archipelago is restricted and 'public transport' in the traditional sense simply doesn't exist. So, in practice, for the overwhelming majority of short-stay visitors, joining guided tours with established operators will provide the most straightforward, enjoyable and safe experience. Visit sysselmesteren.no for the most up-to-date regulations for visitors.

GINGER_POLINA_BUBLIK/SHUTTERSTOCK ©

Northern Lights (p313)

Like being warm? The comfort of **Hurtigruten Svalbard**'s snowcat is probably for you.

During polar night – the period between mid-November and late January when the landscape is blanketed in 24-hour darkness – it's theoretically possible to see the Northern Lights at any time of day. That said, due to Svalbard's high latitude it's a bit more difficult to see them here than it is in mainland Norway.

If you're not lucky with the aurora there's another polar light show to see. In the lead-up to, or just after, polar night, you'll get to experience the blue hour, when the twilight creates just enough light to colour the scenery with a blue tinge.

WHERE TO BUY SVALBARD SOUVENIRS

Barbara Foto & Ramme
Find photographic prints, plushies of Arctic animals and mementoes handcrafted by local makers.

Fruene
Gift your favourite sweet-tooth some Svalbard-made artisan chocolates. Dare you try the chilli-infused Arctic Chill?

Kongsfjordbutikken
Buy and send a postcard from the world's northernmost shop for that famous Ny-Ålesund postmark.

Boutique Isolation at Isfjord Radio
A REMOTE ADVENTURE HOTEL

Bombed by both sides in WWII and rebuilt afterwards, former communications station **Isfjord Radio** is a retreat quite unlike any other. In winter you'll arrive by snowmobile; in summer you'll arrive by boat, docking at a floating jetty beside craggy cliffs and wobbling up a staircase towards a huddle of buildings and satellite installations, before being led into the chic interior of the hotel.

You'll have a short tour of the station with its red-and-white striped lighthouse and see some remnants of the days of hunting and trapping. Depending on when and how long you choose to stay, you can sign up for excursions including RIB boat tours or hikes across the Arctic tundra. At the end of an action-filled day, relax in the sauna and take a dip in the Arctic Ocean for the ultimate refreshment between sessions, then fill up on a gourmet seasonal menu with dishes such as roasted reindeer.

The large picture windows in the guest lounge are perfect for wildlife watching – much of the area immediately outside the station is the **Kapp Linné Bird Sanctuary** so you'll see many avian species, plus reindeer and maybe even a polar bear (they've been known to break into the buildings here in search of food). There's also the peaceful **Prof Åkermans Bibliotek** to while away the hours in solitude, listening to the sound of the howling wind outside the library.

Isfjord Radio is now managed by Basecamp Explorer (p312), which offers a range of experiences to the station.

SVALBARD'S SEASONS

Peder Loso, a snowmobile guide, shares his highlights of Svalbard's nature throughout the year. @pederloso

Late spring through summer the islands come alive with a vibrant array of migrational birds. Various marine mammals, including different whale species, and occasional polar bear sightings add to the appeal of boat journeys towards calving glacier fronts and bird cliffs.

Conversely, winter offers the opportunity to traverse glaciers and snow-covered valleys on snowmobiles. Throughout the season there's a stark contrast in light conditions, ranging from the darkness of polar night and the appearance of the Northern Lights in early January to the eventual arrival of the midnight sun in May.

 SVALBARD BOAT TRIP PROVIDERS

Better Moments
All-round provider with closed RIB boats for walrus-watching, trips to Ny-Ålesund and more.

Henningsen Transport and Guiding
Established outfit offering Isfjorden day cruises covering history, geology and wildlife.

Hurtigruten Svalbard
Get close to glaciers, see Arctic wildlife or eat dinner on a silent hybrid vessel.

GETTING AROUND

Although there are flights to Ny-Ålesund for residents and researchers, visitors can only travel here on an organised boat tour or, less commonly, on one of the few long-distance skiing expeditions available.

Better Moments and Hurtigruten Svalbard are two operators running boat trips to the settlement. It's a long journey – up to 4½ hours each way – and your time in the town is limited, so it helps to reframe the boat journey as part of the overall experience, rather than solely as a means of transport. Use the time to look out for whales and identify the hundreds of seabirds you'll see. Depending on the weather conditions, it can be a choppy ride – be sure to take any medications you may need.

☑ TOP TIP

Enjoy the analogue life during your visit and turn any wi-fi and Bluetooth-enabled devices to flight mode before you arrive. Ny-Ålesund is a 'radio silent community', meaning wi-fi and Bluetooth are avoided to prevent interference with the sensitive scientific instruments here.

Ny-Ålesund

✪OSLO

On the southern edge of Kongsfjorden, isolated Ny-Ålesund lays claim to being the world's northernmost permanently inhabited town. It saw success as a coal-mining centre in the early 20th century but a series of fatal accidents led to the mines' closure in the 1960s and the town's focus shifted to scientific research.

With only 40 year-round residents these days (more in summer when research increases), Ny-Ålesund is a still, echoey place, with just a few streets and a handful of sights. But it's precisely because it's so small that its adventurous past is so captivating. It's best known as the starting point for a number of expeditions to the North Pole, notably those by Roald Amundsen on the airship *Norge* and Umberto Nobile on the doomed *Italia*.

On your way here, you'll see glaciers scratching slowly towards the frigid sea and pass a well-known hauling-out spot for walruses.

In the Footsteps of Explorers
STROLLING THE WORLD'S NORTHERNMOST TOWN

With some planning, you can get around Ny-Ålesund in the short time you'll have without missing out on anything.

Plan for about 20 to 30 minutes in the town's small **museum**, which is open 24/7. Exhibits cover the settlement's past and its present, from the realities of mining at 79° N (the straitjacket is sobering) to scientific research projects that are in progress and the personal stories of some of the town's permanent residents.

Across the road is **Kongsfjordbutikk**, a souvenir emporium with Ny-Ålesund merch aplenty, including plushies, blankets, tote bags and clothes. It's also the place to buy postcards and stamps. There are picnic benches with pens outside so you can write your wish-you-were-heres and post them to get the coveted Ny-Ålesund postmark. Allow about 15 minutes (there's bound to be a queue).

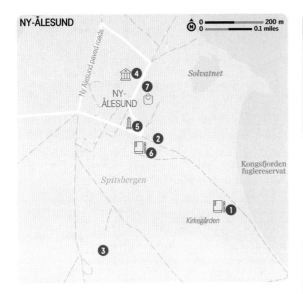

NY-ÅLESUND

0 ——— 200 m
0 ——— 0.1 miles

Solvatnet

NY-ÅLESUND

Spitsbergen

Kongsfjorden fuglereservat

Kirkegården

SIGHTS
1 Amundsen Mast
2 Mess Hall
3 Mining Area
4 Ny-Ålesund Museum
5 Roald Amundsen Memorial
6 Telegraph Station

SHOPPING
7 Kongsfjordbutikk

Factor in around half an hour to walk around town and read the information boards (you can't go inside the buildings). Some highlights include the **Roald Amundsen Memorial**; the **telegraph station** where Amundsen's last communication was received during the fatal rescue mission on the seaplane *Latham* in 1928; and the **mess hall**, where the researchers eat meals together. You'll also stroll past several international research buildings. From a distance (polar bear rules apply here too) you'll be able to see the **Amundsen mast**, to which the *Norge* was tethered in 1926, and the **mining area**, which is mapped out on an information board.

If there's time, pick up an ice cream from the shop for your stroll back to the boat.

AMUNDSEN'S ACHIEVEMENTS

Tales of Roald Amundsen's polar derring-do are covered from different angles at museums across Norway, including the **Fram Museum**, Oslo (p66), the **Polar Museum**, Tromsø (p279) and the **Norwegian Aviation Museum**, Bodø (p248).

WHY I LOVE SVALBARD

Gemma Graham, writer

This snowy, distant island cluster so synonymous with adventure instils a sense of anticipation. I'm always excited by the potential for wildlife encounters here. I'll never forget the thrill of seeing an Arctic fox leap upon a small gaggle of geese when I was walking along a quiet mountainside road in Longyearbyen. The flapping geese saw off the scruffy, mid-moult fox with some aggressive honking and it left the scene hungry. I left feeling like David Attenborough.

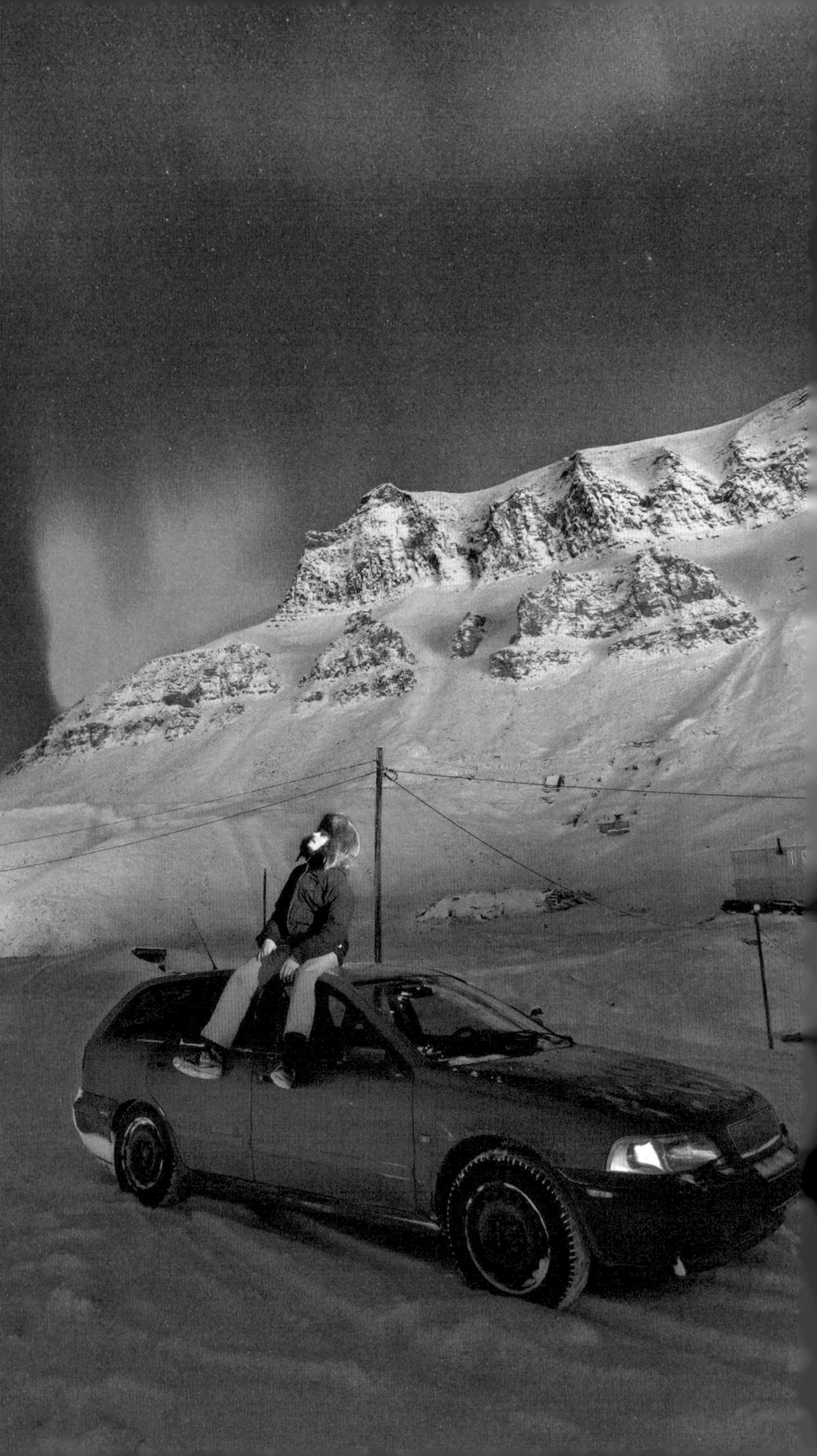

TOOLKIT

The chapters in this section cover the most important topics you'll need to know about in Norway. They're full of nuts-and-bolts information and valuable insights to help you understand and navigate Norway and get the most out of your trip.

Arriving
p320

Getting Around
p321

Money
p322

Accommodation
p323

Family Travel
p324

Health & Safe Travel
p325

Food, Drink & Nightlife
p326

Responsible Travel
p328

LGBTiQ+ Travel
p330

Accessible Travel
p331

How to Hike Safely in Norway
p332

Nuts & Bolts
p333

Language
p334

Viewing the Northern Lights, Longyearbyen (p306)
GINGER_POLINA_BUBLIK/SHUTTERSTOCK ©

✈ Arriving

Oslo Gardermoen is Norway's largest airport, but there are direct flights from many European cities to Stavanger, Bergen, Trondheim and Tromsø too. Oslo airport is well connected to the city centre by public trains and buses; there's also an airport express train. Oslo's arrivals hall has a few shops and (mostly takeaway) food outlets, a currency exchange and ATMs.

Visas

EU nationals don't need a visa for any length of stay. Citizens of the UK, Canada, New Zealand, US and Australia can stay visa-free for up to 90 days in any 180-day period.

Wi-fi

Oslo Gardermoen Airport has fast, free wi-fi for up to four hours. There's coverage throughout the airport and down to the car-rental counters but it starts to get patchy on the train platforms.

Border Crossings

If you're not from an EU or Schengen country, you may be asked to show proof of how long you're staying in Norway (such as an onward ticket) at passport control.

Svalbard

Though it's a Norwegian territory, Svalbard is outside the Schengen Area and has different entry rules; travellers who need a visa to visit Norway will require a double-entry visa to return to the mainland.

Public Transport from Airport to City Centre

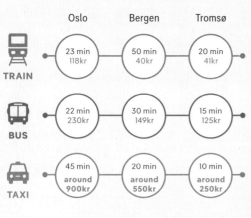

	Oslo	Bergen	Tromsø
TRAIN	23 min 118kr	50 min 40kr	20 min 41kr
BUS	22 min 230kr	30 min 149kr	15 min 125kr
TAXI	45 min around 900kr	20 min around 550kr	10 min around 250kr

ALMOST LIKE BEING IN THE EU

Norway has steadfastly resisted joining the EU – in referenda held in 1972 and 1994, residents narrowly voted against becoming a member. But when it comes to crossing borders, the country and its government is nothing if not pragmatic, meaning most rules are identical to those in most EU countries. If travelling by road, you may not even notice that you've crossed Norway's land borders with Sweden and Finland (both EU members). Also, there are no immigration checks at airports for flights arriving from elsewhere in the EU or another Schengen country.

Getting Around

Norway has excellent road, rail, ferry and domestic flight networks but distances can be long. The Hurtigruten coastal ferry runs between Bergen and Kirkenes.

TRAVEL COSTS

Rental
From 700kr/ day

Petrol/Gas
Approx 22kr/L

EV charging
550–750kr/ kWh

Oslo–Bergen railway ticket (one-way; bought a month in advance)
From 379kr

Hiring a Car

Car-rental companies usually charge per 24 hours. Most cars in Norway have automatic transmission, with an increasing number of hybrid and electric vehicles (EVs). EV rental costs more per day, but you'll save money overall because of significantly reduced fuel costs. Find EV charging stations at ladestasjoner.no.

Road Conditions

Norway's roads are excellent, and tunnels and efficient car ferries help you negotiate the country's challenging terrain. Away from major cities, two-lane, winding roads with a speed limit of 80km/h are the norm, so getting from A to B often takes longer than you expect.

TIP

Norway's road tolls and car ferries have automated payment systems: car rental companies charge your card upon returning your vehicle.

HURTIGRUTEN COASTAL FERRY

Norway's Hurtigruten ferry has been shuttling up and down the convoluted coastline since 1893. Originally a vital ferry link between remote coastal communities, it now stops at 36 ports from Bergen to Kirkenes. These days journeys are promoted as cruises, with optional excursions at some ports (eg to Geirangerfjord from Ålesund). You don't have to book a package though – the option is a bit hidden but you can travel between your own choice of ports. Go to hurtigruten.co.uk/port-to-port.

DRIVING ESSENTIALS

Drive on the right.

The speed limit is 30km/h to 50km/h in urban areas, 80km/h on secondary roads and 110km/h on motorways.

.02

Blood alcohol limit is 0.02%

Bus & Train

Trains reach as far north as Bodø, with an additional line connecting Narvik with Sweden further north. Bus services along major routes are fast and efficient. Although reliable, rural services can be infrequent, especially outside the summer season, sometimes with no services at all on weekends.

Discounted Train Tickets

On most regional Vy train services (vy.no; the state-run transport company), the earlier you book, the cheaper the ticket will be. A limited number of *lavpris* (low-fare) tickets are allocated to each service, so try to book ahead.

Domestic Flights

Flying is an efficient (though environmentally unfriendly) way to travel between some of Norway's more remote destinations. If there's no other feasible option, SAS (flysas.com) and Norwegian (norwegian. com) have extensive domestic networks, while Widerøe (wideroe. no) serves smaller cities.

Money

CURRENCY: NORWEGIAN KRONE (PLURAL KRONER; KR OR NOK)

A Tip for Tipping

Although a tip will always be appreciated in Norway, it's never expected and is usually reserved for stellar service in restaurants and fancier bars. Tipping hotel staff and taxi drivers isn't common practice but welcomed if they've gone above and beyond. If you choose to tip, around 5% to 15% is standard.

Credit Cards

The vast majority of transactions in Norway are now made by card. Some establishments don't accept cash at all, so you might want to consider a travel-specific debit or credit card to save on foreign transaction fees. Visa and MasterCard are widely accepted; American Express and Diners Club less so.

Cash

Although cash is becoming less common, it's handy to have a few kroner to hand, whether for 'honesty box' payments or for museum lockers.

ATMs

Minibanks (Norwegian for ATMs) are widespread and most accept major credit cards as well as Cirrus, Visa Electron and/or Plus bankcards.

HOW MUCH FOR A...

1-day bicycle rental
from 275kr

Museum entry
80–200kr

City parking (24 hours)
200–360kr

Airport express bus
125–230kr

HOW TO... **Save Money**

Cut costs in larger cities with a local discount card (eg a Bergen Card). Valid for periods of one to three or four days, these cards give you free public transport and museum entry, plus a range of discounts around town. If you're planning on visiting a lot of attractions, it could be a sound investment. Buy them online or from the local tourist office.

LOCAL TIP
Many market vendors prefer to be paid via the Vipps payment app, but this only works with Norwegian bank accounts, so you'll need to ask in advance if they'll accept cash or PayPal instead.

TAX REFUNDS

For goods that cost more than 315kr (290kr for food items) at shops displaying the 'Tax Free' logo, you're entitled to a refund for the 25% MVA (value-added or sales tax) or 15% for food items. At the point of sale, you fill out the Tax Free form, then present your sealed goods, passport and form at your departure point from the country to collect the refund. Some shops have now moved to a much smoother app-based system. For more information, pick up a How to Shop Tax Free pamphlet from local tourist offices.

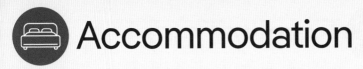

Accommodation

Historic Hotels

Most accommodation in Norway belongs to a handful of smart, but often generic, chain hotels – which is why **De Historiske** (Historic Hotels & Restaurants in Norway; dehistoriske.com) is such a treat. It covers 66 options across the country, from the opulent Britannia Hotel in Trondheim to the Svinøya Rorbuer fishers' cabins in Lofoten.

DNT Mountain Huts

Exploring the Norwegian wilds often means staying in a mountain hut or cabin. **Den Norske Turistforening** (dnt.no) maintains 550 mountain huts or cabins that are a day's hike apart, along the country's 20,000km of well-marked wilderness hiking routes. Of these, more than 400 have beds for sleeping, with the remainder reserved for eating, rest stops or emergency shelter.

Ice Hotels

Norway has four ice hotels: in Alta, Kirkenes, Tromsø and in the Hunderfossen Winter Park, near Lillehammer. Open only in winter, these places have elaborate ice carvings and rooms that rarely rise above -5°C. If you stay in one, you'll usually sleep on an ice bed, topped by reindeer skins and enveloped in an Arctic-grade sleeping bag.

Cheap Accommodation

It's possible to find relief from Norway's expensive accommodation, at least in some cities. Well-kept, reasonably priced hostels *(vandrerhjem)* offer dorm beds, single and double rooms with shared facilities. And recent welcome additions to the budget market include chains such as Citybox and Smarthotel. These stylish no-frills options offer excellent value but you'll only find them in larger cities.

HOW MUCH FOR A NIGHT IN...

a hostel dorm
350kr

a midrange hotel
1400–1900kr

a historic hotel
2000–5000kr

Loyalty Schemes

The majority of Norway's midrange and top-end hotels belong to chains, and this can work to your advantage. Most have loyalty schemes that cost nothing to join and may entitle you to free nights the more nights you stay. These include Scandic Hotels (scandichotels.com), Thon Hotels (thonhotels.com) and Strawberry (strawberryhotels. com), the new name for Nordic Choice Hotels.

NORWAY SEASONS

The main tourist season in Norway runs from around the middle of June to the middle of August, and while it may have once been the case that you'd find good deals during this time, nowadays it's when accommodation prices soar. In some areas, the season begins in mid-May and/or hangs on until mid-September, when prices are a bit lower. Peak winter season runs from December to March in northern Norway where activities such as skiing, snowmobiling and dogsledding abound. Again, this is when prices are correspondingly highest.

Family Travel

Norway is a terrific destination in which to travel as a family. This is a country that has become world famous for creating family-friendly living conditions, and most hotels, restaurants and many sights are accordingly accommodating. Remember, however, that while road trips in Norway can be beautiful, journeys can be winding and long, so careful planning is required.

Supplies

As you'd expect, children's products such as baby food, infant formula, soya and cow's milk and disposable nappies (diapers) are all widely available, in supermarkets, pharmacies and more expensive convenience stores. But you'll find that, like many other things here, these items cost a lot more than back home. Consider bringing a reasonable supply to keep costs down.

Eating Out

Children will be made to feel welcome in most restaurants. Many places offer kids' menus (usually child-pleasing standards such as hot dogs, hamburgers and pizzas) with smaller portions and prices to match. Those that don't are usually willing to serve a smaller portion if you ask. Most restaurants have baby-change areas and a limited number of highchairs.

Public Transport

Children under six travel for free (you still have to book a ticket for them). Those aged between six and 17 travel for half the adult fare. Trains on the Oslo–Bergen line have a family carriage with a children's play area.

Family-Friendly Accommodation

Most accommodation choices have 'family rooms' or cabins accommodating up to two adults and two children. Some hotels advertise that children go free, but ordinarily you're paying for a room, so you'll likely just be saving the cost of a breakfast.

CHILD-FRIENDLY ATTRACTIONS

Whitewater rafting (p128)
Family-friendly trips in Sjoa and elsewhere.

Dogsledding (p311)
Possible from Røros to Svalbard and elsewhere in winter, with wheeled wagons in summer.

Whale-watching (p278)
See whales off the northern coast from Andenes and Tromsø.

Hunderfossen Familiepark (p118)
Water rides, wandering trolls and fairy-tale palaces near Lillehammer.

Natural History Museum (p80)
Dinosaurs, a crystal cave and the wonder of space are covered in Oslo.

Olympic Park (p118)
Everything from simulators to bobsled runs around Lillehammer.

WILDLIFE & NATURAL ATTRACTIONS

Norway's natural world has lots to get children excited, including the midnight sun in summer, polar night in winter and the weird and wonderful Northern Lights. The country also has some incredible wildlife, from the polar bears (pictured), reindeer, Arctic foxes and walruses in Svalbard to the musk-ox safaris (around Oppdal and elsewhere) and elk safaris (from Oppdal, Rjukan and Evje in southern and central Norway). The north also has a couple of decent wildlife parks in case you can't track the animals down in the wild: Polar Park (in Setermoen) and Namsskogan Familiepark (south of Mosjøen).

Health & Safe Travel

INSURANCE

Insurance is not compulsory to travel to Norway, but considering the cost of everything here (including medical treatment), we recommend it. Some policies exclude 'dangerous activities' such as motorcycling, skiing, mountaineering, snowmobiling or even hiking. EU citizens can apply for the European Health Insurance Card (EHIC), which covers medical treatment on the same terms as Norwegian citizens.

Medical Care

Norway has an excellent (if expensive) health system. Most medications are available in Norway but may go by a different name than at home, so be sure to have the generic name as well as the brand name. For minor illnesses, pharmacists can dispense valuable advice and over-the-counter medication.

Insects

In northern Norway, the greatest nuisances are the plagues of blackflies and mosquitoes that swarm out of tundra bogs and lakes in summer. Midsummer is the worst, and hikers should cover exposed skin and may even need head nets. If you're camping, a tent with mosquito netting is essential.

WILDLIFE

Always keep a respectful distance from wildlife both large and small – wild animals can react unpredictably when stressed.

AVALANCHE DANGER SCALE

Danger level 1: Low	Danger level 2: Moderate	Danger level 3: Considerable	Danger level 4: High	Danger level 5: Very High
Only small-sized natural avalanches are possible.	Very large-sized natural avalanches are unlikely.	Large-sized natural avalanches are possible.	Large-sized natural avalanches are expected.	Numerous very large natural avalanches are expected.

Changing Weather

The weather in Norway's high country is notoriously fickle: it can be benign and sunny one minute, and dangerous the next. Always check weather and other local conditions before setting out cross-country, whether on foot, skis or snowmobile. Be prepared for sudden inclement weather at any time of year, and stay aware of potential avalanche dangers.

LOCAL KNOWLEDGE

When setting out into the wilds, always trust the advice of locals – if they say not to go, don't go. As an example of what can happen, two Scottish cross-country skiers died after being caught in snow and freezing fog in March 2007 on the Hardangervidda plateau despite, according to some reports, being warned by local experts not to set out.

Food, Drink & Nightlife

When to Eat

Frokost (breakfast; 7–9am) Usually light, with staples including muesli, rye bread, sliced cheese and cold meats, or scrambled eggs with smoked salmon. Always with coffee.

Lunsj (lunch; noon–3pm) Sandwiches, salads and soups are the usual midday order.

Middag (dinner; 6–10pm) The day's main meal might be a casual burger or a taste-bud-testing adventure at an upscale restaurant.

Where to Eat & Drink

Cafes Essential services for caffeine-hungry Norwegians. Most offer pastries, *boller* (sweet buns) and *kaker* (cakes); some do sandwiches, soups and salads too.

Restaurants Choose from unfussy places offering basic bites to fine dining with seasonal menus celebrating local produce. There's a good choice of international cuisines too.

Bryggerier (breweries/pubs) Sup your choice of beer while filling up on classic pub food. Some larger places offer a dining experience to rival many smart restaurants.

MENU DECODER

Barnemeny Children's menu. Smaller portions of the standard mains or child-friendly bites, such as hamburgers and pasta dishes.

Retter Dishes

Småretter Small dishes

Forretter Starters

Hovedretter Main courses

Dagens rett Dish of the day

Kjøtt Meat

Sjømat Seafood

Biff Beef

Kylling Chicken

Fisk Fish

Torsk Cod

Tørrfisk Stockfish; unsalted cod dried on outdoor racks

Bacalao Salted, dried cod

Reker Prawns/shrimp

Reinsdyr Reindeer

Hvalbiff Whale steak. Though Lonely Planet doesn't promote eating whale meat, we mention it here so you can make an informed decision about what you're eating.

Spekemat Cured meats

Ost Cheese

Iskrem Ice cream

Multebær Cloudberry

Jordbær Strawberry

Blåbær Blueberry

Nøtter Nuts

Skalldyr Shellfish

Bløtdyr Molluscs

Sennep Mustard

Hvete Wheat

Vegetarisk Vegetarian

Vegansk Vegan

Øl Beer

Hvitvin White wine

Rødvin Red wine

Brus Soda

HOW TO... Enjoy a Night Out

Whether it's a leisurely beer in a relaxed pub or a bar crawl and dancing until (almost) dawn, there's a scene to suit your style. In cities, you'll find a venue for after-dark fun any night of the week, but the biggest parties and club nights are usually reserved for Fridays and Saturdays. Revellers tend to go out a bit earlier than in other European countries. Starting the night at 9pm is normal, with pubs, bars and clubs closing at 3am or earlier. Norwegian style trends towards smart-casual, so wear what you feel most comfortable in, whether that's low-key chic or bang on trend. Very few clubs (and almost no bars or pubs) have a strict dress code. Be sure to carry ID – some venues enforce an over-20s-only policy and, though door staff are usually polite and professional, they play by the rules.

HOW MUCH FOR A...

Bolle (sweet bun)
45kr

Filter coffee
40kr (often includes a refill)

Freshly made bakery sandwich
100–150kr

Soda
50kr

Glass of beer
75kr (0.33L), 90kr (0.5L)

Glass of wine
115–150kr

Dinner at a pub
350kr

Dinner at a Michelin-starred restaurant
3500–6000kr (with wine pairing)

HOW TO...

Eat Well for Less

Dining out in Norway can be an exciting and mouth-watering experience. But it's no secret that the price of a restaurant meal here can also make your eyes water. Fortunately, there are a few tried-and-tested strategies to keep costs down.

Although the typical Norwegian breakfast tends to be light, many hotels (especially the chain variety) include breakfast in the cost of a room – take full advantage of it and fill up before you check out.

Try lingering over a later lunch rather than dinner. Many restaurants offer lunch specials – perhaps a dish of the day *(dagens rett)* or a two-course menu – at lower prices compared to à la carte evening options. The quality and service won't diminish, but your bill just might. If you're out for a hike or on the move during the day, make like a Norwegian and prepare a *matpakke,* a packed lunch of open-faced sandwiches.

If you drink alcohol, consider forgoing wine in favour of a non-alcoholic option with your meal. Almost every restaurant offers a range of alcohol-free tipples beyond the usual soda suspects. Locally produced juices can be paired with menus, and imperceptibly non-alcoholic beers and wines are refreshingly common and almost always cheaper than the merry-making versions.

Making a Matpakke

The humble *matpakke* is nothing if not functional. Toppings are usually very simple, such as cheese, ham or peanut butter and, to avoid mess, slices are commonly separated by *matpapir* (greaseproof paper).

WHERE TO BUY ALCOHOL

Despite the lifting of prohibition in 1927, Norwegians remain among the lowest consumers of alcohol in Europe. This may be because of (or perhaps in spite of) the strict laws still in place around sales.

State-run alcohol outlets called *Vinmonopolet* are the only places aside from bars and restaurants where you can buy wine and spirits (and beer over 4.7% ABV). You can buy lower-strength beer and cider in supermarkets.

Vinmonopolet have limited opening hours. They vary slightly from branch to branch, but standard times are 10am to 5pm Monday to Wednesday, 10am to 6pm Thursday and Friday, and 10am to 3pm Saturday. They are always closed on Sundays. Sales of weaker tipples in supermarkets stop at 8pm on weekdays, and 6pm on Saturdays.

Whether in a *Vinmonopolet,* a restaurant or a bar, you'll have to be over 20 to purchase drinks with a 22% ABV or higher; you need to be over 18 to buy any other alcoholic beverage. Be prepared to show ID if you're under 25 (or look it).

It's no secret that booze is expensive in Norway. All alcoholic drinks with more than 0.7% ABV are taxed, and the rates are far higher than in most other countries. Expect to pay around 75kr for 330mL of draught beer and around 115kr for a regular glass of house wine.

Unsurprisingly, given the cost, it's normal to pay for drinks individually, rather than buying rounds. If you're planning a big night out, do as the locals do and *forspill* – enjoy some pre-drinks at home.

Responsible Travel

Climate Change & Travel

It's impossible to ignore the impact we have when travelling, and the importance of making changes where we can. Lonely Planet urges all travellers to engage with their travel carbon footprint. There are many carbon calculators online that allow travellers to estimate the carbon emissions generated by their journey; try resurgence.org/resources/carbon-calculator.html. Many airlines and booking sites offer travellers the option of offsetting the impact of greenhouse gas emissions by contributing to climate-friendly initiatives around the world. We continue to offset the carbon footprint of all Lonely Planet staff travel, while recognising this is a mitigation more than a solution.

Go Electric on a Rental Car

Norway leads the world in electric vehicles per capita, and all major rental companies offer EVs for hire. Download **ElbilAppen** to plan your journey and get realistic ranges based on current driving conditions.

Explore a Sustainable Destination

Consider visiting places with Sustainable Destination accreditation. This national scheme highlights towns and cities committed to developing sustainable tourism over time. Destinations on the list include Lofoten, Geirangerfjord and Røros. Go to **visitnorway.com** for more.

Dine Out on Food 'Waste'

Transform your opinion of leftovers at Oslo's **Rest** (restaurantrest.com), a fine-dining restaurant where exquisite dishes are created from 'waste' ingredients, such as imperfect vegetables or animal parts that might otherwise be discarded.

HANEN (hanen.no) promotes rural tourism and farm food, and its members offer farm stays, as well as activities such as fishing and local food experiences deep in the Norwegian countryside.

There are excellent city-bike schemes in Oslo (oslobysykkel.no), Bergen (bergenbysykkel.no) and Trondheim (trondheimbysykkel.no), with abundant docking stations and well-maintained bikes. On-street e-scooters (most commonly Voi and Ryde) are ubiquitous across the country.

GO BY PUBLIC TRANSPORT

If you're not planning to go very far off the beaten track, public transport will get you around reliably and efficiently. Download the **Entur app** to plan your journey and buy tickets.

LEFT: SKIMGI/SHUTTERSTOCK ©; ABOVE: NRQEMI/SHUTTERSTOCK ©

TOOLKIT

Recycle empty cans and plastic drinks bottles at supermarkets to refund the small *pant* (deposit) applied to them. Drop your empties into the machine (usually by the door) for a voucher to redeem in-store.

Watch Whales Mindfully

See humpback whales and orcas more quietly. **Brim Explorer** (brimexplorer.com) runs 'silent' whale-watching trips from Tromsø on an electric-hybrid catamaran, reducing the excess noise known to affect communication, migratory patterns and wellbeing in cetaceans.

Buy Authentic Sami Duodji

Sami *duodji* (crafts) include knives, jewellery and clothing made from natural materials. To ensure it's authentic, buy directly from Sami people or from vendors who can share information about the maker, such as museum gift shops.

Find Local Flavours

If you're keen to try local produce, **Bondens Marked** (bondensmarked.no) places a focus on traceable, artisanal products and hosts small-scale producers as they bring their goods to market days at locations including Bergen and Tromsø.

Consider Climate Change

Walk deep into an ice tunnel sculpted by Peder Istad at **Klimapark 2469** (klimapark2469.no) in Jotunheimen National Park (p121) to understand 6000 years of geology and human habitation and the effect of climate change.

The right to roam also permits you to pick wild berries, mushrooms and flowers.

Norway's *allemannsretten* ('right to roam') opens the country's landscape to everyone. Follow the rules at environmentagency. no.

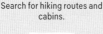

Cutting Carbon

Norway's travel industry plans to cut its greenhouse gas emissions in half by 2030 and, as part of this, aims to reduce the carbon footprint generated by visitor transport by 10% each year.

RESOURCES

environmentagency.no	dnt.no	ladestasjoner.no
Find details about the right to roam.	Search for hiking routes and cabins.	Find electric-vehicle charging stations near your location.

LGBTIQ+ Travellers

An early adopter of anti-discrimination laws, and with equal rights in marriage, adoption and assisted pregnancy, Norway ranks consistently highly as one of the most LGBTIQ+-friendly countries to live and love. April 2022 marked 50 years since Norway decriminalised homosexuality and, while intolerant attitudes still persist in some quarters, this is a country where being yourself is celebrated on stages large and small.

Year-round Pride

The rainbow flag flies over Pride events throughout the year from Svalbard to Stavanger. Plan to visit in June for the biggest festival: **Oslo Pride** (oslopride. no) has been celebrating the LGBTIQ+ community since 1974 and is now a nine-day festival of music, parties and workshops. **Bergen** (bergenpride.no) and **Trondheim** (trondheimpride.no) host the next-biggest events in June and September, respectively. And for some light during a dark northern winter, dress for the elements to experience a parade at 69° north in November at **Arctic Pride** (arcticpride.no) in Tromsø.

LGBTIQ+ VENUES

Because the LGBTIQ+ community is so widely accepted, ironically this means there aren't really LGBTIQ+-specific quarters here. People of all identities party together in most bars and nightclubs but, even so, there's a thriving LGBTIQ+ scene, particularly in the major cities. **London Pub** (londonpub.no) and **Elsker** (facebook .com/ElskerOslo) in Oslo, **Fincken** (fincken. no) in Bergen and **Me** (facebook.com/ menightclub) in Trondheim are well-known LGBTIQ+ hangouts and open to all.

Where Norway Stands

Annual measures such as **ILGA-Europe's Rainbow Europe Index** and the **Spartacus Gay Travel Index** recognise Norway's tolerant culture and strong legal protections for LGBTIQ+ people. Consequently, Norway consistently ranks near the top of the list of countries considered safest for the LGBTIQ+ community to live, love, work and travel.

POP-UP EVENTS

If you identify as female, non-binary or an ally, keep an eye out for pop-up events run by **Karmaklubb°** (karmaklubb.com). This collective brings a movable feast of club nights, drag performances, film screenings, conversations and more to venues primarily in Oslo and Bergen.

THOSE INTOLERANT OF TOLERANCE

Despite its progressive culture, Norway is not exempt from homophobia, transphobia and intolerance. Pride events in Oslo were cancelled in 2022 following a terrorist attack around LGBTIQ+ venues. LGBTIQ+ travellers are very unlikely to have a negative experience during their visit, but might find that public displays of affection are met with disapproval in communities where conservative religious views predominate.

Oslo Fusion

Fan of films? Clear your diary in September, when the annual **Oslo Fusion International Film Festival** (oslofusion.no) celebrates LGBTIQ+-centred films, shorts and documentaries, with screenings at venues across the capital. Past winners include *Finlandia,* an exploration of Oaxaca's Muxe third-gender community.

Accessible Travel

Norway's major cities, towns and attractions are generally well set up for travellers with disabilities, and getting around by public transport is reasonably straightforward. That said, the accessibility information offered on individual attractions' websites is often limited to wheelchair users and travelling around still requires advance planning.

Getting Around Oslo

T-Bane (subway) stations have lifts or ramps to platforms; most have level access to trains. Buses have low floors but tram lines 11, 12 and 19 aren't wheelchair accessible. See ruter.no/en/journey/accessibility.

Airport

Norway's airports are all wheelchair accessible and staff can provide assistance to travellers with a range of disabilities. Contact your airline and the airport 48 hours in advance. Find out the assistance available at avinor.no.

Accommodation

Although newer hotels will be accessible, older buildings often present significant obstacles, such as a lack of step-free access and no lift. With its 159-point accessibility standard, the **Scandic** chain (scandichotels.com) is a safe bet.

AUDIO GUIDES

Many attractions, including Olso's **National Museum**, offer audio guides via an app/QR code, which can be useful for visitors with visual impairments. The **Voice of Norway app** also has downloadable, audio-described city walking tours.

ACCESS FOR ALL

Streets & Sidewalks

Street crossings have lowered kerbs; audible signals speed up as the lights are about to change. Pavements are well maintained in big cities but weather-damaged or unpaved sidewalks are fairly common elsewhere.

Accessible Arctic Adventure

Tromsø Accessible Tours (tromsoaccessibletours.com) aims to make the Arctic inclusive for all. From aurora tours to whale-watching trips, owner Martin coordinates with local providers to ensure the experience is tailored to your needs.

Websites for most organisations and attractions usually provide a good overview of facilities for wheelchair users and those with reduced mobility. It's still best to contact places in advance if you have specific requirements.

RESOURCES

Wheelmap (wheelmap.org) Open-source tool that lets you search the accessibility of mapped attractions, shops, restaurants and more.

Wheelchair Travel (wheelchairtravel.org) Though not Norway-specific, this extensive blog focuses on wheelchair-friendly destinations and offers information about accessible international travel.

Norwegian Association for the Disabled (nhf.no) Organisation advocating for the rights of people living with disabilities in Norway and internationally. It publishes Disability News (handikapnytt.no), which sometimes covers cultural events.

Visit the 'Explorer' section at **ut.no** and filter by 'Suitable for wheelchair' to find a selection of accessible outdoor routes, both easy and challenging. The website is only in Norwegian, so you may need the translation option on your web browser.

How to Hike Safely in Norway

The pull of the wild in this astonishingly beautiful country is irresistible. But it's important to take some common-sense precautions when you're out hiking so that you can enjoy your trip safely and responsibly.

Plan Ahead

Plan your route at **ut.no** (in Norwegian; use your browser's translation function) and check the weather forecast at **yr.no** before heading out. Make someone else aware of your plans, particularly if you're going alone, and check in with them when you return. Always have a plan B (such as a shorter alternative route) and never disregard the advice of locals.

Go Prepared

Make sure you're appropriately dressed for the weather and bring extra layers. At the very least you will need a good pair of hiking boots, base layers (wool is ideal), a fleece or another woollen layer, a windproof jacket and a comfortable backpack. Take a torch and something reflective to make yourself easier to find if you get lost, and bring enough food and water for the whole trip. Always take a paper map and compass and brush up on your map-reading skills if it's been a while since you last used them. Paper maps covering all of Norway are available at **dntbutikken.no**.

Don't Rely Solely on Your Phone

Never rely solely on your phone for directions when you're hiking. Signal is never guaranteed, batteries can drain quickly in extreme temperatures, and phones can fail entirely if they get wet. Having a paper map is essential.

THE NORWEGIAN MOUNTAIN CODE

In 1952, Den Norske Turistforening (DNT; the Norwegian Trekking Association) published its *Fjellvettreglene* (Mountain Code) with the aim of helping everyone to enjoy the outdoors safely. In addition to the general guidance outlined here, find the nine-step code, updated in 2016, at **english.dnt.no/the-norwegian-mountain-code**. Apart from safety information, you can find details about the *allemannsretten* (right to roam) and how to enjoy the outdoors responsibly at **environmentagency.no**.

Know Your Limits

Know the limits of everyone in your hiking party and choose your route accordingly. There's no shame in turning back early or going with your plan B if exhaustion sets in or you realise you've bitten off more than you can chew. This is especially true if weather conditions take a turn for the worse.

IF THINGS GO WRONG

If you get lost, first look for a red DNT 'T' marker or cairn denoting a marked route – they'll guide you back onto an established path. If you can't see any markers, try to find a river or stream and follow it downhill – often this will lead to people. If you find yourself in a genuine emergency and need to be rescued, call the police on 112; they will arrange help.

Nuts & Bolts

OPENING HOURS

Opening hours for attractions are shorter outside of high season (mid-June to mid-August). Standard opening hours for services are:

Banks 9am–4pm Monday to Friday

Bars 6pm–3am

Restaurants Noon–3pm and 6–11pm

Shops 10am–5pm Monday to Saturday

Supermarkets 7am–11pm Monday to Friday, to 10pm Saturday

Toilets

Public toilets are well kept but many charge a fee (around 10kr) and only accept contactless payment cards. To avoid foreign transaction fees, cafes, restaurants and bars are your best bet.

Internet Access

Wi-fi is widely available in hotels, cafes, trains and on some buses. 3G/4G is also widespread.

Tap Water

Norwegian tap water tastes great; it's always safe to drink unless signed otherwise.

GOOD TO KNOW

Time Zone
Central European Time (GMT/UTC plus one hour)

Country Code
47

Emergency Numbers
Fire 110; Police 112; Ambulance 113

Population
5.5 million

Electricity
220V, 50Hz

Type C
220V/50Hz

Type F
230V/50Hz

PUBLIC HOLIDAYS

Though many bars, restaurants and some attractions stay open on public holidays, most shops will be closed. Some establishments also reduce their hours for a few days before and after Constitution Day.

New Year's Day (Nyttårsdag) 1 January

Maundy Thursday (Skjærtorsdag) March/April

Good Friday (Langfredag) March/April

Easter Monday (Annen Påskedag) March/April

Labour Day (Første Mai, Arbeidetsdag) 1 May

Constitution Day (Syttende Mai) 17 May

Ascension Day (Kristi Himmelfartsdag) May/June, 40th day after Easter

Whit Monday (Annen Pinsedag) May/June, eighth Monday after Easter

Christmas Day (Første Juledag) 25 December

Boxing Day (Annen Juledag) 26 December

Language

Norway has two official written language forms: Bokmål, used below, and Nynorsk. They are very similar, and every Norwegian learns both at school.

Basics

Hello. Goddag. *goo-dahg*
Goodbye. Ha det. *hah-day*
Yes. Ja. *yah*
No. Nei. *nai*
Please. Vær så snill. *varr shoo snil*
Thank you. Takk. *tahk*
Excuse me. Unnskyld. *un-shül*
Sorry. Beklager. *beh-klah-gehrr*
What's your name? Hva heter du? *vah hay-tehrr du*
My name is … Jeg heter … *yai hay-tehrr*
Do you speak English? Snakker du engelsk? *snah-kehrr du ehng-ehlsk*
I don't understand. Jeg forstår ikke. *yay for-stohrr i-keh*

Directions

Where's …? Hvor er …? *voor arr*
Which way is …? Hvilken retning er …? *vil-kehn reht-ning arr*
How do I get to …? Hvordan kommer jeg til …? *voor-dahn ko-mehrr yai til*
Can you show me (on the map)? Kan du vise meg (på kartet)? *kahn du vee-seh mai (poh kahrr-teh)*

Signs

Ankomst Arrivals
Avgang Departures
WC/Toaletter Toilet
Gjestgiveri/Pensjonat Guesthouse
Kamping/Leirplass Camping ground
Ledig Vacancy
Vandrerhjem Youth hostel

Time

What time is it? Hva er klokka? *vah arr klo-kah?*
It's … Klokka er … *klo-kah arr*
Half past (9). Halv ti. *hahl too*
morning formiddag. *forr-mi-dahg*
afternoon ettermiddag. *eh-tehrr-mi-dahg*
evening kveld. *kvehl*
yesterday i går. *i-gor-rr*
today i dag. *ee-dahg*
tomorrow i morgen. *ee-mor-rrn*

Emergencies

Help! Hjelp! *yehlp*
Go away! Forsvinn! *foh-shvin*
I'm ill. Jeg er syk. *yai arr sük*
Call …! Ring…! *rring*
a doctor en lege *ehn lay-geh*
the police politiet *poo-li-tee-eh*

Eating & Drinking

What would you recommend? Hva anbefaler du? *vah ahn-beh-fah-lehrr doo*
Cheers! Skål! *skohl!*
That was delicious. Det var nydelig. *Day vahrr nü-deh-lee*

NUMBERS

1 **en** *ehn*
2 **to** *too*
3 **tre** *trray*
4 **fire** *fee-rreh*
5 **fem** *fehm*
6 **seks** *sehks*
7 **sju/syv** *shu/süv*
8 **åtte** *oh-teh*
9 **ni** *nee*
10 **ti** *tee*

DONATIONS TO ENGLISH

Aquavit, fjord, krill, lemming, quisling, ski, slalom...

Useful Phrases

Hvordan sier du? (voorr-dahn see-ehrr doo?) – How do you say ...?
Making an effort to speak the language is always appreciated and Norwegians are usually happy to help.

En kaffe (med melk), takk. (ehn kah-feh (may mehlk), tahk) – One coffee (with milk), please.
If Norway has a national drink, it's coffee. Most Norwegians drink it black and strong, but foreigners requiring milk and/or sugar are normally indulged.

Hvor er toalettene? (voorr aar too-ah-leh-teh-neh?) – Where are the toilets?
This phrase is an oldie but a goodie.

Skal jeg ta av skoene mine? (Skahl yai ta ahv skoo-eh-neh mee-neh?) – Shall I take my shoes off?
Norwegians usually take their shoes off when entering someone's home, particularly when the weather is wintry.

Bokmål

Literally 'book-language', this is the urban-Norwegian variety of Danish, the language of the former rulers of Norway. It's the written language of 80% of the population. Although many Norwegians speak a local dialect in the private sphere, most of them speak Bokmål in the public sphere.

Nynorsk

The other written language is Nynorsk, or 'New Norwegian' – as opposed to Old Norwegian, the language in Norway before 1500 CE, that is, before Danish rule. It's an important part of Norwegian cultural heritage as it is the truly 'Norwegian' language, as opposed to the Danish-based Bokmål.

WHO SPEAKS NORWEGIAN?

Bokmål is the predominant language of Norway's population of more than 4.6 million, except among the Sami minority in the north, where one of three languages from the Finno-Ugric group of the Uralic language family is spoken – though nearly all Sami speak Norwegian as well.

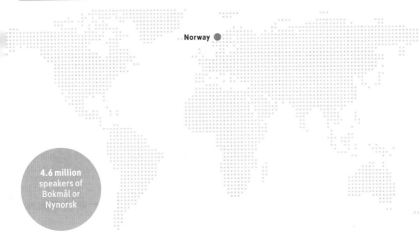

Norway ●

4.6 million speakers of Bokmål or Nynorsk

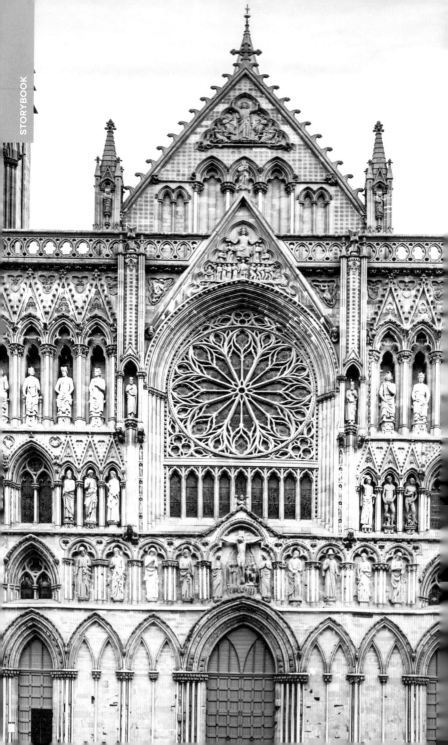

STORYBOOK

Our writers delve deep into different aspects of Norwegian life

A History of Norway in 15 Places

Norway may now be the epitome of a peaceful country, but its history is soaked in blood.

Gemma Graham

p338

Norwegian Noir

Norwegian writers play an influential role in the dark realm of Scandi crime fiction.

Gemma Graham

p347

Meet the Norwegians

Covering hiking, brown cheese, leaving babies out in the fresh air and how the national psyche is changing.

Anita Lillefosse

p342

Plenty of Fish in the Sea

A brief history of *skrei,* the fish that built Norway.

Hugh Francis Anderson

p349

Folklore & Festivities

Norway's folk traditions still thrive in the 21st century.

Gemma Graham

p344

Nidarosdomen (Nidaros Cathedral; p222)
RUBEN M RAMOS/SHUTTERSTOCK ©

A HISTORY OF NORWAY IN
15 PLACES

Norway may now be the epitome of a peaceful country, but its history is soaked in blood. Its story revolves around recurring grand themes, from the Vikings to the battle for supremacy in Scandinavia, from the struggles of the Sami to the dark days of WWII, from extreme poverty to previously unimaginable riches.

THOUGH THIS NORDIC nation's story is much older than the Vikings, between the 8th and 11th centuries Norway gained international recognition as its infamous seafarers set sail to explore Europe and beyond, seeking to trade – and to conquer.

The powerful Viking chieftains were challenged by the influence of a new religion, and King Olav (later St Olav) secured the Christianisation of the country before he was exiled and subsequently killed at the pivotal Battle of Stiklestad in 1030.

Norway lost its independence in the 14th century, first to Sweden and then as part of the Kalmar Union, uniting it with Sweden and Denmark for centuries after.

In the 19th century, the desire for independence grew, and a new constitution was written following the dissolution of the Danish union in 1814. It would be a further 91 years, however, before Norway finally became an independent nation in 1905.

Norway – the north in particular – suffered devastating damage during WWII when it was occupied by Nazi forces. The postwar discovery of oil in the North Sea in the 1960s led to a dramatic change in the country's fortunes: the economy was transformed and the founding of the Oil Fund has secured its continuing prosperity for years to come.

1. Alta
STONE AGE PETROGLYPHS

There's evidence of human habitation in the remote reaches of Norway's Arctic North since around 9000 BCE. Sometime around 4000 BCE, Stone Age peoples found their way to the area close to modern-day Alta and you can see the astonishing marks these peoples made on the landscape – literally. The cliffs around Alta Museum – a UNESCO World Heritage Site – are incised with around 6000 carvings, dating from 6000 to 2000 years ago and rediscovered in the 1960s. Etched into the bedrock, the astonishing petroglyphs depict scenes of Stone Age life and feature animals such as bears, cormorants and fish, as well as human figures and boats.

For more on Alta, see p287.

2. Hafrsfjord
NORWAY IS UNITED

While most Viking chieftains made their name in foreign conquest, Harald Hårfagre (Harald Fairhair) did something no other leader had managed before – he united the disparate warring tribes. Hårfagre controlled Vestfold and the Uplands and was supported by Trønder chieftain Håkon Grjotgardsson.

Commonly dated to 872 (estimates vary between 870 and 900), the Battle of

Hafrsfjord, near Haugesund, saw Harald defeat an enemy fleet allied to the Danish king, led by Kjøtve den Rike (Kjøtve the Rich), to secure trading routes between southwestern Norway and Kaupang (and beyond), thus controlling the country. He remained king for a further 60 years.

For more on Hafrsfjord, see p166.

3. Stiklestad

A KING IS MARTYRED

In 1024, King Olaf II Haraldsson founded the Church of Norway, establishing it as the state religion throughout his realm – a situation that continues to this day. But following an invasion by King Canute (Knut) of Denmark in 1028, Olav was forced to flee. In an attempt to regain power, he returned in 1030 but was killed in the pivotal Battle of Stiklestad, where he faced a peasant army loyal to the Danish monarch.

For Christians, his death amounted to martyrdom and he was canonised as a saint. His most lasting legacy, however, was having forged an enduring identity for Norway as an independent kingdom.

For more on Stiklestad, see p231.

Oslo Cathedral

FRANCESCO BONINO/SHUTTERSTOCK ©

4. Bergen

HANSEATIC HOT SPOT

For over 400 years, Bryggen, the warehouse complex in Bergen's sheltered harbour, was dominated by a tight-knit community of German merchants allied to the Hanseatic League. The League established its first office here around 1360, importing grain and exporting dried fish, among other products. By the 15th century, Dutch and English competitors (and the Black Death, which killed 70% of Bergen's population) brought about the Hanseatic League's decline.

But by the early 17th century, Bergen was the mercantile hub of Scandinavia again and Norway's most populous city, with 15,000 people. Bryggen remained a key trading centre until the League's offices finally closed in 1899.

For more on Bryggen, see p142.

5. Christiania

A NEW OSLO

In 1536 Norway entered a formal coalition with Denmark and all politics and defence matters were managed from Copenhagen. In 1624, Oslo – which was at that time located close to present-day Grønland – burned to the ground.

The Danish king, Christian IV, chose to rebuild the city below Akershus Fortress in the fashionable (late) Renaissance grid pattern. Some of the exquisite 17th-century streetscapes still exist in Kvadraturen (the quad), the area between Akershus Fortress and Oslo Cathedral, Øvre Vollgate and Skippergata. In an early act of Danish brand management, the king renamed the city Christiania; it wasn't until 1925 that Christiania became Oslo again.

For more on Oslo's history, see p71.

6. Røros

COPPER MINING BOOM TOWN

Røros Kobberverk (Røros Copperworks) was established in 1644, following the discovery of copper ore in the region in the early 1640s. The abundant forests surrounding the town provided fuel and the rapids along the river Hyttelva provided hydroelectric power.

The copperworks was especially successful in the 18th century, bringing enormous wealth to the region. Company directors invested heavily in the town, funding a huge church, doctors and schools. But the industry then steadily declined until in 1977, after 333 years of operation, the company went bankrupt. In 1980, Røros was inscribed onto the UNESCO World Heritage List.

For more on Røros, see p234.

7. Eidsvoll

THE BIRTH OF NORWAY'S CONSTITUTION

Following the Napoleonic Wars, the Treaty of Kiel saw the Danes present Norway to Sweden. Tired of being passed between foreign kings, a contingent of farmers, businesspeople and politicians gathered at Eidsvoll Verk in April 1814 to draft a new constitution and elect a Norwegian monarch – it was signed on 17 May.

Sweden resisted this show of independence and forced the new king, Christian Frederik, to yield and accept the Swedish choice of ruler, Karl Johan. War was averted by a compromise accommodating devolved power, but the writing was on the wall for the union. In 1905, Norway gained its independence.

For more on the constitution, see p344.

8. Svalbard

NORTH POLE EXPLORATION

In the late 19th and early 20th centuries, Svalbard became the launching point for pioneering polar expeditions. In 1893, Fridtjof Nansen and his crew set sail from the archipelago on the Fram, aiming to trap the polar ship in ice and drift across the Northwest Passage.

Then in 1926 Roald Amundsen departed Svalbard on the airship *Norge* and completed the first aerial expedition to the North Pole. In 1928, the airship *Italia,* led by Umberto Nobile, crashed upon its return to Svalbard. The rescue operation that followed sadly led to the deaths of rescuers on board the *Latham 47* seaplane, one of whom was Amundsen.

For more on Svalbard, see p302.

9. Ålesund

ART NOUVEAU RECONSTRUCTION

On the night of 22 January 1904, a devastating fire ravaged the coastal city of Ålesund, destroying many of the closely packed wooden buildings and leaving over 10,000 people homeless. Remarkably only one person died.

The city used the fire as an opportunity to rebuild Ålesund in the popular art nouveau style of the day, characterised by ornate facades with organic motifs inspired by nature, as well as turrets, spires and decorative ironwork. The reconstruction process was rapid, and by 1907 Ålesund had transformed into a town known for its cohesive and harmonious art nouveau cityscape.

For more on Ålesund, see p211.

10. Narvik

WWII OCCUPATION

On 9 April 1940, German forces launched a surprise invasion of Norway, targeting several major cities including Oslo, Bergen, Trondheim and Narvik. The latter was a key strategic location for the Germans due to its proximity to Sweden and its significance as a major port city in northern Norway. Narvik was also important for iron ore transport, essential for Germany's war machine. The Battles of Narvik saw the British retake the city in late May 1940, though the situation in mainland Europe prompted them to withdraw, allowing the Germans to regain control of the city on 9 June.

11. Rjukan

SABOTAGING NAZI WEAPONS DEVELOPMENT

The Norwegian resistance carried out many acts of sabotage against the occupying forces during WWII. One such campaign focused on the Norsk Hydro plant in Rjukan, which produced heavy water (deuterium oxide), vital for nuclear research. Fearing the Germans would use it to develop a nuclear weapon, British-backed saboteurs carried out a series of assaults on the plant. Operation Gunnerside in February 1943 proved most successful: infiltrators planted explosives, destroying electrolysis equipment. The Germans attempted to transport the remaining heavy water to Germany on the SF *Hydro,* but in February 1944 resistance operatives sank the vessel on Lake Tinn, thwarting their plan.

For more on Rjukan, see p94.

12. Stavanger

THE DISCOVERY OF OIL

In 1969, Norway struck black gold at the Ekofisk oilfield in the North Sea. Stavanger's proximity to this significant oilfield

UMOMOS/SHUTTERSTOCK ©

STORYBOOK
A HISTORY OF NORWAY IN 15 PLACES

Norsk Oljemuseum (p175), Stavanger

made it the ideal location for the necessary onshore operations and, in the early 1970s, Norway's largest oil company, Statoil (now called Equinor), set up shop in the city.

The economy boomed, transforming the country from one of Europe's poorest into one of its richest. In 1990, the Norwegian government established the Oil Fund (Oljefondet; now known as Statens pensjonsfond utland, the government's pension fund abroad) to safeguard the country's wealth for future generations. As of 2022, it was worth approximately 12.43 trillion kroner (US$1.2 trillion).

For more on Stavanger, see p171.

13. Karasjok/Kárášjohka

THE SAMI PARLIAMENT

Throughout the 19th and early 20th centuries, the Indigenous Sami people in Norway were subjected to forced assimilation policies that suppressed their identity, culture and languages. Government policy changed in the 1960s, but the Sami continued to struggle for rights and political representation. Fierce protests in 1979 and 1981 against a proposed hydroelectric dam on traditional Sami land along the Alta River ultimately led to reform: the Sami are now recognised in the Norwegian Constitution as a separate, Indigenous people, and the Sami Parliament was founded in 1989. In 2001, the new Sami Parliament building was opened in Karasjok (Kárášjohka in Sami).

For more on Karasjok, see p291.

14. Trondheim

THE NATION'S CORONATION CATHEDRAL

Founded in 997 by King Olav I, Trondheim has deep royal roots and the magnificent Nidarosdomen (Nidaros Cathedral), built on Olav II's burial place, was the coronation venue for three kings in the late Middle Ages. When the Norwegian Constitution was written in 1814, Nidarosdomen was named as the official coronation church, and four kings – Karl III Johan, Karl IV, Oscar II and Haakon VII – were crowned there between 1818 and 1905. Though the cathedral lost its constitutional role when the coronation clause was repealed in 1908, both Olav V (1957–91) and Harald V in 1991 held their consecration ceremonies there.

For more on Trondheim, see p222.

15. Oslo & Utøya

A TERRORIST ATTACK ON NORWEGIAN SOIL

On 22 July 2011, Norwegian terrorist Anders Behring Breivik detonated a car bomb in Oslo's government district, targeting the nation's political class and killing eight people. Then, disguised as a policeman, he shot 69 young political activists to death on the island of Utøya, around 30km northwest of Oslo. When he was apprehended, Breivik claimed that he had acted to save Norway and Europe from being taken over by Muslims. The country's measured response to the most deadly attack in its modern history was praised around the world, and Norwegians united in condemning the attacks and its motives.

For more on Oslo, see p42.

MEET THE NORWEGIANS

Covering hiking, brown cheese and leaving babies out in the fresh air, ANITA LILLEFOSSE introduces her fellow Norwegians and explains how the national psyche is changing.

WHEN I WAS growing up our doors were never locked. Though it's changed a bit since then, Norway is still a very safe place and not just from a crime perspective. From the time you are born you have security; growing up, it doesn't matter if your parents are wealthy or not, you will always have enough to get by.

We're not born with skis on our feet like many people think – most Norwegians can't ski. Though we do put our kids outside in the wintertime for fresh air: if you walk past a kindergarten, you'll see a row of buggies, all with sleeping children in them.

We love our homes and no matter how busy or stressed you are, your house is your pride, it's supposed to shine. But, like the other Scandinavian countries, we have the concept of *Janteloven* (the Law of Jante): you should never think that you're better than anyone else. If you have money, you never brag about it. You'll have a good car and a nice house but nothing flashy. It's not as strict as it once was; like everywhere else, Norwegians have been opened up to other influences. Nowadays, we're allowed to show that we can achieve things and be proud of that, but it's a balance.

There isn't any real rivalry between places in Norway – only when it comes to football – but there are stereotypes. For example, people from Bergen would think that *østlandinger* (people from the east) are daddy's boys; people from Oslo think that *bergensere* (people from Bergen) are *brautende* (forward and loud).

Things don't go at 200km/h here. The attitude is: 'OK, we didn't get to do it today, we'll do it tomorrow.' No one is in a hurry really, except between 4pm and 6pm: then people are in a hurry because they know they'll be in a queue in their car. In Norway, five cars in front of you amount to a *kø* (traffic jam).

Norwegians can be difficult to get to know. When you do get to know us though, you'll find that we don't take ourselves very seriously – we make fun of ourselves – but you have to get in first. We don't share our deepest thoughts very quickly. That's also true when it comes to religion and politics: Norwegians don't very often talk about them. We're political, but we like to keep these things to ourselves. We share what you can see, but not what we think.

If anyone has any issues, we'll always say 'walk it off', and suggest taking time out in the mountains. Everything can be fixed by going for a hike. And eating is important: I recommend waffles and brown cheese.

Who & How Many

Norway's population is just over 5.5 million, of whom 16% have arrived from other countries. The greatest proportion of immigrants are from other European nations (7.2%) and countries in Asia (4.8%), while 1.3% are from the other Nordic countries.

I NEEDED SOMETHING DIFFERENT...THEN I MISSED THE CALM

I grew up in Arna and moved to Bergen in my last year of school. But it became too small for me, so I moved to Oslo. Then that felt too small and I got bored. I wanted something different. 'Normal' in Norway would be finish school, get a good education, find a partner, have kids, buy a Volvo. But I was afraid of that. I wanted to travel and I moved to London. My plan was to stay for a year or two – which became 16.

But I missed nature and fresh air. You can feel the difference as soon as you get off the plane, even when you arrive in cities like Oslo and Bergen. And I missed the calmness, which I didn't realise until a year or so after I'd left. A part of me loved London's fast pace, but I appreciate home now I've moved back to Bergen.

FOLKLORE & FESTIVITIES

Norway's folk traditions still thrive in the 21st century. By Gemma Graham

UNDER DANISH RULE for almost three centuries, Norway's identity was for a long time entwined with that of its southern Scandinavian neighbour. Visit the National Museum in Oslo and you'll find an exhibition room titled 'Everything Norwegian is Danish', such was the influence of Norway's association with Denmark. While this may be true of the period glassware and intricately inlaid cabinets on display there, Norway has since forged a unique identity of its own.

Norway was ceded to Sweden in 1814 following the Napoleonic Wars, and leading figures in the newly devolved state set about nation-building, discussing what it meant to be Norwegian and outlining the constitution that was signed on 17 May 1814. Coinciding with the national romanticism sweeping other countries across Europe during this period, interest in Norway's folk traditions grew. Customs were revived, some were newly established following independence in 1905, and several are still celebrated today.

Myths & Tall Tales

Norse mythology and Norwegian folk tales have an enduring appeal far beyond the country itself, made possible by the work of some notable figures who documented the stories many centuries after they were first told.

Much of our knowledge of Norse mythology actually comes from 13th-century Icelandic poets. Historian Snorre Sturlason created a poetry textbook around 1220 CE known as *Snorre's Edda (The Younger Edda)*, which referenced legendary figures, including Thor, from tales first told as early as the 8th century. *The Elder Edda* is another 13th-century manuscript of poetry whose author is unknown but which also tells of Norse gods and heroes.

In the early 19th century, inspired by the work of the Brothers Grimm, folk-tale enthusiasts Peter Christen Asbjørnsen and Jørgen Engebretsen Moe started collecting local and regional fairy tales to ensure their survival for future generations. Their 1841 book *Norske folkeeventyr* (Norwegian Folk Tales) captured the darkly comical, cautionary stories of a host of characters both moral and malevolent, and they're still popular today, commonly ending with the phrase *'Snipp. Snapp. Snute. Så er eventyret ute'* (Snip, snap, snout. Now the adventure is over).

Dugnad to Do Good

While folk tales often warn of grisly consequences for those who take the wrong path, another Norwegian tradition takes a

carrot-and-stick approach to collective responsibility. *Dugnad* (from the Old Norse *dugnaðr,* meaning 'help' or 'good deed') is a form of group volunteering, where a community comes together to complete a task for the benefit of all, usually some form of manual labour. In centuries past, *dugnad* would ensure the survival and prosperity of rural communities.

Although *dugnad* is less commonly practised in large cities these days, the tradition still thrives in smaller towns and rural areas. Locals are invited to take part in various *dugnad* throughout the year, perhaps painting fences, working in a community garden or sprucing up the local area ahead of National Day. Workplaces also organise *dugnad,* and no one is too important – everyone up to and including the CEO is expected to join in to tackle the task at hand.

Though participation is technically voluntary, most Norwegians feel obliged to join in – eyebrows might be raised if one were to skip too many – and the promise of food, drinks and socialising after the job is complete can be just enough of a sweetener. Indeed, many Norwegians are seemingly still community minded: according to Statistics Norway, in 2022, 51.6% of Norwegians had taken part in some form of voluntary work in the previous 12 months.

Bunad: Folk Dress Revived

When it comes to dressing up for special occasions such as weddings, christenings and, of course, National Day, many Norwegians choose to wear a *bunad,* Norway's national dress. In a revival of the traditional folk garments worn in rural communities, the *bunad* was developed in the mid-1800s, and makers looked to local handicrafts for the colours and patterns of the intricate embroidery. As a result, each region's *bunad* is unique and reflects the traditions of the area.

The Norwegian Institute for Bunad and Folk Dress estimates that around 70% of Norwegian women own a *bunad* and around 20% of men own one, though this number is growing. A woman's *bunad* generally consists of a white shirt, a shift, the main dress, an apron and a belt. Depending on the regional variation, there are accessories too, such as a bag, bonnet, shawl or cape, and each *bunad* is completed with jewellery – usually silver – known as *sølje.*

The traditional Sami dress, the *kofte,* is similar to the *bunad* in that there are regional variations, but it has always been in daily use, so it's considered to be a living tradition, rather than a revived one.

Bunader are sometimes handmade by a skilled member of the family and commonly given as a Confirmation gift. If they're purchased, the made-to-measure garments can cost many tens of thousands of kroner, but they're cherished for life, altered as necessary and often handed down from one generation to the next. Such is the deep appreciation of Norway's national dress that it has been nominated for Unesco's List of Intangible Cultural Heritage.

Nasjonaldag, hipp, hipp, hurra!

Few events in the annual calendar bring Norwegians together in quite the same way as *syttende mai* (17 May), also known as *nasjonaldag* (National Day), which marks the birth of Norway's constitution in 1814. Early celebrations were banned by King Carl Johan (then monarch of both Sweden and Norway) because of anti-Swedish sentiment. But in 1836, the *storting* (Norwegian parliament) chose to mark 17 May, and from then on, the date was considered the country's national day.

Every town and city hosts its own celebration, with Norwegian flags aplenty and parades and music throughout the day. Unlike national day festivities in other countries, the main focus isn't on Norway's military but on its regular citizens, particularly its children. The Children's Train *(barnetog)* is a feature of every celebration and sees local youngsters walking a parade route, carrying handmade banners representing their kindergarten or school and waving flags to the music of marching bands. Later in the day, a Citizen Train walks a longer route with participants from various organisations, such as sports teams, majorettes and the emergency services. Hundreds – sometimes thousands in major cities – come out to cheer the parades and eat waffles, hot dogs and ice cream.

The wholesome daytime events are usually followed by a raucous night, as locals, still in their finery, head to bars and clubs to party until the wee hours. Needless to say, 18 May tends to be very quiet around town.

NORWEGIAN NOIR

Norwegian writers play an influential role in the dark realm of Scandi crime fiction. By Gemma Graham

WITH ORIGINS DATING back to the 1960s, the genre that came to be known as Nordic Noir has become a worldwide phenomenon. Set against the bleak backdrop of the harsh, unforgiving Nordic climate and landscape, storylines typically follow a flawed protagonist – more often than not a grizzled detective – as they doggedly pursue justice for the victims of a brutal crime.

Dark, depressing themes of violence, homicide, misogyny and xenophobia contrast sharply with the pervasive perception of the Nordic countries as utopian societies. The veracity of the 'Scandinavian miracle' – happy, prosperous communities buoyed by equality, lack of corruption and a strong social safety net – is called into question through stark narratives that are light on metaphor and heavy on social commentary.

Many point to the works of Swedish writing duo Maj Sjöwall and Per Wahlöö as the earliest pioneers of the genre. Their 10-novel crime-fiction series (written between 1965 and 1975 and known collectively as *The Story of a Crime*), which featured the sullen police detective Martin

Bestselling author Jo Nesbø (p348)

Beck, inspired several TV and film adaptations. Henning Mankell – Swedish creator of the Kurt Wallander series, also successfully translated to TV – is also considered to be a leading figure in the genre's development.

While the 1990s saw this particular brand of crime fiction gaining popularity in the Nordic countries themselves, arguably it wasn't until the mid-2000s that the genre gained significant attention internationally. Notable was the release and subsequent cinematic adaptation of Stieg Larsson's *Millennium Series,* the first being *The Girl with the Dragon Tattoo,* which probed the prevalence of violence against women in Swedish society. On the small screen, series such as *The Killing* (*Forbrydelsen* in Danish, meaning 'the crime') and *The Bridge (Broen)* were similarly pivotal in raising the profile and popularity of Nordic Noir outside of Scandinavia.

In a genre that has translated successfully across the whole of the Nordic region, Norwegian writers have featured front and centre. Gunnar Staalesen is a titan of the Nordic Noir scene, and new novels in his series featuring Verg Veum, a private detective working in Bergen, are always hotly anticipated. Karin Fossum deviates slightly from the Nordic Noir formula. Perhaps influenced by her previous career in healthcare, Fossum has created a protagonist in Inspector Sejer who is compassionate rather than tortured. Meanwhile, Norway's best-selling female author of crime fiction, Anne Holt, is a lawyer and former Minister for Justice in the Norwegian parliament. Her most popular novels include a 10-story collection

THE VERACITY OF THE 'SCANDINAVIAN MIRACLE' – HAPPY, PROSPEROUS COMMUNITIES BUOYED BY EQUALITY, LACK OF CORRUPTION AND A STRONG SOCIAL SAFETY NET – IS CALLED INTO QUESTION THROUGH STARK NARRATIVES THAT ARE LIGHT ON METAPHOR AND HEAVY ON SOCIAL COMMENTARY

Karin Fossum signing books
MARKUS WISSMANN/SHUTTERSTOCK ©

of works featuring Oslo police detective Hanne Wilhelmsen as the lead.

However, no Norwegian crime fiction writer has been more successful internationally than Jo Nesbø, whose bestselling series – comprising 13 titles as of 2023 – following fictional Oslo-based detective Harry Hole has sold more than 55 million copies worldwide. The first title in the series, *The Bat (Flaggermusmannen),* was published in 1997, and a subsequent title in the collection, *The Snowman* (2010), was made into a film starring Michael Fassbender in 2017.

Norway's contributions to Nordic Noir–inspired TV and film might not have received quite the same recognition internationally as some Danish and Swedish productions, but the country has nevertheless created some acclaimed series in the genre.

The first season of *Wisting,* based on crime novels by former police investigator Jørn Lier Horst, aired in 2019 and focuses on detective William Wisting's hunt for a serial killer who has fled to Norway from the USA. While not a crime drama per se, the tense series *Occupied* (*Okkupert;* 2015) garnered significant popularity and certainly explores dark concepts. Executive produced by Jo Nesbø, the series envisages a time when Norway ceases oil and gas production and is subsequently invaded by Russia. The plotline recalls the country's occupation by Nazi Germany during WWII, a parallel which prompted the real-life Russian ambassador to Oslo to voice his disapproval. Decades since Nordic Noir began to excite readers, it would appear that the genre continues to tread a fine line between truth and fiction.

PLENTY OF FISH
IN THE SEA

A brief history of *skrei,* the fish that built Norway. By Hugh
Francis Anderson

ON THE SNOW-DUSTED shores of Svolvær, a fishing town on the south of the Lofoten archipelago in Arctic Norway, vast wooden flakes tower above the cabins and buildings that dot the seafront. On each beam lie thousands of Atlantic cod drying in the polar chill that rides in from the Atlantic. It is an image unchanged in centuries, a tradition started more than 1000 years ago by the Vikings, and subsequently Norway's first export. In Old Norse, this cod was called *skrei,* meaning 'wanderer', a name that remains unchanged to this day.

Large, muscular, and lean, *skrei* is considered the finest cod in the world. Each year between January and April, mature *skrei* migrate 1000km from the Barents Sea, high in the Arctic, to their spawning grounds surrounding Lofoten. Today, this remarkable fish remains an integral part of Norwegian cultural heritage and one of its largest exports.

Humble Beginnings

'As long as *skrei* has existed, there have been people in the Lofoten islands', says Marion Fjelde Larsen, a specialist on the history of fishing in Lofoten at the Lofoten Viking Museum. 'We've found fishing equipment from the very early Iron Age, around 500 BCE, up through the Viking Age and the Medieval Age'.

Tørrfisk, or stockfish, is a simple process by which cod is hung outside until dry, and therefore preserved. Historically, this high-protein food was used throughout lean winters and on extended voyages. While the Vikings had stockfish onboard their ships for sustenance, it also became a valuable trade item, making it one of the first commodities to come from Norway.

The first documented international trade came in 1432 when Venetian merchant Pietro Querini was caught in a storm and rescued by fishermen from Røst, a small island municipality on the far west of Lofoten. When he returned to Venice, he brought stockfish with him, and trade routes opened between the nations. In Venice today, evidence of this tie is found through *baccalà mantecato,* a traditional meal of whipped stockfish served with polenta.

Skrei Worldwide

Italy still maintains its classification of *skrei,* with *prima* being the finest quality, *seconda* the next and the lowest quality called *Africa.* 'One of the first international trades from Norway went through British Columbia to West Africa, where it was used in the slave trade', says Jim Eide, a Lofoten guide and fishing expert. 'Today, the third class and all of the fish heads go directly to Nigeria'. While it originated as a food source for enslaved people, over the centuries it has become an

integral ingredient in Nigerian cuisine and remains a staple today.

When the French exiled the Portuguese and Basque from their fishing grounds in Canada during the 17th century, they soon turned to Iceland and Norway to fish for cod. Their own process of salting and drying cod, which is used in *bacalhau* recipes, was named *klippfisk* in Norway and became an important Norwegian export in the 19th and 20th centuries. Today, almost 80% of *klippfisk* is exported to Portugal.

The Lifeblood of a Nation

As demand grew during the 20th century and the export of fresh *skrei* became viable, questions surrounding sustainable fishing practices became highly important in Norway. *Skrei* is the most lucrative export after oil, so maintaining healthy, thriving fish stocks is of the utmost importance. After years of overfishing, quotas were introduced in 1990 to manage the fisheries so that the fish could be sustained at a viable level both biologically and economically. 'Before 1990, the control on fishing wasn't very good. There were fewer fish, and they were smaller', says Svein Egil Hansen, who first fished these waters in 1974. 'Now it's much, much better'.

Today, researchers and institutions work together to calculate a total allowable catch for each fish stock, which is then shared with the fishing industry and closely monitored by the authorities. In this way, the stocks remain viable year after year. 'We love the fish', says Jonas Walsøe, the former general manager of Berg Seafood, a fish-landing company based in Svolvær. 'It's amazing. It built this country, and we appreciate the way we take care of the cod population'. Penalties for overfishing are high, and catches exceeding quotas are confiscated by the authorities. While stocks fluctuate year to year, the current system forecasts sustainable long-term *skrei* fishing because there's no incentive to overfish and education surrounding viable practices is high.

Cultural Ties

Skrei remains an important part of Norwegian cuisine and culture. Almost every part of the fish is used. *Mølje,* for example, is a meal of *skrei* flesh, liver and roe poached in salted water and served with flatbread or potatoes. The tongues and cheeks are cut out and pan-fried as a delicacy. In a tradition that continues to this day, the *tungeskjaererne* (tongue-cutters) are all children. The job was and still is used to initiate them into the fishing industry, alongside making some pocket money. It's the only work permitted for children in Norway, and they can make more than €10,000 in a single season. 'You need skill and speed to cut tongues well, and many people have found fishing is a nice route to take after school', says 16-year-old Maria Rasmussen. 'When you're born into something, it's part of your identity'.

At Holmen Lofoten, a hotel and restaurant run by Rasmussen's mother, Ingunn, the traditional *skrei* receives a contemporary twist through the Kitchen on the Edge of the World culinary adventure, which often draws famous chefs from across the globe to participate. 'We no longer have to cook in the traditional way', she says. 'It's nice to have new ways of using this wonderful product'.

Holmen Lofoten, like many spots in Lofoten, uses the history and tradition of *skrei* to help bolster tourism, and you can even fish for your own. As an ode to this remarkable fish, the government has funded the construction of SKREI – National Museum of Cod, set to open in Kabelvåg in 2026.

Perhaps the impact and legacy of *skrei* is best summed up by a well-known Norwegian expression: 'In Cod we Trust'.

> LARGE, MUSCULAR AND LEAN, SKREI IS CONSIDERED THE FINEST COD IN THE WORLD. EACH YEAR BETWEEN JANUARY AND APRIL, MATURE SKREI MIGRATE 1000KM FROM THE BARENTS SEA, HIGH IN THE ARCTIC, TO THEIR SPAWNING GROUNDS SURROUNDING LOFOTEN

Racks of drying *skrei* (p349), Svolvær

INDEX

Map Pages **000**

Map Pages **000**

Map Pages **000**

"From a distance, Folgefonna icecap (p164) glistens in the sun. Up close, an otherworldly swatch of ice colours and deep crevasses characterise this richly textured landscape."

ANTHONY HAM

"Among Norway's largest fjord systems, Hardangerfjord (p158) is the heart and soul of Norwegian fjord country."

ANTHONY HAM

Mapping data sources:
© Lonely Planet
© OpenStreetMap http://openstreetmap.org/copyright

THIS BOOK

Destination Editor
Amy Lynch

Production Editor
Katie Connolly

Book Designer
Catalina Aragon

Cartographer
Valentina Kremenchutskaya

Assisting Editors
Ronan Abayawickrema, Sofie Andersen,

Sarah Bailey, Lauren Keith, Alison Killilea, Esther Luettgen, Anne Mulvaney

Cover Researcher
Lauren Egan

Thanks Hannah Cartmel, Karen Henderson, Kate James, Darren O'Connell, Charlotte Orr

MIX
Paper from responsible sources
FSC
www.fsc.org   FSC™ C021741

Paper in this book is certified against the Forest Stewardship Council™ standards. FSC™ promotes environmentally responsible, socially beneficial and economically viable management of the world's forests.

Published by Lonely Planet Global Limited
CRN 554153
9th edition – Apr 2024
ISBN 978 1 83869 853 9
© Lonely Planet 2024 Photographs © as indicated 2024
10 9 8 7 6 5 4 3 2 1
Printed in China